Purls of Wisdom

Knitting Life's Lessons for Little Ones

Lynn Buchheit Janney

Design by Kristen B. Hughes

Photography by Sachs Photography

Library of Congress Control Number 2010936849

ISBN: 978-0-692-01032-7

Published for the author by:

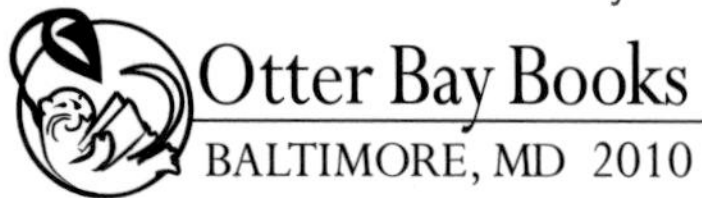

Otter Bay Books, LLC
3507 Newland Road
Baltimore, MD 21218-2513

Direct all inquires to:
lynnbjanney@purls-of-wisdom.com

Printed in the United States of America

{ Table of Contents }

Your Turn

Purls of Wisdom

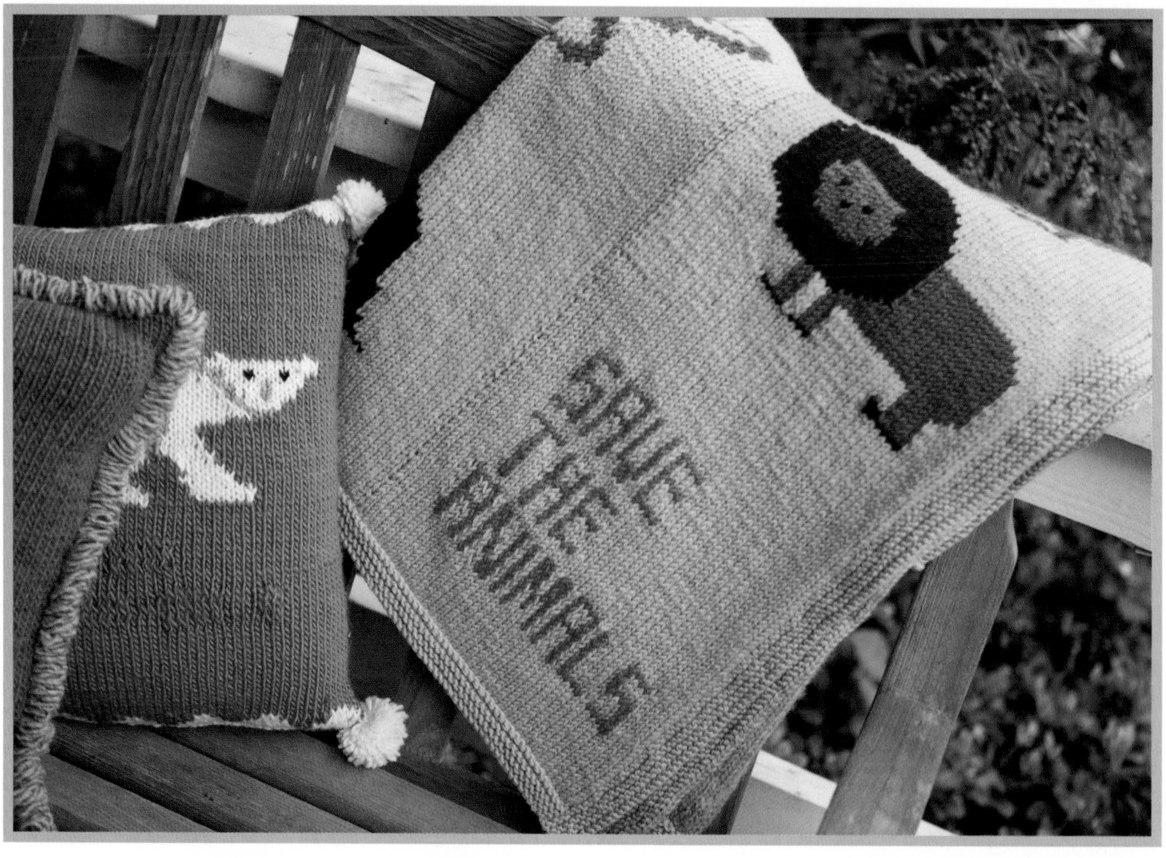

{ Introduction }

How many times do you remember your parents saying, "Be a good sport?" Or "Wait your turn?" And don't forget, "Yes, Please." These are the character-building phrases that we heard when we were growing up, and they are the social courtesies all parents want to teach their children today. They are "Life's Little Lessons."
So I decided to knit these messages into children's sweaters for all to see and read.

This is a book that takes those wonderful pearls of wisdom and translates them into knits and purls. Included in this book are many charming sweaters, blankets and pillows with skill levels ranging from easy to intermediate. For the novice who wants to make that special baby present there is a "Yes, Please" pillow, and for the experienced knitter who is looking for a challenge, an intricate "Stop and Smell the Roses" cardigan.

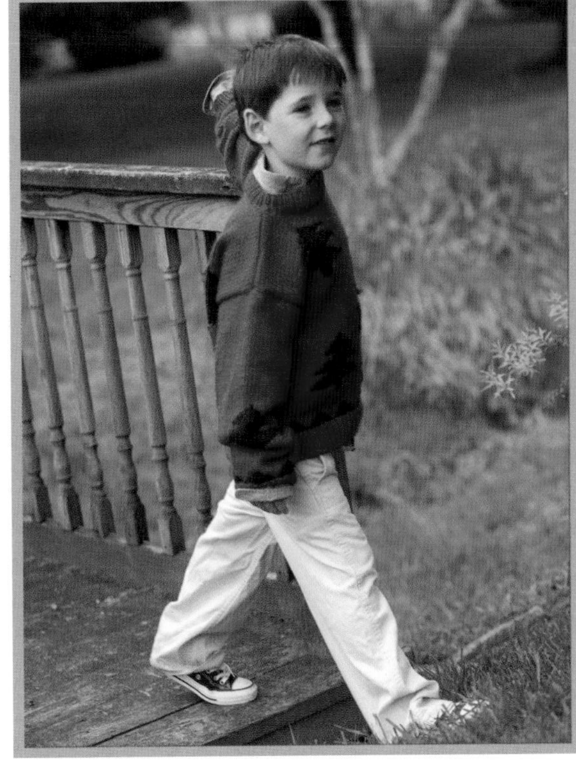

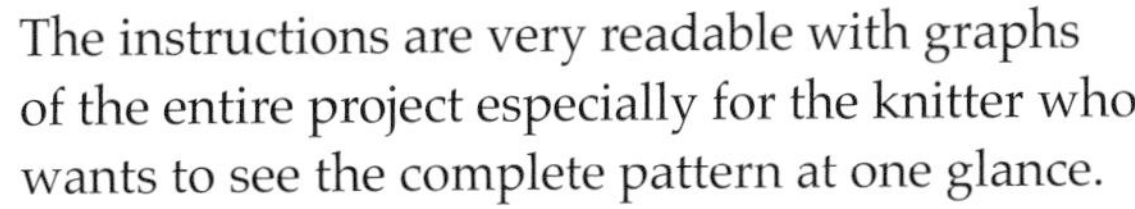

The instructions are very readable with graphs of the entire project especially for the knitter who wants to see the complete pattern at one glance.

The yarns I have used are all natural and there are even buttons you can make from found twigs. I have used lots of color because who can resist seeing children in playful hues. But you can also find some earth tones to match the countryside in which the book was photographed.

Besides my children, my other passion is children's education and literacy. So, as a lifelong knitter, it was natural for me to combine my interests and design sweaters that capture the youthful energy of children while teaching them written words as well.

{ General Instructions }

Because I am a visual person, I have always designed my projects using graphs with one box on a graph equaling one stitch. I like to look at the pattern all at once to get a sense of what it will look like when finished. My sweaters are also very graphic so it is likely that the entire sweater will be shown on the graph. This book utilizes that pattern technique where the entire sweater, in all sizes, is presented to you in graph form with minimal written instructions.

Each sweater pattern starts off with written instructions for the cast on and ribbing or whatever finished band I have chosen. It then instructs you to follow the graph for the body of the sweater. The graphs are in full color, and also indicate where there are special stitches like bobbles and where the embroidery should be placed on the finished sweater. Because of this method, detailed written instructions are not needed for neck shaping and armhole marking, etc. All that information is on the graph in a simple and direct manner.

reading the pattern and charts

First, you may want to go to your local copy center and have the graph enlarged. The side of the sweater that faces out is called the Right Side. All graphs start on the Right Side (RS) of the sweater. When reading rows on RS of chart read from right to left. When on Wrong Side (WS), read from left to right.

At the beginning of each pattern I have given instructions for special stitches or something unique to that pattern. In the interest of saving space, I have not included diagrams for basic knitting instructions for casting on, increasing, etc. Your local yarn shop can be an incredible resource for this kind of information and instruction. Knitters love to share their knowledge. You may also want to check out the Internet, as there are numerous websites with helpful hints as well as videos. I have listed a number of websites on the Yarn Sources page.

sizing

My sweaters are boxy in shape with generous proportions to make the sweater easy to put on, and easy to wear with room to grow. Patterns range from size 2 to size 8. However, these patterns are all designed to either add or subtract stitches or rows to accommodate your individual child. The graphic elements on each sweater (i.e. the soccer ball on "Be a Good Sport") remain the same number of stitches and rows regardless of which size sweater you knit.

materials

Because I wanted to use only natural yarns I have used only wool and cotton. Most of the sweaters are done in wool. This is because though cotton is a wonderful yarn to use for children, it doesn't always work very well for multi-color sweaters. Cotton can often be slippery causing the ends of the yarn to come loose and move to the outside, making your knitting project look sloppy.

gauge

All sweaters are done in the same worsted weight, 4-4 1/2" sts and 6 rows to an inch. At the end of the book I have a list of yarn sources, and with each sweater I also indicate the yarn I used for that particular project. It is, however, very important to check your gauge and the measurements of each sweater. Children come in all sizes so make sure the sweater you are going to knit is the right size for your child. There are measurements along side the graphs, which indicate the length and width of a particular part of the sweater. These may not be an exact translation from stitches to inches, but they are a very close approximation.

measurements

To fit age/size	2	4/6	6/8
Finished chest	28"	31"	33"
Back length with ribbing	14"	17"	18"
Sleeve length with ribbing	12"	15"	16"

buttonhole instructions

For all sweaters using buttonholes, I have used a simple one stitch YO, K2tog buttonhole, and it is done almost exclusively in the ribbing. The directions for this are as follows:
Row of buttonhole: Knit to location of buttonhole. Bringing yarn forward wrap the yarn around the needle and then knit next 2 stitches together. Continue to work in the indicated stitch pattern to the end of row.
Next Row: Knit across row following stitch pattern, which in most cases in this book is rib K1, P1. The buttons on the sweaters may look large, but remember your buttonhole will stretch.

shoulder ribbing and placket instructions

On sweaters with button/buttonhole plackets on the shoulder I did not mark each individual stitch in the Single Rib section of the sweater on the graphs because I thought it might be confusing. This rib section is indicated on the graph usually in a lighter shade of the main color. The first row of the placket is rib K1, P1 across the row. On subsequent rows, K the knit stitches, P the purl stitches. Place buttonholes where indicated.

changing colors

Because of the use of color in these knitting projects, there are two methods that need to be incorporated. You will either use "Weaving" or "Intarsia." Weaving is where you float the yarn on the backside of the knitting being careful not to pull your yarn too tightly when you switch from one yarn to another. The other method is Intarsia, where you pick up the different color from a bobbin or a second ball of yarn and only work in that particular motif. The most important part of color changing is to remember to twist or wrap the two different yarns together before switching from one color to the next or you will have a hole in your knitting. This is done on the wrong side (WS). Make sure to weave in ends of yarn on the backside of the knitted project.

finishing and assembling

Since these patterns are done on a graph you are more likely to have the exact same number of rows for front and back. This makes using the mattress stitch to seam up the sweaters a lot easier, and allows for an almost invisible seam. The Mattress Stitch is done by laying out knitted pieces side by side, RS facing up. Insert a threaded needle under the horizontal bar between the first and second stitch. Then insert the needle into the matching bar on the other knitted piece. Continue this seaming up the sweater alternating from one side to the other. Instructions about using the Mattress Stitch are also in the glossary.

blocking

It is better to block your project before it is seamed together, and I always block on the wrong side of the knitted pieces. When blocking, never apply the iron directly to the finished piece. Use either a steam iron and float it right above the surface of your knitted project.
Or you can place a damp cloth on top of the knitted piece and then use an iron on that surface. Follow manufacturers instructions for care of the particular yarn you have used.

At the end of this book there is also a glossary of terms as well as a list of abbreviations for knitting terms.

You do not need to be an expert knitter to master the projects in this book, but some experience with knitting is helpful. There are some more advanced techniques like color switching and a few different knit stitches, all of which are explained and are readily available in other books and on the Internet. This book doesn't look like many of the other knitting books with its minimal written instructions, but the pattern shapes are simple, and the sweaters are done mostly in a Stockinette Stitch. With a little practice, it will be easy to master these patterns.

{ Yes, Please }

I believe Yes, Please and Thank You are the "magic words" we try to teach our children as early as possible. Perhaps this will help. There are also versions in French and Spanish.

There are different suggestions of yarn to use which all may knit up a little differently. Check measurements on pattern charts and your gauge with your child's measurements to determine how many stitches and rows you should use.

{ Finished Measurements }

size	2	4/6	6/8
chest measurements	29"	31"	33"
length from shoulder with ribbing	14"	16¼"	17¼"
sleeve length from shoulder with ribbing	11"	15"	16"

materials

Wool *(Spanish)*

- 3 (3, 4) skeins 4oz/113grams (190yds/173m) of Brown Sheep Lamb's Pride Worsted in Orange You Glad (A)
- 1 (1, 1) skein 4oz/113grams (190yds/173m) of Brown Sheep Lamb's Pride Worsted in Limeade (B)
- 1 pair #7 and #8 knitting needles or size to obtain gauge
- 3 buttons
- bobbins

Wool *(French)*

- 3 (3, 4) skeins 3.5oz/100grams (220yds) of Cascade Yarn 220 in #8903 Green (A)
- 1 (1, 1) skein 3.5oz/100grams (220yds) of Cascade Yarn 220 in #7827 Yellow (B)
- 1 pair #7 and #8 knitting needles or size to obtain gauge
- 3 buttons
- bobbins

Cotton *(English)*

- 4 (5, 6) skeins 3.5oz/100grams (140 yds) of Plymouth Fantasy Naturale in #9004 Pink (A)
- 1 (1, 1) skein 3.5oz/100grams (140 yds) of Plymouth Fantasy Naturale in #5228 Green (B)
- 1 pair #7 and #8 knitting needles or size to obtain gauge
- 3 buttons
- bobbins

gauge

18 stitches and 24 rows = 4 inches

instructions

Back

With smaller needles and color A cast on 59 (69, 73) sts. Rib K1, P1 for 1½" increasing to 64 (70, 74) sts evenly in last row ending on WS. (RS) Change to larger needles. Continue with color A and in Stockinette Stitch begin following graph for measurements, color and stitch changes, armhole marking and neck shaping. On row 77 (89, 95) bind off 20 (21, 22) sts. Put 24 (28, 30) sts on holder for back neck. *Button Placket:* Work remaining 20 (21, 22) sts on left shoulder in rib K1, P1 for 6 rows. Bind off.

Front

Follow Back for cast on and ribbing instructions. Change to larger needles. Continue with color A and in Stockinette Stitch begin following graph for measurements, color and stitch changes, armhole marking and neck shaping.

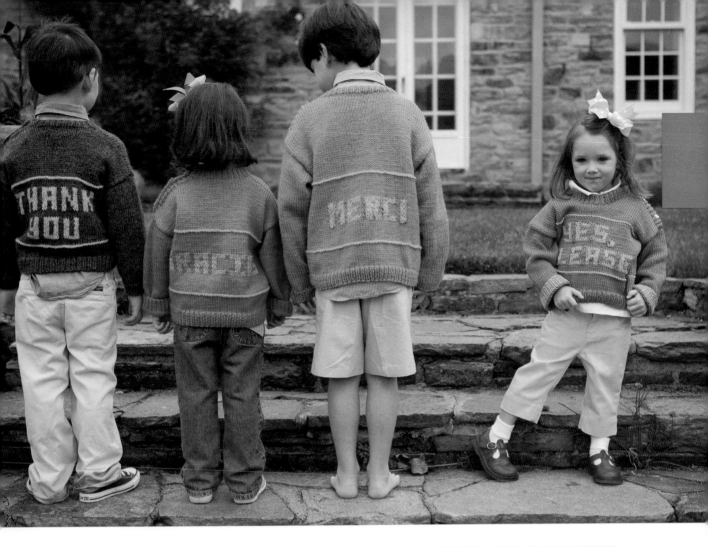

Buttonhole Placket for Left Shoulder: (shown right)
On row 71 (83, 89) (RS) begin rib K1, P1 for 6 rows placing buttonholes according to graph and Buttonhole Instructions in General Instructions. On right shoulder work in Stockinette Stitch to row 77 (89, 95). Bind off.

Sleeve
With smaller needles and color A cast on 37 (39, 39) sts and rib K1, P1 for $1^{1}/_{2}$" ($1^{1}/_{2}$", $1^{1}/_{2}$") increasing to 41 (50, 54) sts evenly in last row ending on WS. Change to larger needles. With color A work sleeve in Stockinette Stitch increasing 1 stitch each edge (2 sts) every 10th (10th, 9th) row 5 (7, 8) times to 51 (64, 70) sts. Bind off.

Sew right front and right back together at shoulder.

Neck Band Ribbing
With RS facing, join yarn at upper corner of front ribbed stitches in color A. With smaller needles, pick up and K63 (65, 69) sts from buttonhole placket, front neck shaping, back neck, and back button placket. Rib K1, P1 for 2 rows.
Buttonhole Row: (K1, P1) 2 times. YO, K2tog to make buttonhole. Continue in rib K1, P1 across row. Rib K1, P1 for 2 more rows. Bind off loosely.

{ Yes, Please }

(A) RPM Pink Raspberry: knit on right side; purl on wrong side

(A) RPM Pink Raspberry: Shoulder Ribbing *(See General Instructions for expanded Placket Instructions)*

(B) Limeade: knit on right side; purl on wrong side

– (B) Limeade: knit on right side; knit on wrong side

X Buttonhole

● Armhole marker

Yes, Please { front }

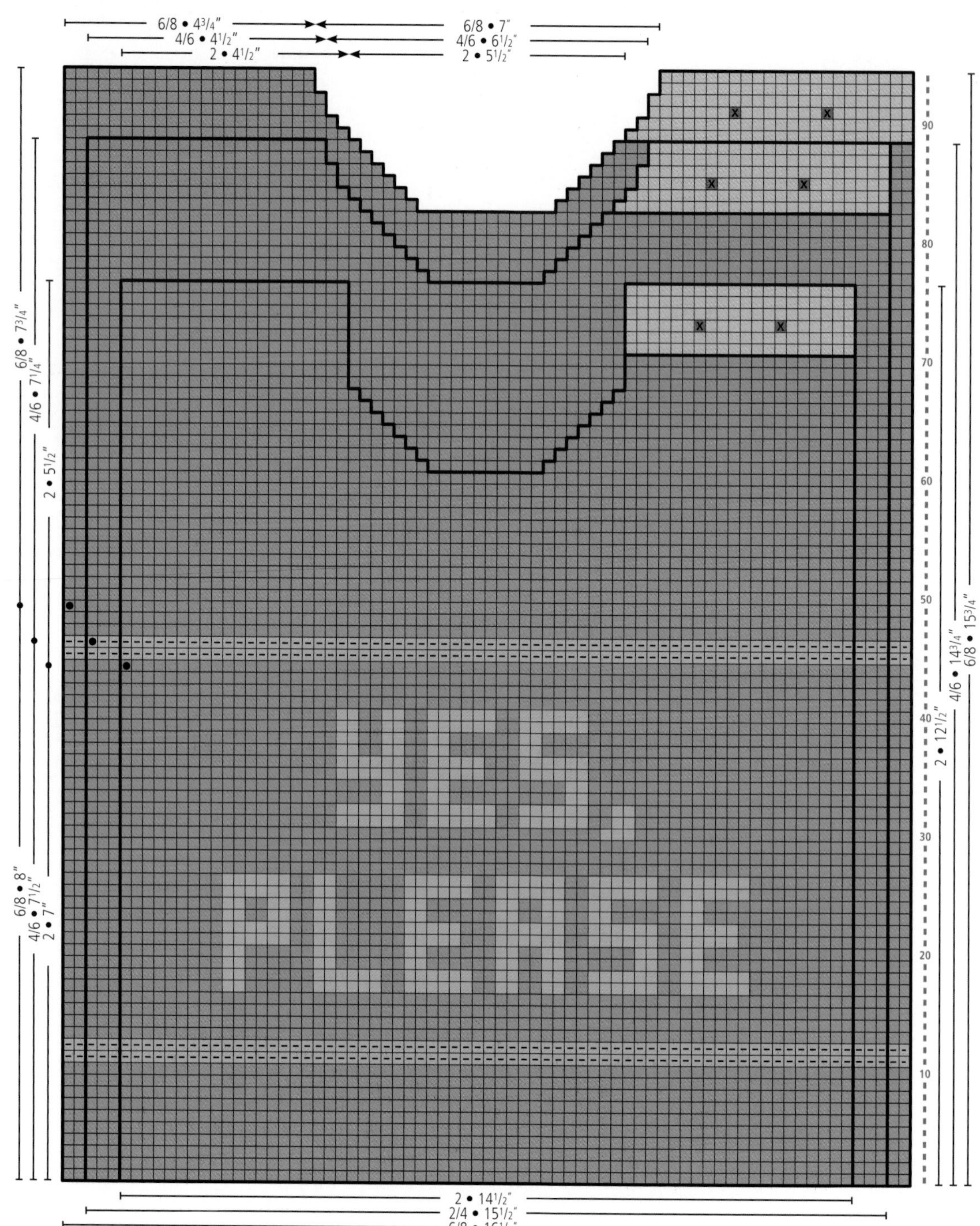

Yes, Please { back }

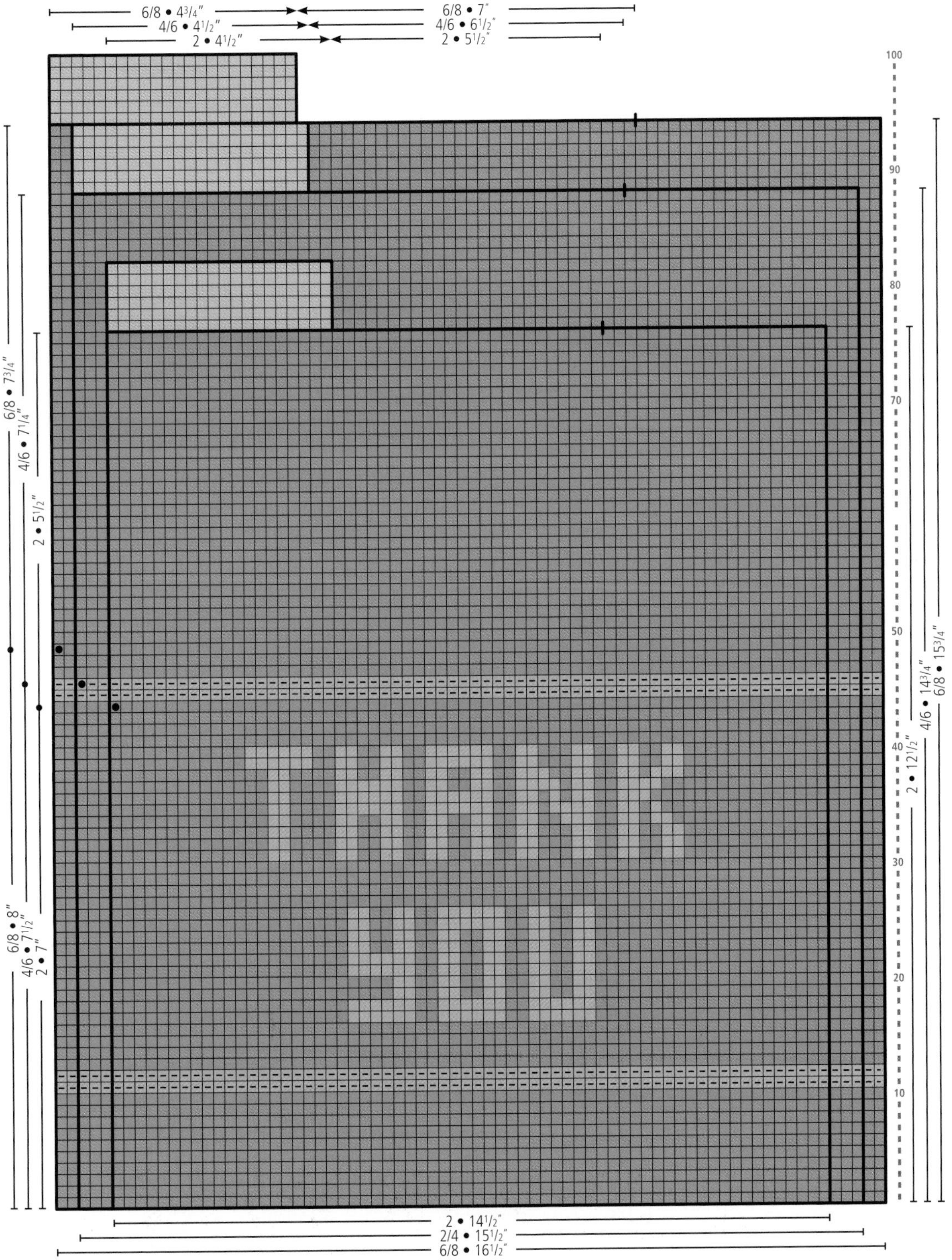

6/8 • 4¾" — 6/8 • 7"
4/6 • 4½" — 4/6 • 6½"
2 • 4½" — 2 • 5½"

6/8 • 7¾"
4/6 • 7¼"
2 • 5½"

6/8 • 8"
4/6 • 7½"
2 • 7"

2 • 12½"
4/6 • 14¾"
6/8 • 15¾"

2 • 14½"
2/4 • 15½"
6/8 • 16½"

THANK YOU

{ Yes, Please }

assembling

Place center of right sleeve on right shoulder seam and within armhole markers. Do not stretch or gather sleeve to fit. Sew in place. Place left front shoulder ribbing (buttonhole placket) on top of back left shoulder ribbing (button placket) overlapping ribbing for 1″. Place center of left sleeve at edge of ribbing and between armhole markers. Sew in place.
Sew up body from bottom ribbing along side and continue down the sleeve to ribbing.

Sew 3 buttons on button placket matching up to buttonholes.

Spanish { front & back }

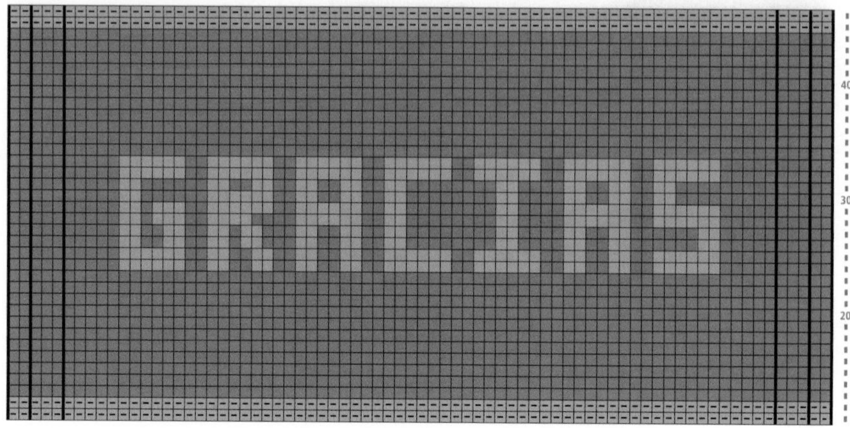

2 • 14½″
2/4 • 15½″
6/8 • 16½″

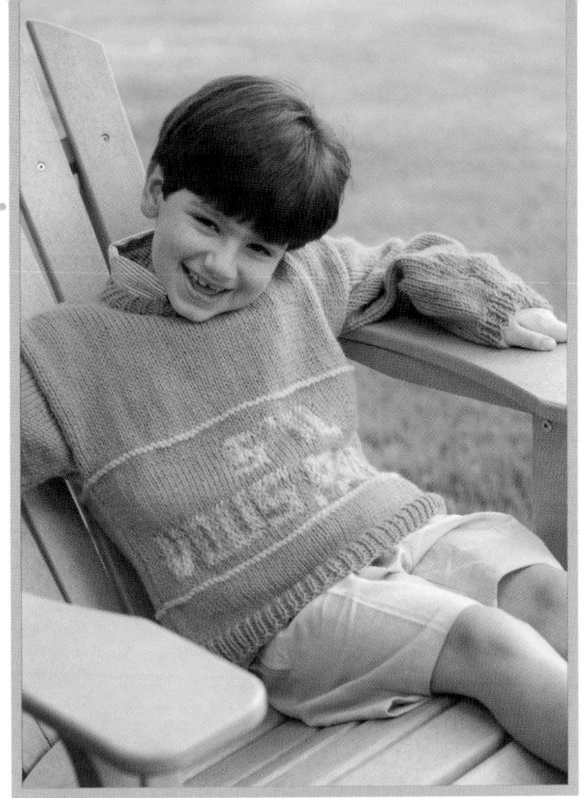

{ Yes, Please; Spanish }

- (A) Orange You Glad: knit on right side; purl on wrong side
- (B) Limeade: knit on right side; purl on wrong side
- (B) Limeade: Knit on right side; knit on wrong side

{ Yes, Please; French }

- (A) Green: knit on right side; purl on wrong side
- (B) Yellow: knit on right side; purl on wrong side
- (B) Yellow: knit on right side; knit on wrong side

French { front & back }

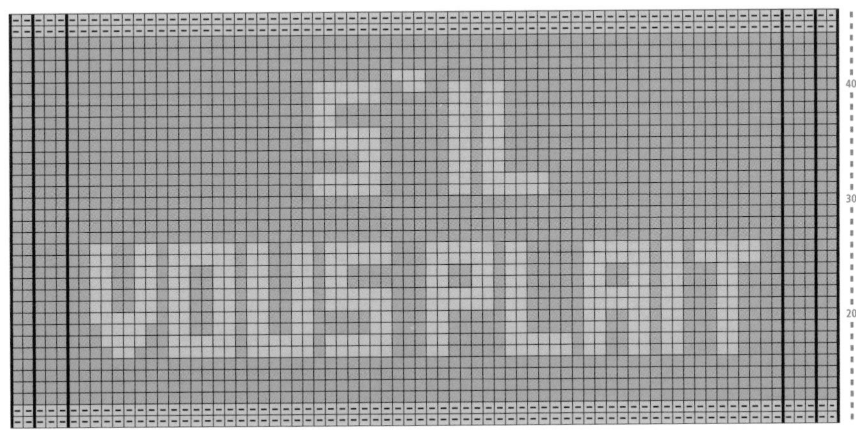

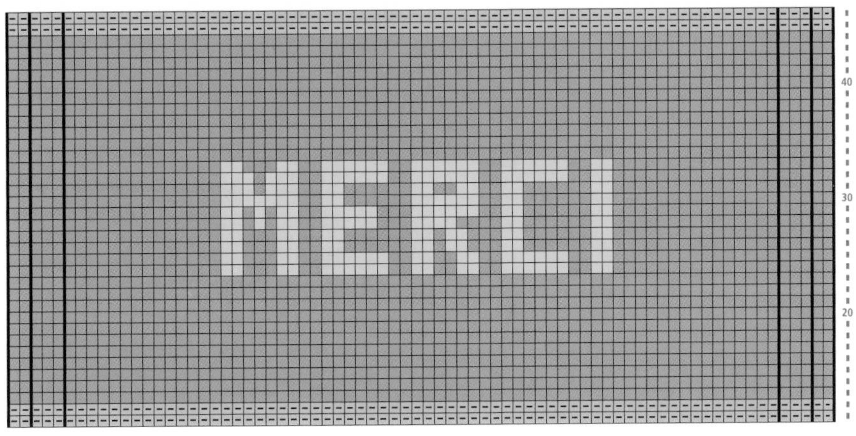

2 • 14½"
2/4 • 15½"
6/8 • 16½"

{ Save the Animals }

My family loves animals, and we have been fortunate to see many creatures in their natural habitat. Living on a farm also gives you an early respect for animals, both domestic and wild. When our children were young we would often play "Twenty Animal Questions" at the dinner table, which involved picking an animal out of a thick encyclopedia and having others guess the answer based on a series of questions. Food played a secondary role in this activity.

My hope in creating this sweater is that our grandchildren and great grandchildren will get to enjoy the wealth of species that exists today.

{ Finished Measurements }

size	4/6	6/8
chest measurement	31"	33"
length from shoulder with ribbing	17 1/4"	18 1/4"
sleeve length from shoulder with ribbing	15 3/4"	16 1/2"

materials

- 4 (5) skeins 4oz/113grams (190yds/173m) of Brown Sheep Lamb's Pride Worsted in Periwinkle (A)
- 1 (1) skein 4oz/113grams (190yds/173m) each of Brown Sheep Lamb's Pride Worsted in Sun Yellow (B), Sable (C), Grey Heather (D), Cream (E), Onyx (F), Oatmeal (G), Autumn Harvest (H)
- 1 pair #7 and #8 straight knitting needles or size to obtain gauge
- 3 buttons
- bobbins

gauge

18 stitches and 24 rows = 4 inches

Along with this sweater I have designed a blanket (p. 70) and pillows (p. 74) with the Save the Animals theme.

instructions

Back

With smaller needles and color A cast on 69 (73) sts. Rib K1, P1 for 2" increasing to 70 (74) sts evenly in last row ending on WS.
(RS) Change to larger needles. Continue with color A and in Stockinette Stitch begin following graph for measurements, color changes, armhole marking and neck shaping.
On row 93 (99) bind off 21 (22) sts for right shoulder. Put 28 (30) sts on holder for back neck.
Button Placket: Work remaining 21 (23) sts on left shoulder in rib K1, P1 for 6 rows. Bind off.

Front

Follow Back for cast on and ribbing instructions ending on WS.
(RS) Change to larger needles. Continue with color A and in Stockinette Stitch begin following graph for measurements, color changes, armhole marking and neck shaping.
Buttonhole Placket for Left Shoulder: On row 87 (93) begin rib K1, P1 for 6 rows placing buttonholes according to graph and Buttonhole Instructions in General Instructions.
On right shoulder work 21 (22) sts in Stockinette Stitch to row 93 (99). Bind off.

{ Save the Animals }

Save the Animals { front }

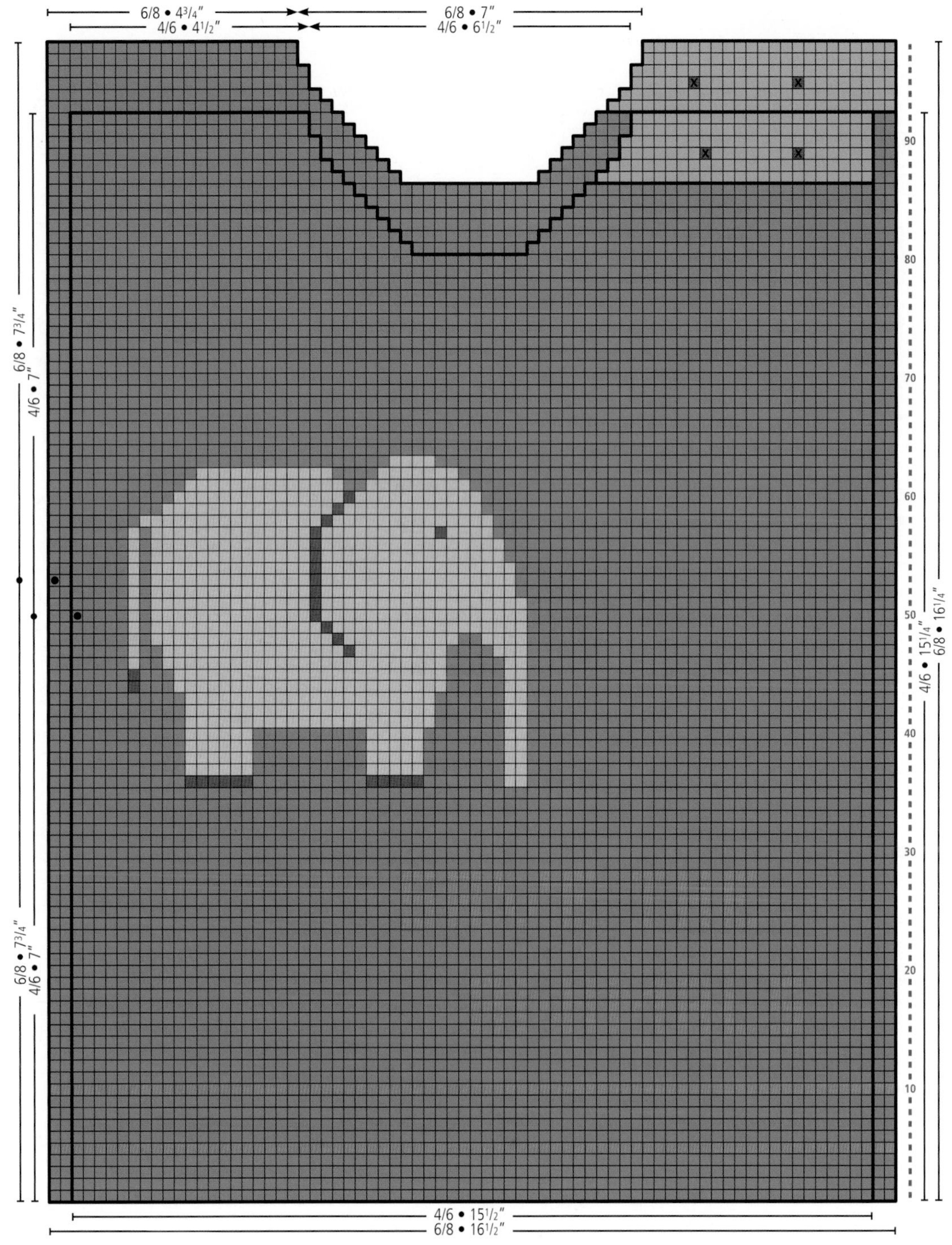

Save the Animals { back }

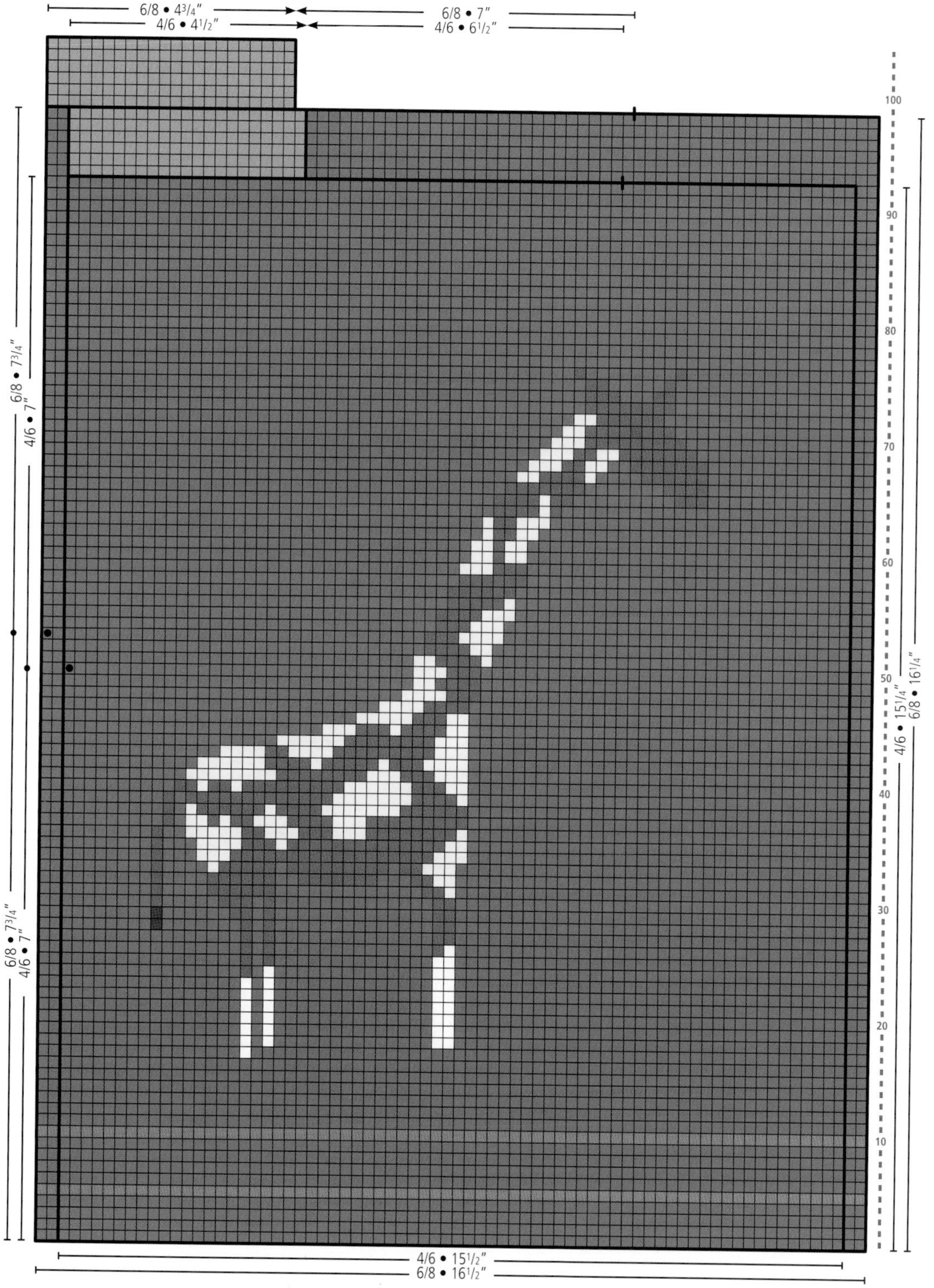

6/8 • 4¾″
4/6 • 4½″
6/8 • 7″
4/6 • 6½″

6/8 • 7¾″
4/6 • 7″

6/8 • 7¾″
4/6 • 7″

100
90
80
70
60
50
40
30
20
10

4/6 • 15¼″
6/8 • 16¼″

4/6 • 15½″
6/8 • 16½″

{ Save the Animals }

- (A) Periwinkle: knit on right side; purl on wrong side
- (A) Periwinkle: Shoulder Ribbing *(See General Instructions for expanded Placket Instructions)*
- (B) Sun Yellow: knit on right side; purl on wrong side
- (C) Sable: knit on right side; purl on wrong side
- (D) Grey Heather: knit on right side; purl on wrong side
- (E) Creme: knit on right side; purl on wrong side
- (F) Onyx: knit on right side; purl on wrong side
- (G) Oatmeal: knit on right side; purl on wrong side
- (H) Autumn Harvest: knit on right side; purl on wrong side
- X Buttonhole
- ● Armhole marker

Save the Animals { right sleeve }

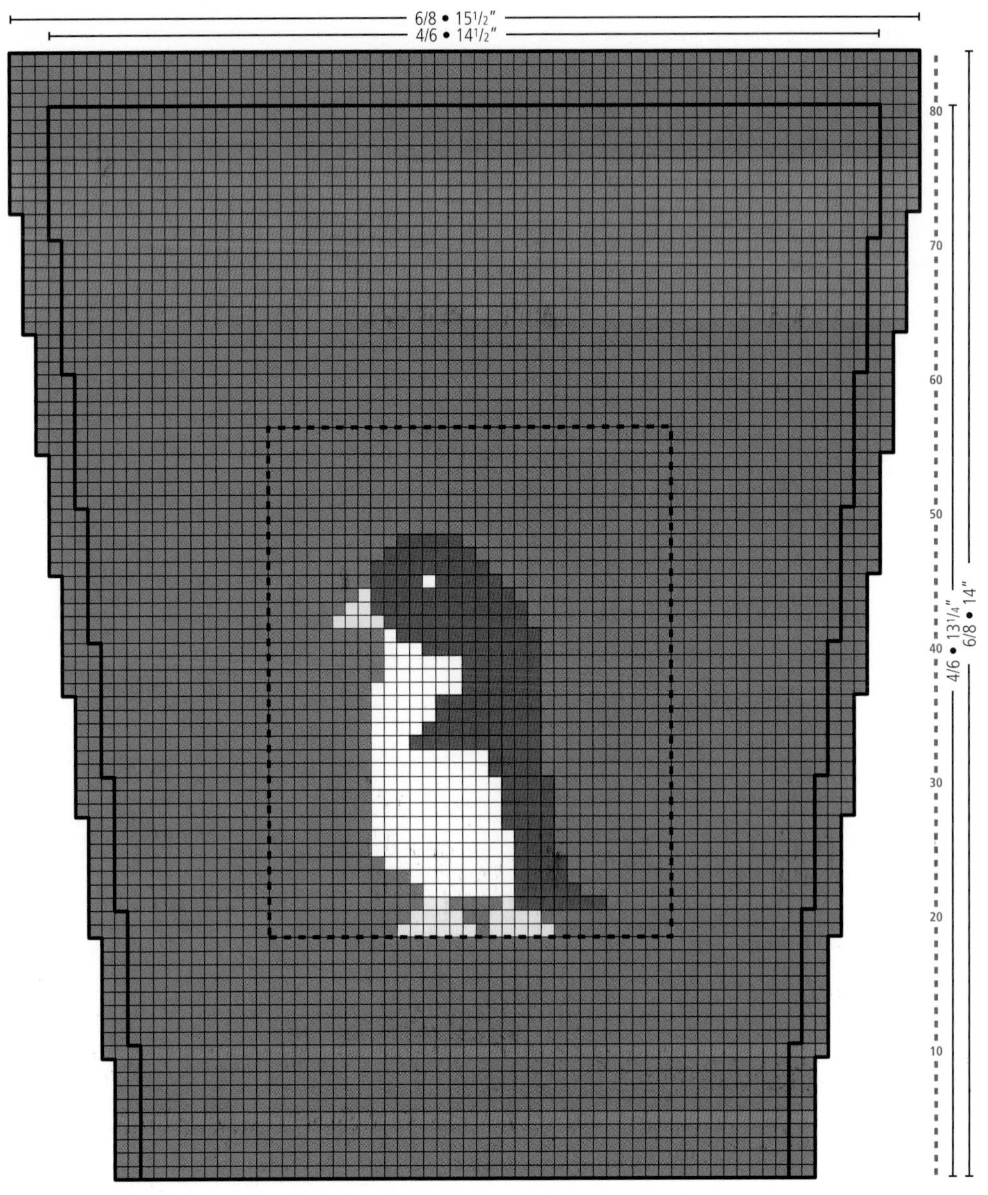

Right Sleeve
With smaller needles and color A cast on 37 (39) sts. Rib K1, P1 for 1½" increasing to 50 (54) sts evenly in last row ending on WS. (RS) Change to larger needles. Continue with color A and in Stockinette Stitch follow graph for measurements, color changes and increases. When graph is completed bind off 64 (70) sts.

Left Sleeve
Follow Right Sleeve for ribbing instructions ending on WS.
(RS) Change to larger needles and in Stockinette Stitch follow graph for Right Sleeve using Left Sleeve Insert starting on row 19.
When graph is completed bind off 64 (70) sts.

Sew right front and right back together at shoulder.

Neck Band Ribbing
With RS facing, join yarn at upper corner of front ribbed stitches in color A. With smaller needles, pick up and K65 (69) sts from buttonhole placket, front neck shaping, back neck, and back button placket. Rib K1, P1 for 2 rows.
Buttonhole Row: (K1, P1) 2 times. YO, K2tog to make buttonhole. Continue in rib K1, P1 across row. Rib K1, P1 for 2 more rows.
Bind off loosely.

assembling
Place center of right sleeve on right shoulder seam and between markers for armhole. Do not stretch or gather sleeve to fit. Sew in place.
Place left front shoulder ribbing (buttonhole placket) on top of back left shoulder ribbing (button placket) overlapping ribbing for 1".
Place center of sleeve at edge of ribbing and between armhole markers. Sew sleeve in place.
Sew up body from bottom ribbing along side and continue down sleeve to ribbing.

Sew 3 buttons on button placket matching up to buttonholes.

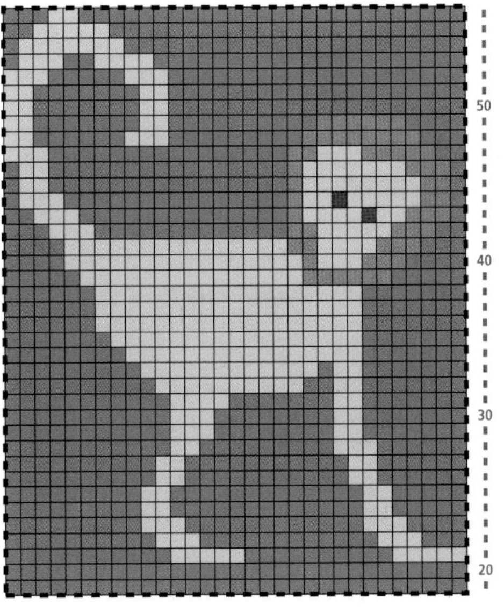

Save the Animals {left sleeve insert}

{ Eat Your Peas }

This sweater may look difficult because of the pea pods and the bobble stitch. Neither is. The bobble stitch just takes practice, and the pea pods are very simple. And maybe it will even inspire your children to eat their veggies.

{ Finished Measurements }

size	4/6	6/8
chest measurements	32″	34″
length from shoulder with ribbing	17″	18″
sleeve length from shoulder with ribbing	16″	17″

materials

- 4 (5) skeins 3.5oz/100grams (131yds/118m) of Brown Sheep Shepherd's Shades in Blue Sky (A)
- 2 skeins 3.5oz/100grams (131yds/118m) of Brown Sheep Shepherd's Shades in Fern (B)
- 1 skein 3.5oz/100grams (131yds/118m) of Brown Sheep Shepherd's Shades in Papaya (C)
- 1 pair #6 or #7 straight knitting needles or size to obtain gauge
- 1 pair #9 or #10 straight knitting needles or size to obtain gauge
- #6 or #7 circular needles (16")
- bobbins

gauge

18 stitches and 24 rows = 4 inches

instructions

Bobble Stitch

Working always on the right side of sweater, pick up stitch that is indicated on the graph. Leaving that stitch on the left needles, knit into front, back, and front again. Turn and purl only these stitches. Turn again knit 3 stitches together. The bobble stitch is done as you are knitting the sweater. On this sweater it is done in color B so you will need to attach yarn B to yarn A before starting your bobble.

Pea Pods

Pea pods are worked separately from sweater and sewn on later.
With B and #6 or #7 needles cast on 1 sts.
Knit inc to 3 sts (Kf,b&f of stitch).
Next Row: Purl.
Next row: Kf&b each stitch. Increase to 6 sts.
Next Row: Purl.
Next row: Starting with first stitch, K inc every other stitch to 9 sts.
Next Row: Purl.
Next Row: Knit.
Next Row: Purl.
Next Row: Knit.
Next Row: Purl.
Next row: K2tog twice. K1, K2tog twice. (6 sts)
Next row: P2tog, P1, P2tog twice. (3 sts)
Next Row: K3tog. Bind off. Sew up seam to make pod leaving tail to attach to sweater.

Back

With smaller needles and color B cast on 72 (76) sts.
Rib 1 row K2, P2.
Change to color A and continue rib K2, P2 for 9 rows (10 rows total) ending on WS.
(RS) Change to larger needles. Continue with color A and in Stockinette Stitch begin following graph for measurements, color and stitch changes, bobble placement, armhole marking and neck shaping. When the graph is completed bind off 20 (21) sts for shoulder. Put 32 (34) sts on holder for back neck and bind off remaining 20 (21) sts for other shoulder.

Front
Follow Back for cast on and ribbing instructions.
(RS) Change to larger needles. Continue with color A and in Stockinette Stitch begin following graph for measurements, color and stitch changes, bobble placement, armhole marking and neck shaping. When graph is completed bind off 20 (21) sts for each shoulder.

Sleeve
With smaller needles and color B cast on 36 (40) sts.
Rib 1 row K2, P2.
Change to color A and continue rib K2, P2 for 9 more rows increasing to 50 (54) sts evenly in last row ending on WS.
(RS) Change to larger needles. Continue with color A and in Stockinette Stitch begin following graph for measurements, color changes, increases and bobble placement. When graph is completed bind off 64 (70) sts.

assembling
Using color B make 6 pea pods and place on front of sweater according to markings on the graph. Stitch top of pea pod securely on inside. Do not secure bottom. Sew shoulders together. Place center of sleeve on shoulder seam and between armhole markers. Do not stretch or gather sleeve to fit. Sew in place. Sew up body from bottom ribbing along side and continue down sleeve to ribbing.

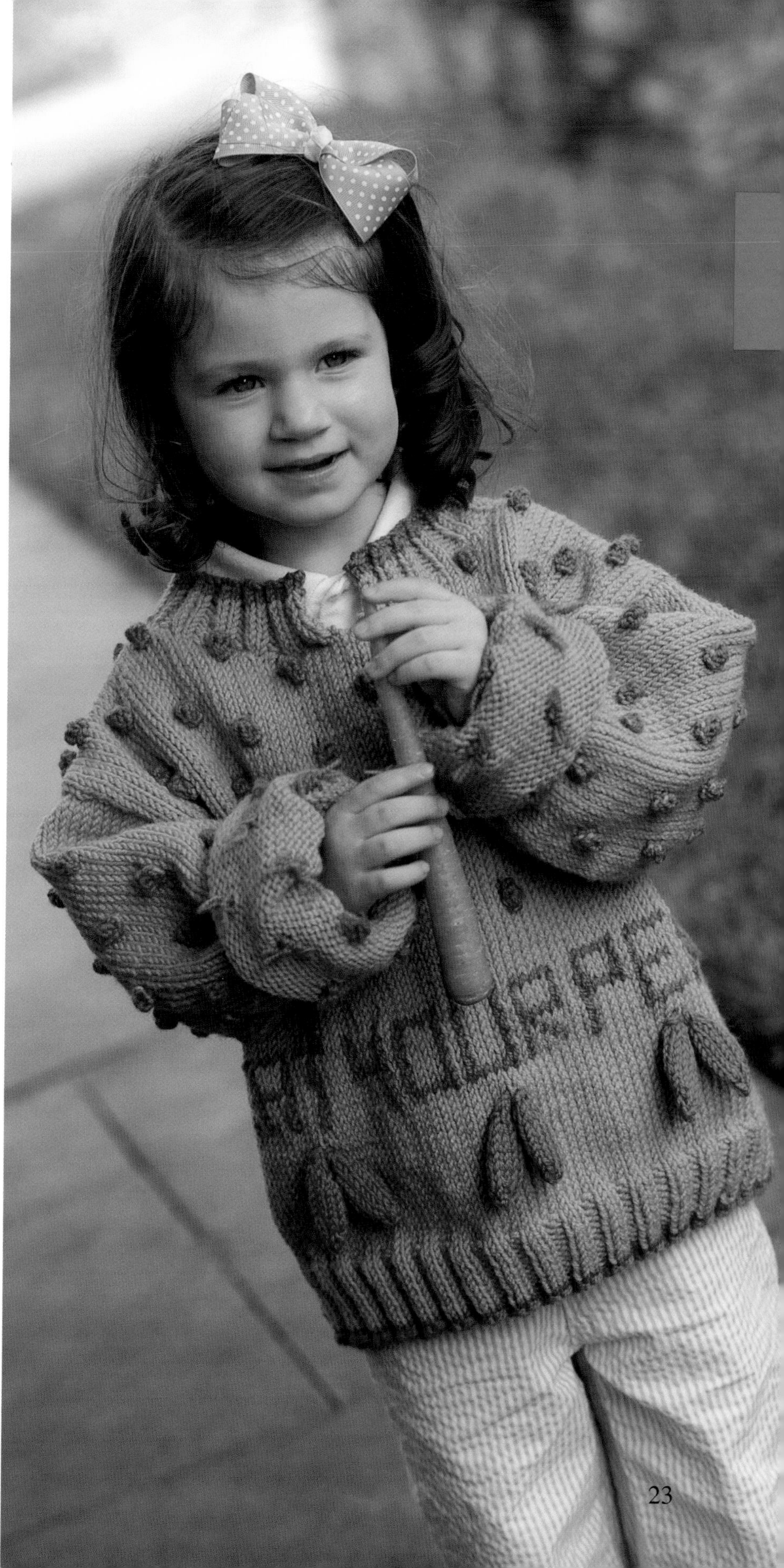

{ Eat Your Peas }

(A) Sky Blue: knit on right side; purl on wrong side

(B) Fern: knit on right side; purl on wrong side

(B) Fern: bobble

(C) Papaya: knit on right side; purl on wrong side

Placement of pea pod

Armhole marker

Eat Your Peas { front }

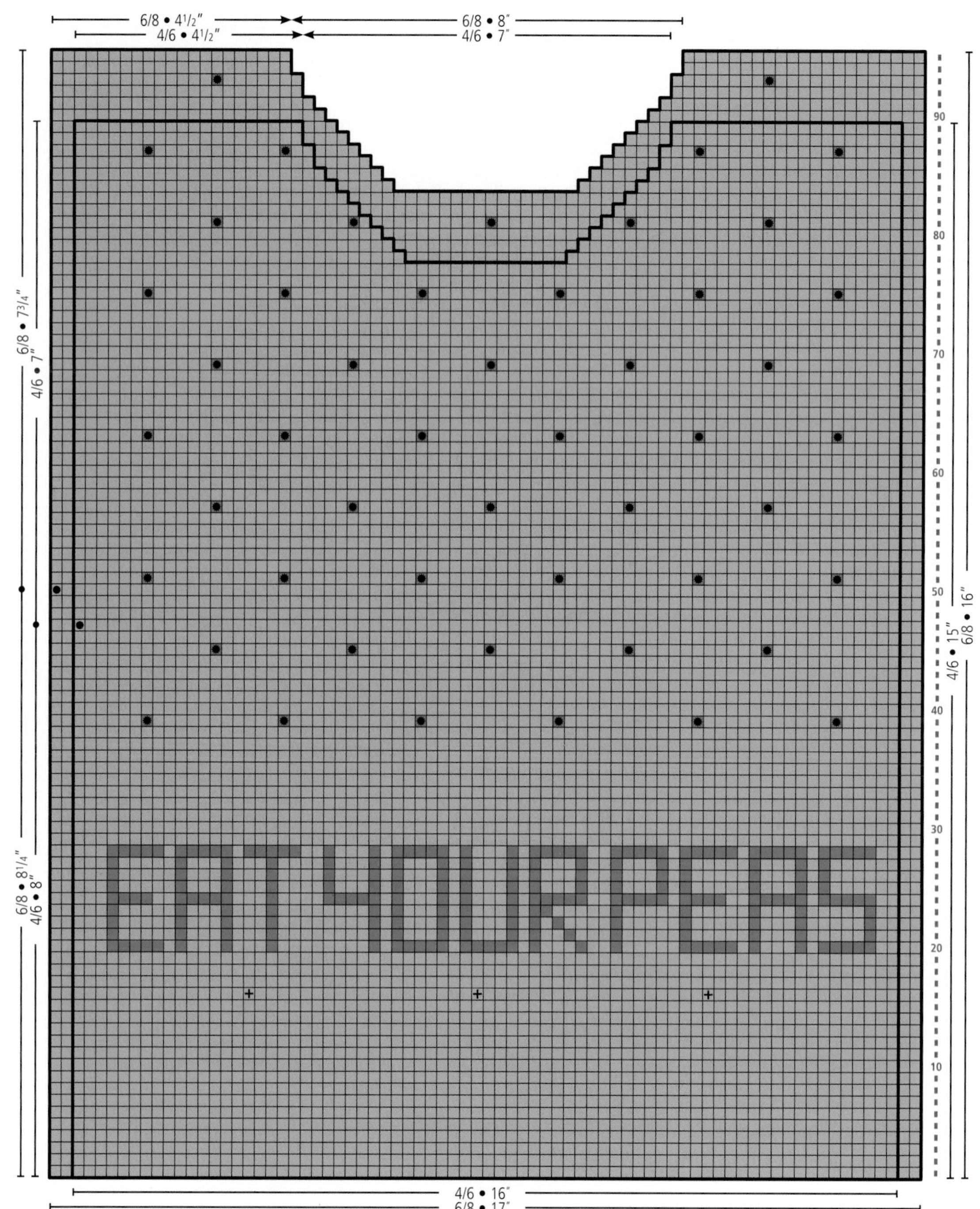

Eat Your Peas { back }

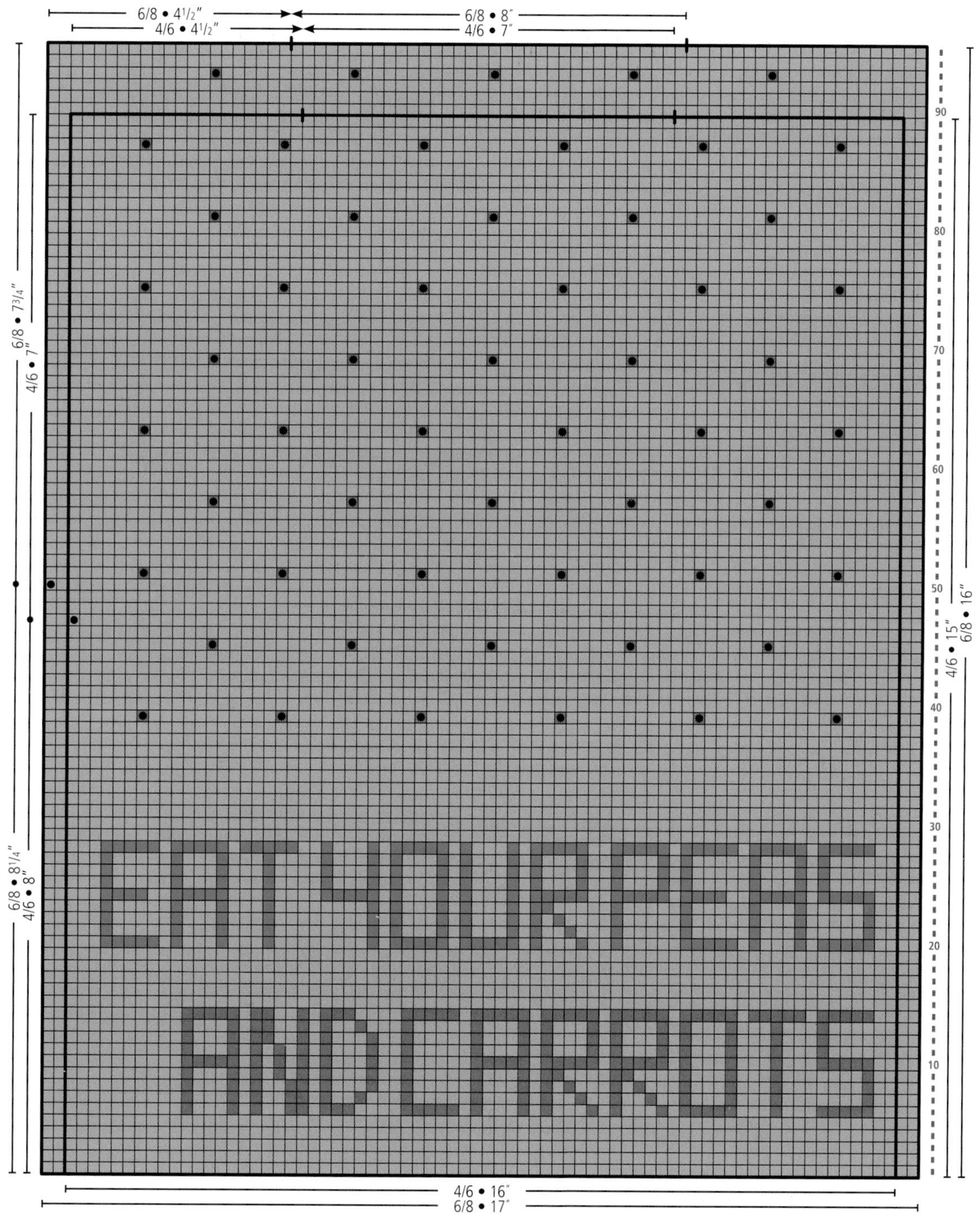

{ Eat Your Peas }

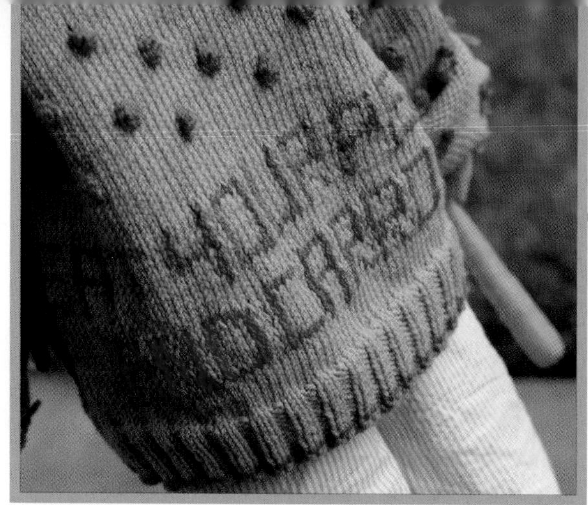

Neck
Starting at center front and with #6 circular needles pick up and K78 (82) sts around neck and in color A rib K2, P2 leaving opening at center front. Rib 6 rows. Switch to color B.
Rib 2 more rows and bind off loosely.

■ Eat Your Peas { sleeve }

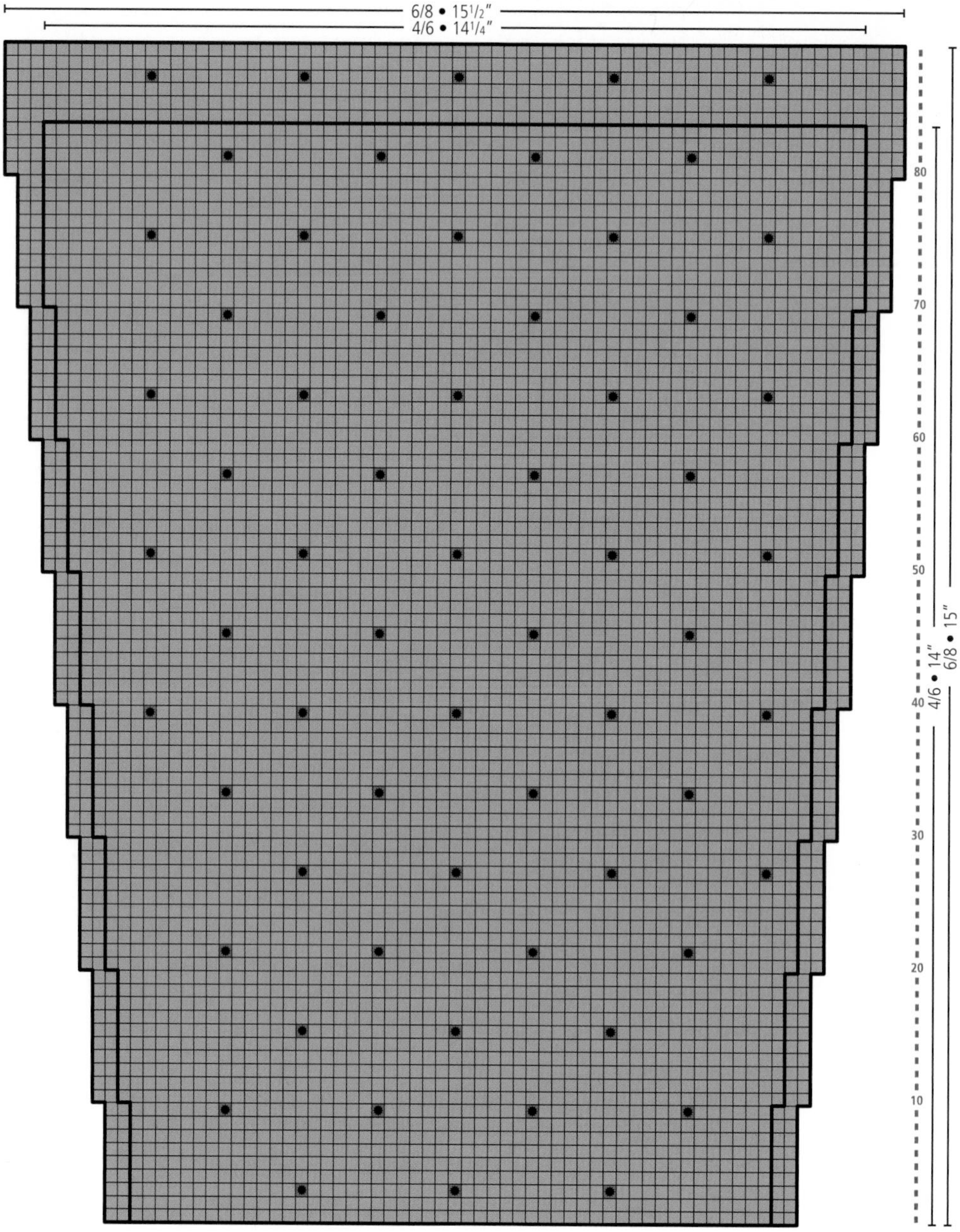

{ Plant a Tree }

When my daughter was in fifth grade, she and her classmates were all given a tree to plant. The tree was 10" tall. We planted it so she could see it from her bedroom window. The tree is now 15' tall, and she still looks out her window to see how it is doing. Her joy in watching that tree grow inspired me to create this pattern when she was still young.

{ Finished Measurements }

size	4/6	6/8
chest measurement	31"	35 1/2"
length from shoulder with ribbing	17"	18"
sleeve length from shoulder with ribbing	14 3/4"	15 1/2"

materials

- 4 (5) skeins 4oz/113grams (190yds/173m) of Brown Sheep Lamb's Pride Worsted in Sandy Heather (A)
- 2 (2) skeins 4oz/113grams (190yds/173m) of Brown Sheep Lamb's Pride Worsted in Kiwi (B)
- 1 pair of #7 and #8 straight knitting needles or size to obtain gauge
- 3 buttons
- bobbins

gauge

18 stitches and 24 rows = 4 inches

instructions

Back

With smaller needles and color A cast on 69 (79) sts. Rib in K1, P1 for 1 1/2" increasing to 70 (80) sts evenly in last row ending on WS. (RS) Change to the larger needles. With color B and in Stockinette Stitch begin following graph for measurements, color changes, armhole marking and neck shaping.

On row 93 (99) bind off 21 (24) sts for right shoulder. Put next 28 (32) sts on holder for back neck.

Button Placket: Work remaining 21 (24) sts on left shoulder in rib K1, P1 for 6 rows. Bind off.

{ Plant a Tree }

(A) Sandy Heather: knit on right side; purl on wrong side

(A) Sandy Heather: Shoulder Ribbing *(See General Instructions for expanded Placket Instructions)*

(B) Kiwi: knit on right side; purl on wrong side

Buttonhole

Armhole marker

Plant a Tree { front }

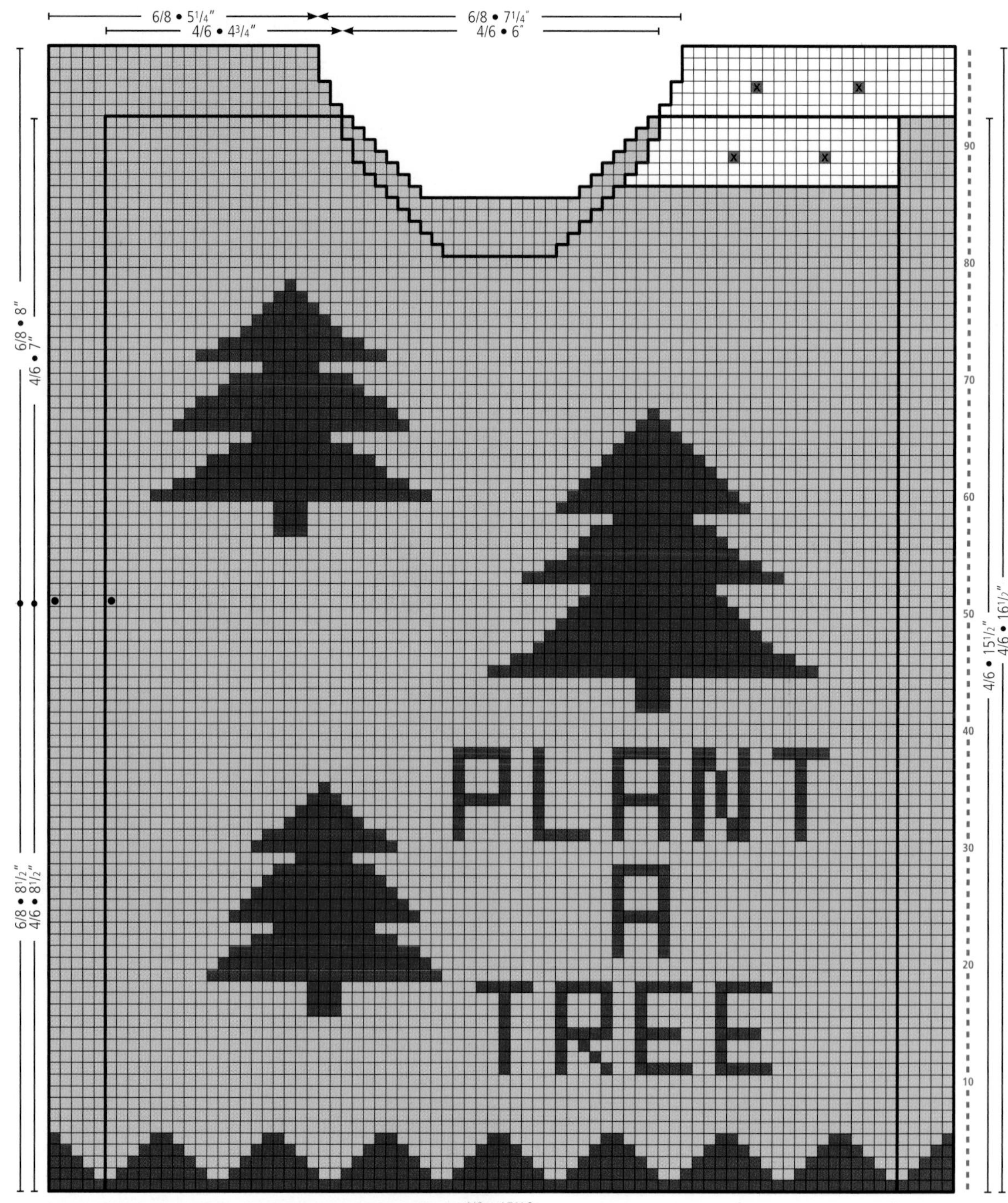

Plant a Tree { back }

{ Plant a Tree }

Front

Follow Back for cast on and ribbing instructions. Change to the larger needles. With color B and in Stockinette Stitch begin following graph for measurements, color changes, armhole marking and neck shaping.

Buttonhole Placket for Left Shoulder: On row 87 (93) begin rib K1, P1 for 6 rows placing buttonholes according to graph and Buttonhole Instructions in General Instructions.

On right shoulder work Stockinette Stitch to row 93 (99). Bind off.

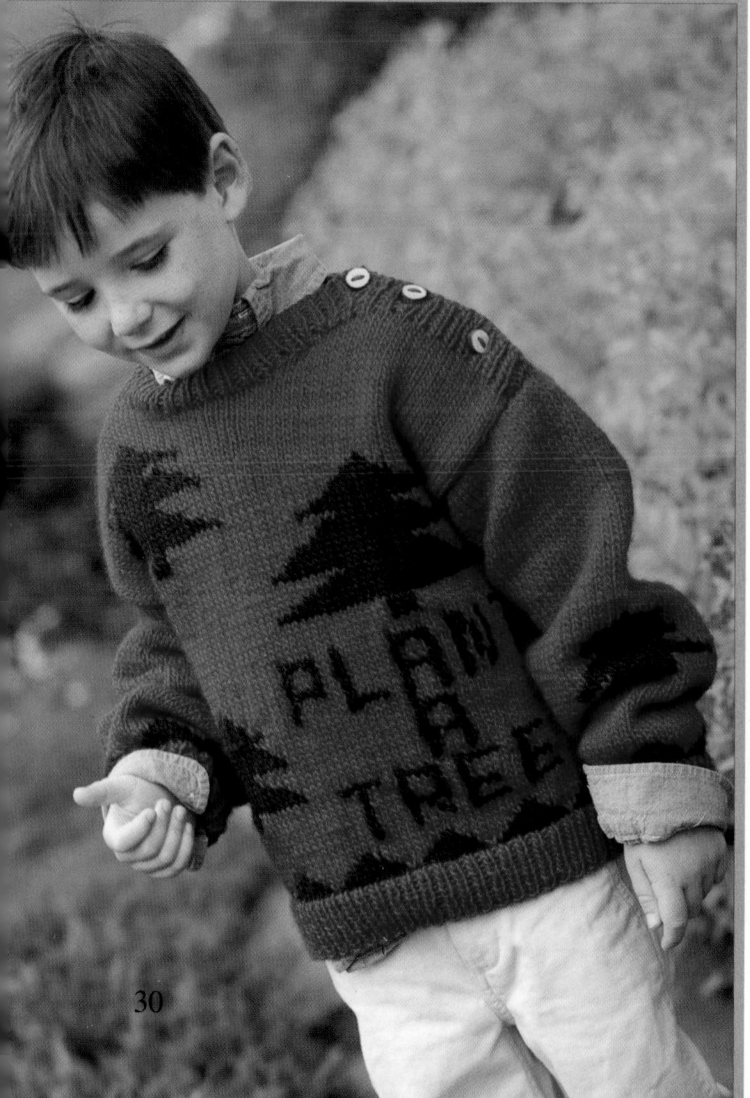

Sleeve

With smaller needles and color A cast on 37 (39) sts. Rib in K1, P1 for $1\frac{1}{2}$" increasing to 50 (60) sts evenly in last row ending on WS. (RS) Change to larger needles. With color B and in Stockinette Stitch begin following graph for measurements, color changes and increases. When graph is completed bind off 64 (70) sts.

Sew right front and right back together at shoulder.

Neck Band Ribbing

With RS facing, join yarn at upper corner of front ribbed stitches in color A. With smaller needles, pick up and K65 (69) sts from buttonhole placket, front neck shaping, back neck, and back button placket. Rib K1, P1 for 2 rows.

Buttonhole Row: (K1, P1) 2 times. YO, K2tog to make buttonhole. Continue in rib K1, P1 across row. Rib K1, P1 for 2 more rows. Bind off loosely.

■ assembling

Place center of right sleeve on right shoulder seam and between markers for armhole. Do not stretch or gather sleeve to fit. Sew in place. Place left front shoulder ribbing (buttonhole placket) on top of back left shoulder ribbing (button placket) overlapping ribbing for 1". Place center of sleeve at edge of ribbing and between armhole markers. Sew sleeve in place. Sew up side seams and along sleeve.

Sew 3 tree buttons on button placket matching up to buttonhole.

{ Holiday Version }

(Shown Left)

- 4 (5) skeins 4oz/113grams (190yds/173m) of Brown Sheep Lamb's Pride Worsted in Ruby Red (A)
- 2 (2) skein 4oz/113grams (190yds/173m) of Brown Sheep Lamb's Pride Worsted in Pine Tree (B)
- 3 buttons

{ Buttons }

In the spirit of recycling I have added buttons to this sweater made from a tree branch. Find a branch in the woods that is approximately 3/4" in diameter and at least 6" long. It needs to be long enough so you can hold on to it while you are cutting it. Cut the stem into rounds of 1/4" width. Cut three. With a small drill place 2 holes in the button about 1/8" apart. Spray entire button with a matte polyurethane finish, and you have your handmade "tree" buttons.

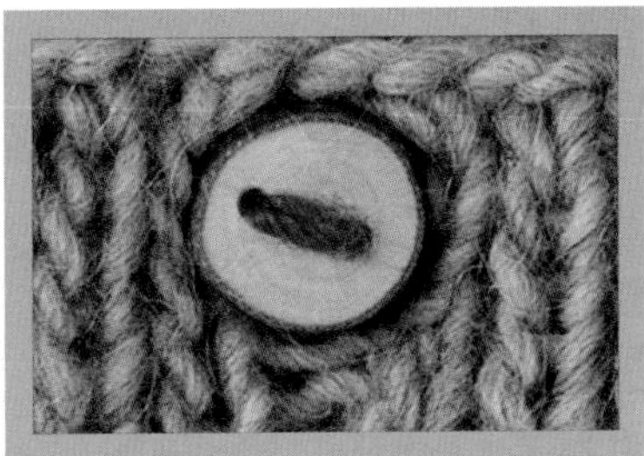

Plant a Tree { sleeve }

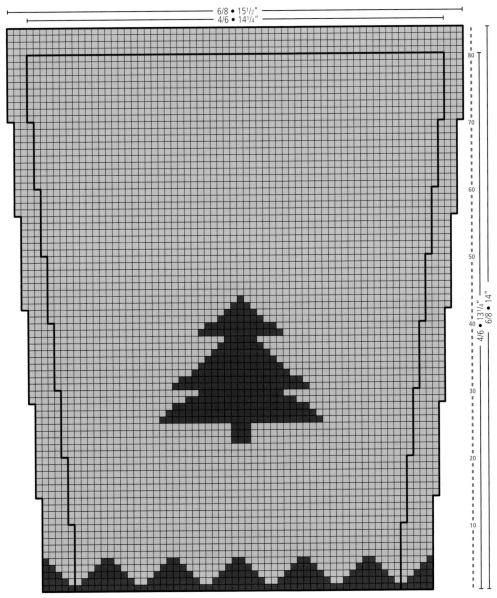

6/8 • 15 1/2"

4/6 • 14 1/4"

4/6 • 13 1/4"

6/8 • 14"

10 20 30 40 50 60 70 80

{ Wait Your Turn }

We all have been told to "wait your turn." That phrase always tested my patience. On the other hand, I felt special because "my" turn was never someone else's. It belonged to me. Maybe I am just rationalizing because I was the third of three girls, and I did a lot of waiting for my turn.

On most of the sweater patterns I start by giving you written instructions for the ribbing and then directing you to the graph for the body of the sweater. On this pattern the sweater starts immediately with the graph, but to avoid confusion I have also given brief written instructions to get you started.
There are embroidered French Knots on the sheep to give texture to our woolly friends.

{ Finished Measurements }

size	4/6	6/8
chest measurement	31"	33"
length from shoulder with ribbing	17"	18"
sleeve length from shoulder with ribbing	13¾"	14¾"

materials

- 4 (5) skeins 4oz/113grams (190yds/173m) of Brown Sheep Lamb's Pride Worsted in Limeade (A)
- 2 skeins 4oz/113grams (190yds/173m) each of Brown Sheep Lamb's Pride Worsted in Lemon Drop (C), Creme (D), Autumn Harvest (E)
- 1 skein 4oz/113grams (190yds/173m) of Brown Sheep Worsted in Onyx (B)
- 1 pair #8 or #9 straight knitting needles or size to obtain gauge
- #8 circular needle (16")
- needle for embroidery
- bobbins

gauge

18 stitches and 24 rows = 4 inches

instructions

Back

With #8 or #9 needles and color E cast on 70 (74) sts.
(RS) Begin graph starting with 2 rows of Garter Stitch still in color E ending on WS.
(RS) Change to color C and begin in Stockinette Stitch. Continue following graph for measurements, color and stitch changes, armhole marking and neck shaping.
When graph is completed bind off 21 (23) sts for shoulder. Put 28 (30) sts on holder for back neck and bind off remaining 21 (23) sts for other shoulder.

Front

Follow Back for cast on instructions.
(RS) Begin graph starting with 2 rows of Garter Stitch still in color E ending on WS.
(RS) Change to color C and begin in Stockinette Stitch. Continue following graph for measurements, color and stitch changes, armhole marking and neck shaping.
When graph is completed bind off 21 (22) sts for each shoulder.

Sleeve

With color E cast on 50 (54) sts.
(RS) Begin graph starting with 2 rows of Garter Stitch still in color E ending on WS.
(RS) Change to color C and begin in Stockinette Stitch. Continue following graph for measurements, color and stitch changes and increases. When graph is completed bind off 64 (68) sts.

assembling

Before putting the sweater together, embroider French Knots on sheep where indicated on graph. Sew shoulders together. Place sleeve within armhole markers and do not stretch or gather sleeve to fit. Sew sleeve in place. Sew up body from bottom ribbing along side and continue down sleeve to ribbing.

Neck

Using circular needle and color E pick up and K66 (72) sts around neck. Rib K1, P1 for 1" and bind off.

{ French Knots }

Thread yarn through needle. From wrong side bring yarn through to right side at required position and hold yarn down where it appears on the surface. Wrap the yarn three times around the needle. While still holding the yarn firmly, twist the needle back to the starting point and insert it close to where yarn first emerged. Pull the needle through to the back, leaving the knot on the surface. Tie off on the inside.
On this sweater they are placed on the sheep.

{ Wait Your Turn }

- (A) Limeade: knit on right side; purl on wrong side
- (B) Onyx: knit on right side; purl on wrong side
- (C) Lemon Drop: knit on right side; purl on wrong side
- (D) Creme: knit on right side; purl on wrong side
- ⌘ (D) Creme: french knot
- (E) Autumn Harvest: knit on right side; purl on wrong side
- (E) Autumn Harvest: knit on right side; knit on wrong side
- ● Armhole marker

Wait Your Turn { sleeve }

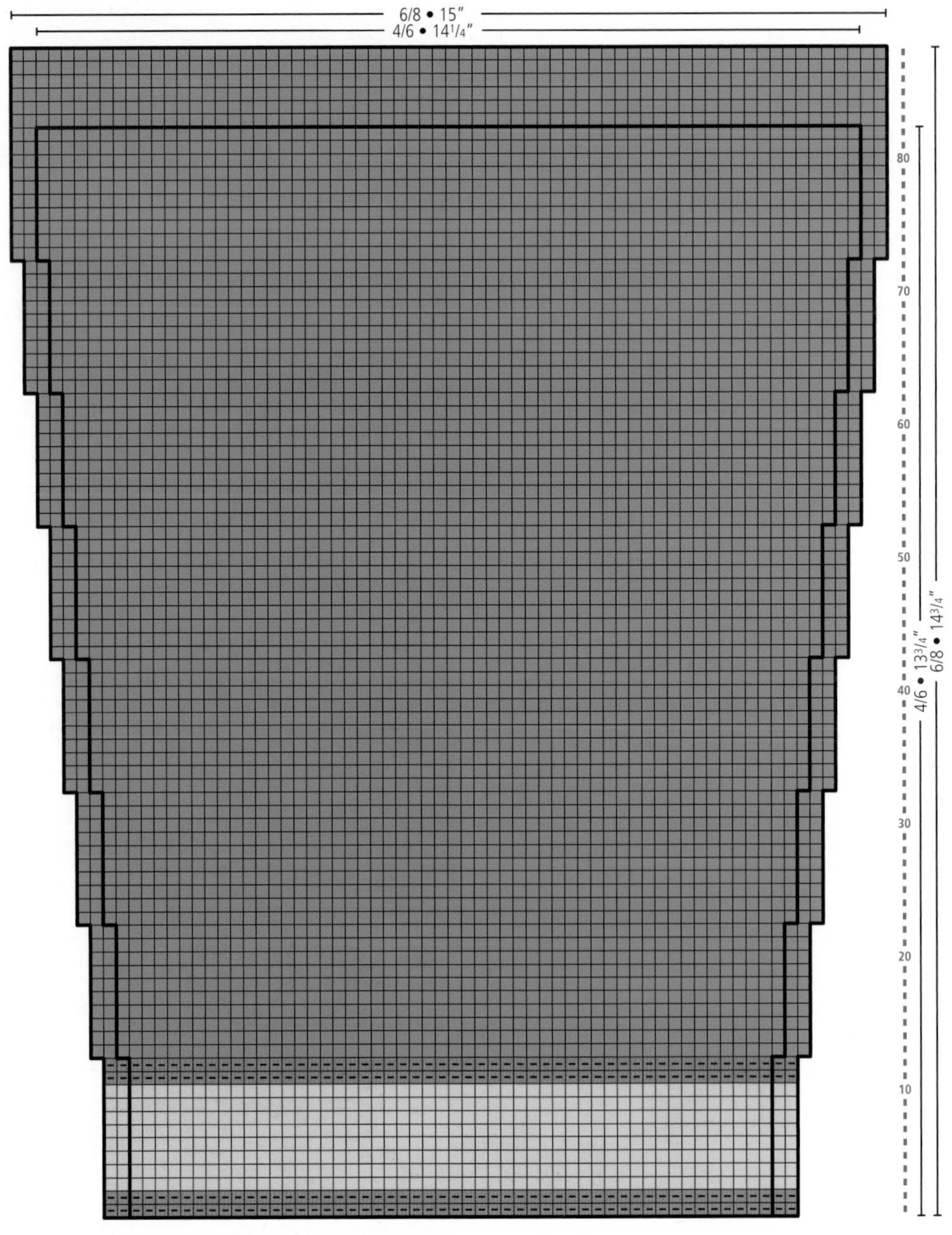

Wait Your Turn { front & back }

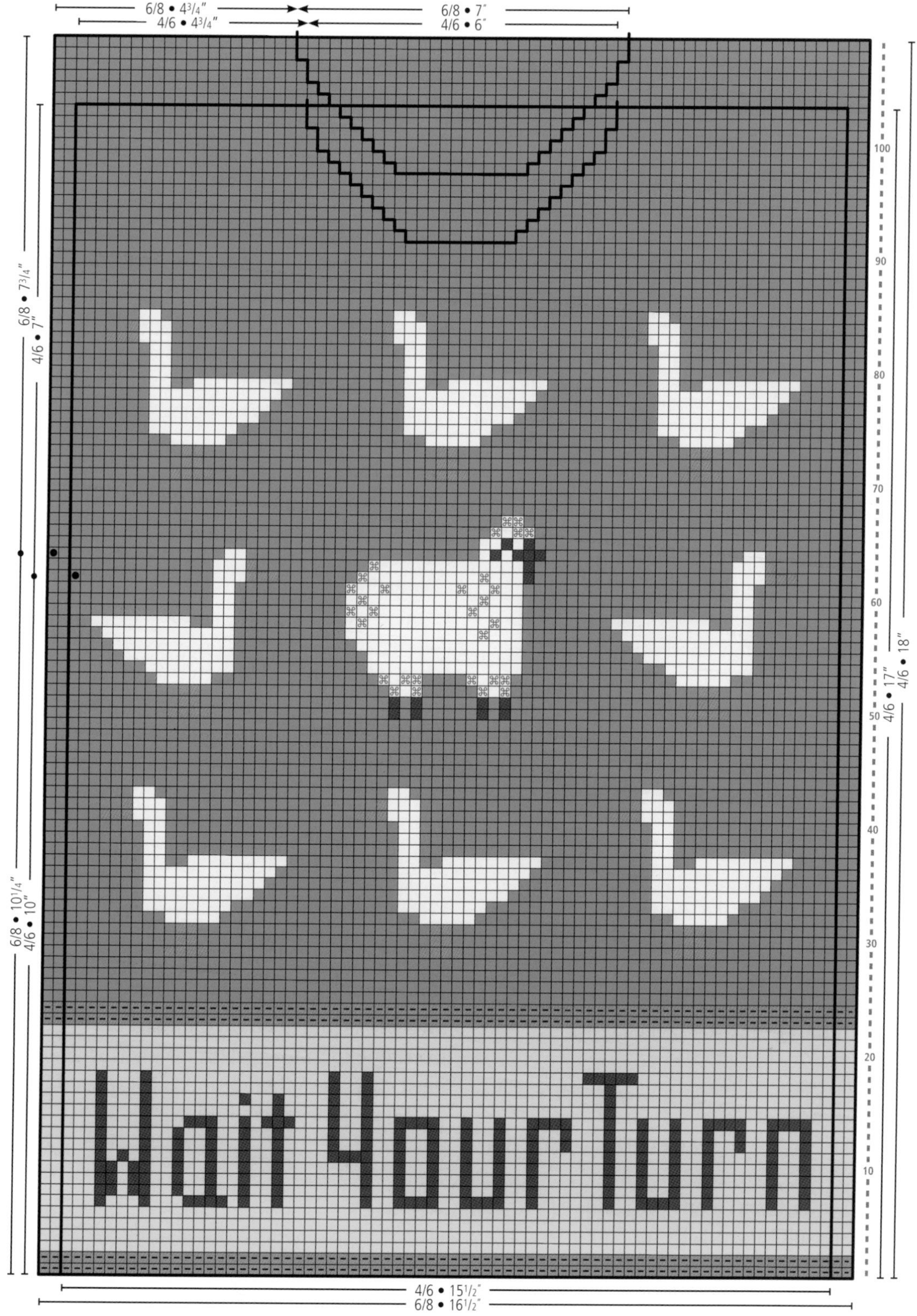

{ Be a Good Sport }

This pattern is sized rather boxy because I can envision an older child wearing this zip cardigan. Again, make sure of your gauge and your measurements before you start the sweater. I have included a baseball graph in case your sports enthusiast prefers that to soccer. Play Ball!

{ Finished Measurements }

size	4/6	6/8
chest measurement	31″	33″
length from shoulder with ribbing	17″	18″
sleeve length from shoulder with ribbing	15″	16″

materials

- 3 (4) skeins 3ozs/85g (158yds/144m) of Lion Brand Wool in Lemongrass (A)
- 1 (2) skein 3ozs/85g (158yds/144m) of Lion Brand Wool in Scarlet (C)
- 1 (1) skein 3ozs/85g (158yds/144m) of Lion Brand Wool in Ebony (D), Winter White (E)
- 1 (1) skein 4oz/113g (190yds/173m) of Brown Sheep Lamb's Pride Worsted in Lemon Drop (B)
- #8 and #9 pair of straight knitting needles or size to obtain gauge
- #0 steel crochet hook
- 16″ jacket zipper in red
- Sewing thread to match zipper
- bobbins

gauge

18 stitches and 24 rows = 4 inches

instructions

Back

With smaller needles and color C cast on 69 (73) sts.
Work K1, P1 for 3 rows.
Change to color B and work 1 row K1, P1.
Change back to C and K1, P1 for 3 more rows.
Change to B and work 1 row K1, P1.
Change back to C, work 2 rows in K1, P1 increasing to 70 (74) sts ending on WS.
(RS) Change to larger needles. Continue with color A and in Stockinette Stitch begin following graph for measurements, color changes, armhole marking and neck shaping. When graph is completed bind off 21 (23) sts for shoulder. Put 28 (28) sts on holder for back neck and bind off remaining 21 (23) sts for other shoulder.

Right Front

With smaller needles and color C cast on 35 (37) sts.
Rib K1, P1 for 3 rows.
Change to color B and work 1 row K1, P1.
Change back to color C and K1, P1 3 more rows.
Change to B and work 1 row K1, P1.
Change back to C, work two rows in K1, P1 ending on WS.
(RS) Change to larger needles. With color A and in Stockinette Stitch begin following graph.
Pocket: At row 11 separate and work for pocket opening as follows: work 16 sts. Break yarn and join 2nd ball of color A and work remaining 19 (21) sts.
Work those 2 sections for 28 rows.
Next row knit across row.
Continue to work pattern following graph and armhole marking. Knit soccer ball (or baseball) on sweater as indicated on the graph.
Continue to follow graph for measurements and neck shaping. When graph is completed bind off 21(23) sts for right shoulder.

Left Front

Follow Right Front for cast on and ribbing instructions. Reverse Right Front graph* for Left Front following graph for measurements, pocket instructions, armhole placement and neck shaping. Bind off 21 (23) sts for left shoulder.

Sleeves

With smaller needles and color C cast on 37 (39) sts and rib K1, P1 for 3 rows. Change to color B and rib K1, P1 for 1 row.
Change back to color C and rib K1, P1 3 more rows. Change to color B and work 1 row K1, P1. Change back to color C, work two rows in K1, P1 increasing to 50 (54) sts evenly in last row ending on WS.
Change to larger needles. Continue with color C and in Stockinette Stitch increasing 1 stitch each edge (2 sts) every 10th (9th) row 7 (8) times until you have 64 (70) sts. Bind off.

assembling

Sew shoulders together.
Place center of sleeve at shoulder seam and between armhole markers.
Do not stretch or gather sleeve to fit.
Sew up sleeve and body of sweater.

Neck

With RS facing, smaller size needles and color C pick up and K61 (65) sts evenly around neck. Rib K1, P1 for 3 rows. Change to color B and rib K1, P1 1 row. Change back to color C and rib K1, P1 for 3 more rows.
Bind off.

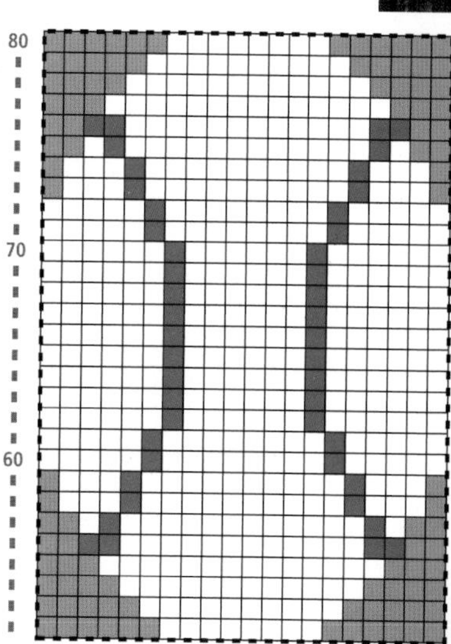

There is no soccer ball on left front

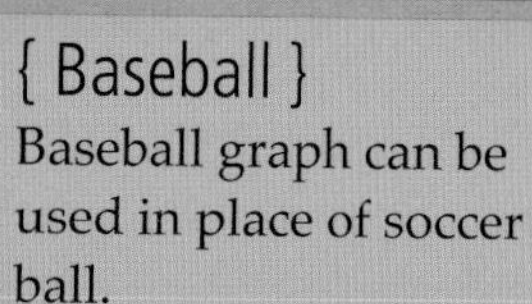

{ Baseball }

Baseball graph can be used in place of soccer ball.

{ Be a Good Sport }

Be a Good Sport { right & left front*}

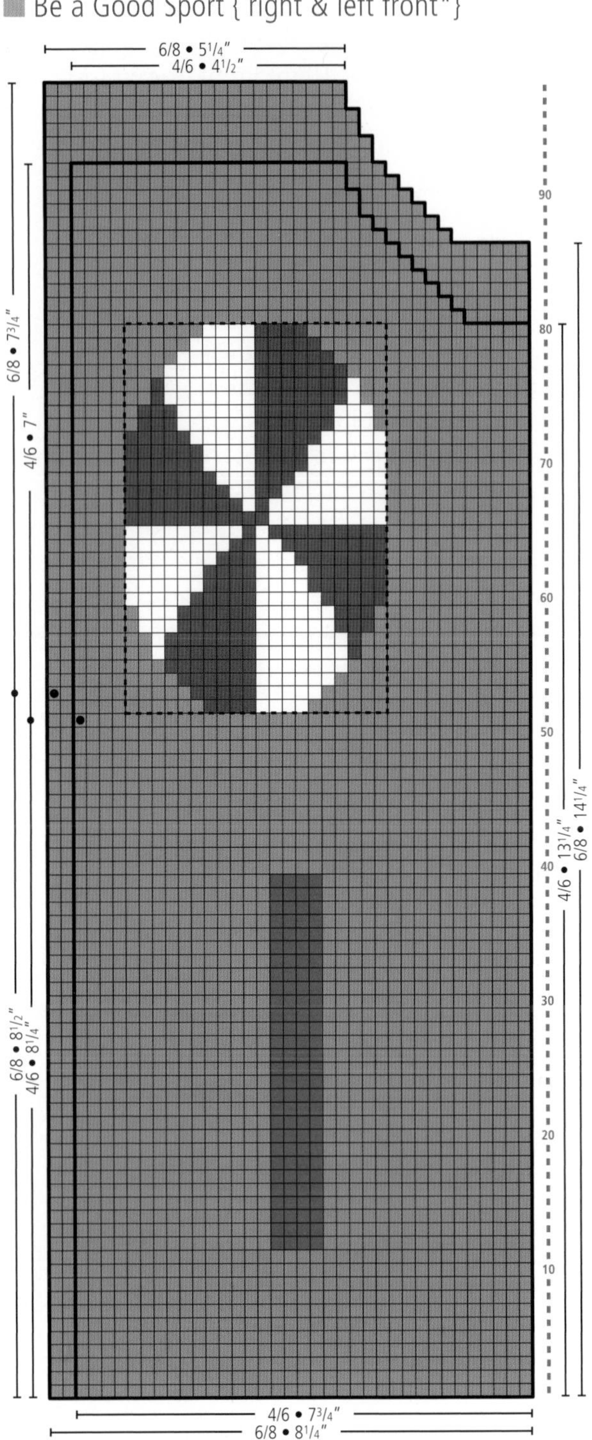

reverse graph for left front; omit ball

With #0 crochet hook crochet 2 rows of single crochet down front openings of the cardigan. Hand stitch zipper in place on cardigan front. Zipper is started at the bottom edge of ribbing and ends just below the neck ribbing. This avoids any scratchiness rubbing against the child's neck on the inside of the sweater.

Finishing Pockets

Pick up 28 sts along pocket on edge closest to front opening and with color A rib K1, P1 for 6 rows and bind off. Sew top and bottom edge of ribbing to sweater.

With color A knit in Stockinette Stitch two rectangles of 14 sts x 28 rows (approximately 6" x 3") for interior of pockets. Sew rectangle to inside of pocket making sure you do not pull too tightly on your stitches or the pocket will show through on front.

- (A) Lemongrass: knit on right side; purl on wrong side
- (B) Lemon Drop: knit on right side; purl on wrong side
- (C) Scarlet: knit on right side; purl on wrong side
- (D) Ebony: knit on right side; purl on wrong side
- (E) Winter White: knit on right side; purl on wrong side
- ● Armhole marker

Be a Good Sport { back }

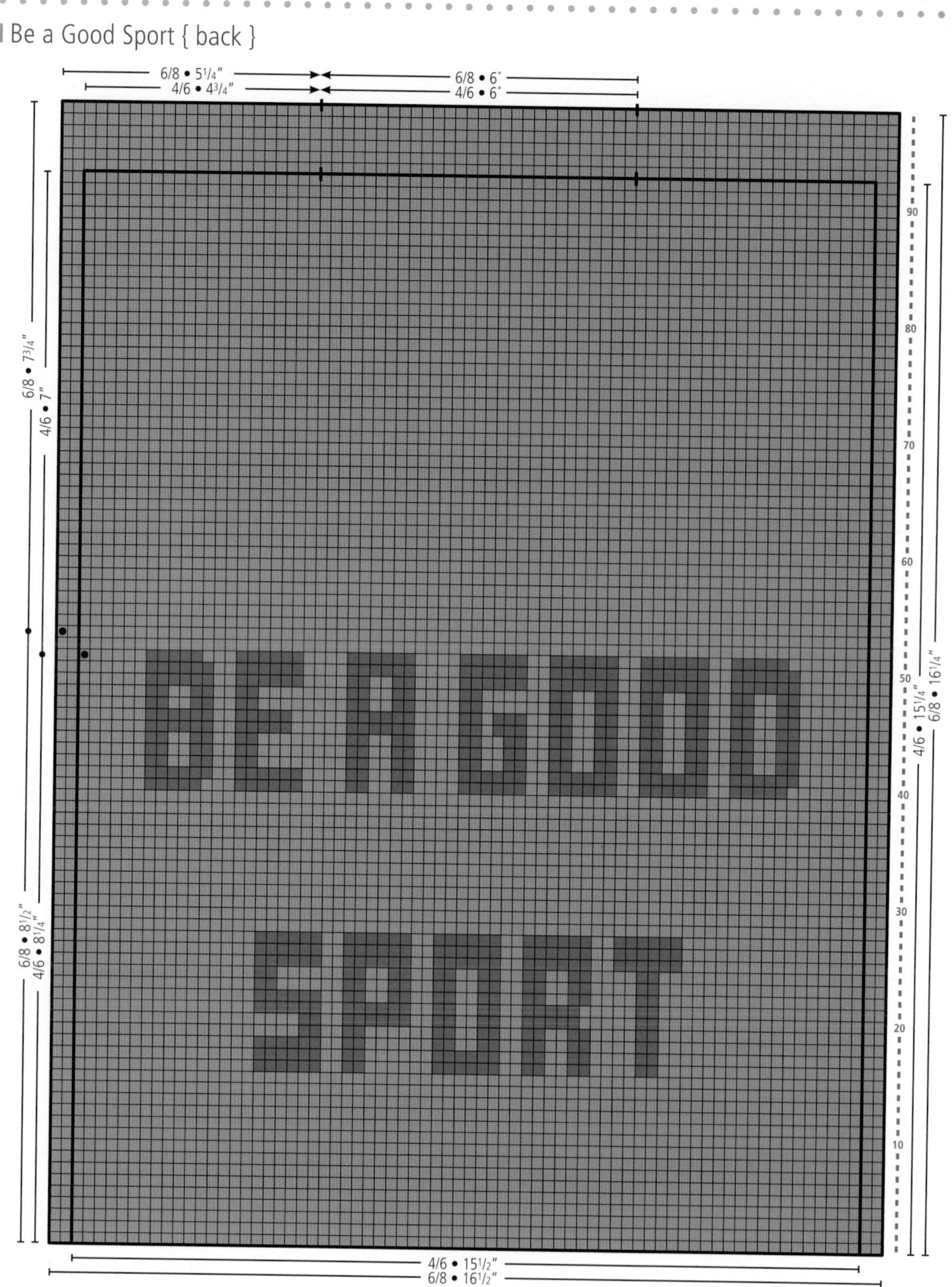

{ Stop and Smell the Roses }

I am a gardener, so obviously I love flowers, and what fun it is to knit them into a sweater. This sweater might look complicated, but when you break down the components, none are particularly complex. The picot edge gives a nice feminine touch to this cardigan.

{ Finished Measurements }

size	4/6	6/8
chest measurement	31″	33″
length from shoulder with ribbing	17″	18″
sleeve length from shoulder with ribbing	14¾″	15½″

materials

- 5 (6) skeins 4oz/113grams (190yds/173m) of Brown Sheep Lamb's Pride Worsted in Creme (A)
- 2 (2) skeins 40z/113grams (190yds/173m) of Brown Sheep Lamb's Pride Worsted in Ruby Red (B)
- 1 (1) skein 4oz/113grams (190yds/173m) of Brown Sheep Lamb's Pride Worsted in Limeade (C)
- 1 pair straight #7 and #8 knitting needles or size to obtain gauge
- 6 buttons
- bobbins

gauge

18 stitches and 24 rows = 4 inches

stitches

Knot Stitch
WYIF (with yarn in front) P3 sts tog leaving these sts on LH needle. WYIB (with yarn in back) knit the same sts tog. P3 sts tog again. Slip sts from LH needle.

Knit Cast On
Cast on one stitch. With that stitch on your LH needle, knit into stitch with RH needle. Without removing stitch from LH needle, and proceeding as if to make a knit stitch, bring out loop from stitch and place that loop back on LH needle. Now 2 sts on needle. Repeat for desired number of cast on sts.

Picot Bind On
With Knit Cast On (described above), cast on 5 sts. Knit and bind off 2 sts. Slip stitch that remains on RH needle back to the LH needle. This creates the picot. Repeat until you have required number of stitches.

Roses
With #8 needle and color B cast on 30 sts.
Rib K1, P1 for 2 rows. Bind off leaving tail to sew flower onto sweater. Form ribbing into a circle and sew ends together to form the roses.
Place rose on sweater in center of red diamond. Sew in place.

instructions

Back
Starting with picot edge using smaller needles and color B *cast on 5 sts using Knit Cast On method. Bind off 2 sts. Slip stitch on RH needle back onto LH needle*. (There are now 3 sts on LH needle).
Repeat from * to * until there are 66 (66) sts on the needle.
Next Row: (RS) In color B K2, P2 across row. Should end with K2.
Next Row: (WS) Change to color A and rib K2, P2 for 2″ increasing to 70 (74) sts evenly in last row ending on WS.
(RS) Change to larger needles. Continue with color A and in Stockinette Stitch begin following graph for measurements, color and stitch changes, armhole marking and neck shaping.

Grey box on graph indicates where you begin knot stitch. When graph is completed bind off with 21 (22) sts for shoulder. Put 28 (30) sts on holder for back neck and bind off remaining 21 (22) sts for other shoulder.

Right Front *(Buttonhole Side)*
Starting with picot edge using smaller needles and color B *cast on 5 sts using Knit Cast On method. Bind off 2 sts. Slip stitch on RH needle back onto LH needle*.

Repeat from * to * until there are 36 (36) sts on the needle.
Cast on 5 more sts. Total of 41 (41).
Next Row: (RS) Rib K1, P1, K1, P1, K1, (These 5 stitches become the front band) Begin Double Rib (K2, P2) starting with P2 and continue across row ending with K2.
Next Row: (WS) Change to color A and K2, P2 across row changing to Single Rib (K1, P1) for the last 5 sts.
Next Row: *Buttonhole Row* (RS) K1, YO K2tog, P1 K1. Continue P2, K2 across row.

{ Stop and Smell the Roses }

Continue in rib K2, P2 for 2" keeping 5 sts of front band in Single Rib.
For size 6/8 increase to 43 sts in last row ending on WS.
Size 4/6 remains 41 sts.
(RS) Change to larger needles.
Continue with color A and in Stockinette Stitch begin following graph for measurements, color and stitch changes, armhole marking, neck shaping and knot stitch keeping front band in K1, P1 rib.

Place buttonholes according to graph and Buttonhole Instructions in General Instructions. When graph is completed bind off 21 (22) sts for right shoulder.

Left Front
Follow Right Front for cast on and ribbing instructions without placing buttonholes.
Begin following graph for Left Side. When graph is completed bind off 21 (22) sts for left shoulder.

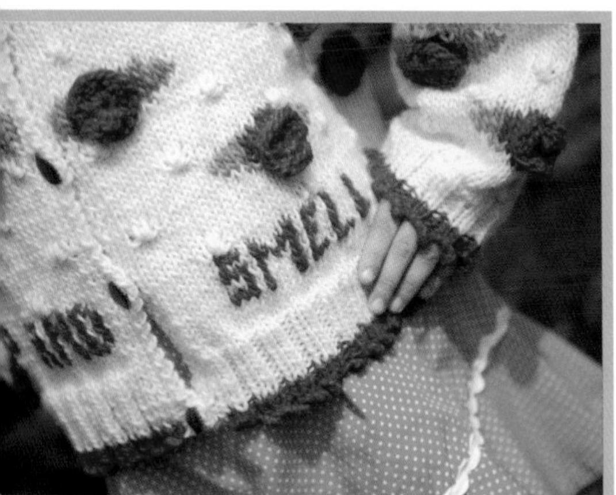

Stop and Smell The Roses { right front }

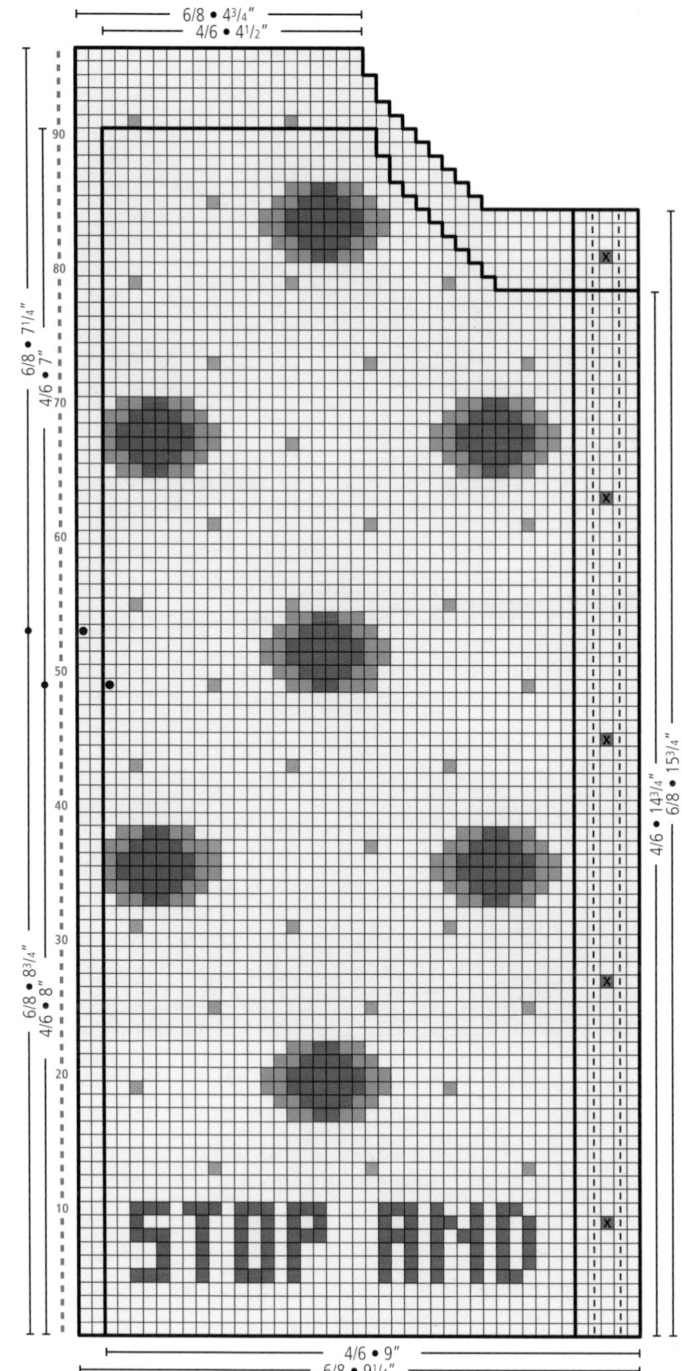

Stop and Smell the Roses { left front }

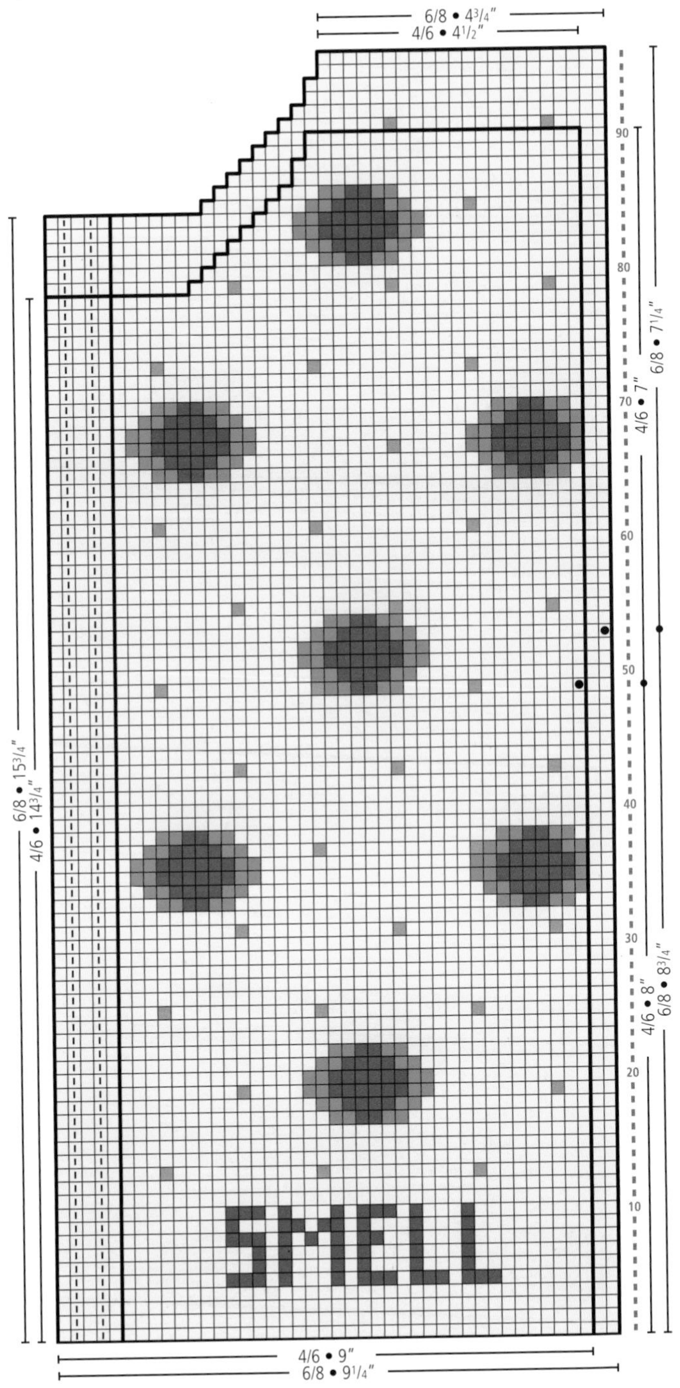

Sleeve

With smaller needles and color B cast on 5 sts and follow instructions for picot edge until there are 36 (39) sts on the needle.

Next Row: (RS) rib K2, P2.

Next Row: (WS) Change to color A. Rib K2, P2 for 1½" increasing to 50 (54) sts evenly in last row ending on WS.

(RS) Change to larger needles and in Stockinette Stitch begin following graph for measurements, color and stitch changes and increases.

When graph is completed bind off bind off 64 (70) sts.

assembling

Make 45 roses for both size 4/6 and 6/8 and sew to sweater in center of red diamond as indicated on the graph.

Sew shoulder seams together.

Find center of sleeve top edge and place at center seam on sweater. Place sleeves within armhole markings and remember not to stretch or gather sleeve to fit.

Neck

With RS facing, smaller needles and color A pick up and K81 (89) sts starting at right front edge and spaced evenly around neck edge. Work 6 rows rib K1, P1 placing last buttonhole in center of band centered above buttonholes on right front band. Bind off.

Sew buttons in place.

{ Stop and Smell the Roses }

- (A) Creme: knit on right side; purl on wrong side
- I (A) Creme: purl on right side; knit on wrong side
- (A) Creme: knot stitch
- (B) Ruby Red: knit on right side; purl on wrong side
- (C) Limeade: knit on right side; purl on wrong side
- X Buttonhole
- ● Armhole marker

Stop and Smell the Roses { back }

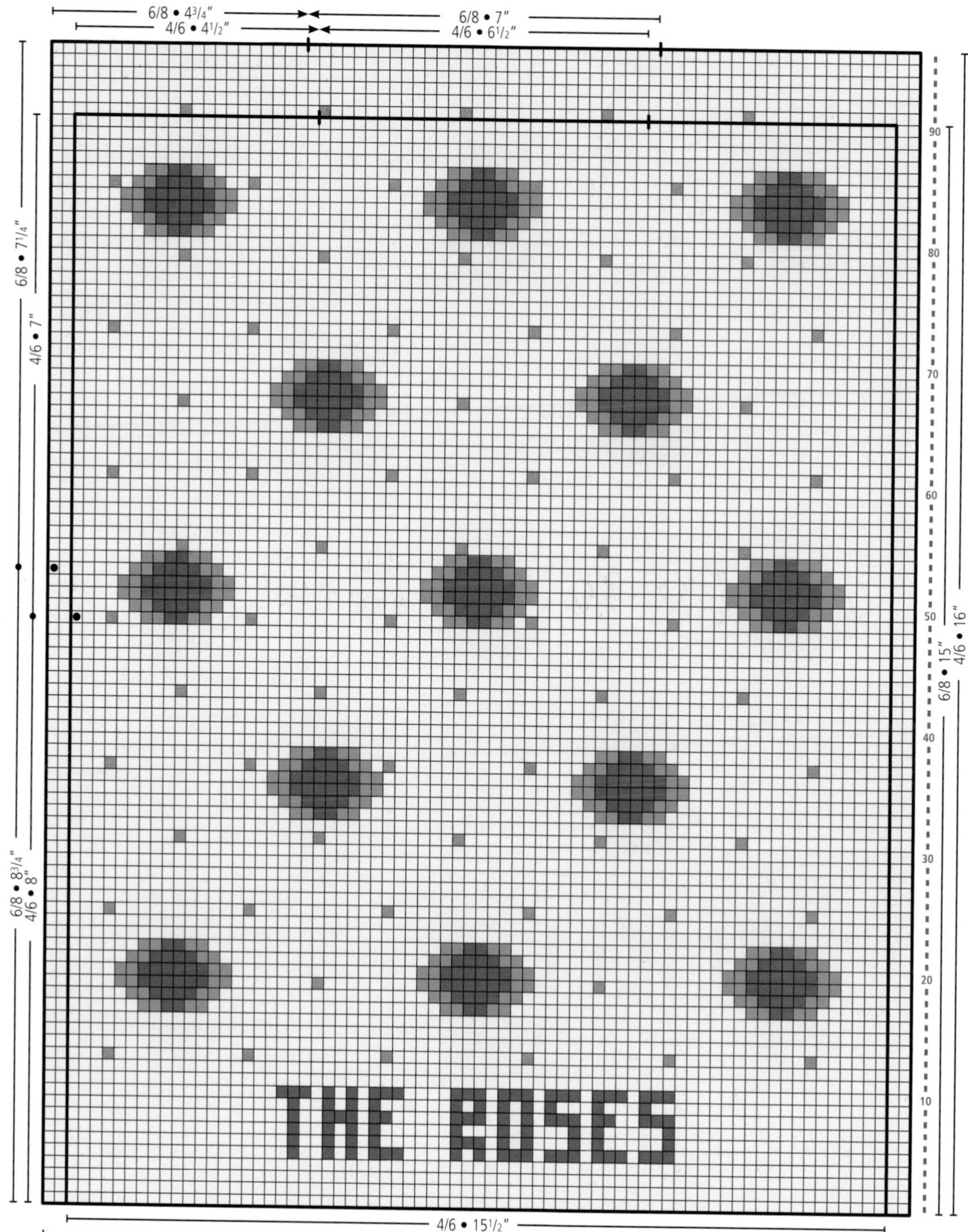

This hat is done on straight needles and is very simple. The circumference of this hat is 18". To increase or decrease size work in multiples of 2 plus 2.

With #8 and color A cast on 82 sts. Work in Stockinette Stitch for 6 1/2". End on WS.
Next Row: K1, K2tog across row until last stitch, K1. (42 sts)
Next Row: Purl across row.
Next Row: K1, K2tog across row, K1. (22 sts)
Next Row: Purl across row.
Next Row: K1, K2tog, K1. (12 sts)
Next Row: Purl across row.
Thread tapestry needle and thread through stitches. Pull tight and sew hat together along seam.
Make 3 roses in color B and sew onto hat.

■ Stop and Smell the Roses { sleeve }

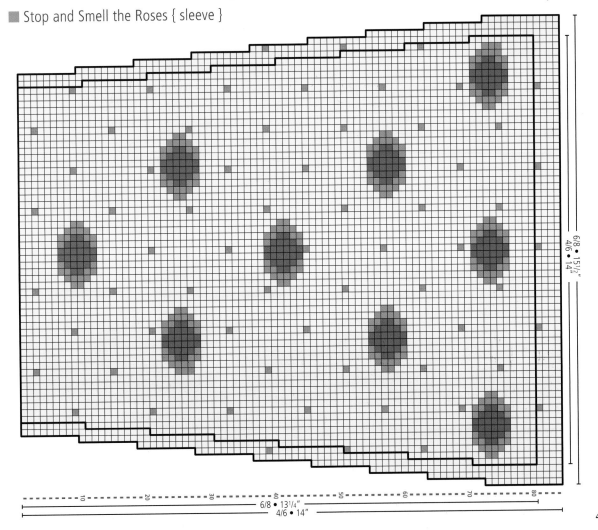

{ Stop Look and Listen }

Young children love toy cars. They power them across the floor with just the push of a tiny hand. My son used to sit in the kitchen surrounded by an assortment of colorful cars, racing them across the tiles, always accompanied by his vroom-vroom sound effects. This sweater embodies the playfulness of little toy cars, and the words teach them to respect the big cars.

{ Finished Measurements }

size	4/6	6/8
chest measurement	31″	33″
length from shoulder with ribbing	17½″	18½″
sleeve length from shoulder with ribbing	15″	16″

materials

- 4 (5) skeins 1.75oz/50grams (77yds/70m) of Fiatura DiCrosa Zara Plus in Charcoal Grey (A)
- 1(1) skeins 1.75oz/50grams (77yds/70m) each of Fiatura DiCrosa Zara Plus in White (B), Royal Blue (C), Mustard (D), Red (E) Deep Sage (F)
- 1 pair #8 and #9 straight knitting needles or size to obtain gauge
- #7 circular needle (16″)
- bobbins

gauge

18 stitches and 24 rows = 4 inches

instructions

Back

With smaller needles and color A cast on 69 (73) sts. Rib K1, P1 for 4 rows. Change to color E and rib 1 row. Change back to color A and rib 5 more rows increasing to 70 (74) sts evenly in last row ending on WS.

(RS) Change to larger needles. Continue with color A and in Stockinette Stitch begin following graph for measurements, color changes, armhole marking and neck shaping. When graph is completed bind off 20 (21) sts for shoulder. Put 30 (32) sts on holder for back neck and bind off remaining 20 (21) sts for other shoulder.

Front

Follow Back for cast on and ribbing instructions. (RS) Change to larger needles. Continue with color A and in Stockinette Stitch begin following graph for measurements, color changes, armhole marking and neck shaping. When graph is completed bind off 20 (21) sts for each shoulder.

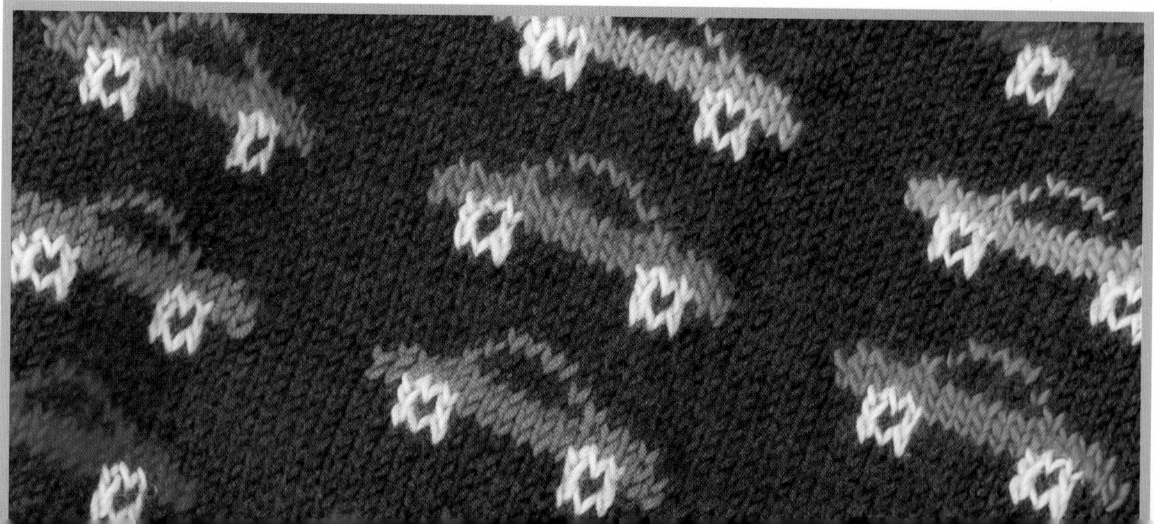

Sleeves

With smaller needles and color A cast on 37 (39) sts and rib K1, P1 for 4 rows. Change to color E and rib 1 row. Change back to color A and rib for 5 rows increasing to 50 (54) sts evenly in last row ending on WS.

(RS) Change to larger needles. With color A work sleeve in Stockinette Stitch increasing 2 sts every 10th row 7 times for size 4/6 (64 sts). For size 6/8 increase 2 sts every 9th row 8 times (70 sts). Bind off.

■ assembling

Sew shoulders together. Place sleeve within armhole markers. Do not to stretch or gather sleeve to fit. Sew sleeve in place. Sew up body from bottom ribbing along side and continue down the sleeve to ribbing.

Neck

Pick up and K70 (74) sts around neck and rib K1, P1 for 6 rows or 1". Bind off loosely.

- ■ (A) Charcoal Grey: knit on right side; purl on wrong side
- □ (B) White: knit on right side; purl on wrong side
- ■ (C) Royal Blue: knit on right side; purl on wrong side
- ■ (D) Mustard: knit on right side; purl on wrong side
- ■ (E) Red: knit on right side; purl on wrong side
- ■ (F) Deep Sage: knit on right side; purl on wrong side
- ● Armhole marker

{ Stop Look and Listen }

Stop Look and Listen { front }

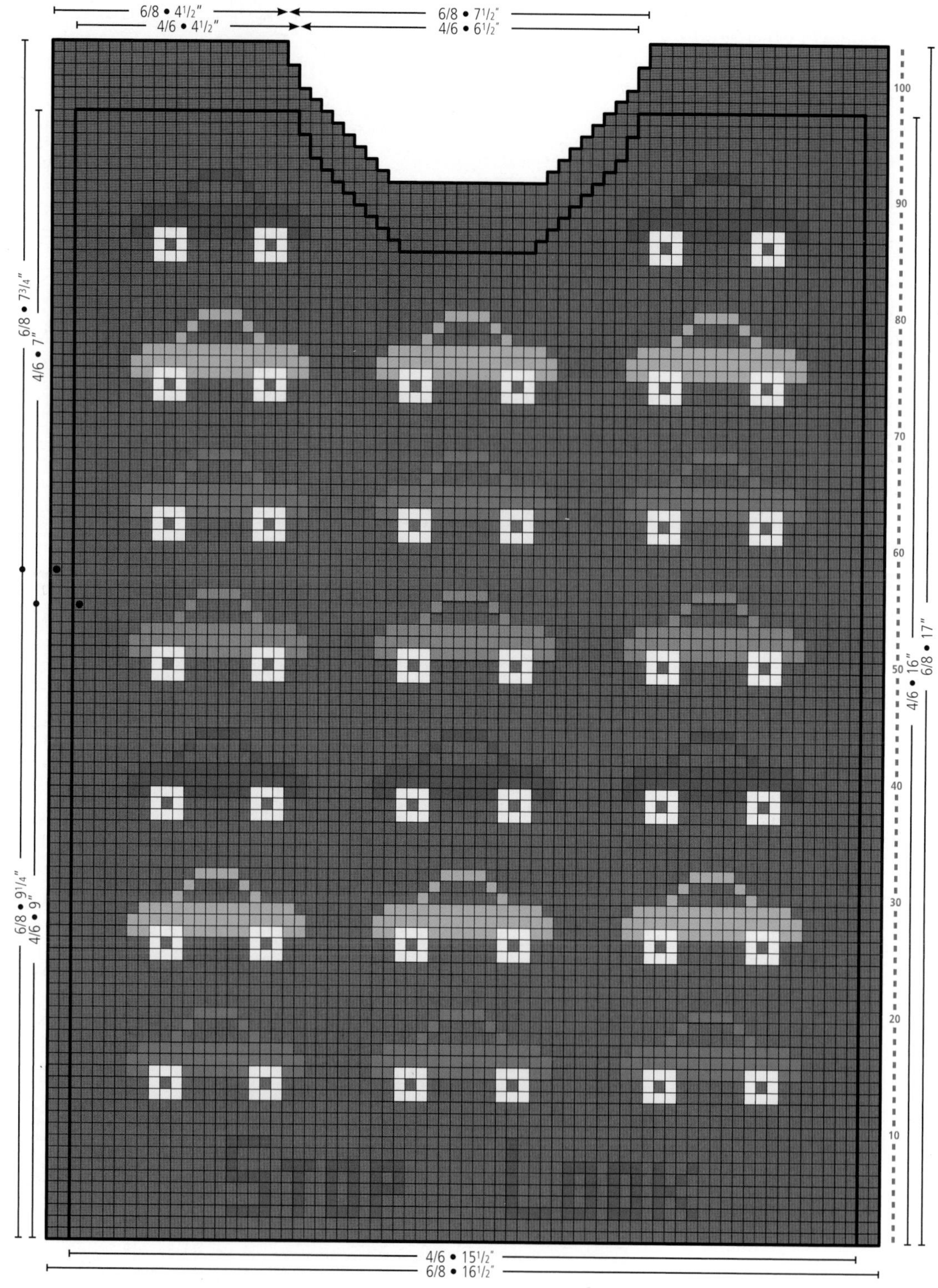

Stop Look and Listen { back }

{ Be Yourself }

I have always encouraged my children to be individuals and appreciate their uniqueness. It makes the world more interesting. This sweater is designed to inspire children to embrace their personal style, and make them smile.

The cardigan is sized in 2/4 and 6, so check your measurements before you start. The "B-E-Y-O-U-R-S-E-L-F" buttons are simple square alphabet buttons found at a local craft store. The yarn balls are made by crossing yarn over the already knitted in balls on the sweater.

{ Finished Measurements }

size	2/4	6
chest measurement	28"	30"
length from shoulder with ribbing	14¼"	15¼"
sleeve length from shoulder with ribbing	15¼"	16"

■ materials

- 4 (5) skeins 4oz/113grams (190yds/173m) of Brown Sheep Lamb's Pride in Color Onyx (A)
- 1 (1) skein 4oz/113grams (190yds/173m) each of Brown Sheep Lamb's Pride in Creme (B) Grey Heather (C), Wild Oak (D), Limeade (E), Brite Blue (F), Autumn Harvest (G), RPM Pink (H), Lemon Drop (I), Oatmeal (J)
- 1 pair #7 and #8 straight knitting needles or size to obtain gauge
- 10 Alphabet Buttons
- 1 Star Button or any button to separate B-E from Y-O-U-R-S-E-L-F
- bobbins

■ gauge

18 stitches and 24 rows = 4 inches

■ instructions

Back

With smaller needles and color A cast on 61 (67) sts. Rib K1, P1 for 2" increasing to 64 (68) sts evenly in last row ending on WS. (RS) Change to larger needles. Continue with color A and in Stockinette Stitch begin following graph for measurements, color changes, armhole marking and neck shaping. When graph is completed bind off 19 (21) sts for shoulder. Put 26 (26) sts on holder for back neck and bind off remaining 19 (21) sts for other shoulder.

Right Front

With smaller needles and color A cast on 29 (35) sts. Rib K1, P1 for 2" ending on WS. (RS) Change to larger needles. Continue with color A and in Stockinette Stitch begin following graph for measurements, color changes, armhole marking and neck shaping. When graph is completed bind off 19 (21) sts for right shoulder.

Left Front

Follow instructions for Right Front for cast on and ribbing instructions. (RS) Change to larger needles and begin following graph for Left Front. When graph is completed bind off 19 (21) sts for left shoulder.

Left Sleeve
With smaller needles and color A cast on 37 (39) sts. Rib K1, P1 for 2″ increasing to 50 (54) sts evenly in last row ending on WS. (RS) Change to larger needles. Continue with color A and in Stockinette Stitch begin following Left Sleeve graph for measurements, color changes and increases. When graph is completed bind off 64 (70) sts.

Right Sleeve
Follow Left Sleeve for cast on and ribbing instructions. (RS) Change to larger needles and in Stockinette Stitch follow graph for Left Sleeve using Right Sleeve Insert starting on row 7. When graph is completed bind off 64 (70) sts.

Left Front Edge *(Button Band)*
With RS facing, smaller needles and color A, begin at left front neck edge and pick up and K 77 (83) sts evenly to lower edge. Begin with WS, work 8 rows in rib K1, P1. Bind off. Place markers on band where buttons should go starting 1/4″ from lower edge and 1/4″ from upper edge with others spaced evenly between. There are 10 buttons on this band starting at the top with "E", followed by a star (or any non-alphabet button) finishing with "F". "B" will be placed in the neck band.

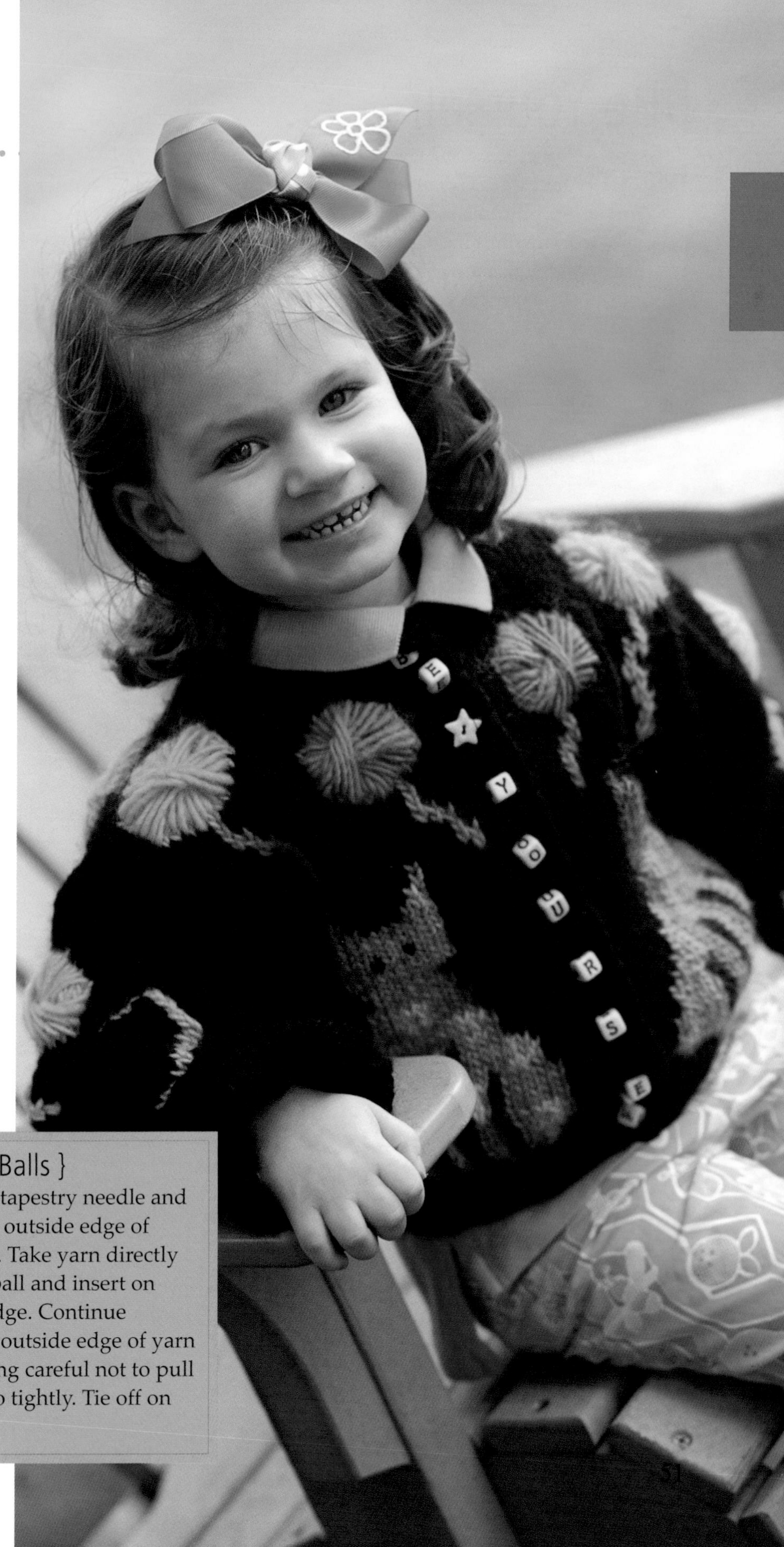

{ Yarn Balls }
Thread tapestry needle and start on outside edge of the ball. Take yarn directly across ball and insert on other edge. Continue around outside edge of yarn ball being careful not to pull yarn too tightly. Tie off on inside.

Right Front Edge *(Buttonhole Side)*
Work as for button band beg at right front neck edge, working buttonholes (on 4th row) to correspond with markers for buttons following Buttonhole Instructions in General Instructions. Bind off.

Sew shoulder seams together.
Place sleeves into sweater within armhole markings and do not stretch or gather sleeve to fit. Sew up body from bottom ribbing along side and continue down sleeve to ribbing.

Be Yourself { right & left front }

(A) Onyx: knit on right side; purl on wrong side

(B) Creme: knit on right side; purl on wrong side

(C) Grey Heather: knit on right side; purl on wrong side

(D) Wild Oak: knit on right side; purl on wrong side

(E) Limeade: knit on right side; purl on wrong side

(F) Brite Blue: knit on right side; purl on wrong side

(G) Autumn Harvest: knit on right side; purl on wrong side

(H) RPM Pink: knit on right side; purl on wrong side

(I) Lemon: knit on right side; purl on wrong side

(J) Oatmeal: knit on right side; purl on wrong side

X Button hole

● Armhole marker

Be Yourself { back }

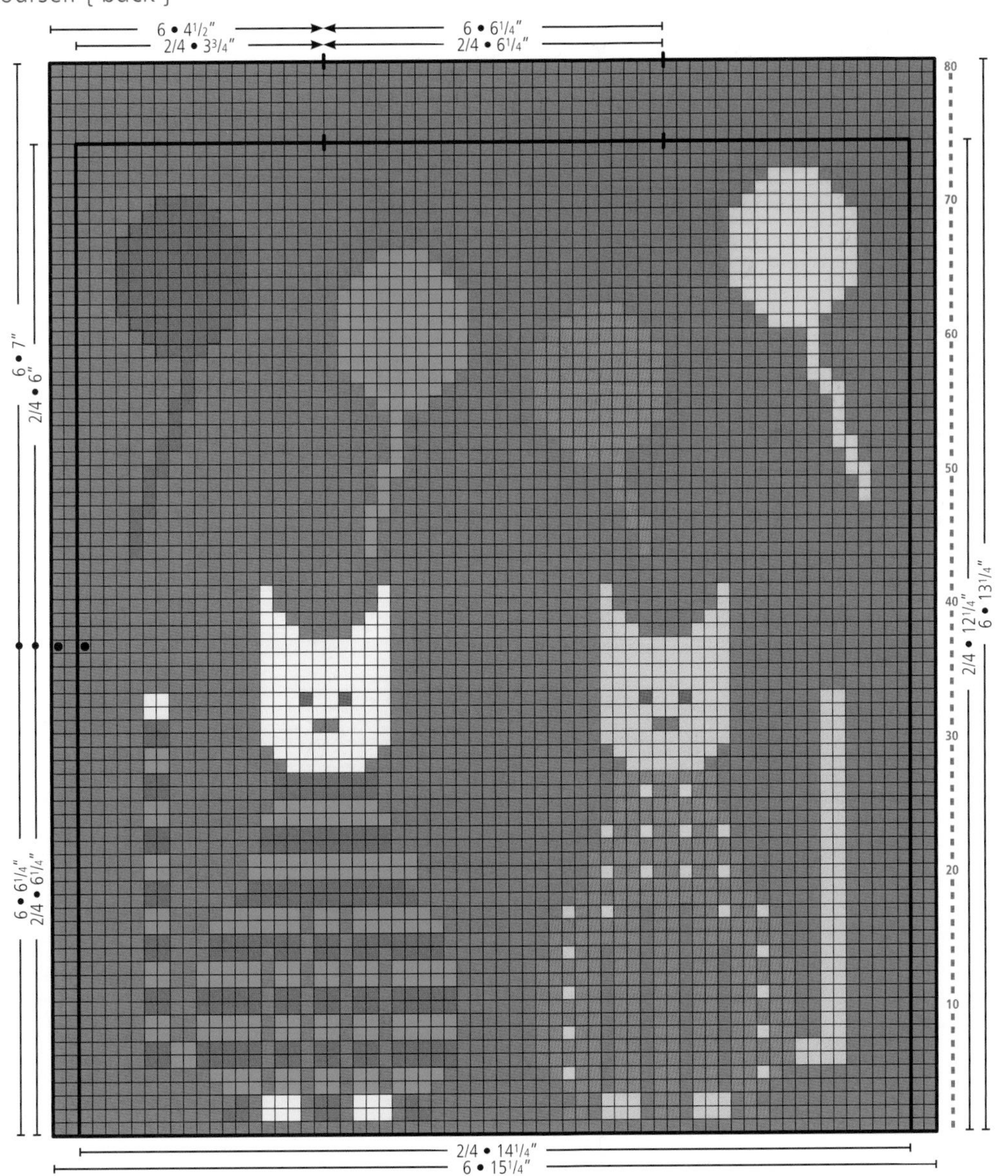

{ Be Yourself }

Neck
With RS facing, smaller needles and color A pick up and K71 (75) sts starting at right front edge and spaced evenly around neck edge.

Work 6 rows rib K1, P1 placing last buttonhole in center of band centered above buttonholes on right front band. Bind off.

Sew buttons in place.

Be Yourself { left sleeve }

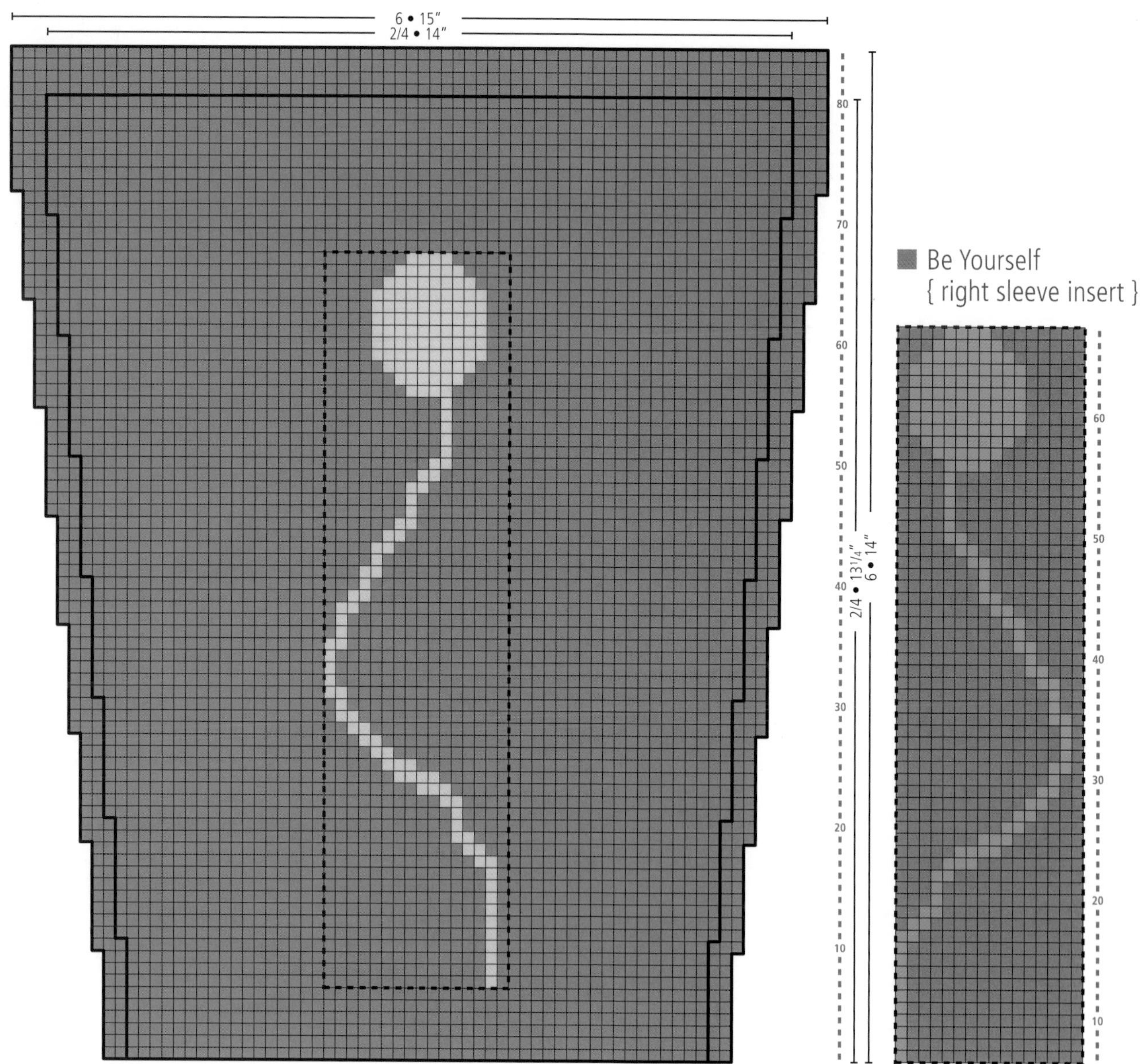

{ Be Kind }

We have always had dogs in our house, and when my children were young we were constantly saying "Be Kind" when they reached out to pull the dog's hair. The phrase then transferred to the flowers in the garden. As they grew older it took on another broader meaning applying to both friends and strangers, and it is a phrase that cannot be taught too often or too early.

{ Finished Measurements }

size	2/4	6
chest measurement	28″	30″
length from shoulder with ribbing	15″	16″

materials

- 2 (3) skeins 35oz/100grams (183yds/167m) of Tahki Donegal Tweed Homespun in Color Light Olive (A)
- 1 (1) skein 1.75oz/50grams (77yds/70m) each of Filatura Di Crosa Zara Plus in Red (B), Black (C), Lemon (D), White (E)
- 1 pair #7 and #8 straight knitting needles or size to obtain gauge
- #7 circular needle (16″)
- needle for embroidery
- bobbins

gauge

18 stitches and 24 rows = 4 inches

{ Be Kind }

instructions

French Knot

Thread yarn through needle. From wrong side bring yarn through to right side at required position and hold yarn down where it appears on the surface. Wrap the yarn three times around the needle. While still holding the yarn firmly, twist the needle back to the starting point and insert it close to where yarn first emerged. Pull the needle through to the back, leaving the knot on the surface. Tie off on the inside.

Back

With smaller needles and color B cast on 63 (67) sts. Rib K1, P1 for 2 rows. Change to color A and continue to rib for 2" ending on WS. (RS) Change to larger needles. Continue with color A and in Stockinette Stitch begin following graph for measurements, color changes, armhole marking and neck shaping.
When graph is completed bind off 12 (13) sts for shoulder. Put 27 (29) sts on holder for back neck and bind off remaining 12 (13) sts for other shoulder.

Front

Follow Back for cast on and ribbing instructions. (RS) Change to larger needles. Continue with color A and in Stockinette Stitch begin following graph for measurements, color changes, armhole marking and neck shaping. When graph is completed bind off 12 (13) sts for each shoulder.

Neck

With RS facing, circular needle and color A pick up and K60 (66) sts evenly around neck.
Rib K1, P1 for 5 rows.
Change to color B and work rib K1, P1 for 1 row.
Bind off loosely.

Sew side seams together.

Armhole

With RS facing, circular needle and color A pick up and K52 (56) sts evenly around armhole.
Rib K1, P1 for 5 rows.
Change to color B and work K1, P1 for 1 row.
Bind off loosely.

(A) Light Olive: knit on right side; purl on wrong side

(B) Red: knit on right side; purl on wrong side

⌘ (C) Black: French Knot

⌘ (D) Lemon: French Knot

● Armhole marker

Be Kind Vest { front & back }

{ Don't Bee a Litterbug }

I grew up in the 1950's with the "Litterbug" ads, and I was sorry to see them fade away. That campaign left a huge impression on me. So I am glad to see its return because the message is clearly an example of a simple expression having a very big impact. My very clever daughter had the idea to make it a play on bees.

The bumblebees are embroidered on this sweater to give it some texture. You could knit them in if you are less comfortable with embroidery

{ Finished Measurements }

size	4/6	6/8
chest measurement	32″	34½″
length from shoulder with ribbing	16½″	17½″
sleeve length from shoulder with ribbing	14¾″	15¾″

materials

- 5 (6) skeins 4oz/113grams (190yds/173m) of Brown Sheep Lamb's Pride Worsted in Grey Heather #03 (A)
- 1 (1) skein 4oz/113grams 190yds/173m) each of Brown Sheep Lamb's Pride Worsted in Ruby Red (B), Onyx (C), Autumn Harvest (D), Limeade (E), Winter Blue (F), Lemon Drop (G), Cream (H), Sable (I)
- 1 pair #8 straight knitting needles or size to obtain gauge
- #7 circular needle (16")
- needle for embroidery
- bobbins

gauge

18 stitches and 24 rows = 4 inches

instructions

French Knot

Thread yarn through needle. From wrong side bring yarn through to right side at required position and hold yarn down where it appears on the surface. Wrap the yarn three times around the needle. While still holding the yarn firmly, twist the needle back to the starting point and insert it close to where yarn first emerged. Pull the needle through to the back, leaving the knot on the surface. Tie off on the inside.

Back

With #8 needles and color A cast on 70 (74) sts. Work in Garter Stitch for 1½" increasing to 72 (78) sts evenly in last row ending on WS. (RS) Continue with color A and in Stockinette Stitch begin following graph for measurements, color changes, armhole marking and neck shaping. When the graph is completed bind off 22 (23) sts for shoulder. Put 28 (32) sts on holder for back neck and bind off remaining 22 (23) sts for other shoulder.

Front

Follow Back for cast on and Garter Stitch border. (RS) Continue with color A and in Stockinette Stitch begin following graph for measurements, color changes, armhole marking and neck shaping. Bees are embroidered after sweater front is finished. When graph is completed bind off 22 (23) sts for each shoulder.

Sleeves
With #8 needles and color A cast on 37 (39) sts. Work in Garter Stitch for $1^{1}/_{2}$" increasing to 50 (54) sts evenly in last row ending on WS.
(RS) Continue with color A and in Stockinette Stitch begin following graph for measurements, increases and ladybug placement*.
When graph is completed bind off 64 (68) sts.

assembling

Embroider bees on front as indicated on graph.
Sew shoulders together. Place sleeve within armhole markings and remember not to stretch or gather sleeve to fit.
Sew sleeve in place.
Sew up body from bottom ribbing along side and continue down sleeve to ribbing.

Neck
Using #7 circular needle pick up and K72 (78) sts. Put marker at beginning. Work Garter Stitch in rounds as knit 1 row, purl next row for 1". Bind off.

**For Size 4/6 do not knit the top row of bugs on the sleeve graph (shown faded out).*

{ Don't Bee a Litterbug }

Don't Bee a Litterbug { front }

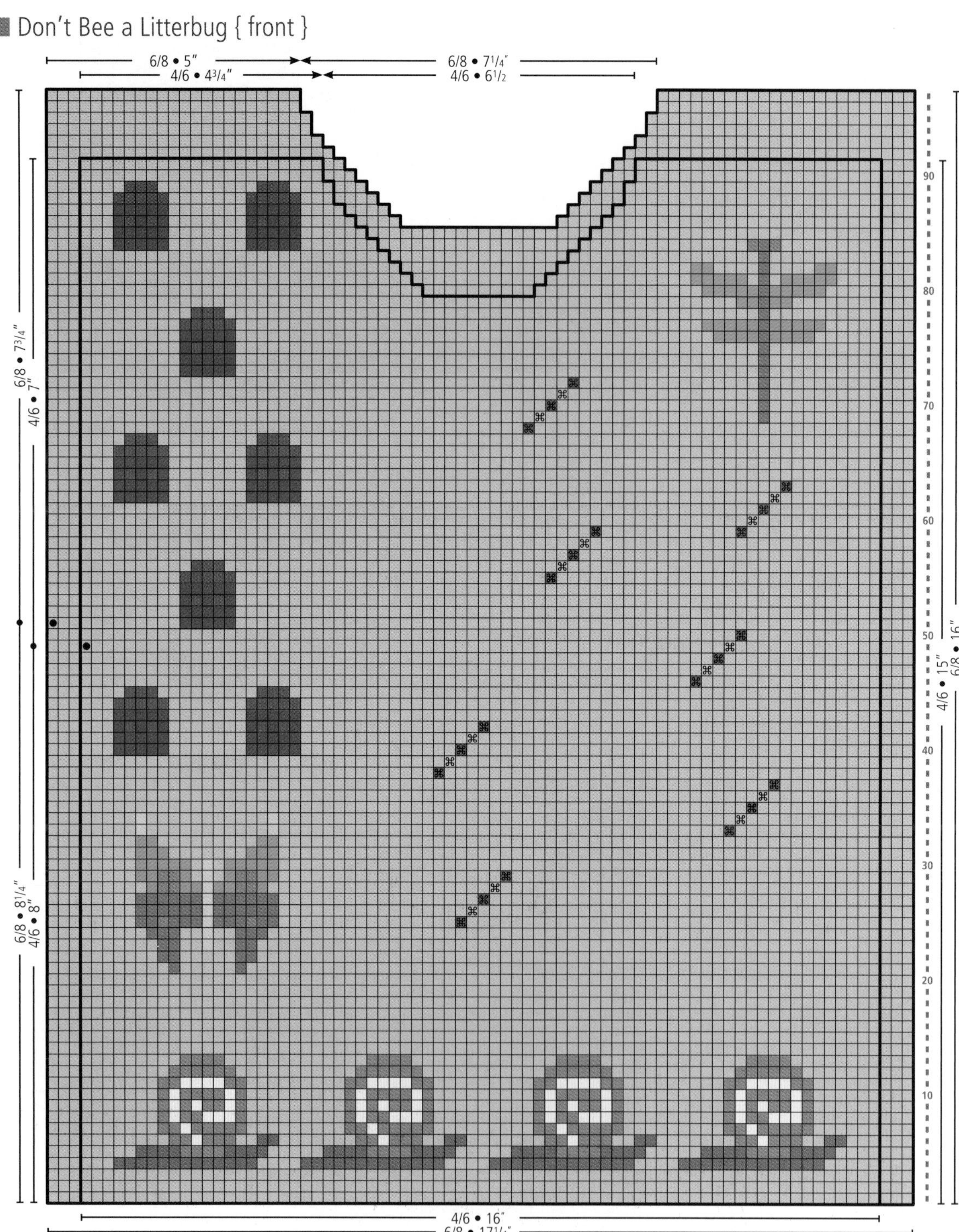

Don't Bee a Litterbug { back }

{ Don't Bee a Litterbug }

- (A) Grey Heather: knit on right side; purl on wrong side
- (B) Ruby Red: knit on right side; purl on wrong side
- (C) Onyx: knit on right side; purl on wrong side
- ⌘ (C) Onyx: French Knot
- (D) Autumn Harvest: knit on right side; purl on wrong side
- (E) Limeade: knit on right side; purl on wrong side
- (F) Winter Blue: knit on right side; purl on wrong side
- (G) Lemon Drop: knit on right side; purl on wrong side
- (H) Cream: knit on right side; purl on wrong side
- (I) Sable: knit on right side; purl on wrong side
- X Buttonhole
- ● Armhole marker

Don't Bee a Litterbug { sleeve }

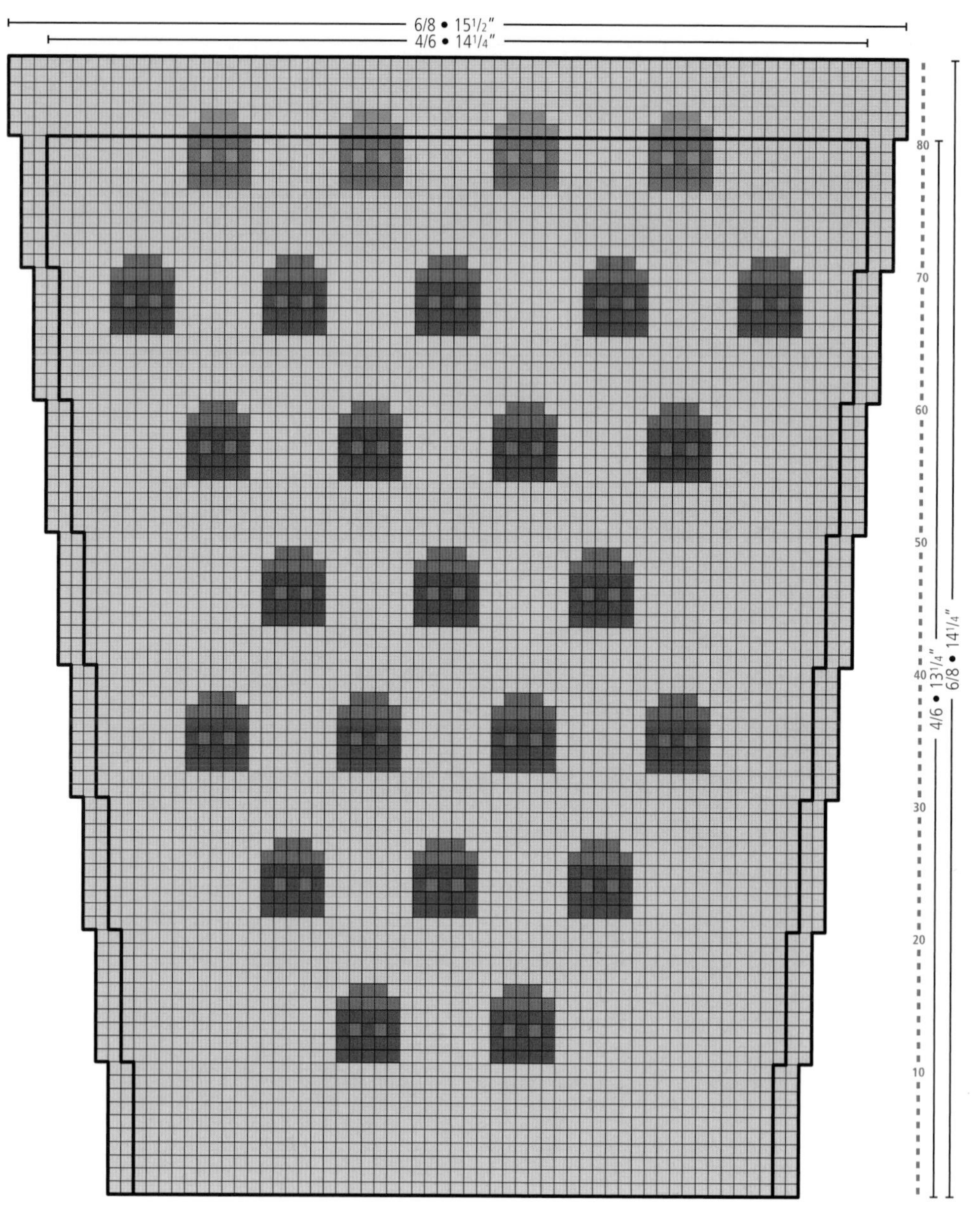

{ Reach for the Stars }

Whether we are "wishing on" or "reaching for" a star there is something magical about evening when the stars first appear. I thought the texture and color of this yarn captures some of that nighttime, dreamy feeling. The added "glitter" helps to bring those stars within reach when we do our very best to make our dreams come true.

{ Finished Measurements }

size	4/6	6/8
chest measurement	31 1/2"	33 1/2"
length from shoulder with ribbing	17 1/2"	18 1/2"
sleeve length from shoulder with ribbing	15 1/2"	16 1/2"

materials

- 3 (4) skeins 3.5oz/100grams (183yds/167m) of Tahki Donegal Tweed Homespun in Midnight Blue (A)
- 2 (2) skeins 1.75oz/50grams (77yds/70m) of Filatura Di Crosa in Mustard (B), Off White (C)
- 1 skein 1.75oz/50grams (77yds/70m) of Filatura Di Crosa in Bright Orange (D)
- 1 skein of any gold metallic yarn gauge 3 1/2"-4 sts to the inch.
- 1 pair # 8 straight knitting needles or size to obtain gauge
- 6 Star Buttons
- embroidery needle
- bobbins

gauge

18 stitches and 24 rows = 4 inches

instructions

French Knot

Thread yarn through needle. From wrong side bring yarn through to right side at required position and hold yarn down where it appears on the surface. Wrap the yarn three times around the needle. While still holding the yarn firmly,

{ Reach for the Stars }

twist the needle back to the starting point and insert it close to where yarn first emerged. Pull the needle through to the back, leaving the knot on the surface. Tie off on the inside.

Back

With #8 needles and color A cast on 71 (75) sts. Rib K1, P1 for 4 rows ending on WS.

(RS) Change to color D and in Stockinette Stitch begin following graph for measurements, color changes, armhole marking and neck shaping. When graph is completed bind off 21 (22) sts for shoulder. Put 29 (31) sts on holder for back neck and bind off remaining 21 (22) sts for other shoulder.

Right Front

With #8 needles and color A cast on 36 (38) sts. Rib K1, P1 for 4 rows ending on WS.

(RS) Change to color D and in Stockinette Stitch begin following Right Front graph for measurements, color changes, armhole marking and neck shaping. When graph is completed bind off 21 (22) sts for right shoulder.

Left Front

Follow directions for Right Front for cast on and ribbing instructions.

(RS) Change to color D and reverse Right Front graph for Left Front and begin following graph for measurements, color changes, armhole marking and neck shaping. When graph is completed bind off 21 (22) sts for left shoulder.

Sleeves

With #8 needles and color A cast on 47 (49) sts and rib K1, P1 for 4 rows ending WS.

(RS) Change to color D and in Stockinette Stitch begin following graph for measurements, color changes and increases. When graph is completed bind off at top of sleeve 63 (69) sts.

Left Front Band *(Button Band)*

With RS facing, #8 needles and color A and pick up and K90 (96) sts along left front edge.

Reach for the Stars { right front* }

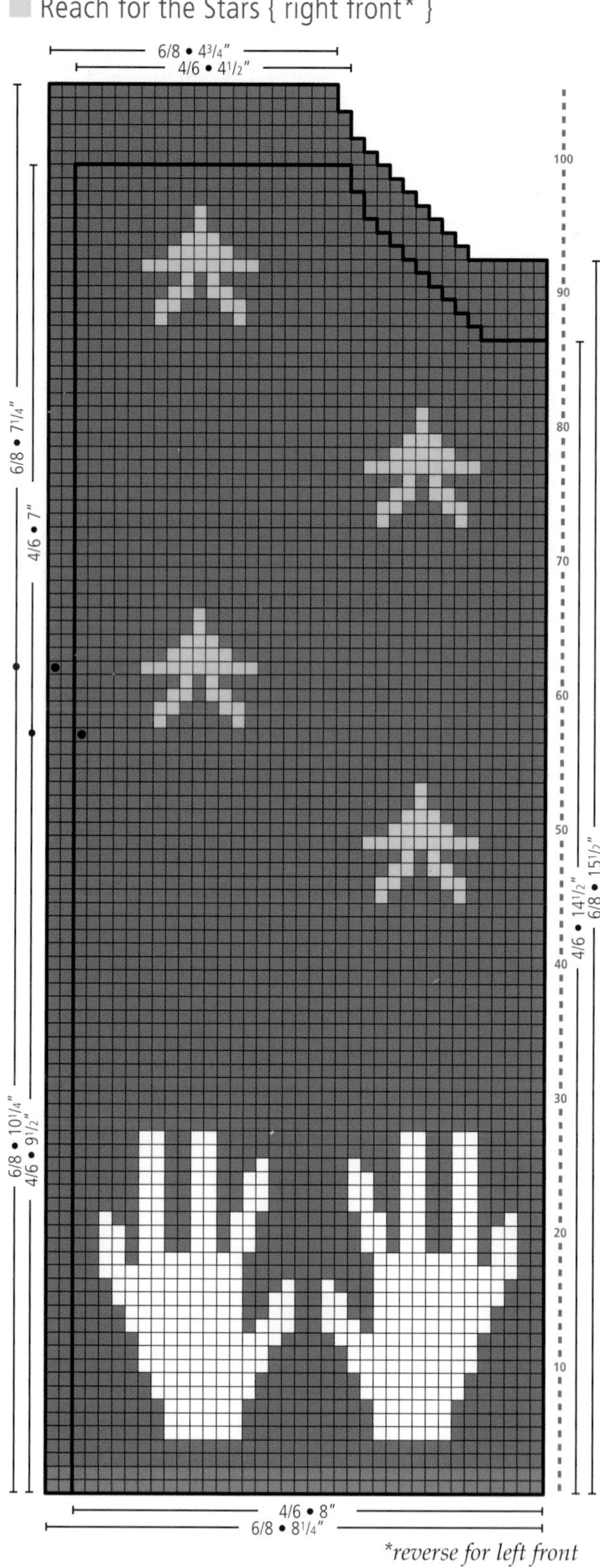

**reverse for left front*

Work K1, P1 for 8 rows. Bind off. Place 5 markers on band where buttons should go starting at 1/2" from lower edge and 2 1/2" (2 1/2") from top edge. The remaining 3 buttons are spaced evenly between.

Right Front Band
(Buttonhole Band)
Work as for button band, working buttonholes (on fourth row) to correspond with markers for buttons following buttonhole instructions in General Instructions. Bind off.

Sew shoulder seams together.

assembling

Place French Knots on big star as indicated on graph with decorative gold metallic yarn. Place sleeves into sweater within armhole markers and do not stretch or gather sleeve to fit. Sew up body from bottom ribbing along side and continue down sleeve to ribbing.

Neck
With RS facing, #8 needles and color A pick up and K73 (79) sts starting at right front edge and spaced evenly around neck. Work 6 rows in rib K1, P1 placing last buttonhole in center of band centered above buttonholes in right front band. Bind off.

Sew on buttons.

{ Reach for the Stars }

Reach for the Stars { back }

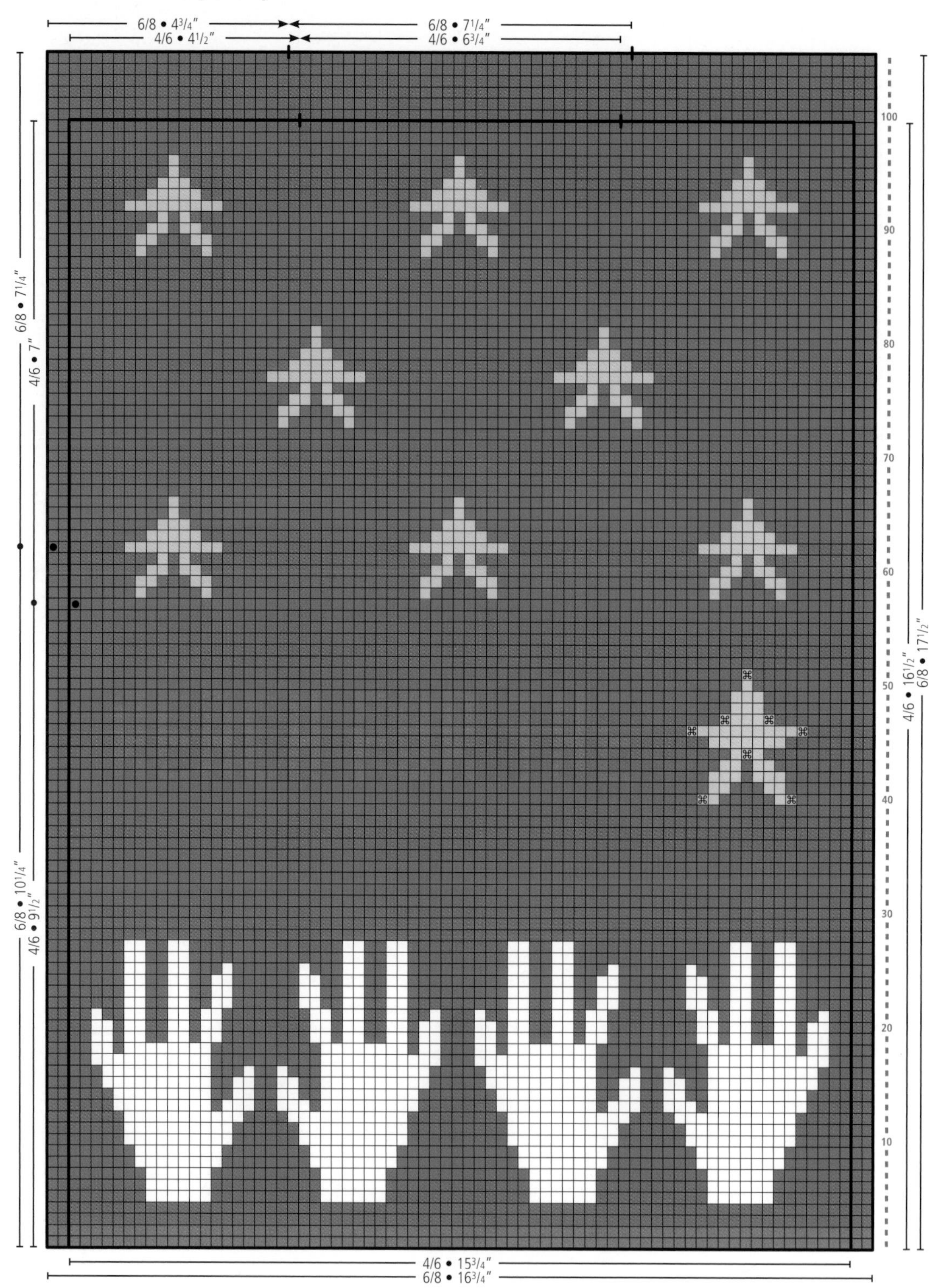

■ (A) Midnight Blue: knit on right side; purl on wrong side

□ (B) Mustard: knit on right side; purl on wrong side

□ (C) Off White: knit on right side; purl on wrong side

■ (D) Bright Orange: knit on right side; purl on wrong side

⌘ (B) gold metallic: french knot

X Buttonhole

● Armhole marker

Reach for the Stars { sleeve }

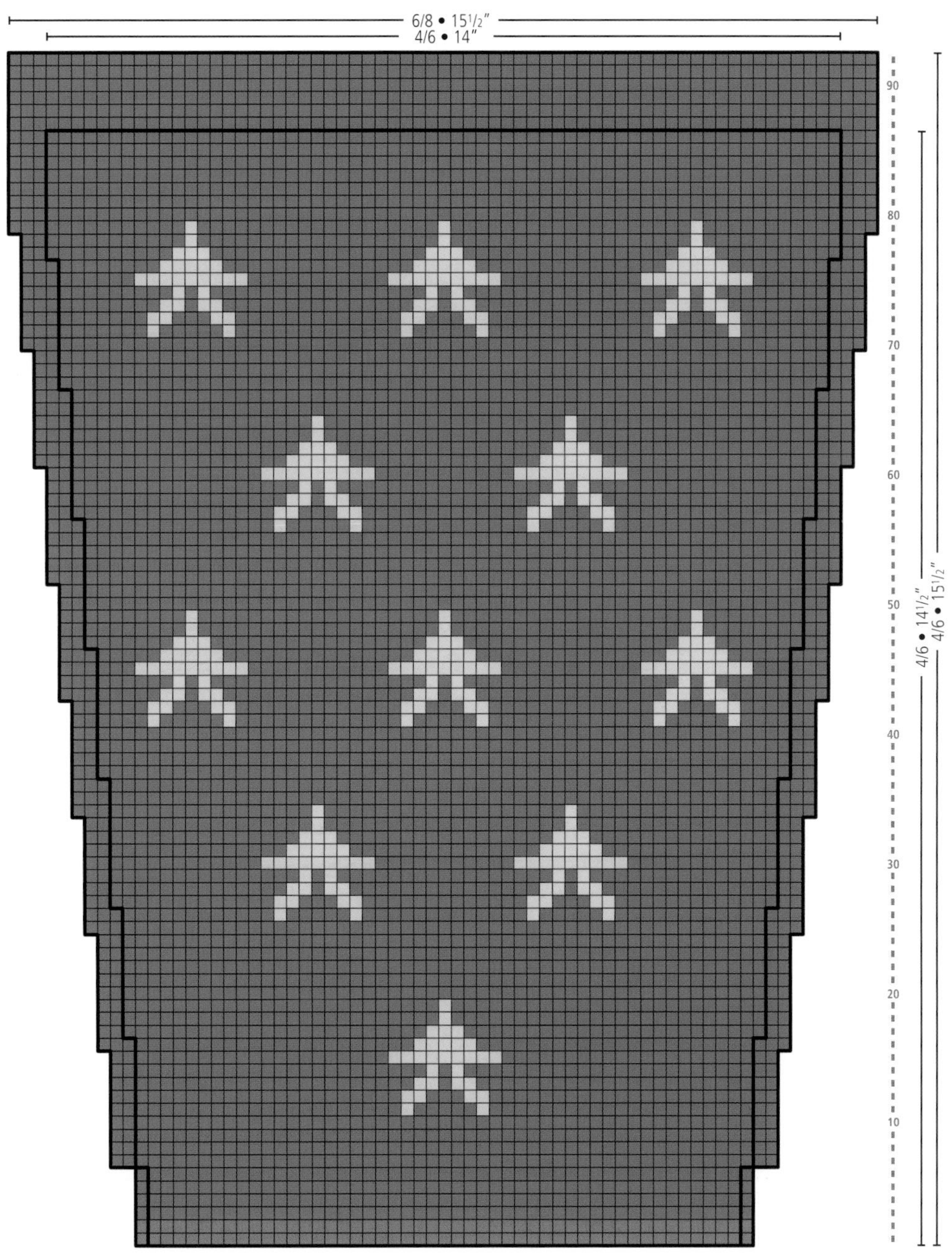

{ Hi & Bye Mittens }

I would have preferred to put Hello and Goodbye on these mittens, but I ran out of space. So in the interest of brevity–probably more appropriate in our shorthand culture–I used Hi and Bye. Certainly a greeting of any kind is preferable to none at all. If you want to knit on a much smaller gauge you could possibly fit, "It is very nice to meet you." But that may be too ambitious for all of us.

I made these mittens in one size because I found my models who ran the ages of 3 to 8 could all wear them. On the older children the mittens just stretched a little more. The only tricky part of making these mittens is to remember to put "HI" on the inside palm of the RIGHT HAND and "BYE" on the inside palm of the LEFT HAND.

■ materials

- 1 skein 3.5oz/100grams (220yds) of Cascade 220 yarns in Christmas Red as Main Color (MC) and Natural as Contrasting Color (CC)
- 1 pair #7 and #8 straight knitting needles or size to obtain gauge.
- bobbins
- markers

■ gauge

16 stitches and 24 rows = 4 inches

■ instruction

Kf&b

Knit in front of stitch and without removing stitch, knit into the back of the stitch which creates an additional stitch.

Left Hand Mitten *(BYE Mitten)*

Rows 1-2: With smaller needles and Contrasting Color (CC) cast on 29 sts and rib K1, P1 for 2 rows.

Rows 3 - 13: Change to Main Color (MC) and continue rib K1, P1 for 2" increasing 4 sts evenly in last row ending on RS. (33 sts)

Rows 14 - 19: (WS) Change to larger needles and MC. Begin Stockinette Stitch starting with a purl row.

Continue in Stockinette Stitch for 6 rows ending on RS.

Row 20: (WS) P15 sts and slip on marker, P3 sts, slip on another marker, P15 sts.

Row 21: (RS) K15, Kf&b to make an additional stitch, K1, Kf&b, K15. (35 sts)

Row 22: (WS) P across row.

Start Graph

Row 23: (RS) With MC K2 sts. Add CC and start graph for color changes in lettering for next 11 sts. K2 sts in MC, slip marker onto needle. Continuing in MC, Kf&b, K3, Kf&b, slip marker onto needle and K15. (37 sts)

Row 24: (WS) P across row following graph.

Row 25: (RS) K15 following graph for color changes, Kf&b, K5, Kf&b, K15. (39 sts)

Row 26: (WS) P across row following graph.

Row 27: (RS) K15 following graph for color changes, Kf&b, K7, Kf&b, K15. (41 sts)

Row 28: (WS) P15 following graph. Put 11 sts on holder for thumb. (You will return to these stitches later.) Continue across row and P15 sts. (30 sts)

Row 29: (RS) This should be the last row of incorporating the graph into the palm of the mitten. Continue to work in Stockinette Stitch in MC until mitten measures 6 1/2" or fits child's hand. End on WS.

Next Row: (RS) K1, K2tog, K1. (16 sts)

Next Row: (WS) Purl.

Next Row: (RS) K1, K2tog, K1. (9 sts)

Next Row: (WS) Purl.

Next Row: (RS) K1, K2tog. (5 sts)

Pass needle through 5 sts and pull tight.

Sew mitten side seam.

Thumb
Pick up 11 sts for thumb and work in Stockinette Stitch for 6 more rows ending on WS.
Next Row: (RS) K1, K2tog across row. (5 sts) Pass needle through 5 sts and pull tight. Sew thumb.

Right Hand Mitten *(HI Mitten)*
Follow Left Hand Mitten instructions to row 23.
Row 23: (RS) With MC K15 sts, slip marker onto needle, Kf&b, K3, Kf&b, slip marker onto needle and K4. Adding CC start graph for color changes in lettering for next 7 sts. Finish row with K4 in MC. (37 sts)
Continue in Stockinette Stitch following HI graph for color changes, making all increases indicated and following instructions for Left Hand Mitten.

■ Right { hi } & Left Mitten { bye }

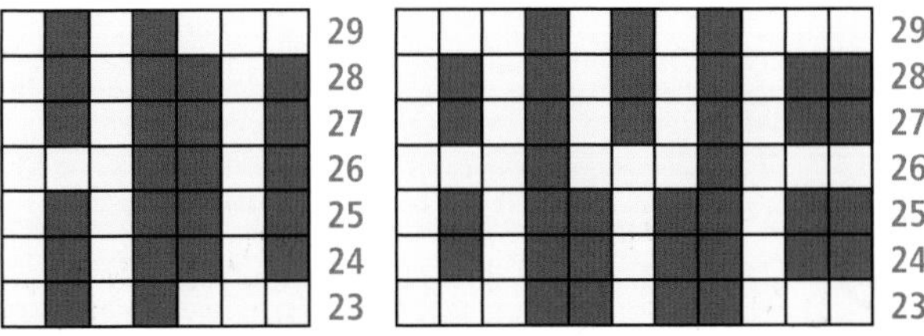

■ (MC) Christmas Red: knit on right side; purl on wrong side

□ (CC) Natural: knit on right side; purl on wrong side

{ Save the Animals Blanket }

Is there a child who doesn't love animals? Animals' names are often the first words children learn after "Mommy" and "Daddy… cow, dog." I have designed a blanket that is not only colorful, but also helps your child to recognize the animals we unfortunately can't find in our backyard unless you live in Africa, Asia, Australia or Antarctica. Maybe we can teach a little geography, too.

{ Finished Measurements }

size approximately 32" wide x 32" long

materials

- 5 skeins 3.5oz/100grams (131yds/118m) of Brown Sheep Shepherd's Shades in Blue Sky (A)
- 2 skeins 3.5oz/100grams (131yds/118) Brown Sheep Shepherd's Shades in Pineapple (B)
- 1 skein 3.5oz/100grams (131yds/118m) each of Brown Sheep Shepherd's Shades in English Oak (C), Steel (D), Pearl (E), Obsidian (F), Rose Petal (G), Buckskin (H), Maple Sugar (I), Lemon Juice (J)
- #9 circular knitting needle (36 ")
- bobbins

(A) Blue Sky: knit on right side; purl on wrong side

(B) Pineapple: knit on right side; purl on wrong side

(C) English Oak: knit on right side; purl on wrong side

(D) Steel: knit on right side; purl on wrong side

(E) Pearl: knit on right side; purl on wrong side

(F) Obsidian: knit on right side; purl on wrong side

(G) Rose Petal: knit on right side; purl on wrong side

(H) Buckskin: knit on right side; purl on wrong side

(I) Maple Syrup: knit on right side; purl on wrong side

(J) Lemon Juice: knit on right side; purl on wrong side

(K) Papaya: knit on right side; purl on wrong side

instructions

With #9 circular needle cast on 45 stitches in color A, cast on 45 sts in color B, and then 45 sts in color A for a total of 135 sts. This blanket is worked in blocks of 45 stitches x 60 rows. Follow graph for all color changes and graphs of animals. Body of blanket is worked in Stockinette Stitch. When graph is completed bind off.

edging and finishing

With #9 needle in color A pick up 135 sts on top edge of blanket and work in Garter Stitch for 6 rows. Bind off. Repeat along bottom edge. Bind off.
Along one side of blanket pick up 173 sts including stitches on top and bottom edge, skipping every 10th stitch. Work Garter Stitch for 6 rows. Bind off. Repeat on opposite edge.

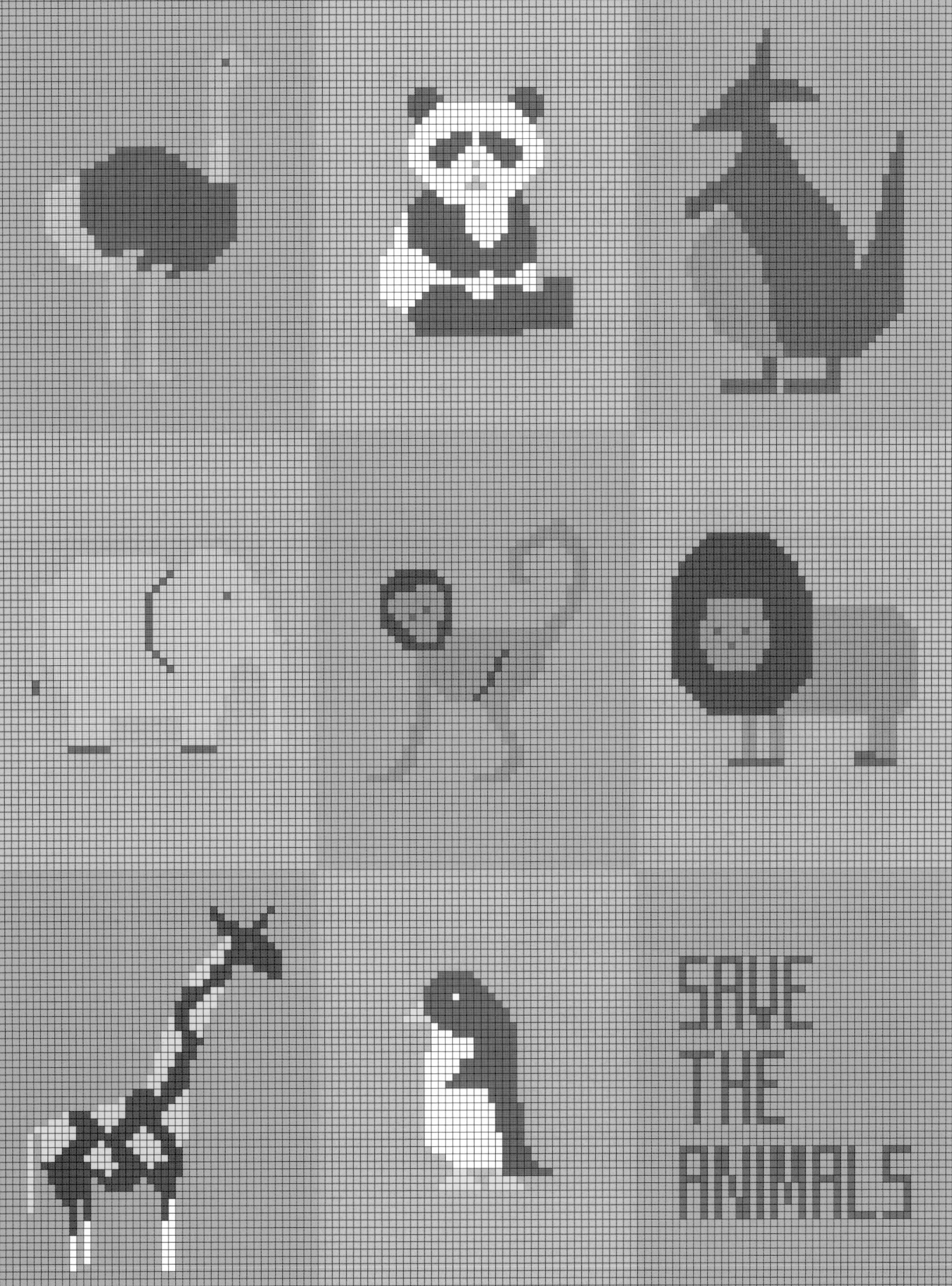
SAVE
THE
ANIMALS
180
170
160
150
140
130
120
110
100
90
80
70
60
50
40
30
20
10

{ Plant a Tree Blanket }

This blanket has been done in earth tones, but you can certainly do it in brighter, less realistic colors to give it punch. If you are going to use this blanket as more of a blanket for your child to sit and play on you may want to add a similarly-sized fabric backing. Remember blankets have a tendency to grow as you are knitting them.

{ Finished Measurements }

size approximately 34" wide x 45" long

materials

- 2 skeins 8oz/227grams (465yds/425m) of Lion Brand Fisherman's Wool in Oatmeal (A)
- 2 skeins 3.5oz/85grams (158yds/144m) of Lion Brand Fisherman's Wool in Rich Cool Green (B)
- #9 circular knitting needle (36 ")
- bobbins

gauge

16 stitches and 24 rows = 4 inches

instructions

Blanket

With #9 needle and color B cast on 142 sts. Follow graph for all color changes. Body of blanket is worked in Stockinette Stitch. When graph is completed bind off.

edging and finishing

With #9 needle in color A pick up 142 sts on top edge of blanket.
Garter Stitch for 8 rows. Bind off.
Repeat along bottom edge. Bind off.
Along one side of blanket pick up 193 sts including stitches on top and bottom edge, skipping every 10th stitch. Work Garter Stitch for 8 rows. Bind off. Repeat on opposite edge.

(A) Oatmeal: knit on right side; purl on wrong side

(B) Cool Green: knit on right side; purl on wrong side

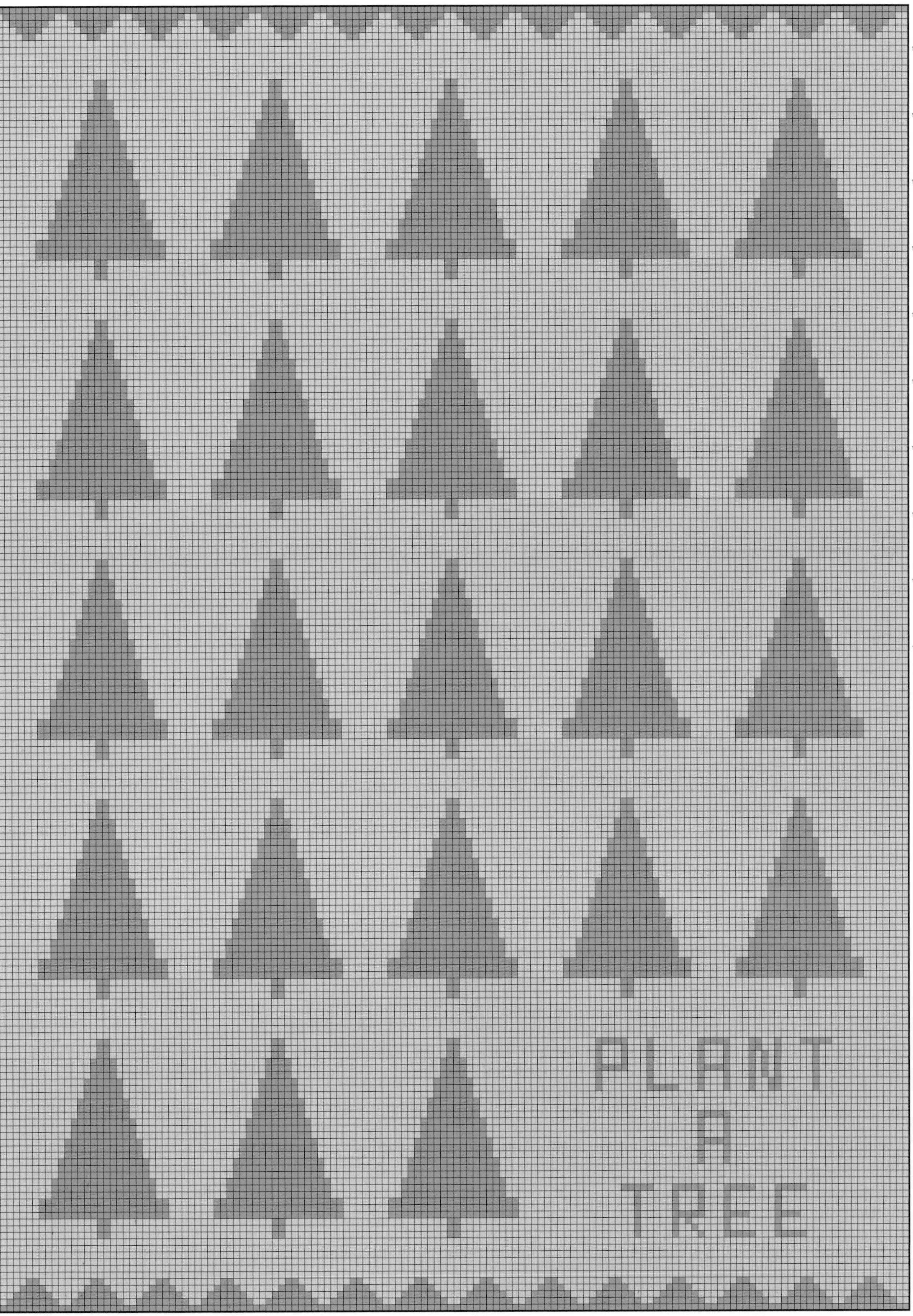

PLANT
A
TREE
190
180
170
160
150
140
130
120
110
100
90
80
70
60
50
40
30
20
10

{ Pillows }

All the pillows are the same gauge $4\frac{1}{2}$ sts and 6 rows = 1 inches and measure 16 inches by 16 inches (72 sts and 96 rows).

You may want to change one of the animals on the "Save The Animals" pillow or put a different animal on the front from the back. To do so, use the graphs from the "Save the Animals" blanket.

{ Yes, Please Pillow } boys

materials

- 6 skeins 1.75oz/50grams (77yds/70m) of Filatura Di Crosa Zara Plus in Royal Blue (A)
- 1 skein 1.75oz/50grams (77yds/70m) of Filatura Di Crosa Zara Plus in Bright Red (B)
- 1 skein 1.75oz/50grams (77yds/70m) Filatura Di Crosa Zara Plus Color White (C)
- 1 pair #8 knitting needles or size to obtain gauge
- #10 double pointed knitting needle
- 14" blue zipper
- 16" x 16" pillow insert
- bobbins*

I-cord

Using 2 strands in color A cast on 3 stitches on #10 double pointed needles. Knit into these 3 sts. Instead of turning the needle, slide the sts down on the needle and knit the same 3 sts again pulling slightly on the yarn so it tightens the cord. Continue to knit in this manner to create the I-cord.

instructions

With color A cast on 72 sts and in Stockinette Stitch follow graph for pillow front. When graph is completed bind off. Repeat cast on instructions for pillow back. Follow graph and when completed bind off.

When completed sew pillow front to pillow back along 3 sides leaving bottom edge open for 14". Hand sew zipper in the pillow.

Make I-Cord approximately 66" long. The length may vary depending on how tight you make your knot at the corner. I would suggest that after you have made a 10" length, make a knot to determine how much more of an I-cord you will need. Once you have determined length, place knot on one end and secure to bottom edge of pillow. Sew I-Cord to the pillow along seam line making knots at each of the top corners.

**Bobbins may be used for each of the pillows found in this section*

Finish at opposite bottom edge making one last knot on bottom corner. There is no I-cord running along bottom edge next to zipper, but you could continue there if you wanted one.

{ Yes, Please Pillow } girls

■ materials

- 2 skeins 3.5oz/100grams (215yds/197m) of Brown Sheep Cotton Fleece in Pink-A-Boo (A)
- 1 skein 3.5oz/100grams (215yds/197m) of Brown Sheep Cotton Fleece in Peridot (B)
- 1 pair #8 knitting needles or size to obtain gauge
- 14″ pink zipper
- 16″ x 16″ pillow insert

Yes, Please girls is continued on p. 78

{ Pillows }

(A) Royal Blue: knit on right side; purl on wrong side

(B) Bright Red: knit on right side; purl on wrong side

(C) Bright Red: knit on right side; purl on wrong side

Yes, Please Pillow (boys) { front }

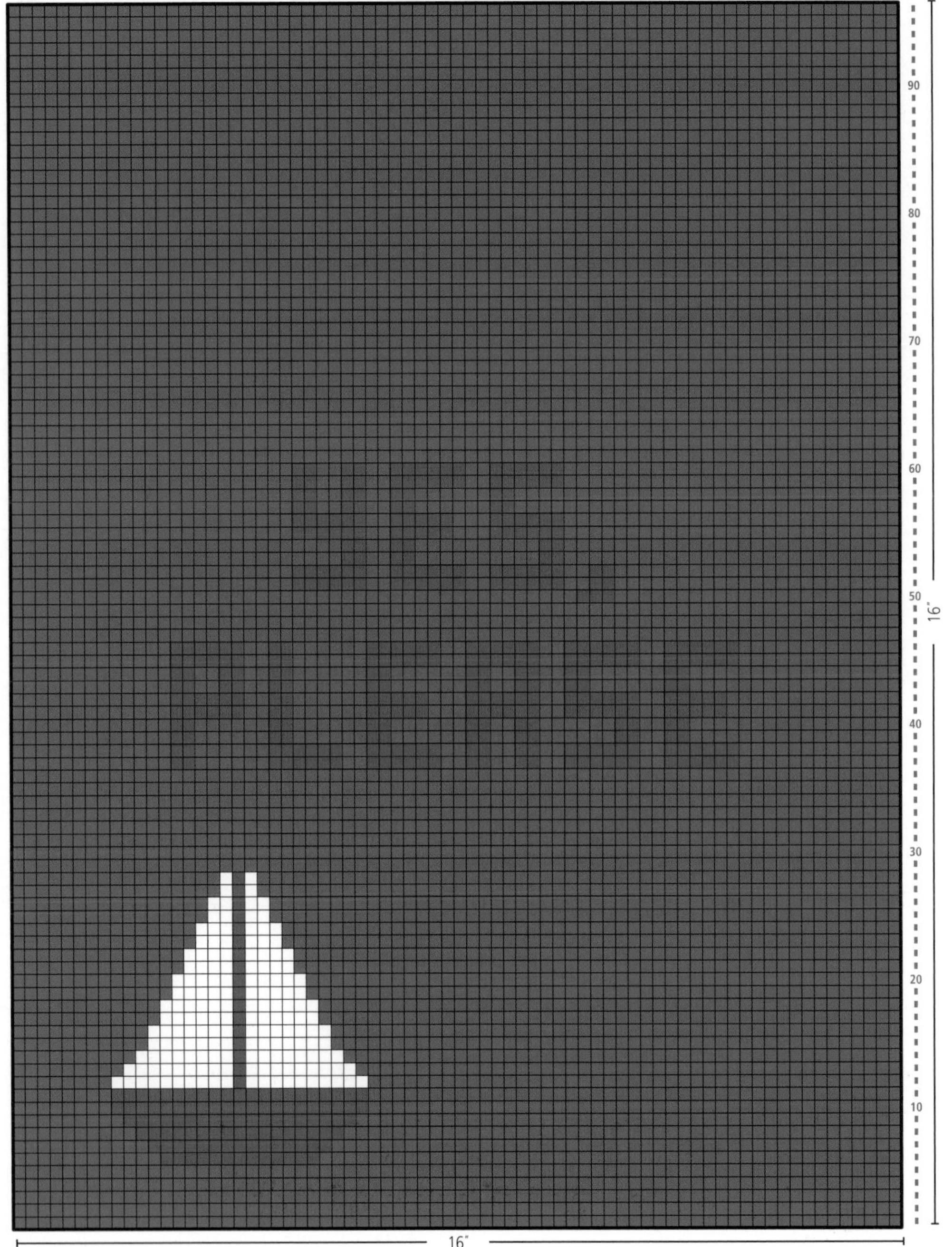

Yes, Please Pillow (boys) { back }

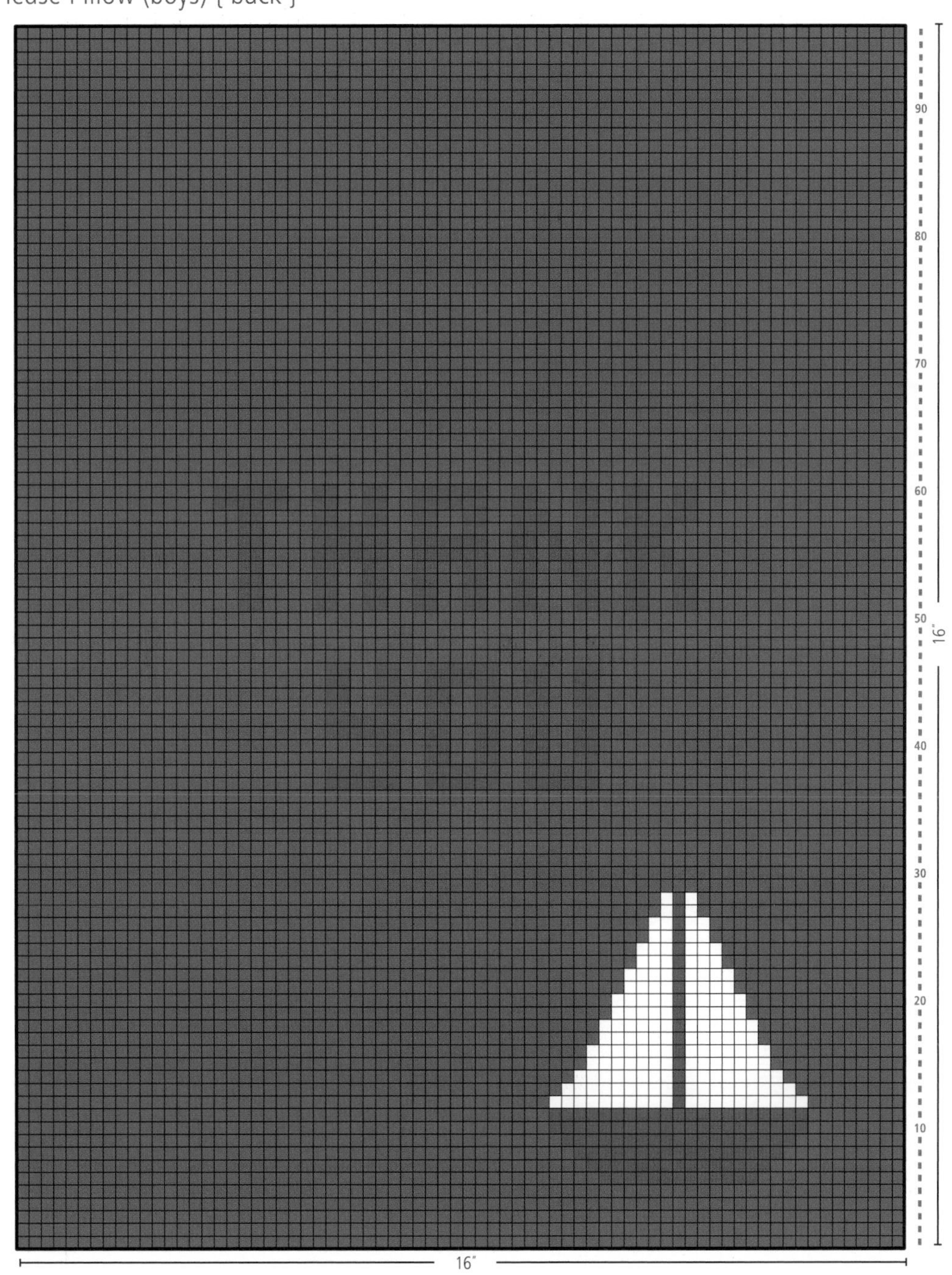

{ Pillows }

(A) Pink-A-Boo: knit on right side; purl on wrong side

(B)Peridot: knit on right side; purl on wrong side

instructions

With color A cast on 72 sts and in Stockinette Stitch follow graph for pillow front. When graph is completed bind off.

Repeat cast on instructions for pillow back. Follow graph and when completed bind off.

Yes, Please Pillow (girls) { front }

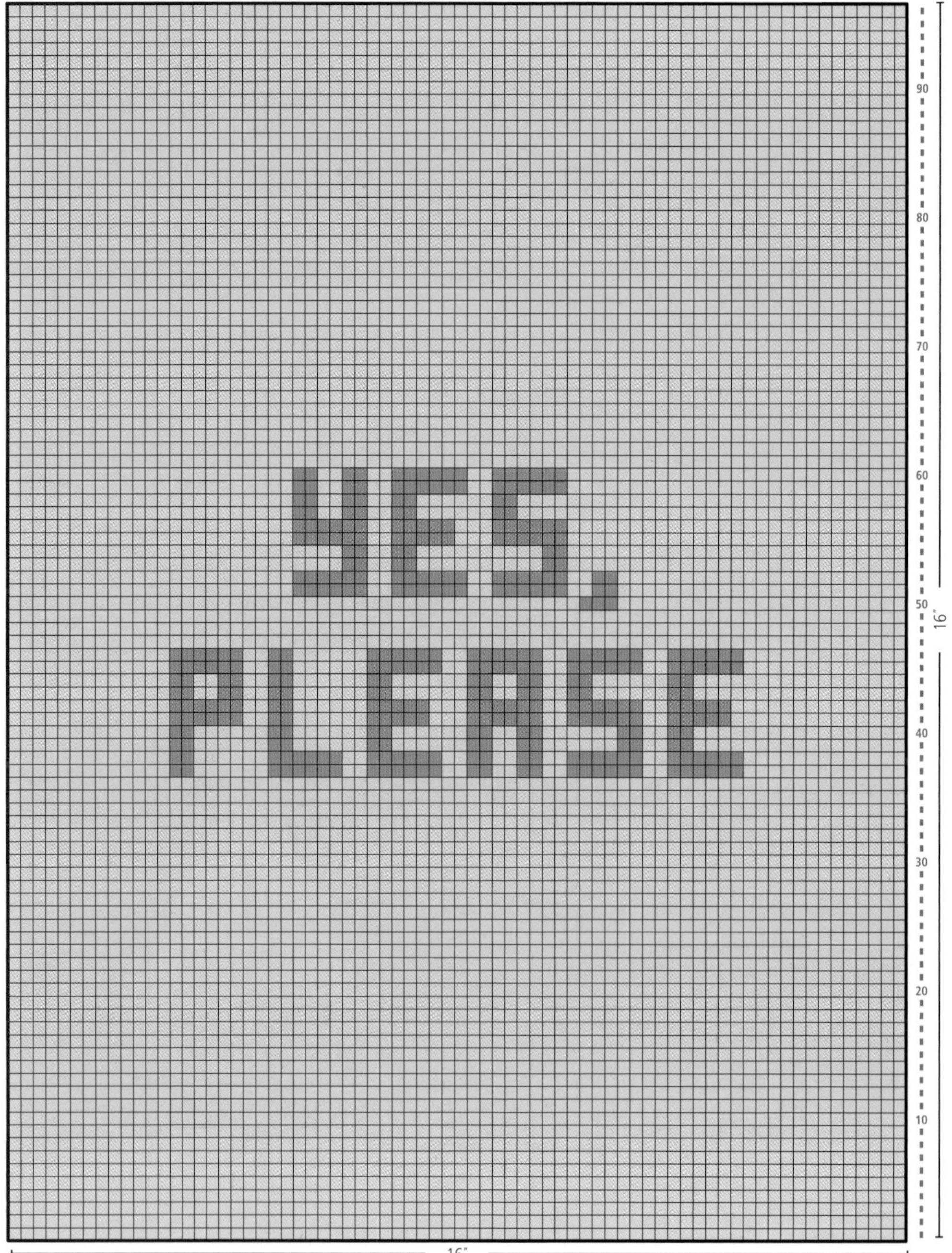

Trim

Pick up 72 sts along bottom edge of pillow front. Knit into front and back of each stitch (144 sts). Knit in Garter Stitch for 8 rows and bind off. Repeat for top edge of pillow front. Working one side at a time pick up 72 sts among the 96 rows on side edge. Knit in front and back of each stitch (144 sts) and knit for 8 rows. Bind off. Repeat on the other sides.

When completed sew pillow front to pillow back along 3 sides leaving bottom edge open for 14″. Hand sew zipper in the pillow.

■ Yes, Please Pillow (girls) { back }

{ Pillows }

{ Save The Animals Pillow} polar bear

■ materials

- 2 skeins 4oz/100grams (190yds/173m) of Brown Sheep Lamb's Pride in Brite Blue (A)
- 1 skein 4oz/100grams (190yds/173m) each of Brown Sheep Lamb's Pride in Creme (B), Grey Heather (C), Orange (D)
- 1 pair #8 knitting needles or size to obtain gauge
- 14″ zipper
- 16″ x 16″ pillow insert

■ instructions and assembling

With color A cast on 72 sts and in Stockinette Stitch follow graph for pillow front. When graph is completed bind off. Repeat cast on instructions for pillow back. Follow graph and when completed bind off.* When completed sew back and front together along 3 sides leaving bottom edge open for 14″ zipper. Hand sew zipper in the pillow. Sew a pompoms on each corner

Pompoms

The snowball on the corners is a classic 1 1/2″ pompom. I did mine on a ready made pompom maker. You can also find pompom making instructions on the Internet.

**If you don't want to put the graphic on the back of the pillow you can knit up a solid back. (72 sts x 96 rows in color A)*

{ Save The Animals Pillow } elephant

■ materials

- 2 skeins 4oz/100grams (190yds/173m of Brown Sheep Lamb's Pride in Kiwi Green Color (A)
- 1 skein 4oz/100grams (190yds/173m) each of Brown Sheep Lamb's Pride in Heather Grey (B), Onyx (C), Orange (D)
- 1 pair #8 knitting needles or size to obtain gauge
- 14″ zipper
- 16″ x 16″ pillow insert

■ instructions and assembling

With color A cast on 72 sts and in Stockinette Stitch follow graph for pillow front. When graph is completed bind off. Repeat cast on instructions for pillow back. Follow graph and when completed bind off.* When completed sew back and front together along 3 sides leaving bottom edge open for 14″ zipper.
Hand sew zipper in the pillow.

Fringe

The fringe around three sides of the pillow is sewn on after completion. Thread an embroidery needle with grey yarn doubled. Attach onto lower left corner and secure in place. Take any 3/4″ diameter round tube. You may choose a larger or smaller tube depending on the size fringe you want to make. I used a round magic marker. Place tube on the seam line and while holding the tube in place wrap yarn around tube and sew through to other side. Continue to do this along entire edge. When you arrive at the corner, place tube along top edge perpendicular to side and continue making fringe. You need to repeat threading needle and securing the yarn. I did this by guiding the needle to the inside and making it come out on right side, securing with one knot and then continuing to make loops over tube. Do reverse when ending yarn.

{ Pillows }

■ (A) Bright Blue: knit on right side; purl on wrong side

□ (B) Creme: knit on right side; purl on wrong side

■ (C) Grey Heather: knit on right side; purl on wrong side

■ (C) Orange: knit on right side; purl on wrong side

■ Save the Animals Pillow { polar bear }

■ (A) Kiwi Green: knit on right side; purl on wrong side

□ (B) Heather Grey: knit on right side; purl on wrong side

■ (C) Onyx: knit on right side; purl on wrong side

■ (C) Orange: knit on right side; purl on wrong side

■ Save the Animals Pillow { elephant }

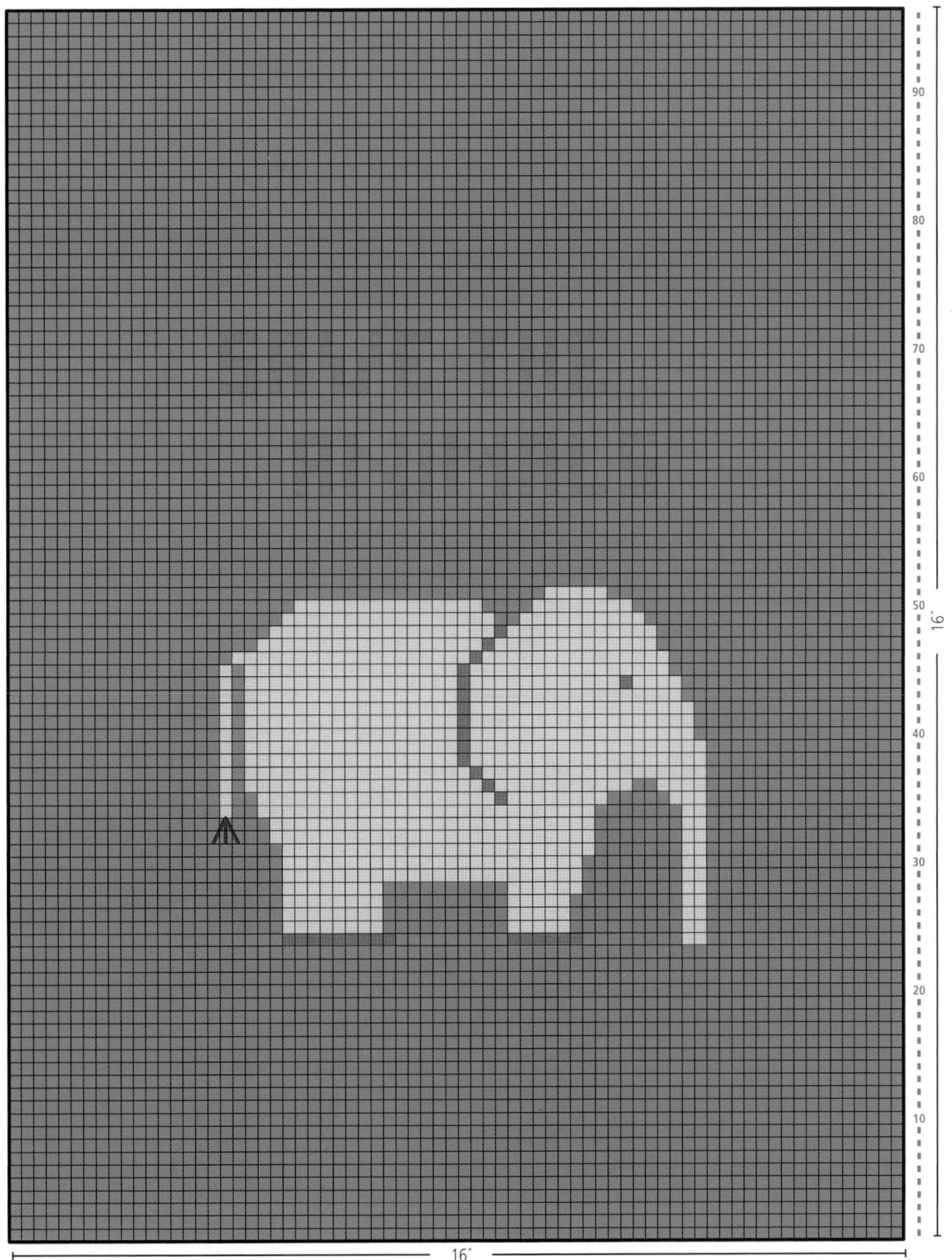

{ Glossary & Abbreviations }

glossary

Cast Off/Bind Off
Most of my sweaters are worked in Stockinette Stitch. Knit two stitches and lift first over second. Continue across row until one stitch remains. Cut thread and pull through remaining loop.

Cast On
There are several different ways to cast on. On most of my sweaters I use a Long Tail Cast On using one needle. The only trick to this method is figuring out how long the tail should be. You can either wrap the needle with the number of stitches you will need plus a couple of inches extra. Or for these worsted weight yarns, I have found that for every 10 stitches I need about 6 inches of yarn. Another method is Knitted Cast On which uses 2 needles. This is described in "Stop and Smell the Roses".

Decreasing a stitch
The most common and simplest method is knitting 2 stitches together, written as K2tog.

Single Rib
Row 1: K1, P1
Row 2: P1, K1 (K knit stitches and P purl stitches)

Double Rib
Row 1: K2, P2
Row 2: P2, K2 (K knit stitches and P purl stitches)

Garter Stitch
Knit every row when using straight needles.
When knitting in the round as is done with the neck on "Don't Bee a Litterbug", knit first row and purl the second row. Continue to alternate knit and purl rows.

I-Cord
Described in "Pillows"

Increasing a stitch
The most common and simplest method is to knit into the front and back of stitch (written as K1f&b).

Intarsia
This is a method of using blocks of color in a sweater where yarn is picked up from either a bobbin or a second ball of yarn and is not carried or woven in across the entire row. When switching from one yarn to another, remember to twist or wrap the old and the new yarn so you do not create a hole. Do this twisting on the wrong side.

Mattress Stitch
(Used for seaming)
For a half-stitch seam, pick up the horizontal bar at the base of the stitches in every other row. For a full stitch allowance pick up two horizontal bars on either side of stitches.

Stockinette Stitch
Row 1: Knit every stitch
Row 2: Purl every stitch

abbreviations

C	color
CC	contrasting color
CO	cast on
dec	decrease
inc	increase
K	knit
Kf&b	knit into front and back of a stitch
K2tog	knit 2 sts together
LH	left hand
MC	main color
oz	ounce
PU	pick up
P	purl
P2tog	purl 2 sts together
P3tog	purl 3 sts together
RH	right hand
RS	right side
sts	stitches
WS	wrong side
WYIB	with yarn in back
WYIF	with yarn in front
YO	yarn over needle

{ Yarn Sources }

The following yarns are yarns I have used for the knitting projects in this book. All fall in the same worsted weight gauge. If your local yarn shop does not have these yarns ask for a substitute recommendation.

Brown Sheep Company, Inc.
100662 County Road 16
Mitchell, Nebraska 69357
1-800-826-9136 • FAX 1-308-635-2143
Brown Sheep Lamb's Pride Worsted
Brown Sheep Shepherd's Shades
Brown Sheep Cotton Fleece

Cascade Yarns
1224 Andover Park East
Tukwila, WA 98188
www.cascadeyarns.com
Cascade 220

Lion Brand Yarn Co
135 Kero Road
Carlstadt, NJ 07072
www.lionbrand.com
Lion Brand Cotton
Lion Brand Organic Cotton
Lion Brand Fisherman's Wool
Lion Brand Wool

Plymouth Yarn Company
500 Lafayette Street
Bristol, PA 19007
215-788-0459
pyc@plymouthyarn.com
Plymouth Fantasy Naturale

Tahki • Stacy Charles, Inc.
70-30 80th St. Building 36
Ridgewood, NY 11385
info@tahkistacycharles.com
1-800-338-YARN
Filatura D Crosa Zara Plus
Tahki Cotton
Tahki Donegal Tweed

helpful Internet sites

www.knitty.com
www.knittyhelp.com
www.ravelry.com

{ Acknowledgments }

There are so many people to thank I am glad I was given a full page to do so. When I started this project I had no idea of the amount of work it would require, but is has been a lot of fun. I have enjoyed every moment.

First, I must thank my niece, Kristen Hughes, who is a multi-talented graphic designer. She designed the book, and it is more beautiful than I hoped it would be. Kristen was extremely patient with me and was able to quickly produce what I envisioned for this book. Besides laughing our way through this entire project, I also learned a great deal from her. I am so fortunate to have Kristen as my niece.

I now want to thank my ace knitter, pattern checker and friend, Sandy Light. Sandy has been working with me for nearly 25 years, and I would not be writing this text today if had she not been part of the team, creating exquisitely knitted sweaters. I hope that we can continue to work together another 25 years because she was invaluable in this project, and I hope more to come.

I want to thank my other expert pattern checkers and friends, Melanie Heacock, Lynn Rauch, Mary Reath, and Ann Reid. Together they caught a lot of mistakes.

The beautiful photographs were taken by the husband and wife team, Ann and Joe Sachs, who own Sachs Photography, based in Baltimore. Ann and Joe got a feel for what I wanted immediately and produced these delightful photos with very little effort. The adorable and cooperative models also contributed to the smoothness of the photo shoot. So many thanks to the gorgeous and handsome Annie, Connor, Hadley, Margaret and William, and to their great moms, Muffy Fenwick, Rebecca Bausman, and once again, Kristen Hughes.

I was fortunate to meet Ann Hughes of Otter Bay Books in Baltimore, who is not only a wonderful publisher and editor, but also a knitter and speaks my language. Her assistance guiding me through this process of which I knew nothing cannot be minimized. Thank you, Ann

There are also a number of people who helped me get this project started and gave me the needed support throughout this endeavor. I will start with Margie Weeks of Outloud Advertising in Baltimore, Marian Hoffman, Barbie Horneffer, and Barbara Schweizer. In addition I want to give a special thanks to my lovely sister, Geri Redfield, who has helped me with many of my knitting projects over the years, including this one.

I must express my gratitude to my mother who taught me to sew, knit and most importantly, the belief I could make anything, simply because she always did so herself.

And finally, I need to thank my family; my husband, Stuart and my children, Emily and Matthew who inspire me every single day.

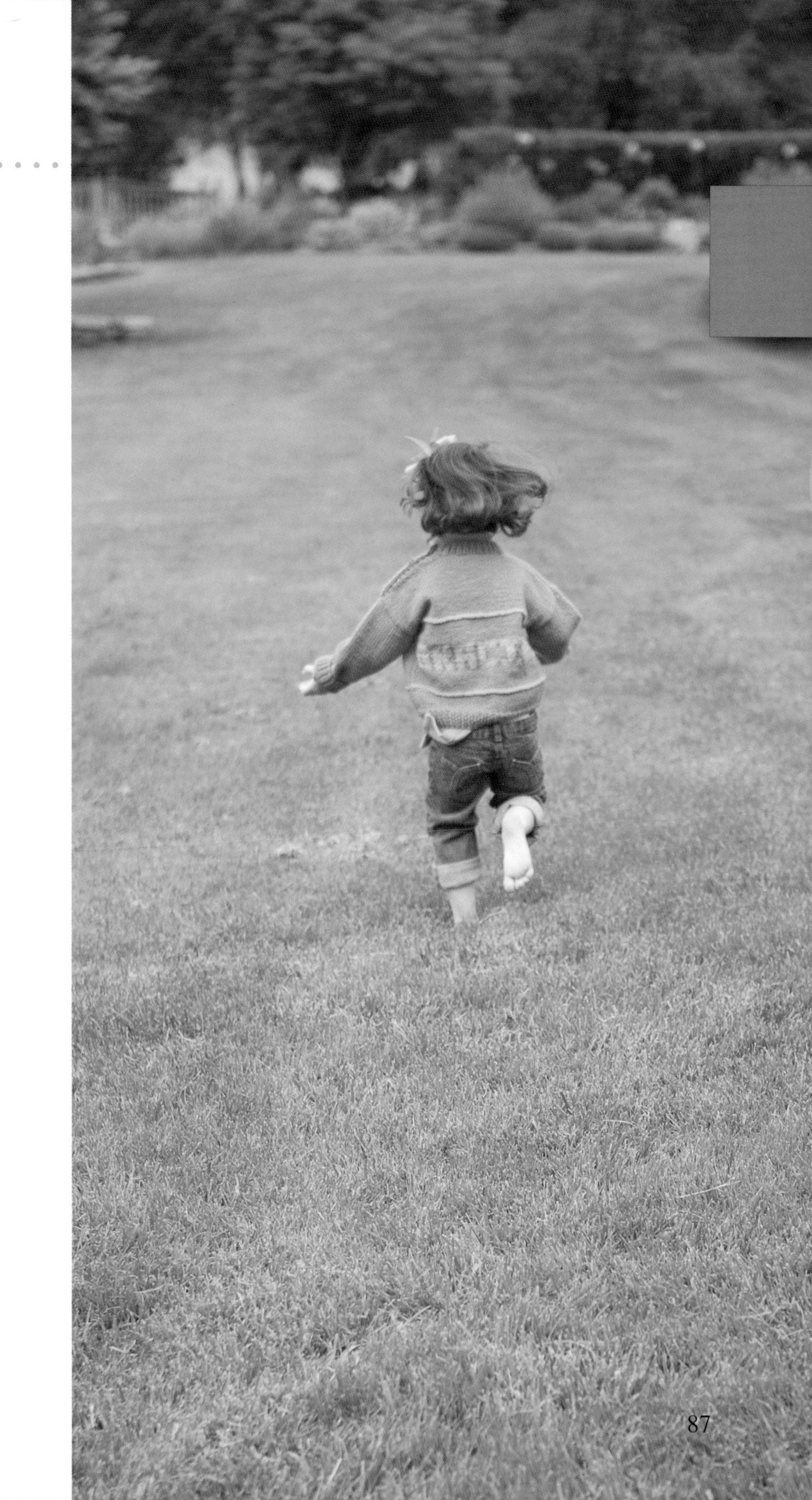

{ About the Author }

Lynn Buchheit Janney has been fascinated with design since she was in elementary school. She began by making doll's clothes and followed by designing her own clothes through high school and college. After college, Lynn worked for a number of years designing women's fashions before she moved into graphic design. Eventually she turned her focus to knitwear. She has now been involved in designing and producing knitted items for 30 years. Her designs have been published in Vogue Knitting, McCall's and Women's Day. In the process of raising her children she spent a lot of time volunteering at several elementary schools and discovered her passion for children's literacy. Her idea of producing a children's sweater pattern book with written messages, came out of her love for design and teaching. She lives on a farm in Maryland with her husband and has two grown children who have had "a few" knitted sweaters in their lifetime.

■ contact
web: www.purls-of-wisdom.com
email: lynnbjanney@purls-of-wisdom.com

SOUND IDEAS

Advanced Listening and Speaking

TAPESTRY

The **Tapestry** program of language materials is based on the concepts presented in ***The Tapestry of Language Learning:*** *The Individual in the Communicative Classroom* by Robin C. Scarcella & Rebecca L. Oxford.

Each title in this program focuses on:

- Individual learner strategies and instruction
- The relatedness of skills
- Ongoing self-assessment
- Authentic material as input
- Theme-based learning linked to task-based instruction
- Attention to all aspects of communicative competence

TAPESTRY

SOUND IDEAS

Advanced Listening and Speaking

Helen Fragiadakis
Virginia M. Maurer

Heinle & Heinle Publishers
An International Thomson Publishing Company
Boston, Massachusetts, 02116, USA

The publication of *Sound Ideas* was directed by the members of the Heinle & Heinle Global Innovations Publishing Team:

Elizabeth Holthaus, Global Innovations Team Leader
David C. Lee, Editorial Director
John F. McHugh, Market Development Director
Lisa McLaughlin, Production Editor

Also participating in the publication of this program were:

Publisher: Stanley J. Galek
Assistant Editor: Kenneth Mattsson
Manufacturing Coordinator: Mary Beth Hennebury
Full Service Project Manager/Compositor: PC&F, Inc.
Interior Design: Maureen Lauran
Cover Design: Maureen Lauran

Manufactured in the United States of America

ISBN: 0-8384-4700-7

Heinle & Heinle Publishers is an International Thomson Publishing Company.

10 9 8 7

To Melissa and Jerzy

PHOTO CREDITS

1, Michael Newman/PhotoEdit; 13, John Henley/The Stock Market; 28, David Bartruff/FPG International; 37, Comstock, Inc.; 41, Fran Ortiz. SABA Press Photos, Inc.; 63, Joseph Schuyler/Stock, Boston; 78, North Wind Picture Archives; 81, Bettmann Archives; 88, Culver Pictures; 95, Elizabeth Crews/Stock, Boston; 97, Lee Foster/FPG International; 106, Culver Pictures; 117, R. Rathe/FPG International; 119, Paul Barton/The Stock Market; 132, AP/Wide World Photos; 138, Culver Pictures; 143, Arthur Grace/Stock, Boston; 145, PEOPLE Weekly © 1991 Penny Wolin; 152, Alan Dorow; 169, Akos Szilvasi/Stock, Boston; 179, Culver Pictures; 183, Culver Pictures; 195, Courtesy of NASA; 201, Jim Harrison; 202, Courtesy of NASA; 214, Ellis-Sawyer/FPG International; 221, Bettmann Archives

TEXT CREDITS

38, 122, 148, 173, © National Public Radio® 1992. Excerpts and audio actualities from National Public Radio's news magazine are used with permission of National Public Radio. All rights reserved.

73, Humor in Japan was produced by Jim Metzner for Public Radio International's "Marketplace Radio," produced at KUSC radio.

100, Adaptation of "Ash Girl" (Aschenputtel), from The Grimms' German Folk Tales, pp. 86-92, translated by Francis P. Magoun Jr. and Alexander H. Krappe. Copyright © 1966 by Southern Illinois University Press. Reprinted by permission of the publisher.

Welcome to Tapestry

Enter the world of Tapestry! Language learning can be seen as an ever-developing tapestry woven with many threads and colors. The elements of the tapestry are related to different language skills like listening and speaking, reading and writing; the characteristics of the teachers; the desires, needs, and backgrounds of the students; and the general second language development process. When all these elements are working together harmoniously, the result is a colorful, continuously growing tapestry of language competence of which the student and the teacher can be proud.

This volume is part of the Tapestry program for students of English as a second language (ESL) at levels from beginning to "bridge" (which follows the advanced level and prepares students to enter regular postsecondary programs along with native English speakers). Tapestry levels include:

Beginning
Low Intermediate
High Intermediate
Low Advanced
High Advanced
Bridge

Because the Tapestry Program provides a unified theoretical and pedagogical foundation for all its components, you can optimally use all the Tapestry student books in a coordinated fashion as an entire curriculum of materials. (They will be published from 1993 to 1996 with further editions likely thereafter.) Alternatively, you can decide to use just certain Tapestry volumes, depending on your specific needs.

Tapestry is primarily designed for ESL students at postsecondary institutions in North America. Some want to learn ESL for academic or career advancement, others for social and personal reasons. Tapestry builds directly on all these motivations. Tapestry stimulates learners to do their best. It enables learners to use English naturally and to develop fluency as well as accuracy.

Tapestry Principles

The following principles underlie the instruction provided in all of the components of the Tapestry program.

EMPOWERING LEARNERS

Language learners in Tapestry classrooms are active and increasingly responsible for developing their English language skills and related cultural abilities. This self direction leads to better, more rapid learning. Some cultures virtually train their students to be passive in the classroom, but Tapestry weans them from passivity by providing exceptionally high interest materials, colorful and motivating activities, personalized self-reflection tasks, peer tutoring and other forms of cooperative learning, and powerful learning strategies to boost self direction in learning.

The empowerment of learners creates refreshing new roles for teachers, too. The teacher serves as facilitator, co-communicator, diagnostician, guide, and helper. Teachers are set free to be more creative at the same time their students become more autonomous learners.

HELPING STUDENTS IMPROVE THEIR LEARNING STRATEGIES

Learning strategies are the behaviors or steps an individual uses to enhance his or her learning. Examples are taking notes, practicing, finding a conversation partner, analyzing words, using background knowledge, and controlling anxiety. Hundreds of such strategies have been identified. Successful language learners use language learning strategies that are most effective for them given their particular learning style, and they put them together smoothly to fit the needs of a given language task. On the other hand, the learning strategies of less successful learners are a desperate grab-bag of ill-matched techniques.

All learners need to know a wide range of learning strategies. All learners need systematic practice in choosing and applying strategies that are relevant for various learning needs. Tapestry is one of the only ESL programs that overtly weaves a comprehensive set of learning strategies into language activities in all its volumes. These learning strategies are arranged in eight broad categories throughout the Tapestry books:

Forming concepts
Personalizing
Remembering new material
Managing your learning
Understanding and using emotions
Overcoming limitations
Testing Hypotheses
Learning with Others

The most useful strategies are sometimes repeated and flagged with a note, "It Works! Learning Strategy . . ." to remind students to use a learning strategy they have already encountered. This recycling reinforces the value of learning strategies and provides greater practice.

RECOGNIZING AND HANDLING LEARNING STYLES EFFECTIVELY

Learners have different learning styles (for instance, visual, auditory, hands- on; reflective, impulsive; analytic, global; extroverted, introverted; closure-oriented, open). Particularly in an ESL setting, where students come from vastly different cultural backgrounds, learning styles differences abound and can cause "style conflicts."

Unlike most language instruction materials, Tapestry provides exciting activities specifically tailored to the needs of students with a large range of learning styles. You can use any Tapestry volume with the confidence that the activities and materials are intentionally geared for many different styles. Insights from the latest educational and psychological research undergird this style-nourishing variety.

OFFERING AUTHENTIC, MEANINGFUL COMMUNICATION

Students need to encounter language that provides authentic, meaningful communication. They must be involved in real-life communication tasks that cause them to *want* and *need* to read, write, speak, and listen to English. Moreover, the tasks—to be most effective—must be arranged around themes relevant to learners.

Themes like family relationships, survival in the educational system, personal health, friendships in a new country, political changes, and protection of the environment are all valuable to ESL learners. Tapestry focuses on topics like these. In every Tapestry volume, you will see specific content drawn from very broad areas such as home life, science and technology, business, humanities, social sciences, global issues, and multiculturalism. All the themes are real and important, and they are fashioned into language tasks that students enjoy.

At the advanced level, Tapestry also includes special books each focused on a single broad theme. For instance, there are two books on business English, two on English for science and technology, and two on academic communication and study skills.

UNDERSTANDING AND VALUING DIFFERENT CULTURES

Many ESL books and programs focus completely on the "new" culture, that is, the culture which the students are entering. The implicit message is that ESL students should just learn about this target culture, and there is no need to understand their own culture better or to find out about the cultures of their international classmates. To some ESL students, this makes them feel their own culture is not valued in the new country.

Tapestry is designed to provide a clear and understandable entry into North American culture. Nevertheless, the Tapestry Program values *all* the cultures found in the ESL classroom. Tapestry students have constant opportunities to become "culturally fluent" in North American culture while they are learning English, but they also have the chance to think about the cultures of their classmates and even understand their home culture from different perspectives.

INTEGRATING THE LANGUAGE SKILLS

Communication in a language is not restricted to one skill or another. ESL students are typically expected to learn (to a greater or lesser degree) all four language skills: reading, writing, speaking, and listening. They are also expected to develop strong grammatical competence, as well as becoming socioculturally sensitive and knowing what to do when they encounter a "language barrier."

Research shows that multi-skill learning is more effective than isolated-skill learning, because related activities in several skills provide reinforcement and refresh the learner's memory. Therefore, Tapestry integrates all the skills. A given Tapestry volume might highlight one skill, such as reading, but all other skills are also included to support and strengthen overall language development.

However, many intensive ESL programs are divided into classes labeled according to one skill (Reading Comprehension Class) or at most two skills (Listening/Speaking Class or Oral Communication Class). The volumes in the Tapestry Program can easily be used to fit this traditional format, because each volume clearly identifies its highlighted or central skill(s).

Grammar is interwoven into all Tapestry volumes. However, there is also a separate reference book for students, *The Tapestry Grammar,* and a Grammar Strand composed of grammar "work-out" books at each of the levels in the Tapestry Program.

Other Features of the Tapestry Program

PILOT SITES

It is not enough to provide volumes full of appealing tasks and beautiful pictures. Users deserve to know that the materials have been pilot-tested. In many ESL series, pilot testing takes place at only a few sites or even just in the classroom of the author. In contrast, Heinle & Heinle Publishers have developed a network of Tapestry Pilot Test Sites throughout North America. At this time, there are approximately 40 such sites, although the number grows weekly. These sites try out the materials and provide suggestions for revisions. They are all actively engaged in making Tapestry the best program possible.

AN OVERALL GUIDEBOOK

To offer coherence to the entire Tapestry Program and especially to offer support for teachers who want to understand the principles and practice of Tapestry, we have written a book entitled, *The Tapestry of Language Learning. The Individual in the Communicative Classroom* (Scarcella and Oxford, published in 1992 by Heinle & Heinle).

A Last Word

We are pleased to welcome you to Tapestry! We use the Tapestry principles every day, and we hope these principles—and all the books in the Tapestry Program—provide you the same strength, confidence, and joy that they give us. We look forward to comments from both teachers and students who use any part of the Tapestry Program.

Rebecca L. Oxford
University of Alabama

Robin C. Scarcella
University of California at Irvine

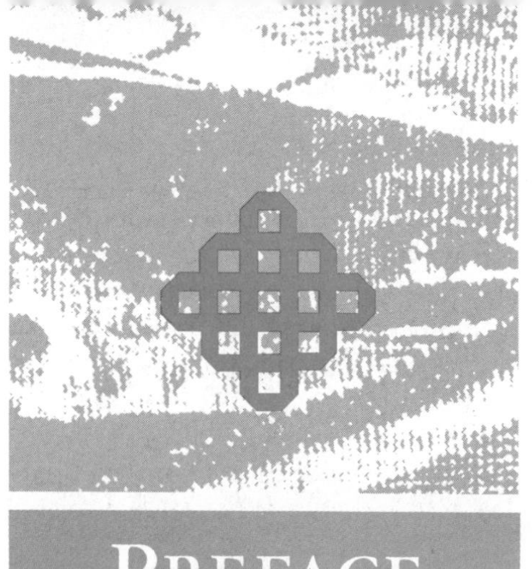

PREFACE

Sound Ideas—Advanced Listening and Speaking is designed to draw students step-by-step into meaningful discussions of topics of universal interest. By providing authentic input in the form of listening and reading passages, this book arms students with a great deal to talk about both in and out of class. Chapter by chapter, from the introductory "Warm-Up" to the concluding "Follow-Up," it introduces students to themes they first explore in depth, after which they can branch out to investigate related topics. As students progress, they acquire listening, note-taking, and summarizing skills, absorb an abundance of new vocabulary, and actively engage in communication with classmates and others through activities such as surveys and interviews. The text offers opportunities throughout for visual, verbal, and auditory input.

Our goal, as we provide enjoyable activities and interesting information to students, is to encourage them to acquire the confidence they need to communicate successfully in English-speaking environments, both academic and social. To engage the students, to draw them in, we deal with each theme in depth.

Recognizing that our students come from a variety of backgrounds and have wide-ranging interests, we have made an effort to choose rich, diverse themes that would be new to advanced-level students who have progressed through the traditional topics typically found in the beginning and intermediate levels. At the advanced level, students want to and are able to learn and talk about a myriad of subjects. When these students enter into discussion with native speakers of English, they will encounter a broad range of unrelated topics under discussion. It is important for them to learn how to approach and develop conversations about topics they may not have thought much about previously. Thus, we have purposely chosen widely varying themes so that students, after exploring in great depth the particular theme of one chapter, can move on to explore with a fresh approach a completely different theme in the next chapter.

These diverse themes allow the students to examine different aspects of our lives from the perspectives of the past, the present, and the future and give them an opportunity to reflect on what forces in our world influence and affect how we live and what we think. The book and the accompanying tape expose students to the same materials that native speakers read, watch, listen to, and talk about: radio and television programs, films, books-on-tape, lectures, stories told aloud, articles from newspapers and magazines, and passages taken from books.

Chapter Organization

Except for the introductory chapter, "Preview—Getting Started," which asks students to identify their own learning strategies, each chapter follows the organizational pattern outlined below. References within the chapters refer students to the numerous appendices for additional information.

BACKGROUND KNOWLEDGE CHECK

The "Background Knowledge Check" is a classroom assessment technique designed to reveal students' prior knowledge of a topic. It gives the teacher and the class a sense of the students' general familiarity or unfamiliarity with a particular topic and helps to set a direction for further inquiry.

SETTING GOALS

The "Setting Goals" questionnaire at the beginning of each chapter requires students to bring their personal language-learning goals to a conscious level. While the first 9 items are the same in each chapter, item 10 is chapter-specific, and item 11 allows students to add other goals that they may want to achieve.

WARM-UP

The "Warm-Up," usually in the form of a cartoon, photograph, or quotation, introduces the topic of each chapter, with the intention of sparking the interest and curiosity of everyone in the class.

LISTENING

Each "Listening" section is divided into three parts:

- Before You Listen

To prepare for taped listening passages, students often read newspaper and magazine articles and short excerpts from books. This reading material is glossed to make the reading go more smoothly since our focus is on listening and speaking. Besides reading, before they listen to the tape, students are frequently asked to make predictions based on prior knowledge, and do vocabulary preparation exercises.

- As You Listen

As students listen to the passages, they listen for main ideas, details, and opinions, taking notes in a variety of formats.

- After You Listen

After they listen to the passages, students often discuss and compare notes, present oral and written summaries, provide definitions and oral reconstructions, analyze the language and pronunciation of the speakers, and answer comprehension questions.

LISTENING LOGS

To encourage students to increase their exposure to English outside the classroom, two listening log entries based on TV and/or radio programs are assigned each week. Toward the end of each chapter, students in small groups give their "Listening Log Reports." These logs are not related to the chapter themes.

ANY QUESTIONS?

This is a classroom assessment technique that appears between the "Listening" and "Speaking" sections of each chapter. It allows students to anonymously reveal what was most valuable to them to that point in the chapter and what may still be unclear. Before continuing with the "Speaking" part of the chapter, the teacher may share the feedback with the class and take time to focus on any topics that remain unclear.

SPEAKING

The "Speaking" sections of *Sound Ideas* contain numerous activities, probably more than most classes would attempt to complete. Those who use this text should pick and choose, reading over the possible activities and choosing to use those that are most interesting and practical for their particular needs. Activities include discussions, reading and orally responding to authentic written material, surveys, simulations, role-plays, speeches, informal debates, movie reviews, guest speakers, interpretation of cartoons and charts, and analyses of case studies. Each chapter contains a questionnaire that asks students to self-evaluate the conversational and group skills they used in these speaking activities.

FOLLOW-UP

"Follow-Up" activities come in many forms. Students may be given contact assigments in which they ask questions of people outside their classes. Students may also be asked to visit the library to find particular material or to rent a videotape on a certain subject. Other follow-up activities involve students in writing letters, watching TV, conducting surveys, making telephone calls, and visiting community organizations, museums, and local colleges and universities. When possible, students report to their class on their follow-up activities.

LEARNING ASSESSMENT

So that they may take charge of their own learning, students assess their efforts and progress as they complete each chapter. Thus, they can identify when and why they were successful or unsuccessful. And, to come full circle, they consider whether or not they achieved any of the goals they set down at the beginning of the chapter.

Appendices

Fifteen comprehensive Appendices filled with information, directions, suggestions, and forms related to listening and speaking are provided. Throughout *Sound Ideas* we refer teachers and students to particular Appendices, but we suggest that users of the text look through these resources early in their course to know exactly what is available.

Teacher's Manual and Tapescript

The teacher's manual contains the following: suggestions for the first day of class, chapter-by-chapter notes, answer key for chapter exercises, additional classroom assessment techniques, sample essay test questions, and tapescript.

Acknowledgments

We would like to express our appreciation to the *Tapestry* editorial director, Dave Lee, and assistant editor, Ken Mattsson, for the support and encouragement that they provided as we developed *Sound Ideas.* In addition, we would like to thank Rebecca Oxford and Robin Scarcella for creating the project, and editors Elaine Hall, Amy Jamison, Lisa McLaughlin, and Shirley Simmons for their work on the production of our text.

To our reviewers, Paul Abraham (Simmons College); Kimberly Brown (Portland State University); Barbara Campbell (State University of New York at Buffalo); Leilani Cook (University of Florida); and Lee Culver (Miami-Dade Community College), we also send our gratitude for your very insightful and valuable comments. And we thank John Fitzer (State University of New York at Buffalo) who also piloted the material.

Helen Fragiadakis
Contra Costa College

Virginia Maurer
Harvard University

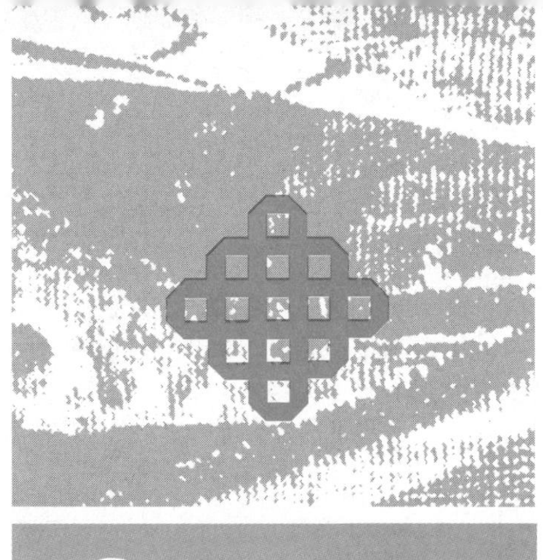

CONTENTS

7 *Smells and Behavior—How We Are Influenced* 169

8 *Understanding Our World—Science and the Citizen* 195

Appendices 227

Preview—Getting Started

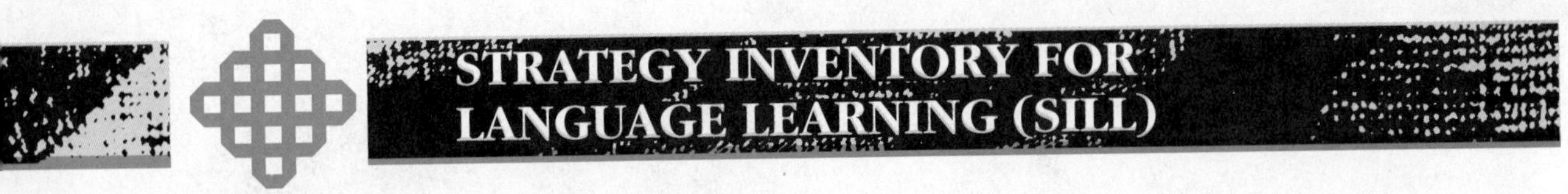

STRATEGY INVENTORY FOR LANGUAGE LEARNING (SILL)

Threads

A strategy is a method for obtaining a specific goal or result.

The best way for you to get started with *Sound Ideas* is to think about language learning. In this lesson, you will answer survey questions to find out exactly what you yourself consciously do to learn English. You will also become more aware of new strategies that you can use to speed up and improve your progress.

On the following pages you will find a survey called the "Strategy Inventory for Language Learning" (SILL) which was created for students to find out exactly what they do (what *strategies* they use) to learn a new language. Complete the survey to discover more about your own language learning process.

Strategy Inventory for Language Learning (SILL)

Version 7.0 (ESL/EFL)
(c) R. Oxford, 1989

Directions

This form of the STRATEGY INVENTORY FOR LANGUAGE LEARNING (SILL) is for students of English as a second or foreign language. You will find statements about learning English. Please read each statement. On the separate Worksheet on page 8, write the response (1, 2, 3, 4, or 5) that tells HOW TRUE OF YOU THE STATEMENT IS.

1. Never or almost never true of me
2. Usually not true of me
3. Somewhat true of me
4. Usually true of me
5. Always or almost always true of me

NEVER OR ALMOST NEVER TRUE OF ME means that the statement is very rarely true of you.

USUALLY NOT TRUE OF ME means that the statement is true less than half the time.

SOMEWHAT TRUE OF ME means that the statement is true of you about half the time.

USUALLY TRUE OF ME means that the statement is true more than half the time.

ALWAYS OR ALMOST ALWAYS TRUE OF ME means that the statement is true of you almost always.

Answer in terms of how well the statement describes you. Do not answer how you think you should be, or what other people do. There are no right or wrong answers to these statements. Put your answers on the separate Worksheet on page 8. Please make no marks on the items. Work as quickly as you can without being careless. This usually takes about 20–30 minutes to complete. If you have any questions, let the teacher know immediately.

EXAMPLE

I actively seek out opportunities to talk with native speakers in English.

On this page, put an "X" in the blank underneath the statement that best describes what you actually do in regard to English now. Do not make any marks on the Worksheet yet.

Never or Almost Never	Generally Not True of Me	Somewhat True of Me	Generally True of Me	Always or Almost Always True of Me
1	2	3	4	5
______	______	______	______	______

If you have answered the question above, you have just completed the example item.

Now wait for the teacher to give you the signal to go on to the other items. When you answer the questions, work carefully but quickly. Mark the rest of your answers on the Worksheet on page 8, starting with item 1.

Strategy Inventory for Language Learning

Version 7.0 (ESL/EFL)

(c) R. Oxford, 1989

1. Never or almost never true of me
2. Usually not true of me
3. Somewhat true of me
4. Usually true of me
5. Always or almost always true of me

(Write answers on Worksheet)

Part A

1. I think of relationships between what I already know and new things I learn in English.
2. I use new English words in a sentence so I can remember them.
3. I connect the sound of a new English word and an image or picture of the word to help me remember the word.
4. I remember a new English word by making a mental picture of a situation in which the word might be used.
5. I use rhymes to remember new English words.
6. I use flashcards to remember new English words.
7. I physically act out new English words.
8. I review English lessons often.
9. I remember new English words or phrases by remembering their location on the page, on the board, or on a street sign.

Part B

10. I say or write new English words several times.
11. I try to talk like native English speakers
12. I practice the sounds of English.
13. I use the English words I know in different ways.
14. I start conversations in English.
15. I watch English language TV shows spoken in English or go to movies spoken in English.
16. I read for pleasure in English.
17. I write notes, messages, letters, or reports in English.
18. I first skim an English passage (read over the passage quickly) then go back and read carefully.

1. Never or almost never true of me
2. Usually not true of me
3. Somewhat true of me
4. Usually true of me
5. Always or almost always true of me

(Write answers on Worksheet)

19. I look for words in my own language that are similar to new words in English.
20. I try to find patterns in English.
21. I find the meaning of an English word by dividing it into parts that I understand.
22. I try not to translate word-for-word.
23. I make summaries of information that I hear or read in English.

Part C

24. To understand unfamiliar English words, I make guesses.
25. When I can't think of a word during a conversation in English, I use gestures.
26. I make up new words if I do not know the right ones in English.
27. I read English without looking up every new word.
28. I try to guess what the other person will say next in English.
29. If I can't think of an English word, I use a word or phrase that means the same thing.

Part D

30. I try to find as many ways as I can to use my English.
31. I notice my English mistakes and use that information to help me do better.
32. I pay attention when someone is speaking English.
33. I try to find out how to be a better learner of English.
34. I plan my schedule so I will have enough time to study English.
35. I look for people I can talk to in English.
36. I look for opportunities to read as much as possible in English.
37. I have clear goals for improving my English skills.
38. I think about my progress in learning English.

1. Never or almost never true of me
2. Usually not true of me
3. Somewhat true of me
4. Usually true of me
5. Always or almost always true of me

(Write answers on Worksheet)

Part E

39. I try to relax whenever I feel afraid of using English.
40. I encourage myself to speak English even when I am afraid of making a mistake.
41. I give myself a reward or treat when I do well in English.
42. I notice if I am tense or nervous when I am studying or using English.
43. I write down my feelings in a language learning diary.
44. I talk to someone else about how I feel when I am learning English.

Part F

45. If I do not understand something in English, I ask the other person to slow down or say it again.
46. I ask English speakers to correct me when I talk.
47. I practice English with other students.
48. I ask for help from English speakers.
49. I ask questions in English.
50. I try to learn about the culture of English speakers.

Directions for Worksheet for Answering and Scoring

the Strategy Inventory for Language Learning (SILL)

Version 7.0 (ESL/EFL)

1. The blanks (_____) are numbered for each item on the SILL.
2. Write your response to each item (that is, write 1, 2, 3, 4, or 5) in each of the blanks.
3. Add up each column. Put the result on the line marked SUM.
4. Divide by the number under SUM to get the average for each column. Round this average off to the nearest tenth, as in 3.4.
5. Figure out your overall average. To do this, add up all the SUMS for the different parts of the SILL. Then divide by 50.
6. When you have finished, complete the Profile of Results on page 9. Copy your averages (for each part and for the whole SILL) from the Worksheet to the Profile.

SILL Worksheet

Version 7.0 (ESL/EFL)

Part A	Part B	Part C	Part D	Part E	Part F	Whole SILL
1. ____	10. ____	24. ____	30. ____	39. ____	45. ____	SUM Part A ____
2. ____	11. ____	25. ____	31. ____	40. ____	46. ____	SUM Part B ____
3. ____	12. ____	26. ____	32. ____	41. ____	47. ____	SUM Part C ____
4. ____	13. ____	27. ____	33. ____	42. ____	48. ____	SUM Part D ____
5. ____	14. ____	28. ____	34. ____	43 ____	49. ____	SUM Part E ____
6. ____	15. ____	29. ____	35. ____	44. ____	50. ____	SUM Part F ____
7. ____	16. ____		36. ____			
8. ____	17. ____		37. ____			
9. ____	18. ____		38. ____			
	19. ____					
	20. ____					
	21. ____					
	22. ____					
	23. ____					

Part A	Part B	Part C	Part D	Part E	Part F	Total
SUM ____	SUM ____	SUM ____	SUM ____	SUM ____	SUM ____	SUM ____
÷ 9 = ____	÷ 14 = ____	÷ 6 = ____	÷ 9 = ____	÷ 6 = ____	÷ 6 = ____	÷ 50 = ____ (OVERALL AVERAGE)

Your Name ______________________________ Date ____________________

Profile of Results on the Strategy Inventory for Language Learning (SILL)

Version 7.0 (ESL/EFL)

Complete this Profile after you have finished the Worksheet. This Profile will show your SILL results. These results will tell you the kinds of strategies you use in learning English. There are no right or wrong answers.

To complete this profile, copy your averages for each part of the SILL, and your overall average for the whole SILL. These averages are found on the Worksheet on page 8.

Part	What Strategies Are Covered	Your Average on This Part
A.	Remembering new material	____________
B.	Forming concepts	____________
C.	Overcoming limitations	____________
D.	Managing your learning	____________
E.	Understanding and using emotions	____________
F.	Learning with others	____________
YOUR OVERALL AVERAGE		____________

SILL Profile of Results (continued)

Version 7.0 (ESL/EFL)

(c) R. Oxford, 1989

Key to Understanding Your Averages

High	Always or almost always used	4.5 to 5.0
	Usually used	3.5 to 4.4
Medium	Sometimes used	2.5 to 3.4
Low	Usually not used	1.5 to 2.4
	Never or almost never used	1.0 to 1.4

Graph Your Averages Here

If you want, you can make a graph of your SILL averages. What does this graph tell you? Are you very high or very low on any part?

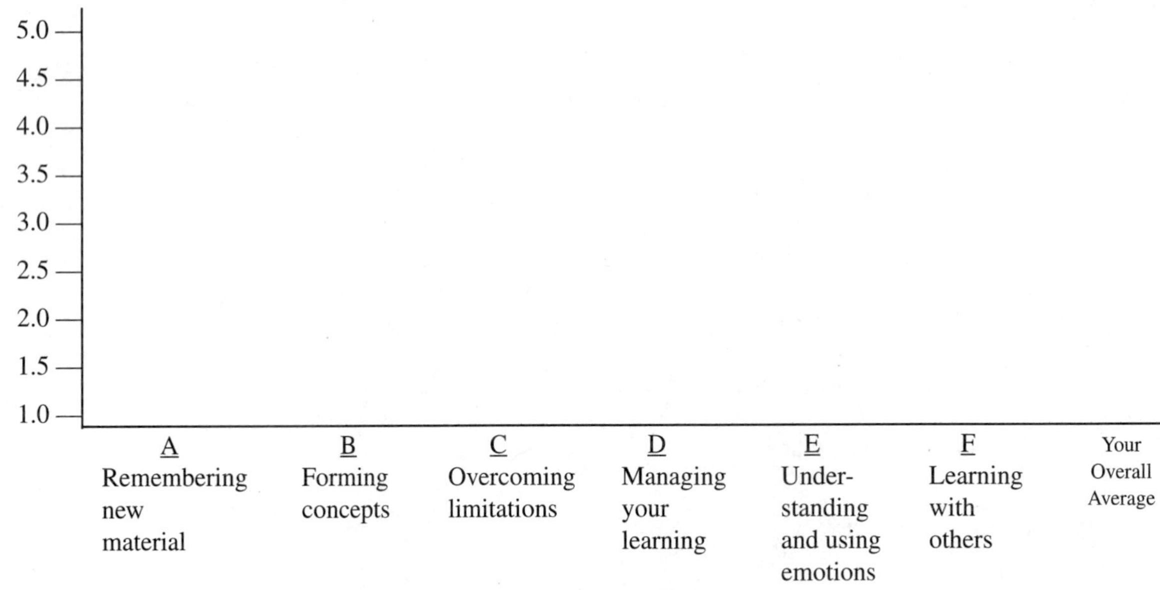

What These Averages Mean to You

The overall average tells how often you use strategies for learning English. Each part of the SILL represents a group of learning strategies. The averages for each part of the SILL show which groups of strategies you use the most for learning English.

The best use of strategies depends on your age, personality, and purpose for learning. If you have a very low average on one or more parts of the SILL, there may be some new strategies in these groups that you might want to use.

Source: *Language Learning Strategies: What Every Teacher Should Know* by Rebecca L. Oxford, 1990. Boston: Heinle & Heinle, pp. 293–300.

Discussion

Talk about the results of the SILL in small groups. One student should serve as the discussion leader who will make sure that group members stay focused on discussing language-learning strategies.

1. Look at your graph on page 10 and tell your classmates which of the six groups of learning strategies you use the most. Turn back to the actual survey and point out exactly which strategies you use.

Give details: for example, if you had a very high score for "Remembering New Material," you should turn to Part A of the survey and explain which of the strategies help you the most. Perhaps, for example, you use flashcards to remember English words.

The other members of the group should ask for details and examples. They might ask questions such as "Do you tape flashcards around your house?" "Do you draw pictures?" "Does anyone test you?"

2. Next, look at the graph and tell your classmates which of the six groups of learning strategies you use the least. Turn back to the actual survey to find the individual strategies you don't use, and explain why you don't use them. Perhaps, for example:

a. You never thought of using that strategy.
b. You've thought of using it, but you never took the time.
c. You'd be uncomfortable using it.
d. Other reason:

____

Also discuss which new strategies you would like to try as you work on improving your English.

Many activities in this book are preceded by labels naming the Learning Strategies that you are using. These help make you aware of exactly what you are doing as you work to improve your English. As you learn many new strategies and practice those you have used in the past, you will find out which strategies work best for you.

Small Talk—Not Deep, but Important

1

CHAPTER

INTRODUCTION

In this chapter, you will listen to an expert on communication skills talk about how to start a conversation, keep it going, and end it. You will also have opportunities to read about and discuss small talk, a light kind of conversation.

LEARNING STRATEGY

Forming Concepts: Using background knowledge can help you understand what you read and hear.

Background Knowledge Check*

The following items reflect some of the content that you will find in this chapter. Write **a, b, c,** or **d** next to each item in the list according to the following:

(a) I have never heard of this.
(b) I have heard of this, but I don't really know what it means.
(c) I have some idea of what this means, but I'm not sure about it.
(d) I have a clear idea of what this means and can explain it.

_____ **1.** Small talk

_____ **2.** An embarrassing silence

_____ **3.** A good conversationalist

Students who have chosen **d** for any of the items should *briefly* explain what these items mean. If no one has chosen **d,** don't worry. You will have a chance to learn more about these as you progress through the chapter.

*This activity is based on the Background Knowledge Probe developed by Thomas A. Angelo and K. Patricia Cross and presented in their handbook, *Classroom Assessment Techniques,* Jossey-Bass Publishers, San Francisco, California, © 1993.

LEARNING STRATEGY

Managing Your Learning: Setting goals and objectives helps you improve skills that are important to you.

Setting Goals

Complete the following statement by checking the goals you want to achieve in this chapter.

While working on this chapter, I will make an effort to:

_____ **1.** speak more while I am working in a small group.

_____ **2.** give others a chance to speak while working in a small group.

_____ **3.** show others that I am actively listening by looking into their eyes and nodding as they talk.

_____ **4.** ask more questions in front of the whole class.

_____ **5.** make more comments in front of the whole class.

_____ **6.** monitor one aspect of my pronunciation, such as ________________.

_____ **7.** monitor one aspect of grammar as I speak, such as ________________.

_____ **8.** use some of the new vocabulary when speaking, both in and out of class.

_____ **9.** listen to the radio and watch TV outside of class.

_____ **10.** start a conversation with a native speaker of English.

_____ **11.** try to achieve another goal, such as ____________________________

____.

Threads

"Lord grant that I may always desire more than I can accomplish."

Michelangelo

LEARNING STRATEGY

Overcoming Limitations: Letting your imagination take over can help you feel free to be creative.

Take a look at this cartoon.

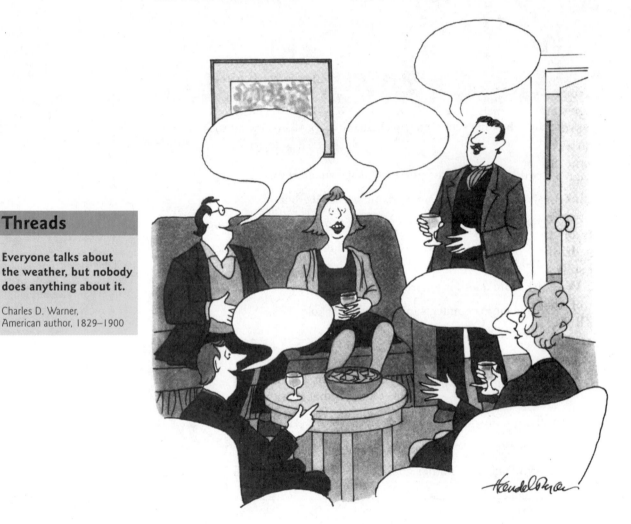

Threads

Everyone talks about the weather, but nobody does anything about it.

Charles D. Warner, American author, 1829–1900

Running on Empty

1. With a partner, fill in the empty balloons with what the people might be saying.
2. Would you say that the people in the cartoon are having a light or a serious conversation?
3. Notice the cartoon caption: "Running on Empty." What do you think that means?
4. What do you think is the cartoonist's message?

Before You Listen

PROFILE OF THE SPEAKER

Read the following "bio" of the speaker that you will listen to.

Dr. Lillian Glass

Known as the "First Lady of Speech," Dr. Lillian Glass is recognized as one of the world's foremost authorities on communication skills and image. She is also a highly sought-after motivational speaker and a best-selling author.

Dr. Glass has a successful private practice in Beverly Hills, California, where she trains many top celebrities, heads of corporations, and politicians to improve their personal image through improving the way they speak and communicate.

Dr. Glass has coached many celebrities on their voices, accents, and dialects. She herself is an expert dialectician and can imitate dialects from all over the world. Dr. Glass taught Dustin Hoffman how to perfect his "female" voice for the film, "Tootsie," and Julio Iglesias to improve his accent in his award-winning song, "To All the Girls."

Lillian Glass's expertise has been extremely valuable to corporate executives, politicians, and the general public in improving their images through enhancing their speech and communication skills.

LEARNING STRATEGY

Forming Concepts: Predicting what you are about to hear helps focus your listening.

PREDICTING

In the passage you will listen to, which has been taken from her tape-recorded book called *Say it Right: How to Talk in Any Social Situation,* Dr. Glass explains how to start a conversation, how to keep it going, and how to end it. Before you hear her talk, predict what you think she will say, using the "concept map" below. A concept map is a graphic way for you to organize your ideas and take notes. You can add as many items around each circle as you wish.

How to Start a Conversation

How to Keep a Conversation Going

How to End a Conversation

LEARNING STRATEGY

Overcoming Limitations: Seeking out and using language-based clues help you guess the meaning of unfamiliar words.

VOCABULARY PREPARATION FOR LISTENING TO "SAY IT RIGHT—HOW TO BE A GOOD CONVERSATIONALIST"

Try to guess the meanings of the **boldfaced** words by looking for the definitions already given in the sentences:

1. Starting a conversation usually means coming up with an opening line, or **ice breaker.**
   - An ice breaker is ____________________.
   - In what situations do you need ice breakers? ____________________
2. To keep a conversation going, you keep asking questions based on the last thing a person says. This is called the **elaboration technique.**
   - The elaboration technique involves ____________________.
   - When would you use this technique? ____________________
3. When ending a conversation, if you're not interested in talking to someone again, don't mention the possibility of a future meeting just to be polite. That's **hypocritical.**
   - Hypocritical probably means ____________________.

As You Listen

LISTEN FOR THE MAIN IDEA

The "How to Be a Good Conversationalist" listening passage has been divided into three parts. Stop the tape at the sound of each beep, and for each question write one or two very *general* sentences that give the main idea—not details.

It would be a good idea to read over these three questions *before* you listen to the passage.

Part 1. What can you do to start a conversation?

____

____

Part 2. How can you keep a conversation going?

____

____

Part 3. How can you politely end a conversation?

____

____

LISTEN FOR DETAILS

LEARNING STRATEGY

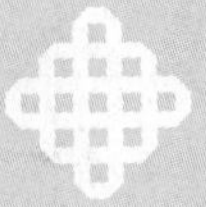

Remembering New Material: Learning how to take good notes helps you remember and organize what you have heard or read.

As you listen to the tape again to focus on details, you are going to take notes. There are two note-taking formats that you can use: an outline (Format A) or a concept map (Format B). Choose whichever format you are most comfortable with. (Refer to Appendix B for more information on note-taking.)

By the way, notice that your answers to the main idea questions above are now the headings for your notes below.

Format A: Outline of "How to Be a Good Conversationalist"

Part 1. How to start a conversation:

Icebreakers: ______________________________

____

____

Part 2. How to keep a conversation going:

Questions/Descriptions: ______________________________

____

____

Tips: ______________________________

____

____

____

____

____

____

Part 3. How to end a conversation:

Signals: ______________________________

____

____

____

____

Threads

Conversationalists in competition tend to sit face to face. Conversationalists in cooperation tend to sit side by side. Camera studies reconfirm it.

L. M. Boyd, *San Francisco Chronicle*, March 6, 1994

Format B: Concept Map of "How to Be a Good Conversationalist"

Part 1. How to Start a Conversation:

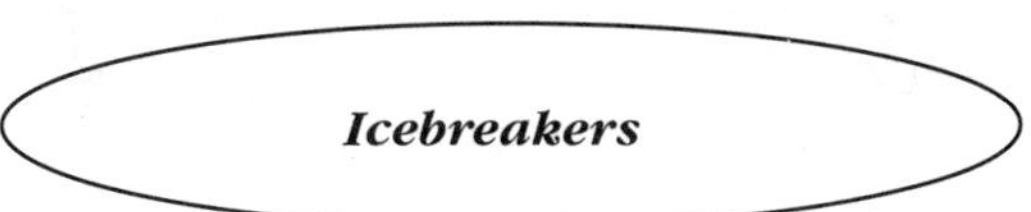

Part 2. How to Keep a Conversation Going:

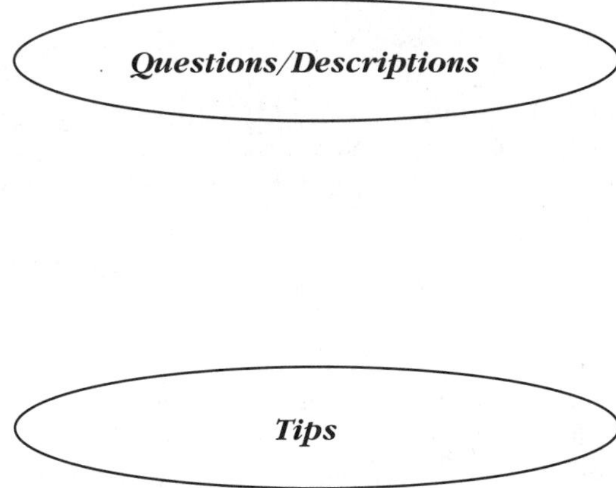

Part 3. How to End a Conversation:

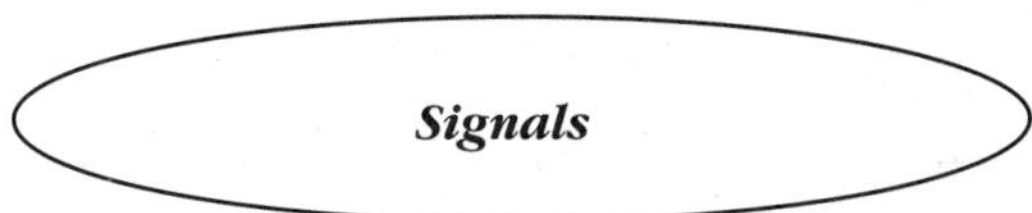

After You Listen

LEARNING STRATEGY

Managing Your Learning: Understanding what works best for you helps you become a more efficient learner.

FOCUS ON THE LISTENING/NOTE-TAKING PROCESS

1. Compare your notes to your predictions on page 18. Did Dr. Glass say anything that you expected her to say?
2. Which note-taking format did you choose? Why did you choose it? Were you comfortable with it? Would you use it again?
3. Do you now see that listening for the main idea first and then listening again for details helps your comprehension?

LEARNING STRATEGY

Forming Concepts: Summarizing helps you structure new information and show that you understand it.

FOCUS ON GIVING AN ORAL SUMMARY

We give summaries to people who haven't seen or heard what we have seen or heard. Generally, we start by giving them the main idea, and then some (but not all) details for clarification. (See Appendix A for details about summarizing.)

Imagine that you are at a cafe talking to some friends. You want to tell them about what you listened to in class about being a good conversationalist. Do the following orally, in pairs. Take turns so that each of you has a chance. Then choose one pair of students to perform the following conversation in front of the entire class.

NOTE: A very useful way to start a conversation is to say, "I heard/saw . . . today." You might try to use this when you want to start a conversation.

X: I heard a pretty interesting tape in class today.

Y: What about?

X: It was about [give a one-sentence summary] ____________________

____

Y: What does a good conversationalist do?

X: [Give some details about the three parts] ____________________

____

FOCUS ON WRITING A SUMMARY

Now you are ready to write a one-paragraph summary of the listening passage. Follow the writing guide below so that you will end up with a brief summary that moves from the general main idea to a few specific details.

1st sentence: Give Lillian Glass's name and the main idea, which you can get from the title of the passage.
2nd sentence: Mention the three parts of the tape.
3rd and possibly 4th sentence: Give a few details about Part 1.
Subsequent sentences: Give a few details about Parts 2 and 3.

LEARNING STRATEGY

Remembering New Material: Repeating and imitating a native speaker's speech patterns helps you get the feel of the language.

FOCUS ON STRESS AND INTONATION

You can improve your use of stress and intonation by consciously becoming aware of how they are used by native speakers. Lillian Glass makes great use of "word stress" (emphasis) and "rising intonation" (pitch) to convey the importance of certain words.

Play the tape again at the beginning of the listening passage. Notice how strongly Dr. Glass says the words "connects" and "important" in this sentence, and how her voice rises: "A great conversationalist is someone who *connects* with people and makes them feel *important.*"

Now, listen to the sentences that follow the one above and underline the words given special emphasis by Dr. Glass. More than one word in a sentence may receive this special emphasis.

Threads

A good listener is a good talker with a sore throat.

Katherine Whitehorn

1. When they talk to you, they make you feel like you're the only person in the room.
2. Becoming a good conversationalist requires knowing three things: first, how to start a conversation; second, how to keep it going; and third, how to end it.
3. Starting a conversation usually means coming up with an opening line or ice breaker.
4. The best kind of ice breaker is one that's positive.
5. The last thing people want to hear from a stranger is how noisy the party is, how awful the food is, or how ugly the people are dressed.
6. A compliment is always a good ice breaker and will usually be appreciated.

Continue listening to the tape, and notice where Dr. Glass's voice gives special emphasis and rising intonation. As a speaker, she decides what words are important and then uses stress and intonation to communicate that importance to the listener.

Read the preceding seven sentences aloud, giving special attention to the words that you feel should be emphasized.

LISTENING LOG

LEARNING STRATEGY

Forming Concepts: Listening to English outside the classroom gives you ongoing input that will become more and more comprehensible over time.

As you know, it is necessary to expose yourself to English outside the classroom in order to speed up your language learning. One way to do this is to systematically document what you listen to. In a section of your binder, or in a separate small notebook, start a "Listening Log." In it you will take notes as well as write short summaries and commentaries on TV and radio programs that you choose. (See Appendix F for examples of and details about listening logs.)

Why should you keep a Listening Log? Because doing so will help you

- practice focused listening, that is, listening for the main idea and details.
- practice note-taking, summarizing, and giving personal reactions.
- practice conversational techniques by telling your classmates in small groups about a radio or TV program and then answering their questions with clarification and details.
- inspire your classmates to watch or listen to certain programs that you found entertaining, newsworthy, or just interesting.

At the end of the next section, entitled "Speaking," you will be asked to report on one of your Listening Log entries in a small group. Your teacher will decide how many log entries will be required each week and how often the logs will be collected.

LEARNING STRATEGY

Managing Your Learning: Clarifying your progress helps keep you focused on your goals.

ANY QUESTIONS?

Before you go on to read about and discuss more issues about small talk, answer the following questions on a separate sheet of paper. Do not write your name on the paper. Your teacher or a classmate will collect the papers and share everyone's answers with the class.

1. What has been the most valuable aspect of this chapter for you so far?
2. What is still unclear?

Discussion

The following discussion questions deal with different aspects of having conversations. Choose the topic or topics you would like to discuss. Also, feel free to add questions of your own that are related to the questions asked here.

When appropriate for the activity, work in small groups. Assign one person to act as discussion leader and another person to act as recorder. The discussion leader will make sure that everyone talks and stays on the subject. The recorder will take notes and later report briefly to the class on the main points of your group's discussion. (See Appendix C for more information on small-group discussion roles and Appendix E for information on turn-taking strategies.)

LEARNING STRATEGY

Learning with Others: Becoming aware of others' thoughts and feelings helps you understand more clearly what is being communicated.

1. Answer the following questions related to Lillian Glass's talk:
   - **a.** To you, is the hardest part of a conversation (1) starting it, (2) keeping it going, or (3) ending it? Be sure to explain your answer.
   - **b.** Do you think you are a good conversationalist? Why or why not?
   - **c.** What are some other ice breakers besides giving a compliment or talking about the news?
   - **d.** Glass suggests that to keep a conversation going, it helps to ask *who, what, where, when, why,* and *how* questions. In your native culture, would doing this be considered acceptable or impolite?
   - **e.** Glass tells her listeners to be aware of their "facial language." This means that in addition to looking into each other's eyes, people in a conversation should focus on each other's faces. What do you think? Would this be comfortable for you?
   - **f.** Glass also recommends that people not interrupt each other. In your native culture, is interrupting during a conversation considered natural, or is it impolite? Please explain.
   - **g.** To end a conversation, Glass suggests that people break eye contact or say a few transitional words that hint that the conversation is over. Can you suggest any other ways to politely end a conversation?

LEARNING STRATEGY

Understanding and Using Emotions: Taking risks in class can help give you the confidence to take risks in the outside world.

2. Imagine that your classroom is the scene of a party. Everyone should get up and start a conversation (using an ice breaker) with a person standing near them. Then, the speakers should try to keep the conversation going by asking "Wh——" questions and using the "elaboration technique" described by Glass. Those answering the questions should try to give detailed responses.

When your teacher signals you (by clapping hands or ringing a bell), stay with your partner, but find a polite and natural way to end the conversation. Then walk over to another student and use an ice breaker to start another conversation. Continue this procedure for as long as your class wishes.

Once everyone sits down again, form small groups and discuss how you felt. Explain what was easy for you and what produced the most tension.

LEARNING STRATEGY

Managing Your Learning: Highlighting what you find interesting in a reading later helps you focus your discussion.

3. Read the following newspaper article. Don't worry about understanding every word. Just try to get the main points. Highlight any ideas you would like to discuss by (1) underlining, (2) using a colored pen, or (3) adding a star or bracket in the margin.

In social interactions, small talk has a big role

by Craig Tomashoff

Hi there. How's it going?

Oh, fine. Fine. How about this weather, huh? . . . Well, I guess we can always use the rain.

What's that? This story? Oh, just a little look at **small talk.** You know, **those seemingly meaningless conversations you have dozens of times a day.** Maybe you're waiting for the elevator. Or in a line at the bank. Or in a hallway or at a party.

Yeah, I know. It all seems pretty trivial. Idle chatter about traffic doesn't do much more than fill the air with empty words that are quickly forgotten. But you should know that small talk actually has a big place in our lives.

"We need it," says Dana Gould, a Los Angeles-based comedian. "We need to seize any form of communication with each other because we have so few left."

Then there's Small Talk Gone Bad.

Pat Oliver, assistant professor and chair of the communication arts department at Loyola Marymount University, says that, left unchecked, small talk can be "an invasion. It's so powerful. It does something to you."

Almost without exception, small talk is done right, according to the pros.

"I come into my office every morning and start the day with small talk with my secretary," Oliver says. "I come in after spending an hour and a half on the freeway raring to do business, but that doesn't always happen . . . **If I don't make that small connection with another person, I can't work. I need that bonding that will carry me through the day."**

What causes it?

As a rule, you're either trying to yank somebody into your life, or you're using conversation as an invisible force field to keep them out.

"You can be wanting to connect with another person, and small talk is your entree to more meaningful conversation. Each approach is probably used with the same frequency."

The way people use small talk is usually determined by where they happen to be at the time. Take the elevator, for instance. Now there's prime territory. Nobody knows anyone and there's no reason to start a conversation, but invariably, someone does.

Making conversation in such peaceful social settings, according to Oliver, "Can confirm your territory. It's a way of feeling liked and accepted."

Or it can be a geographical thing.

"Being a Southerner, that's the hardest thing for me," explains actress Park Overall, co-star of the NBC sit-com "Empty Nest." **"I just can't stand those embarrassing silences. . .** When I'm at a Beverly Hills party, I'll ask the wives of powerful men what it's like to be married to those men."

"I actually hate to hear silence," says Mark K. Smith, who works as an administrative assistant in the personnel department for the May Co. "If I'm in a car and it's quiet, I always have to start a conversation."

The topics of small talk don't matter. In fact, you don't want anything more taxing than weather or traffic. **It's non-threatening talk in a threatening situation.** However, the rules change quickly when you're with lots of people doing lots of talking.

Let's say you're at a party. Or perhaps you've gone to a bar with friends. There's no way to avoid social interaction. Now it's time to use small talk as a way of making others feel more comfortable around you, so you don't look silly standing by the food table alone all night.

Kenny Green hears it all the time. He's a bartender for the Red Onion, a restaurant and nightclub in Huntington Beach, and he knows exactly what it takes to make successful small talk.

"The guys talk about themselves—their jobs, their finances, whatever. Girls talk about everything but the guy and themselves," he explains. "Talking about the music that's playing is usually a pretty good call. That's easy small talk. And things like, 'Come here often?' That gives you some security."

This verbal mating ritual can go on for as long as 20 minutes, according to Green's unscientific observations. If the talk remains small, it's probably time to move on.

"It varies a little from person to person, but I think most people intuitively know how long small talk should go on," says Oliver.

Source: San Francisco Chronicle, May 10, 1993 (Section D, pp. 3-4).

Now, comment on the following sentences that are taken from the article. If no comment occurs to you right away, then do one of the following:

- Express your feelings—fear, dread, enjoyment, etc.
- Say whether or not you identify with what has been said. If you identify, then give a personal example.
- Explain why you agree or disagree with what has been said.
- Talk about cultural and male-female differences that relate to what has been said.

a. "Small talk . . . Those seemingly meaningless conversations you have dozens of times a day."

b. "If I don't make that small connection with another person, I can't work. I need that bonding that will carry me through the day."

c. "As a rule, you're either trying to yank somebody into your life, or you're using conversation as an invisible force field to keep them out."

d. "The way people use small talk is usually determined by where they happen to be at the time. Take the elevator, for instance. Now there's prime territory. Nobody knows anyone and there's no reason to start a conversation, but invariably, someone does."

e. "I just can't stand those embarrassing silences . . . I actually hate to hear silence."

f. "It's (small talk) non-threatening talk in a threatening situation."

g. "The guys talk about themselves—their jobs, their finances, whatever. Girls talk about everything but the guy and themselves."

4. Dr. Deborah Tannen, a world-famous sociolinguist, has studied communication styles and made the following analyses:

a. **[About business & small talk]** "American men's information-focused approach to talk has shaped the American way of doing business. Most Americans think it's best to 'get down to brass tacks' as soon as possible, and not 'waste time' in small talk (social talk) or 'beating around the bush.' But this doesn't work very well in business dealings with Greek, Japanese, or Arab counterparts for whom 'small talk' is necessary to establish the social relationship that must provide the foundation for conducting business."

Source: Excerpted from *That's Not What I Meant,* 1986.
New York: William Morrow & Co., p. 32.

b. **[About male perceptions of small talk]** "In response to an article I had written, a journalist remarked that my claim that many men have little use for small talk, since they believe talk is designed to convey information, rang a bell with him. He deplores chit-chat and believes that talk should have significant content, be interesting and meaningful. This is fine so long as there is a business meeting with lots of substance to discuss. But he finds himself verbally hamstrung when the meeting breaks up, and he has to embark on the long walk down the hall with a stranger. Opposed in principle to, and simply unpracticed in, making small talk, he is at a loss when there is no 'big talk' available."

Source: Excerpted from *You Just Don't Understand,* 1990.
New York: William Morrow and Co., p. 104.

c. **[About female perceptions of small talk]** "Small talk is crucial to maintain a sense of camaraderie when there is nothing special to say. Women friends and relatives keep the conversational mechanisms in working order by talking about small things as well as large. Knowing they will have such conversations later makes women feel they are not alone in life. If they do not have someone to tell their thoughts and impressions to, they *do* feel alone."

Source: Excerpted from *You Just Don't Understand,* 1990.
New York: William Morrow and Co., p. 102.

Decide whether you want to discuss excerpts a, b, or c above. Then get into a group with others who have chosen the same topic, and do the following activities:

- Help each other with the vocabulary, referring to your dictionaries when necessary.
- Have each member of your group write one or two discussion questions related to the paragraph.
- Go around the group and respond to everyone's questions.
- Have the group recorder report on the most interesting aspects of your discussion.

If there is time, do the same with another one of the three paragraphs.

5. According to Dr. Leonard Zunin in his book *Contact: The First Four Minutes,* "In our culture it is apparent that a rule of social courtesy and congeniality has evolved when two strangers are introduced. Following the introduction, if neither party wishes to be rude, the two will converse for three to five minutes, or an average of four. This is the first courteous breaking-off point."

   Dr. Zunin came to this conclusion after observing "hundreds of people at parties, offices, schools, homes and in recreational settings." His point is that during the first four minutes of conversation, the speakers decide whether or not they want to get to know each other better. Ending a conversation too soon would be considered impolite.

Source: From *Contact: The First Four Minutes,* 1972.
Los Angeles: Nash Publishing, p. 8 & p. 17.

Think about people at a gathering in your native country. Imagine that two strangers are introduced and start a conversation. Would Dr. Zunin's theory about four minutes apply? Why or why not?

LEARNING STRATEGY

Understanding and Using Emotions: Using a checklist can help you discover feelings, attitudes, and motivations that apply to how *you* learn a language.

6. Now that you have spent some time working in groups, it is time to analyze your experiences. Complete the "Classroom Work Style Survey" on pages 30 and 31 to find out if you usually prefer an *independent* work style or a *collaborative* work style.

   When you have finished, it will be useful to have a class discussion on the pros and cons of working in groups.

Classroom Work Style Survey

Last name ______________________ First name ______________________

In your classes, how would you describe your past experiences working in small groups?

Mostly Positive ______ Just OK ______ Mostly Negative ______

Directions: This survey has been designed to help you and your teacher better understand **the way you usually prefer to work on assignments in class.**

Please read each statement, and then based on your past educational experiences, decide whether you mostly agree or disagree with each statement.

	AGREE	DISAGREE
1. When I work by myself in class (instead of with a partner or small group), I usually do a better job on assignments.	_____	_____
2. When I work by myself in class, I often feel frustrated or bored.	_____	_____
3. When I work by myself on assignments in class, I usually concentrate better and learn more.	_____	_____
4. I enjoy having opportunities to share opinions and experiences, compare answers, and solve problems with classmates.	_____	_____
5. I prefer working with a single partner than with a group.	_____	_____
6. Most of the time, I prefer to work by myself in class rather than with a partner or a small group.	_____	_____
7. When I work with a partner or a small group in class instead of by myself, I often feel frustrated or like I am wasting time.	_____	_____
8. When I work with a partner or a small group in class, I usually learn more and do a better job on the assignment.	_____	_____
9. Most of the time, I would prefer to work in class with a single partner rather than by myself.	_____	_____
10. Most of the time, I would prefer to work with a group rather than with a single partner or by myself.	_____	_____

	AGREE	DISAGREE
11. I am more comfortable working in groups when I can select the group of classmates with whom I will be working.	_____	_____
12. Usually, I prefer my teacher to select the small groups.	_____	_____
13. I prefer working in groups when there is a mixture of students from different backgrounds.	_____	_____
14. I prefer working in groups when my teacher assigns a specific role to each group member.	_____	_____
15. I prefer working in groups when the teacher lets us figure out for ourselves which group member roles and responsibilities we each want.	_____	_____
16. Usually, I find working in a group to be a waste of time.	_____	_____
17. Usually, I find working in a group to be more interesting and productive than working alone in class.	_____	_____
18. I hope we will not do too much group work in this class.	_____	_____
19. I hope we will have regular opportunities in this class to work with a partner or with a small group.	_____	_____
20. I mainly want my teacher to give us classroom assignments that we can work on by ourselves.	_____	_____

Directions: Give yourself 1 point if you AGREED with the following questionnaire items and 0 points if you DISAGREED. Next, add the points under each heading.

The greatest total indicates the way you usually prefer to work in class.

INDEPENDENT WORK STYLE	COLLABORATIVE WORK STYLE
1. ____	2. ____
3. ____	4. ____
6. ____	8. ____
7. ____	9. ____
16. ____	10. ____
18. ____	17. ____
20. ____	19. ____
TOTAL ____	TOTAL ____

LEARNING STRATEGY

Managing Your Learning: Practicing English outside of class creates a bridge between your classroom and the outside world.

Survey

In his book, *Why Things Are,* Joel Achenbach asks the question, "Why Don't People Talk on Elevators?" (pp. 319-320, Ballantine Books, N.Y., 1991)

In his answer, he gives three reasons: First, it is rude because some people would be left out of the conversation. Second, it's stupid because there's no way elevator conversations can be meaningful. Third, in an elevator we experience "an invasion of personal space," so we become tense and uncomfortable. All of this discomfort, Achenbach says, can create the feeling that time passes very slowly on an elevator.

What do you think? When you are in an elevator,

a. What do you look at?
b. Do you feel free to talk? Why or why not?
c. Do you feel uncomfortable when people stand very close to you?

Answer these questions with a partner and then go out separately or together and conduct a survey. Interview five to ten people, using the same questions. Be sure to ask the people where they are from. Their answers, together with their backgrounds, may reveal how people from different cultures deal with space, eye contact, and small talk in an elevator. (For details on how to conduct a survey, refer to Appendix K.)

Listening Log Report

Bring your Listening Log to class and report on one entry in a small group. Take turns doing the following:

- Tell your group members what you watched or listened to.
- Give a short oral summary followed by your personal reaction. Do not read what you have written.
- Check your listeners' comprehension by asking questions such as "Do you understand what I mean?" and "Am I being clear?"
- Rephrase or restate to make your points clear.
- Answer your listeners' questions and ask for their reactions.

LEARNING STRATEGY

Managing Your Learning: Practicing outside the classroom in a natural setting makes language learning more rewarding.

FOLLOW-UP

Choose any of the following activities to do outside of class and then report on what happened or what you found out. These activities can be done individually, in pairs, or in small groups. (Refer to Oral Presentation Feedback forms in Appendix L.)

1. Write a letter to an advice columnist (such as Ann Landers or Dear Abby) in your local newspaper. Explain how you feel when you want to start, continue, or end a conversation, and ask her for tips.
2. Analyze how characters on TV programs start, continue, and end conversations. Find out if it is true that TV characters end telephone conversations by hanging up without saying good-bye.
3. When watching a TV comedy, notice how the actors use stress and intonation to emphasize the importance of words. (The higher the intonation, the more intense the emotion.)

   If you have a VCR, record five minutes of a show and take the role of one of the characters to imitate. After your character says a line, pause the tape and repeat what you hear. Get to know this character and watch this comedy every week.
4. Conduct a survey on how people feel about small talk and the techniques that they use in conversations. (See Appendix K for guidelines on how to conduct a survey.)

5. Go to the library or a bookstore to see what more you can learn about the subject of small talk. You might want to look at these books (some of which are also on tape):

By Dr. Lillian Glass:

- Say it Right: How to Talk in Any Social Situation
- Talk to Win
- He Says, She Says—Closing the Communication Gap Between the Sexes

By Dr. Deborah Tannen:

- You Just Don't Understand—Women and Men in Conversation
- That's Not What I Meant!—How Conversational Style Makes or Breaks Your Relations with Others

By Dr. Leonard Zunin:

- Contact: The First Four Minutes

6. Find out what volunteer activities exist in your community so you can help people and also practice using small talk. You might consider contacting hospitals, libraries, retirement homes, soup kitchens, or museums.

LEARNING STRATEGY

Managing Your Learning: Evaluate your own progress so you become a better learner.

LEARNING ASSESSMENT

1. Look back at Part I (Listening) of this chapter. What activities helped you most in understanding the listening passages?

___

___

___

2. Give an example of when you had trouble understanding what you heard.

___

___

___

Why did you have difficulty?

_____ **a.** I didn't know the vocabulary.

_____ **b.** I wasn't paying attention.

_____ **c.** The speaker wasn't clear.

_____ **d.** The speaker spoke too fast.

_____ **e.** Other: ________________________________

3. Were you more successful than you expected to be in understanding the listening material on the subject of being a good conversationalist? Were you less successful than you expected? Why?

____

____

____

4. Look back at Part II (Speaking) of this chapter. Give one or two examples of your most successful efforts at oral communication. Try to explain why you were able to succeed.

____

____

____

5. Give an example of a discussion in which you had trouble communicating with your classmates.

____

____

____

Why did you have difficulty?

_____ **a.** My classmates didn't understand my pronunciation.

_____ **b.** I didn't understand my classmates' pronunciation.

_____ **c.** I had trouble finding the main ideas in the readings.

_____ **d.** There was a lot of new vocabulary.

_____ **e.** Other: ________________________________

6. What could you do next time to:

a. better prepare for a listening passage?

____

____

____

b. improve your effectiveness when speaking in a group?

____

____

____

7. Look back at the goals you set at the beginning of this chapter.

a. Which goals did you achieve?

____

____

____

b. What will be your primary goal in the next chapter?

____

____

____

Telephone Technology —a Curse or a Blessing?

2

CHAPTER

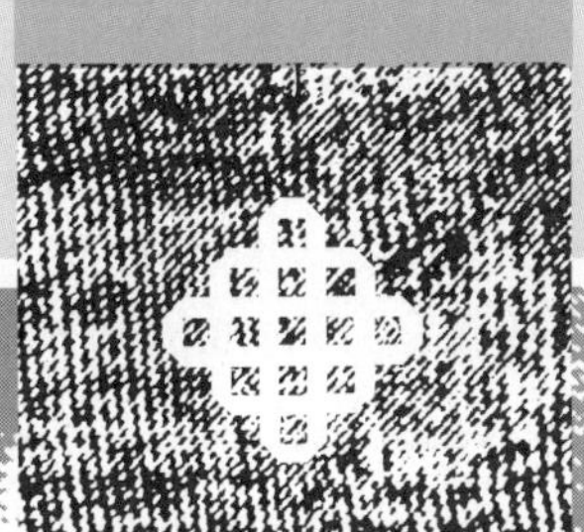

In the previous chapter, you looked at small talk—one of many ways we communicate with each other daily. In this chapter, we will continue to focus on communication—communication aided by modern technology. You will listen to two National Public Radio discussions, one about "voice mail" and the other about "call waiting," two forms of telephone technology that some people love and others hate.

You will also have opportunities to read about and discuss these and other technological innovations.

Background Knowledge Check

IT WORKS! Learning Strategy: Using Prior Knowledge

The following items reflect some of the content that you will find in this chapter. Write **a, b, c,** or **d** next to each item in the list according to the following:

(a) I have never heard of this.
(b) I have heard of this, but I don't really know what it means.
(c) I have some idea of what this means, but I'm not sure about it.
(d) I have a clear idea of what this means and can explain it.

_____ **1.** Voice mail

_____ **2.** Call waiting

_____ **3.** Answering machine

_____ **4.** Cellular phone

_____ **5.** Fax

_____ **6.** Technophobia

Students who have chosen **d** for any of the items should *briefly* explain what these items mean. If no one has chosen **d**, don't worry. You will have a chance to learn more about these as you progress through the chapter.

Setting Goals

IT WORKS! Learning Strategy: Setting Goals

Complete the following statement by checking the goals you want to achieve in this chapter.

While working on this chapter, I will make an effort to:

_____ **1.** speak more while I am working in a small group.

_____ **2.** give others a chance to speak while working in a small group.

_____ **3.** show others that I am actively listening by looking into their eyes and nodding as they talk.

_____ **4.** ask more questions in front of the whole class.

_____ **5.** make more comments in front of the whole class.

____ **6.** monitor one aspect of my pronunciation, such as ________________.

____ **7.** monitor one aspect of grammar as I speak, such as ________________.

____ **8.** use some of the new vocabulary when speaking, both in and out of class.

____ **9.** listen to the radio and watch TV outside of class.

____ **10.** learn more about and maybe even try to use a form of telephone technology.

____ **11.** try to achieve another goal, such as ________________________________

____.

LEARNING STRATEGY

Understanding and Using Emotions: Laughing helps you relax so that you will be able to learn more easily.

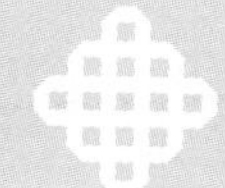

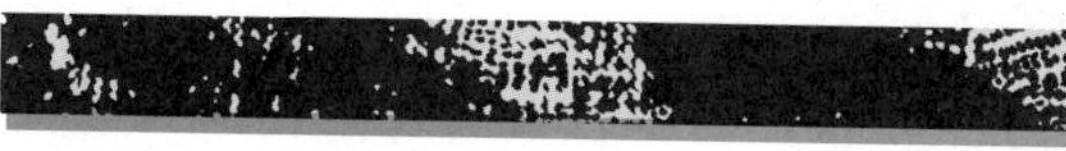

WARM-UP

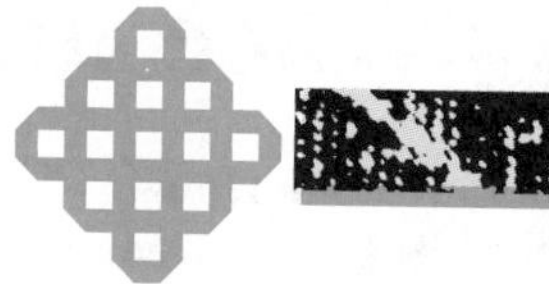

In the cartoon below, the man has just called "911," the emergency number used throughout the United States. To his surprise, he hears a recording of a "voice-mail menu."

1. Why do you think this is called a "menu"?
2. Notice the musical notes at the end of the recording. And notice that the man sarcastically says, "Oh, great. Muzak." Can you guess what "Muzak" is and where people usually hear it played?
3. What is absurd about the situation portrayed in this cartoon?
4. Have you ever heard of or had to use a voice-mail menu? If so, how do you feel about it?

BIZARRO By DAN PIRARO

Source: The "BIZARRO" cartoon by Dan Piraro is reprinted by permission of Chronicle Features, San Francisco, California

Threads

There were approximately 423,619,000 telephones in the world on January 1, 1989.

Guinness, 1993

PART I: LISTENING

Before You Listen: Listening Passage 1

LEARNING STRATEGY

Forming Concepts: Learning more about a topic through reading helps you prepare for new ideas and vocabulary you will hear.

BACKGROUND READING

Read the following newspaper article. Don't worry about getting every word; just try to get the main idea, because it will help you understand the listening passage that you will hear.

Voice mail: not the answer?

by John Flinn

It's **a long shot,** but if this revolt ever succeeds, grateful telephone users may someday erect a statue to Ed Crutchfield, the man who fired the shot heard 'round the world against **voice mail.**

Joyful employees stood and applauded last month when Crutchfield, chairman of First Union Bank in Charlotte, N.C., sent out a memo ordering the bank to *"press 1 to disconnect now"* from its hated voice-mail system.

"The next time I call and get an answering machine, we're going to be minus one telephone answering machine operator," warned Crutchfield's memo.

His memo has become a rallying point of voice-mail haters, who say the computerized phone answering systems symbolize the **contempt** some businesses display for their customers and that government agencies show for the taxpayers. . . .

One reason we **chafe at** voice mail may be buried deep within the human psyche, according to new research conducted at Stanford University. The technology violates basic rules of human communication that have existed since the first cavemen **grunted at** each other, according to Clifford Nass, an assistant professor of communication at Stanford.

"When people hear a human voice, it sets off strong cues within their brain, and it sets up certain expectations," Nass said. "This is a very hard-wired, **visceral** response."

One Bay Area business is even capitalizing on our **loathing** of voice mail in its advertising campaign.

TakeCare Health Plan, the Concord-based **health maintenance** plan that covers 230,000 members in California, doesn't advertise that it has the most liberal coverage or doctors with the warmest bedside manner.

It advertises that its members don't have to suffer through voice mail when they call.

"If you have a question, press 1, now. If you would like it answered, press 2, now. If you would like to be put on hold for 10 minutes, press 3, now," the ads say, **lampooning** their competitors' **impenetrable** voice-mail systems. *"If you want a membership card, please punch in Beethoven's Fifth, now, in D minor."*

Instead of using a computer, TakeCare employs 12 human operators to handle calls from its customers on its toll-free line. On an average day, they handle 1,170 inquiries.

"Voice mail erects a wall between service industries and their customers," said Mike Massaro of Goldberg Moser O'Neill, the agency that created the campaign.

The people who make voice mail say none of this is the fault of the technology. The problem, they insist, lies with users who do a **shoddy** job of programming their systems.

"People will love it eventually," predicts Maria DeMarco, marketing director for Pacific Bell Voice Mail.

Most of the **acrimony** toward voice mail could be eliminated, says DeMarco, if system users made sure callers always had an easy way to punch out of the system and talk to a live human being.

And voice-mail supporters point out that pushing buttons or talking to a recording can't be any more irritating than listening to a busy signal or a phone ringing endlessly without being answered.

There's one person who never gets tired of hearing that **disembodied** voice say, ". . . or, press 1, for more options." That's because Joan Kenley of Oakland loves hearing her own voice.

Kenley, a former singer who has performed with Ethel Merman, is the voice of voice mail. Northern Telecom, Pacific Bell and other major system suppliers have hired her because **oscilloscope** tests show her intonations retain warmth and "smile" on a computer chip. "I'm everywhere," she says. "I'm **ubiquitous.**"

Former singer Joan Kenley is the voice of voice mail, hired by companies for the "smile" she brings to the recorded messages.

Reprinted with permission from the San Francisco Examiner.

NOTE: Some people use *voice mail* and *phone mail* as synonyms.

a long shot: not a likely possibility
voice mail: computerized phone-answering system
contempt: feeling that someone is worthless
chafe at: become very irritated at
grunted at: made deep, wordless sounds at
visceral: instinctive
loathing: extreme hate
health maintenance: health insurance
lampooning: making fun of
impenetrable: unable to be entered
shoddy: poorly done
acrimony: bitterness
disembodied: without a body
oscilloscope: electronic device that shows voice patterns
ubiquitous: everywhere

Now, complete the following chart:

NAME	OCCUPATION	OPINION OF VOICE MAIL
1. Ed Crutchfield	__________	__________
2. Maria De Marco	__________	__________
3. Joan Kenley	__________	__________

VOCABULARY PREPARATION FOR LISTENING TO "VOICE MAIL MAY COST COMPANY'S BUSINESS"

Try to guess the meanings of the **boldfaced** words and phrases.

1. An automated phone system aimed at saving companies money may be **turning off** their customers.

    HINT: Many customers don't like this system.

    ____

IT WORKS! Learning Strategy: Guessing Meanings

2. Five years ago, when voice mail was first introduced, many companies were **wary of** the technology.

    HINT: Today, in contrast, many companies use voice mail a lot.

    ____

3. TakeCare, a large **health maintenance** organization (HMO) **lampooned** the **disembodied** voices with their menu options. . .

    HINT: These words are all contained in the reading passage that you just read.

    ____

    ____

    ____

4. President Jud Jessup says the **spoof** on voice mail has been a huge success.

    HINT: When they lampooned or made fun of voice mail, they did a "spoof."

    ____

5. The majority felt frustration, even **fury,** over their **run-ins** with voice mail.

    HINT: "Run-ins" are experiences, but not good ones. So how did people feel?

    ____

    ____

6. **Flawed** systems easily can be fixed.

    HINT: If something needs to be fixed, it's "flawed."

    ____

7. Many voice-mail systems could use an **overhaul,** but that technology is here to stay.

    HINT: Many voice-mail systems aren't perfect, so what do they need?

    ____

8. He sees a growing **backlash** against voice mail.

    HINT: Some people don't like voice mail. They reject it. A "backlash," then, is a

    ____

As You Listen: Listening Passage 1

LISTEN FOR OPINIONS

As you listen, complete the following chart:

NAME	OCCUPATION	OPINION OF VOICE MAIL
1. Jud Jessup	________________	________________
2. Sandy Hale	________________	________________

LISTEN FOR DETAILS

First, read the TRUE/FALSE items below. Then listen to the tape again and circle **T** for "true" or **F** for "false" to the left of each item.

T F **1.** A company's main goal in using voice mail is to be efficient and save money.

T F **2.** Companies that use voice mail may lose business.

T F **3.** Five years ago, everyone wanted to use voice mail.

T F **4.** To attract customers, TakeCare used a serious voice-mail message in its advertisements.

T F **5.** The TakeCare spoof on voice mail was a successful advertising effort.

T F **6.** According to many consumers, voice mail increases contact between companies and customers.

T F **7.** According to Sandy Hale, the voice-mail menus are fine. The problem lies with the technology.

T F **8.** To prevent the problem of "voice jail," callers should always have the option of talking to a human being.

T F **9.** Voice mail is valuable in that it saves companies money.

T F **10.** TakeCare, a large HMO, does not use voice mail with its customers, but it does use voice mail internally, among its employees.

LEARNING STRATEGY

Learning with Others: Checking your answers with someone else helps confirm that you understood correctly.

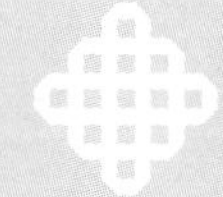

After you complete this exercise, check your answers with your class. Then, with a partner, rewrite the false sentences to make them true.

Before You Listen: Listening Passage 2

PREPARATION FOR LISTENING TO "CALL WAITING COULD COST YOU FRIENDS"

Call Waiting," according to Pacific Bell Calling Customer Information, "gives a special tone when someone calls while you are already on the phone. You can answer the second call and then return to your original call without hanging up."

Many people say that it is rude to ask someone you are talking to to hold on while you see who's on the other line.

You are going to hear a listening passage which has two parts:

a. a dialogue between two friends, Wanda and Pat. Pat is very upset. (Stop the tape when you hear the beep at the end of the dialogue so that you can answer the questions under **A** below.)

b. a conversation between interviewer Bob Edwards and newspaper columnist Judith Martin, otherwise known as "Miss Manners"®, who answers letters from readers about manners and politeness. They talk about the dialogue between Wanda and Pat, and about the subject of call waiting.

As You Listen: Listening Passage 2

LEARNING STRATEGY

Remembering New Material: Picturing scenes in your mind helps you remember and understand what you hear.

A. Close your eyes and listen to the dialogue once or twice. Then, write as many words as you can that describe the three people:

Pat is: [for example: upset, a close friend, etc.]

Wanda is:

Gary is:

With members of your class,

a. share the above descriptions and why you chose them.

b. predict what the interviewer and Miss Manners will say about Pat's and Wanda's specific situation and call waiting in general.

B. Continue listening, and then answer the following questions:

1. What bothers Miss Manners the most about call waiting?
2. According to Miss Manners, what is a better way for a caller to find out that you are already on the phone?
3. Did Pat really jump off a bridge? How do you know?
4. What did Miss Manners mean when she asserted that "if it's a genuine emergency, it is one of these 'drop everything and attend to your friend' situations"?

After You Listen

LEARNING STRATEGY

Overcoming Limitations: Using standard expressions and formulas makes you more fluent in idiomatic English and helps you overcome limitations.

FOCUS ON GIVING DEFINITIONS AND SUMMARIES

Imagine that you are at a cafe talking to some friends. You want to tell them about what you listened to in class about voice mail and call waiting.

Voice Mail

X: I heard a pretty interesting radio program about voice mail today.

Y: What's voice mail?

X: It's [give a definition] ______________________________

____

____

The tape was about [give a brief summary in two or three sentences]

____

____

____

Y: Oh, that's really interesting.

Call Waiting

Y: I heard a pretty funny radio program about call waiting today.

X: What's call waiting?

Y: It's [give a definition] ______________________________

____

The tape was about [give a brief summary in two or three sentences]

____

____

____

X: Uh-huh.

Y: And there was a really hilarious dialogue to show how rude call waiting can be.

X: Oh yeah? Tell me about it.

Y: Well, two women were talking, and ______________________________

____

____

FOCUS ON STARTING AND CONTINUING A CONVERSATION

IT WORKS! Learning Strategy: Practice Outside the Classroom

Start a conversation in English with someone using one of the following:

I saw [an interesting movie last night; you working hard in the library yesterday, etc.]

I heard [that you were going to get married; that the teacher's going to give a test, etc.]

I read [that the President is going to come here; that the next Olympics will be in . . ., etc.]

Keep the conversation going by using turn-taking strategies that are explained in Appendix E.

After you finish your conversation, write up what you remember in dialogue form and bring it to class. In class, discuss whether it was easy or difficult to start the conversation and keep it going. Give reasons for your answers.

Threads

The first telephone for domestic use was installed in April, 1877 at the home of Charles Williams, Jr. of Somerville, Massachusetts.

LISTENING LOG

Reminder: Keep up your Listening Log with as many entries as your teacher requires. At the end of Part II (Speaking), you will report on one of your entries in a small group. (If necessary, see Appendix F for more details on Listening Logs.)

ANY QUESTIONS?

Before you go on to read about and discuss more issues about modern telephone technology, answer the following questions on a separate sheet of paper. Do not write your name on the paper. Your teacher or a classmate will collect the papers and share everyone's answers with the class.

IT WORKS! Learning Strategy: Clarifying

1. What has been the most valuable aspect of this chapter for you so far?
2. What is still unclear?

PART II: SPEAKING

Discussion

The following discussion questions deal with different aspects of modern telephone technology. Choose the topic or topics you would like to discuss. Feel free to add related questions of your own to the questions that are asked here. And as always, you should focus on using new vocabulary and appropriate conversation skills.

IT WORKS! Learning Strategy: Learning with Others

When appropriate for the activity, work in small groups. Assign one person to act as discussion leader and another person to act as recorder. The discussion leader will make sure that everyone talks and stays on the subject. The recorder will take notes and later report briefly to the class on the main points of your group's discussion.

Before you begin, take a look at the group work questionnaire on page 54 of this section. You will respond to the items on the questionnaire after one of your discussions has been completed. As you work in groups, keep the items on the questionnaire in mind.

1. In the cartoon at the right, the woman is answering her phone as if she were an answering machine. What is the message of this cartoon?

BIZARRO
By DAN PIRARO
YOU HAVE REACHED KIM AT JL5-3220. I AM HOME RIGHT NOW, BUT I DON'T WANT TO TALK TO YOU. AT THE SOUND OF THE TONE, I WILL HAVE HUNG UP.
©CHRONICLE FEATURES 1993
PIRARO

Source: The "BIZARRO" cartoon by Dan Piraro is reprinted by permission of Chronicle Features, San Francisco, California

2. Now that we have answering machines and voice mail, it is possible for people to avoid talking to each other directly. This phenomenon has led to a new expression in English: "telephone tag." It occurs when one person leaves a message on a machine, and the person who receives the message responds with another recorded message. The machines convey the messages, but the two people just can't seem to make personal contact.

Writer Ellen Goodman discusses this in her article, "Telephone Tag of the '90s." Read the following quotes from her article. Highlight whatever you would like to discuss:

IT WORKS!
Learning Strategy:
Highlighting

a. "A hundred years ago, the telephone was invented to allow people to talk to each other. Now it's being used to help people avoid talk."

b. "A growing number of Americans have come to prefer voice mail to voices. Have you ever prayed for an answering machine when you called up to break a date? Have you ever deliberately phoned people you knew were out so you could just leave a message? Have you ever RSVPed, apologized, lied, by voice mail? Ever wished you could? Have you ever turned on the answering machine when you were in and then monitored the calls?"

c. "Communication . . . implied that words went two ways, back and forth. Communication was a people skill. Information, on the other hand, is a sequence of facts to be delivered and received. I dump information on you; you dump it on me. It's a game you can play by machine or by those other telephone toys of the information era, the fax and the modem."

d. "In the much vaunted time-crunch of the '90s, it is faster to leave a message on a machine. You don't have to ask the machine whether it had had a nice weekend. Voice mail doesn't want to know why you can't have lunch. Telephone technology doesn't have opinions or feelings. It can't correct you, argue, or engage in what we once thought of as social discourse."

e. "So it is that haste has become the new status symbol. Talking is considered wasteful. The powerful are those who eliminate that messy, time-consuming and unpredictable business liability: people."

Write some questions to ask about Goodman's points. Three questions are started for you; make up the last one.

- What does Goodman think ______________________________?
- Do you agree with ______________________________?
- Have you ever ______________________________?
- ______________________________?

Working in a small group, answer everyone's questions. After your discussion, choose one person to report the most interesting points to the entire class.

3. Answer the following questions, and then have a student at the board compile a master list of your class's experience with technology.

a. Have you ever: **Yes** **No**

- used a computer?
- used E-mail?
- set a VCR to record a television show?
- programmed your favorite stations on a car radio?
- set a digital alarm clock?
- used a fax machine?
- bought an answering machine?

b. Do you have "technophobia" (a fear of technology)? Read the following newspaper article.

Most Americans suffer from fear of technology, study says

F**ear of technology** afflicts most Americans, and one-fourth of the nation's adults would not use a computer unless they were forced to, according to a survey released yesterday.

A quarter of U.S. adults have never used a computer, **set a VCR** to record a television show or programmed favorite stations on their car radio, the survey by Dell Computer Corp. showed.

The survey was conducted of 1,000 adults and 500 teens across the country, Dell said.

Teenagers are more technically literate than adults, with 92 percent of the younger set more comfortable using a variety of **technical devices,** compared with 74 percent of adults.

Computers produced the most anxiety among adults, with 23 percent saying they were **not comfortable using a computer** on their own. Thirty-two percent of the adults were intimidated by computers and afraid they might damage the machine if they used it without help. Of that group, 22 percent were **uncomfortable setting a digital alarm clock,** the survey said.

Teenagers were more comfortable using a computer than an answering machine.

Other survey findings:

Women are more inclined to suffer from technophobia than men, 55 percent vs. 45 percent, with technophobia showing up in 55 percent of the survey's respondents overall.

Source: San Francisco Chronicle, July 26, 1993. Reprinted with permission from Reuters America Inc.

LEARNING STRATEGY

Managing Your Learning: Use checklists to make sure that you are actively using new vocabulary.

Answer the questions in the lettered list below, and as you are speaking, make a point to use some of the phrases from the previous article in your discussion. A checklist is provided for you.

Vocabulary Use Checklist

_____ **1.** fear of technology

_____ **2.** set a VCR

_____ **3.** technical devices

_____ **4.** not comfortable using a computer

_____ **5.** uncomfortable setting a digital alarm clock

_____ **6.** other: ________________________________

(a) What do you think "technophobia" means?
(b) Do any of the results of this survey surprise you?
(c) Why do you think teenagers were more comfortable using a computer than an answering machine?
(d) Would you expect the same survey results in your native country? Explain.
(e) What do you think can be done to decrease "technophobia," especially among adults, in the United States and elsewhere?

4. In the modern world, people move about so much that multicultural societies are becoming more and more common. One of the first barriers that immigrants (and travelers in general) face is the telephone. The difficulty arises not only because of language differences, but also because of a lack of information about how to use the phone, as can be seen from this article about immigrants in the United States:

Phones can perplex recent immigrants

by L. A. Chung

A new nationwide survey shows that recent immigrants from Asia and Latin America often fall victim to phone **scams** and probably pay for more telephone services in general because they do not fully understand the American phone system.

The survey shows that 14 percent of Chinese, Korean, and Latino immigrants were victims of telephone **fraud** and that 50 percent did not know they could dial 411 for **directory assistance,** said Ken McEldowney, director of Consumer Action in San Francisco.

Sprint, an international telecommunications company, commissioned the survey, which **queried** Chinese, Korean, and Latino consumers in San Francisco, Los Angeles, New York, Miami, Chicago, and the Brownsville, Texas, area. Consumer Action, with the help of the U.S. Office of Consumer Affairs, will conduct a one-year educational campaign in those cities beginning in June.

"This is a multicultural society, and to do business in the United States—certainly in California—you have to recognize that reality," said McEldowney, whose group has worked on consumer telephone and banking issues for several years.

The telecommunications industry has become increasingly sophisticated, and many new immigrants—particularly from countries where telephone systems are significantly different—are at a disadvantage because of language barriers.

The study also showed that:

—20 percent did not know to call 911 for emergencies.

—28 percent did not know operator-assisted international calls were more expensive than **direct-dial calls.**

—67 percent did not use the phone for personal business.

—40 percent felt someone might be **listening in on** phone conversations without their knowledge.

—28 percent did not know the difference between a local company and the **plethora** of long-distance companies.

The results indicate that recent immigrants may have trouble during medical emergencies, and many might not be receiving reduced-rate service even if they are **eligible,** said McEldowney.

"This is a big concern for us," said Sylvia Ramirez, executive director of Latino Information Center, who added that her help is often needed when newly arrived immigrants need phones installed. "A lot of our clients are from countries where these kind of services are not even available."

scams: dishonest tricks
fraud: deception/dishonesty
directory assistance: help in finding a phone number
queried: asked
direct-dial calls: calls made without an operator
listening in on: eavesdropping; listening when others aren't aware
plethora: superabundance; great number of
eligible: qualified/able

After reading the preceding article, the class should divide into groups of three. In each group, one student will be called the "speaker," another student will be called the "listener," and the third student will be called the "observer." (See Appendix D for information on active listening.)

IT WORKS! Learning Strategy: Developing Cultural Awareness

The **speaker** should talk about *one* of the following subjects:

- Specific difficulties in using the telephone when he or she first arrived in a foreign country
- What a newcomer to the speaker's native country should know about the telephone system (the number for emergencies and for directory assistance, the cheapest way to make local and long-distance calls, whether or not anyone might be listening in on a call, etc.)
- Advice for newcomers to the United States about using the telephone.

While speaking, the speaker should make eye contact with the listener and check his or her comprehension occasionally by asking, "Do you know what I mean?"

The **listener** should listen *actively* to show interest in what the speaker is saying. To do this, the listener should do *all* of the following:

- Nod, smile, make eye contact
- Say uh-huh, um-hm, "I know what you mean" to show understanding
- Ask questions for clarification, such as: "What do you mean by . . .?" or "Could you give me an example of that?" and so on
- Restate or rephrase what the speaker says, in order to confirm understanding, such as "So you're saying that . . .?"

The **observer** should be a silent participant and take notes in the chart below. After the discussion, the observer should give a report and then ask the speaker and listener how they felt during their discussion.

	SPEAKER	LISTENER
used eye contact	__________	__________
showed comprehension (said um-hm, nodded, smiled, spoke)	__________	__________
checked comprehension	__________	__________
asked for clarification	__________	__________
restated or rephrased	__________	__________

Threads

Fifty-four percent of cellular phone users say that their phone has improved their marriage.

Harper's Magazine

5. Today it is not unusual to see people talking on cellular phones in their cars or in restaurants. The use of cellular phones has brought up the question of *etiquette,* meaning manners and behavior. Imagine that you are in a restaurant and someone at the next table is making and receiving phone calls. Would it bother you?

Read these "Etiquette Guidelines for the Cellular Set" by writer Alice Kahn, and then give your reaction to each of the guidelines. If you've had any experience with cellular phones, let your classmates know.

ETIQUETTE GUIDELINES FOR THE CELLULAR SET

1. Don't listen in on other people's calls. The Electronic Privacy Act of 1986 made it a crime. Last year Congress passed another law that prohibits the manufacture or importation of scanners to help you listen to cellular calls.

2. Don't force other people to listen in on your calls by phoning in public places.

Miss Manners says, "It is rude to annoy other people with the sounds you make doing business." In Japan managers and waiters will ask you not to use your phone in fine restaurants. "Use of portable telephones at your seat may be a disturbance to other passengers, so please use the vestibule even if it is inconvenient," says a sign on the Japanese Bullet Train.

3. If you know people who carry a cellular phone for emergencies, don't call them unless it's an emergency. "Interruptions are interruptions," says Miss Manners, and they are rude.

4. Phone unto others as you would have them phone unto you. Use the same good manners in cellular phoning that you expect in any situation. "Users imagine themselves to be in an etiquette-free zone," says Miss Manners.

5. Don't drive under the influence of an absorbing phone call. If you can't get two hands on the wheel and your undivided attention on the road, you shouldn't be operating a moving vehicle.

ALICE KAHN

LEARNING STRATEGY

Learning with Others: Ask questions to clarify what you don't understand.

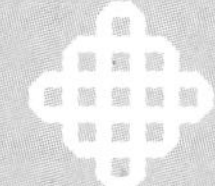

6. What's so funny about the following cartoon? If you don't know, go out and ask someone and report to the class.

Source: The "BIZARRO" cartoon by Dan Piraro is reprinted by permission of Chronicle Features, San Francisco, California

7. Now, think about one group that you worked with while discussing topics in this section. Evaluate your group experience by filling out the group work questionnaire on page 54.

LEARNING STRATEGY

Learning with Others: Awareness of what makes a group work well makes your discussions more productive.

Group Work Questionnaire for Discussion Question # ____

1. What one word would you use to describe how well the group worked together?

   ____

2. What one word would describe the way you would have liked the group to work together?

   ____

3. Did everyone participate?

   Always ____ Usually ____ Occasionally ____ Rarely ____ Never ____

   If not, why not?

4. Did you try to help each other feel able to talk and say what each one thought?

   Always ____ Usually ____ Occasionally ____ Rarely ____ Never ____

5. Did you listen to each other?

   Always ____ Usually ____ Occasionally ____ Rarely ____ Never ____

6. Did you show you were listening by nodding at each other?

   Always ____ Usually ____ Occasionally ____ Rarely ____ Never ____

7. Did you use such expressions as "That's good" to each other when you liked something?

   Always ____ Usually ____ Occasionally ____ Rarely ____ Never ____

8. Did you ask each other questions?

   Always ____ Usually ____ Occasionally ____ Rarely ____ Never ____

9. Did you listen and really try to answer those questions?

   Always ____ Usually ____ Occasionally ____ Rarely ____ Never ____

10. Did you pay attention to each other?

    Always ____ Usually ____ Occasionally ____ Rarely ____ Never ____

11. Did your group stay on the assigned task?

    Always ____ Usually ____ Occasionally ____ Rarely ____ Never ____

12. Did any one person do most of the talking?

    Yes ____ No ____

13. Was any one person quiet most of the time?

    Yes ____ No ____

Adapted from Scarcella and Oxford, 1992. *The Tapestry of Language Learning.* Boston, Mass.: Heinle & Heinle, (p. 159); and Aronson, Blaney, Stephan, Sikes, and Snapp, 1978. *The Jigsaw Classroom.* Beverly Hills, California: Sage.

LEARNING STRATEGY

Understanding and Using Emotions: Playing a role can help lower anxiety in speaking.

Simulation

For this simulation, you will be taking on the roles of various people engaged in a debate about whether or not to install a voice-mail system in a language school. You may either have one group perform the simulation for the rest of the class or have several groups conduct simultaneous simulations. (For more information on debates, see Appendix J.)

The situation: This language school in the United States has become very popular. It receives hundreds of phone calls daily from around the world. People are inquiring about taking intensive courses in the many languages that are offered.

The problem is that the office staff has a lot of paperwork and doesn't have much time to answer all the questions that people call to ask. Also, some of the staff members complain that many people who call don't understand English.

A number of staff members have asked for a voice-mail system through which they could connect people to messages in various languages that would give basic information about the programs. The first voice-mail message would say, for example, "If you would like information in English, press 1. If you would like information in Japanese, press 2," and so on. After pressing the appropriate number, callers would get information about how to apply in the language they chose. After they heard that information, they would be able to press another number if they wanted to speak to a "warm body."

Some members of the office staff fear that such a voice-mail system would scare people off. They say it would be too impersonal and that students who call knowing little or no English would not be able to understand the voice-mail menu. They point out that people can't ask a recording to "Please slow down" or "Please say that again."

Because staff members have such opposing opinions, the director of the school has called a meeting with both office staff and faculty to decide whether or not a voice-mail system should be installed.

Step One: Preparation

- Choose roles (see role descriptions on the following page).
- With the other person who is "on your side," complete the PRO-CON chart below. You will find information for this in Part I in the article, "Voice mail: not the answer?" on page 40 as well as in the opinion charts following the article. Feel free to add any other arguments that occur to you.
- Using this PRO-CON chart, decide on the points that you would like to make when you take on your role. Also, write down any questions you want to ask during the discussion. Try to anticipate the arguments that the opposing side will make and think of possible replies.

(PRO)	(CON)
Arguments for Voice Mail	Arguments Against Voice Mail
______________________	______________________
______________________	______________________
______________________	______________________
______________________	______________________
______________________	______________________
______________________	______________________
______________________	______________________

Step Two: Acting out the Simulation

- Hold the meeting. The director of the school will run the meeting. She or he will:
  —make sure that everyone gets a chance to speak.
  —ask questions for clarification as necessary.
  —occasionally rephrase what has been said to confirm understanding.
- Everyone will try to use the active listening skills listed under "Listener" on page 51 and in Appendix D.
- At the end of the meeting, the group should vote on whether or not to have a voice-mail system installed. If the group votes "yes," then, if there is time, everyone should decide on the actual voice-mail menu that would be used.

Step Three: Debriefing

IT WORKS! Learning Strategy: Discussing Your Feelings

- Participants should discuss how they felt the discussion and vote went.
- If part of the class observed the simulation, those students should voice their reactions to the simulation and the issues presented.
- If more than one simulation was going on at the same time, the groups should compare notes on what took place in each simulation.

THE ROLES

Director: You have a wonderful group of people working in the office. They are dedicated to their jobs because they really enjoy working with people from around the world. You think a voice-mail system would probably be helpful in this busy office, but are concerned about using it with such an international population. You want to hear the points made by both sides.

Office Manager: You find that the office has become extremely busy. While students, teachers, and others are standing in line waiting for information, members of your office staff are often on the phone answering inquiries. You don't want to hire any more people; the office is too crowded already. You want a voice-mail system.

Receptionist: You really enjoy talking to people on the phone, and know how to communicate very well with people who don't know much English. When you think of voice mail, you get the feeling that many of the callers would just hang up when they hear a recording. You think that rather than getting voice mail, the school should hire another person to work in the office.

Office Assistant: You hate all the ringing phones and people standing in line, waiting for help. The office is crazy. To you, voice mail would reduce the noise and let you help the people who are already there. And you strongly believe that with a good voice-mail menu and with clear information in numerous languages, callers would be satisfied.

Teacher: To you, voice mail is just another example of the world becoming more impersonal, and you feel strongly that anything so impersonal has no place in a school whose primary goal is effective communication. You also feel that when people around the world call your school, their first contact should be warm and personal, not cold and mechanical. You can imagine how awful it would be to enter "voice-mail jail" in a foreign language.

Listening Log Report

Bring your Listening Log to class and report on one entry in a small group. Take turns doing the following:

- Tell your group members what you watched or listened to.
- Give a short oral summary followed by your personal reaction. Do not read what you have written.
- Check your listeners' comprehension by asking questions such as "Do you understand what I mean?" and "Am I being clear?"
- Rephrase or restate to make your points clear.
- Answer your listeners' questions and ask for their reactions.

FOLLOW-UP

IT WORKS! Learning Strategy: Practice Outside the Classroom

Choose any of the following activities to do outside of class and then report on what happened or what you found out. These activities can be done individually, in pairs, or in small groups. (Refer to Oral Presentation Feedback Forms in Appendix L.)

1. To find out how people feel about modern telephone technology, conduct a survey on one or more of the following:

- Voice Mail
- E-Mail
- Answering Machines
- Cellular Phones
- Technophobia
- Dealing with phones in a foreign country
  (To get ideas on how to prepare for a survey, see Appendix K.)

Threads

The city with the most phones in the world is Tokyo, Japan with 5,511,000.

2. In a library or bookstore, find the answer to this question: Why do we have time-saving gadgets like fax machines and personal computers and yet feel just as rushed and harried as ever?
   The answer to this question is located on pages 228–230 in the book *Why Things Are, Volume II: The Big Picture,* by Joel Achenbach (Ballantine Books, 1993).
3. Go to the periodical index in your library and look up "TTY" ("Two-Text Telephones"). Find out how this technology helps the deaf.
4. Call the Customer Services office of your local telephone company and ask if they have any information that they can send you on voice-mail tips and etiquette.
5. Newspapers and magazines have articles on modern technology every day. Find and read an article that you choose, and then bring it to class to explain it either to a small group or in a speech to the entire class.
6. Read the list of optional services on page 59 provided by Pacific Bell in California. Call your phone company for an explanation of any services that you would like to know more about, and ask if they have any translated material.

Optional Services

Custom Calling Services

Call Waiting (including Cancel Call Waiting where available)—gives a special tone when someone calls while you are already on the phone. You can answer the second call and then return to your original call without hanging up. Cancel Call Waiting, where available, lets you temporarily turn off this feature before you make a call, so you won't be interrupted. It automatically turns on again as soon as you hang up.

Three-Way Calling—lets you call two different locations at once. You can also add a third party to a conversation.

Priority Ringing—gives a distinctive ring when you get a call from up to 10 preselected phone numbers.**

Repeat Dialing—redials the last number you called and signals you when the line is free.**

Call Return—returns the last call you received, whether or not you answered it.**

Call Screen—blocks calls from up to 10 telephone numbers you select. When someone calls from one of those numbers, you are not disturbed, and the caller hears a message informing them that you are not receiving their call at this time.**

Call Forwarding—lets you automatically transfer incoming calls to another telephone number.*

Speed Calling 8—lets you dial up to eight frequently called numbers by pressing only one number on your telephone.

Busy Call Forwarding and Busy Call Forwarding-Extended—send any incoming calls to another number when you're on your line—a number that you choose ahead of time.*

Delayed Call Forwarding—lets your home phone ring for the number of times you specify, and then automatically forwards the call to a number you have preselected.*

Select Call Forwarding (where available)—lets you forward only calls from certain preselected numbers.*

**Additional charges apply to calls forwarded outside your local calling area.*

Intercom Plus—effectively turns your telephone into an intercom system. It also allows you to either transfer calls, put an extension on hold (Call Hold) or add a third party (Three-Way Calling). Some restrictions apply.

Call Trace—allows you to have Pacific Bell trace an offending call immediately by dialing a special code after hanging up. We will record the telephone number from which the call originated. The traced number will only be released to the law enforcement agency handling the harassment complaint. Pacific Bell will not release a traced telephone number to any customer, even the person being bothered.**

***These services are available in limited areas served by modern switches.*

COMMSTAR[sm] II—links two to 30 phone lines in a single system. Features include Call Hold, Intercom, Call Transfer, Three-Way Calling and Call Pickup. Other optional features are available.

Source: Reprinted By Permission of Pacific Bell.

LEARNING ASSESSMENT

IT WORKS!
Learning Strategy: Evaluating Your Progress

1. Look back at Part I (Listening) of this chapter. What activities helped you most in understanding the listening passages?

____

____

____

2. Give an example of when you had trouble understanding what you heard.

____

____

____

Why did you have difficulty?

_____ **a.** I didn't know the vocabulary.

_____ **b.** I wasn't paying attention.

_____ **c.** The speaker wasn't clear.

_____ **d.** The speaker spoke too fast.

_____ **e.** Other: ______________________________

3. Were you more successful than you expected to be in understanding the listening material about telephone technology? Were you less successful than you expected? Why?

____

____

____

4. Look back at Part II (Speaking) of this chapter. Give one or two examples of your most successful efforts at oral communication. Try to explain why you were able to succeed.

____

____

____

5. Give an example of a discussion in which you had trouble communicating with your classmates.

____

____

____

Why did you have difficulty?

_____ a. My classmates didn't understand my pronunciation.

_____ b. I didn't understand my classmates' pronunciation.

_____ c. I had trouble finding the main ideas in the readings.

_____ d. There was a lot of new vocabulary.

_____ e. Other: ______________________________

6. What could you do next time to:
   a. better prepare for a listening passage?

____

____

____

   b. improve your effectiveness when speaking in a group?

____

____

____

7. Look back at the goals you set at the beginning of this chapter.
   a. Which goals did you achieve?

____

____

____

   b. What will be your primary goal in the next chapter?

____

____

____

3

CHAPTER

Humor—Its Role in Our Lives

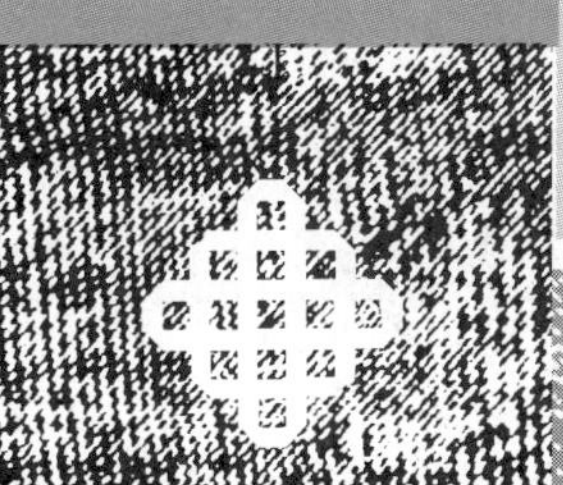

INTRODUCTION

In the previous chapters you had a chance to look at some of the ways we communicate with each other today. But what about how we communicate through humor? Have you ever thought about what makes people laugh? In this chapter you will have the chance to explore humor from different perspectives—the perspectives of various people who have thought a lot about laughter and its role in our lives: cartoonists who interpret our society with sharp wit; a Japanese interpreter who considers how humor crosses cultural boundaries; newspaper reporters who look at the dark side of humor; a columnist who sees humor as a positive force in dealing with stress and frustration; and a Polish-born writer who reflects on her early, unsuccessful attempts to express her sense of humor in English.

IT WORKS! Learning Strategy: Using Prior Knowledge

Background Knowledge Check

The following items reflect some of the content that you will find in this chapter. Write **a, b, c,** or **d** next to each item in the list according to the following:

(a) I have never heard of this.
(b) I have heard of this, but I don't really know what it means.
(c) I have some idea of what this means, but I'm not sure about it.
(d) I have a clear idea of what this means and can explain it.

_____ **1.** satire
_____ **2.** black humor
_____ **3.** nonsense humor
_____ **4.** pun
_____ **5.** rakugo
_____ **6.** April Fool's Day
_____ **7.** laughter is the best medicine
_____ **8.** how some humor can stereotype people

Students in the class who have chosen **d** for any of the items should *briefly* explain what these items mean. If no one has chosen **d,** don't worry. You will have a chance to learn more about these as you progress through the chapter.

Setting Goals

Complete the following statement by checking the goals you want to achieve in this chapter.

While working on this chapter, I will make an effort to:

_____ **1.** speak more while I am working in a small group.
_____ **2.** give others a chance to speak while working in a small group.

_____ **3.** show others that I am actively listening by looking into their eyes and nodding as they talk.

_____ **4.** ask more questions in front of the whole class.

_____ **5.** make more comments in front of the whole class.

_____ **6.** monitor one aspect of my pronunciation, such as _______________.

_____ **7.** monitor one aspect of grammar as I speak, such as _______________.

_____ **8.** use some of the new vocabulary when speaking, both in and out of class.

_____ **9.** listen to more radio programs outside of class.

_____ **10.** watch television comedies outside of class.

_____ **11.** try to achieve another goal, such as _______________

____.

IT WORKS! Learning Strategy: Setting Goals

LEARNING STRATEGY

Understanding and Using Emotions: Sharing laughter together with others helps lower anxiety about language learning.

WARM-UP

1. How is YOUR sense of humor?
   a. Look at the following cartoons and rate each cartoon on a scale of 1–5.

   1 = not funny at all
   2 = mildly funny
   3 = definitely funny
   4 = *very* funny
   5 = *extremely* funny

   b. Compare your ratings with a partner. Do you agree on what is and isn't funny? If you disagree on certain cartoons, explain why you rated the cartoons as you did.

(a)

BIZARRO By DAN PIRARO

The Bizarro cartoon by Dan Piraro is reprinted by permission of Chronicle Features, San Francisco, California.

Threads

The most perfect humor and irony is generally quite unconscious.

Samuel Butler, 1835–1902

(b)

Source: Drawing by Donnelly;
©1992, *The New Yorker* Magazine, Inc.

(c)

HERMAN

"It's the barman's little joke. First drink's on the house."

Universal Press Syndicate

(d)

"We're fighting like—well, we're fighting."

Drawing by Leo Cullum;
©1992, *The New Yorker* Magazine, Inc.

(e)

FARLEY

Source: © *San Francisco Chronicle.*
Reprinted by permission.

(f)

Source: Drawing by Toles; ©1993, Universal Press Syndicate

(g)

Source: Drawing by Cheney; ©1992, *The New Yorker* Magazine, Inc.

(h)

Source: The Bizarro Cartoon by Dan Piraro is reprinted by permission of Chronicle Features, San Francisco, California.

(i)

INTERACTIVE TELEVISION

©1993 NORMAN DOG

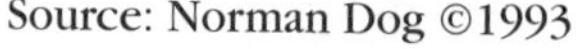

Source: Norman Dog ©1993

(j)

Source: Drawing by Wiley.
©1994, *The Washington Post* Writer's Group.
Reprinted with permission.

(k)

THE LAST CARTOON

"And now, as an experiment in democracy, I'm decreeing free elections to choose the national bird."

Source: Drawing by Chas. Adams; © 1993, *The New Yorker* Magazine, Inc.

2. After you have rated the cartoons, work with a partner or in small groups to categorize the kind of humor in each cartoon. Read the following definitions of the kinds of humor, look at the cartoons, and then put the letter of each cartoon under the category in the chart that best describes the humor in that cartoon. (Some of the cartoons can fit in more than one category.)

satire—humor that makes fun of practices and institutions of our society
black humor—humor dealing with the unpleasant side of human life
nonsense humor—humor that portrays an absurd, ridiculous situation
word play or puns—humor that comes from the amusing double meaning of words
aggressive humor—humor that portrays violence or that is mean in nature

SATIRE	BLACK HUMOR	NONSENSE HUMOR	WORD PLAY/PUNS	AGGRESSIVE HUMOR
______	______	______	______	______
______	______	______	______	______
______	______	______	______	______
______	______	______	______	______
______	______	______	______	______

Now that you have categorized the cartoons, look at the cartoons you rated the funniest. Do you prefer a particular kind of humor? Explain your answer.

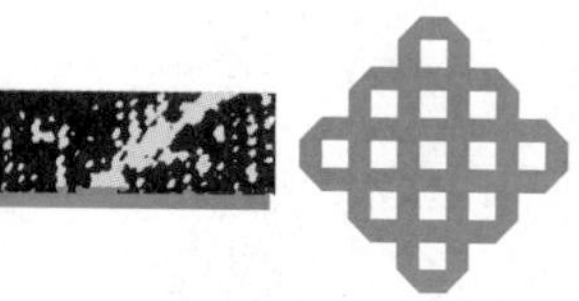

PART I: LISTENING

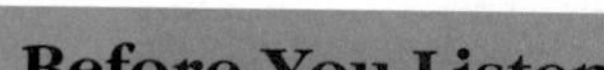

Before You Listen

VOCABULARY PREPARATION FOR LISTENING TO "HUMOR IN JAPAN"

IT WORKS! Learning Strategy: Learning Through Reading

Read the following article, in which Massachusetts graphic designer Susan Marsh shares some of her views about humor. The boldfaced words are vocabulary items you will hear in the listening passage. You may already know many of them. Do not look the words up—you will have a chance to guess their meanings from the context.

When moving to a new town, often where they don't know anyone, many people find it very difficult and uncomfortable to begin a conversation with a complete stranger. Using humor can be one way **to break the ice.** A **lighthearted** remark to the person standing in front of you in line at the post office can result in a smile and ignite a conversation. At a party or other gathering, a humorous **anecdote** can stimulate not only laughter and interest, but also a similar amusing story from someone else. Even people who prefer more serious conversations admit that amusing stories and jokes are not necessarily **frivolous,** but can be a way to connect with other people.

Susan Marsh, a graphic designer who moved to Holden, Massachusetts, from Cambridge a few years ago, agrees.

"When we first moved here, I was afraid it would be hard to meet people. When you've lived in one community for a long time, as we had, you almost forget what it's like to have to start making new friends again. You imagine that there will be a lot of **obstacles** to getting to know people—people in this country seem to have so little free time; we're always working or taking care of our families or running errands and doing chores. But almost right away, we met one couple who have children about the same age as our children, and we really hit it off. One thing I remember is that we laughed a lot together the first time we met. It made me realize how laughing with someone can help form a **bond** between you. If you find the same things funny, it's some **common ground** you have. We're now really good friends with that family."

Marsh **cautions** that when you first meet someone you have to be careful about the kind of funny stories or jokes you tell. "Obviously, not everybody finds the same things funny. A lot of popular jokes seem to **perpetuate stereotypes** such as the dumb blonde or the greedy lawyer with no morals who would do anything for money. These jokes **caricature** certain people, professions, **ethnic** groups and so on, and some people are offended by these kinds of jokes. And if you're a member of the group which is the **butt** of the joke, it can be pretty painful even if you want to be **a good sport** about it. It can be tricky. On one hand, you don't want to take yourself so seriously that you can't make fun of or laugh at anything, including yourself. On the other hand, you don't want to be mean."

When pressed for her favorite joke, Marsh laughs. "I don't know," she answers. "In fact, I can never remember the **punch line** to any of the jokes I've heard. I'm a terrible joke teller. You should ask my six year old son, Joe. He loves funny stories and can sit **mesmerized** for hours listening to them. He likes nonsense jokes a lot, but he also loves jokes that depend on word play, like **puns.** Once he gets them, he laughs and laughs and tries them out on everybody."

"Joe has a wonderful sense of humor and you would be amazed at how well he can **mimic** people; sometimes he has us in stitches when he's imitating someone. But anyway, he's the one you should ask for a joke—he's the joke **connoisseur** in the family!"

"Let me add something else," Marsh continues, "along different lines. I think it's important to have a sense of humor just to help you **cope with** daily life. Sometimes you can turn a bad situation into a funny story. Let's say you have a flat tire and are on your way to a job interview and get completely dirty while you're changing it. It's not funny at the time, but afterwards, turning it into a funny story can help you deal with an otherwise terrible situation."

Threads

Q: What's the largest punctuation mark in the world?
A: The 100-yard dash.

List two positive points and one negative point that Ms. Marsh makes about humor:

Positive: **1.** ______________________

2. ______________________

Negative: **1.** ______________________

IT WORKS! Learning Strategy: Summarizing

Can you think of any additional positive or negative aspects to humor? If so, what? Write them here:

Positive: ______________________

____

____

Negative: ______________________

____

____

Now, on your own or with a partner, write each vocabulary word from the reading next to the definition that best fits it.

- A connection: ______________________
- A person or thing that people make fun of: ______________________
- To remove feelings of awkwardness or nervousness: ______________________
- A short interesting or amusing story about a person or event: ______________________
- Someone who has good knowledge and understanding of a subject: ______________________
- A person who accepts defeat or trouble in an uncomplaining, cheerful way: ______________________
- Cheerful, happy, not serious: ______________________
- To warn: ______________________
- To deal successfully with a difficult situation: ______________________
- Of a racial, national, or tribal group: ______________________
- An amusing use of a word or phrase that has two meanings: ______________________
- To have similar opinions on certain things: ______________________
- Something which prevents action or success: ______________________
- To copy someone in order to make people laugh: ______________________
- To be so fascinated by something that it completely holds your attention: ______________________

- To make something continue to exist for a long time: ____________________
- To exaggerate certain physical or behavioral characteristics of someone: ____________________
- A fixed set of ideas of what a person is like: ____________________
- The last few words of a joke that cause amusement or surprise: ____________________

As You Listen

IT WORKS! Learning Strategy: Getting the Idea

LISTEN FOR THE MAIN IDEA

You are about to hear a listening passage by radio producer Jim Metzner on humor in Japan. The piece has been divided into three parts. Stop the tape at the sound of each beep, and for each question write one or two sentences that answer the question.

Read over the following questions *before* you listen to the passage.

Part 1
What is the difference between the ways that Japanese and Americans regard the use of humor in public speaking?

Part 2
What is rakugo?

Part 3
What is the main theme of Mr. Muramatsu's joke?

NOTE: "Yank," from the word "Yankee," is a slang word for an American.

LISTEN FOR DETAILS

First, read the questions below. Then listen to the tape again. When you hear the sound of the beep, stop the tape and write, on a separate piece of paper, short answers to the comprehension questions in each section.

Part 1

1. Who is Masumi Muramatsu?
2. According to Mr. Muramatsu, how would a Japanese interpret a joke or humorous remark given in a public speech?
3. When do Japanese tend to exchange jokes?
4. What kind of humor does Mr. Muramatsu say that the Japanese enjoy?
5. What kinds of jokes does Mr. Muramatsu say are both hard to understand and to translate?

Part 2

6. What does a rakugo storyteller do during a performance?
7. How long is a rakugo performance?
8. Why do people who enjoy rakugo come again and again to hear the same stories?
9. How have Western audiences responded to rakugo translated into English?

Part 3

10. According to Mr. Muramatsu, how do the Japanese caricature Americans?
11. In Mr. Muramatsu's joke about the overcrowded lifeboat, what does the captain tell:
    a. the Englishman?
    b. the Italian?
    c. the German?
    d. the Canadian?
    e. the American?
    f. the Japanese?

LEARNING STRATEGY

Learning with Others: Verifying your answers with a classmate helps you check your comprehension.

How sure are you about your answers? Before you check your answers to the questions, fill out the chart below, recording the certainty with which you think each of your answers is correct and complete. Place the number of the question in the appropriate column.

CERTAINTY CHART			
I'm Absolutely Certain My Answer Is Correct	I Think My Answer Is Correct, but I'm Not Quite Sure	I Think My Answer Is Probably Wrong, but I'm Not Quite Sure	I Know My Answer Is Wrong
______	______	______	______
______	______	______	______
______	______	______	______

- When you have finished, compare your answers to the comprehension questions with those of a classmate. If your answers differ, discuss them and decide together which answer is right.
- Now that you have gone over your answers with a classmate, do you want to change any of your responses on the certainty chart?
- Listen to the tape again to verify your answers.

After You Listen

FOCUS ON GETTING MEANING FROM CONTEXT

*IT WORKS!
Learning Strategy:
Guessing
Meanings*

As you know, often when you hear new words, you can guess their meanings from context. Look at the following excerpt from the tape:

"No . . . we like to see people with a sense of humor. If you, for example, tell a story about how you tried to speak Japanese but have failed, that's a humorous situation, and Japanese hosts will act favorably. They will laugh and they say, oh, he's a good sport. **Self-deprecating** is very much a part of our custom. We do it constantly among ourselves. Therefore, we should understand when visitors do that in the form of humor."

Write a definition of **self-deprecating:**

____

____

____

Share your definition with a partner. Do you have similar definitions? Use a dictionary or check with your teacher to verify your definition.

LEARNING STRATEGY

Remembering New Material: Repeating new words in context helps fix them in your memory.

FOCUS ON RETELLING WHAT YOU HEARD

bond	pun	break the ice	connoisseur
mesmerized	sense of humor	butt of the joke	stereotype
common ground	self-deprecating	to caricature	to mimic
frivolous	a good sport	punch line	to perpetuate
anecdote	lighthearted	to caution	rakugo

At home, prepare an oral reconstruction of the listening passage about humor in Japan by preparing notes on $3'' \times 5''$ cards. Before you begin, underline six or more words or phrases that you will use from the vocabulary list.

FOCUS ON MORE LANGUAGE ABOUT HUMOR

The following words and phrases are all terms related to humor:

tongue in cheek	a farce	hilarious	to make fun of
a buffoon	slapstick humor	a corny joke	to pull one's leg
sick humor	an off-color joke	a practical joke	to giggle
gallows humor	to fall flat	a good one	to get it
parody	a riot	funny bone	to kid
wit	to fall for	a gag	to play a prank
a ribbing	to quip, a quip	to jest, a jest	

1. Choose one or more terms (all the terms should be assigned) and look them up in the dictionary, or ask a native speaker how they are pronounced and what they mean. If you use a dictionary and find that a word has several meanings, be sure to use the meaning that would make sense in the context of humor. Ask a native speaker for several examples that show what the word means and how it can be used.
2. Present the terms to your class or to a small group and do the following for each term:

   - Explain its definition and give one or two clear examples to illustrate its meaning.
   - Check to make sure that the other students are following you.

3. As you listen to other students explaining their terms:

   - Take notes.
   - Ask questions about anything you don't understand.

LISTENING LOG

Reminder: Keep up your Listening Log with as many entries as your teacher requires. At the end of Part II (Speaking), you will report on one of your entries in a small group. (If necessary, see Appendix F for more details on Listening Logs.)

ANY QUESTIONS?

IT WORKS!
Learning Strategy:
Clarifying

Before you go on to read about and discuss more issues about humor, answer the following questions on a separate sheet of paper. Do not write your name. Your teacher or a classmate will collect the papers and share everyone's answers with the class.

1. What has been the most valuable aspect of this chapter for you so far?
2. What is still unclear?

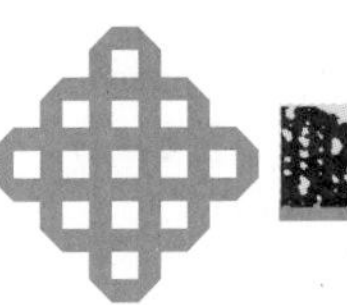

Telling Jokes And Funny Stories

1. What's your favorite joke? Before you tell it, look at the jokes in the box. Do you find them funny? Why or why not?

WHAT'S *YOUR* FAVORITE JOKE?

Sam, age 10, student, Holden, Mass.:
A man was lost and went up to a farmer's house to ask directions. He saw a mean-looking dog in the yard and stopped to ask, "Does your dog bite?" The farmer said, "No." So the man came into the yard, and the dog bit him on the leg, which upset him. "I thought you said your dog doesn't bite," the man said angrily. The farmer replied, "That's not my dog."

Richard, age 45, writer, Holden, Mass.:
One day, a wealthy Texan was driving through Massachusetts when he saw a farmer out plowing in a field. The Texan stopped his Cadillac and started talking to the farmer. "Say, how much land do you have on your farm?" the Texan asked in a thick drawl. The farmer answered, "Well, a little over 150 acres." The Texan then told the farmer, "Man, if I got in my pickup truck and started driving as soon as the sun came up, it would take me till after sunset to drive across all the land I've got." The farmer said, "Yeah, I used to have a pickup truck like that myself, but I got *mine* fixed."

a. Tell the class one of your favorite jokes. If you can't think of one, ask some friends outside of class to tell you some of their favorite jokes. Practice telling the jokes back to your friends to make sure you can tell them correctly, and then share the jokes in class.
b. Compile a booklet of international jokes made up of the jokes told by your classmates, teachers, and friends.

2. As an oral presentation exercise, tell a true story to the class of something funny that once happened to you. Your story should take from three to five minutes to tell. Include plenty of details so that your audience can get the whole picture. Use gestures, facial expressions, and mime to help communicate the situation.

IT WORKS!
Learning Strategy:
Setting Goals

For evaluation, design your own evaluation sheet with your speaking goals clearly stated at the top of the page. Before you begin your presentation, give the evaluation sheet to your teacher to fill out as you are speaking.

3. Is there any kind of tradition of story telling, such as rakugo, in your native country? Describe your storytelling traditions, and if possible, tell one such traditional story. Use gestures, facial expressions, and mime to help you tell your story.

4. On April 1st, known as April Fools' Day, it is the custom to play tricks on people. Often people fall for these pranks and don't realize that they are being tricked. Here are some examples of past April Fools' tricks:

Threads

The first newspaper cartoon was published on May 9, 1754 in Philadelphia, Pennsylvania.

- In Great Britain, a well-respected BBC-TV journalist reported on the spring spaghetti harvest in an isolated Swiss canton. BBC staffers had covered the branches of several trees with strands of long, white, cooked spaghetti. Actresses, dressed as Swiss farm girls, were shown collecting the spaghetti into baskets and taking it to market. Some BBC viewers fell for the gag and called the BBC to ask how to grow spaghetti at home.
- In Kenya, the front page of *The Standard,* a Nairobi newspaper, carried a story reporting that a multimillion-dollar international effort was going to be made to pile enough rock on top of snow-capped Mount Kenya to make it Africa's highest peak.
- A respected magazine for wine lovers, *Wine Spectator,* ran a number of made-up stories about wine in one April issue a few years ago. One story reported that workers in California's Mondavi vineyards had been instructed to speak only French in the fields since the French vines were extremely sensitive and would thus be soothed.

Source: Adapted from *Hemispheres* Magazine, April 1993

Now, answer the following questions:

a. Are April Fools' Day pranks a custom in your country? If so, what are some tricks you can remember? These can be tricks you played on people, tricks that were played on you, or tricks you heard about. When you describe the tricks, use as many details as possible to provide a rich description. You want to create a vivid picture for your classmates.

b. What is the origin of April Fools' Day? If you don't know, several students can volunteer to go to the library to find out. Each of you can check a different source to find out. When you have finished researching, combine your notes to make a full report back to the class.

5. The cartoon to the right is an editorial cartoon. This kind of cartoon usually appears on the editorial page of a newspaper and deals with current public issues or people, often satirically.

a. What point is this cartoon making?

b. Find an editorial cartoon that you like and bring it to class. Explain what issue or person is being satirized.

Source: Reprinted by permission of Kirk Anderson, © 1993, Ladysmith, Wisconsin.

Discussion

The following discussion questions deal with different aspects of humor. Choose the topic or topics you would like to discuss. Feel free to add related questions of your own to the questions that are asked here. And as always, you should focus on using new vocabulary and appropriate conversation skills.

When appropriate for the activity, work in small groups. Assign one person to act as discussion leader and another person to act as recorder. The discussion leader will make sure that everyone talks and stays on the subject. The recorder will take notes and later report briefly to the class on the main points of your group's discussion.

Before you begin, take a look at the checklist in question 6 of the following section. After one of your discussions has been completed, respond to the items on the checklist. As you work in groups, keep the checklist in mind.

IT WORKS! Learning Strategy: Developing Cultural Awareness

1. The following joke, a variation on Mr. Muramatsu's joke, appeared in the *Boston Globe.*

> What's the difference between heaven and hell? In heaven the police are British, the mechanics German, the lovers Italian, the cooks are French, and it's all run by the Swiss. In hell, the police are German, the mechanics French, the chefs British, the lovers Swiss, and it's all run by the Italians.

Do you find this joke funny? Why or why not?

Do you know any jokes like these, which rely on stereotypes of different nationalities for their humor? If so, share them with the class.

Do you think jokes like these are funny? Are jokes that stereotype a particular group popular in your native country? Explain your answer.

How much can humor extend across cultures? Are certain things universally funny? Explain your answer fully.

2. Both the preceding *Boston Globe* joke and Mr. Muramatsu's joke are based on commonly held stereotypes of certain cultures, and therein lies their humor. But are jokes that stereotype or make fun of certain groups always harmless?

Read the following articles to find out more. As you read, highlight any interesting points you may want to bring up in your discussion. After you complete each reading, write down the main point of the article and your reaction to it.

Sexist jokes affect reality, study says

Jokes that play on stereotypes of women may or may not make you laugh, but they might affect your judgments of women you meet, a new study suggests.

College students who heard sex-stereotyped jokes before watching female lecturers later rated the women in a more stereotyped fashion than did students who heard non-sexist jokes.

"This study suggests that exposure to stereotyped humor can affect people's judgments of other people, and that we should be on guard about that," said study co-author Christine Weston.

Weston, a graduate psychology student at Boston University, did the work with Cynthia Thomsen of Tufts University. Weston presented it at the annual meeting of the American Psychological Association.

For the study, 52 male and 50 female students were told they were participating in a study of the effects of television on learning. Each watched one of two 12-minute tapes of stand-up comedy routines by male comedians that had appeared on cable television.

All the students also watched tapes of four 3-minute lectures, by two men and two women, on issues surrounding construction of a hydroelectric dam.

Analysis found that, on average, students who had seen stereotyped comedy rated the female lecturers higher than the men in the category covering likeability, sensitivity and caring, while the other students rated the men higher than the women. The opposite pattern appeared for ratings of professional abilities.

Source: San Francisco Chronicle. Reprinted by permission.

Main point: ______________________________

____

Your reaction: ______________________________

____

Tell me if you've heard this one and hate it

by Mike Kennedy

For presidents and celebrities as well as ordinary people, **cracking jokes** can be risky business today, **provoking** anger and resentment instead of laughter.

The problem is that humor, like beauty, often is in the eye of the **beholder.**

Consider a jest by President Clinton. At a trade fair on the White House lawn, Clinton and his cabinet came upon a three-foot-high **replica** of the White House.

With the 4-foot-10 inch secretary of labor, Robert Reich, at his side, Clinton **quipped,** "Secretary Reich could almost live in there."

Lighthearted **ribbing** between longtime pals? Or a remark offensive to those sensitive about their height?

Experts who train people to use humor in business and social relationships say it can be an **invaluable** tool—but it must be used with sensitivity.

Of course, the line between laughing with someone and laughing at someone isn't always so clear.

So in today's **litigious** and sensitive society should we all take the safest course and avoid any attempts at humor? That would make for a dull world, experts said.

U.S. Labor Secretary Robert Reich and President Bill Clinton

The wrong kind of humor, though, can be **destructive.** Jokes that attack often cause people to withdraw, or worse, seek revenge.

Supervisors need to be especially careful. Because of the power they hold, their attempts at humor **demean** an employee.

Of course, some people just can't take a joke. So what can you do?

"On the politically correct front, there are certain people whose mission is to be offended," Langley said. "There's not really much you can do about them."

Source: Kansas City Star
Reprinted by permission.

cracking jokes: telling jokes
provoking: causing
beholder: person who is watching or seeing
replica: close copy
quipped: joked
ribbing: teasing
invaluable: extremely useful
litigious: habitually taking matters of disagreement to a court of law
destructive: damaging
demean: make inferior in the eyes of others

Main point: ______________________________

____

Your reaction: ______________________________

____

Nasty lawyer jokes

by Roni Rabin

The scene is a dusty rodeo. As the crowd cheers, the **chute** opens and out pops an **attorney** in suit and tie, clutching his briefcase and running for his life.

"There's Billy Bugh, going after that divorce lawyer that took away his **bass boat!**" the rodeo announcer **belts,** as a cowboy on horseback whirls his **lasso** in the air and gives chase.

"Yee haw!" erupts from the **bleachers.**

"Get him!"

This particular lawyer wound up roped and **hog-tied** in a beer commercial. And Miller Brewing Co. knows exactly what it's doing. In just about 30 seconds of **air time,** they're selling beer by acting out the sweetest **revenge** fantasies of millions of level-headed American citizens.

After decades of lawyer jokes and lawyer cartoons, lawyer-inspired song lyrics, T-shirts and "Saturday Night Live" skits, **assaults** on attorneys have reached a new intensity.

The humor has developed a darker, sharper edge. At best, it **depicts** members of **the Bar** as thieving, **conniving shysters;** at worst, as far less than human.

Source: Newsday
Reprinted by permission.

chute: a narrow, sloping passage
attorney: a lawyer
bass boat: a recreational fishing boat
belts: shouts
lasso: a rope with one end tightened in a circle, used for catching horses and cattle
bleachers:cheap, unroofed seats in the far end of a stadium or ballpark
hog-tied: hands and feet all tied together with a rope
air time: the duration of time an ad is aired, or shown, on TV
revenge: punishment given to someone in return for harm done to oneself
assaults: attacks
depicts: shows, illustrates
the Bar: the professional association of lawyers
conniving:conspiring, working together secretly for an illegal purpose
shyster: a dishonest person, especially a dishonest lawyer or politician

Main point: ______________________________

____

Your reaction: ______________________________

____

After you have finished reading, discuss in small groups what you find most interesting about the articles. Feel free to develop your own questions. You may want to consider the following questions:

- Why are jokes that stereotype or make fun of certain groups of people so popular?
- Are all stereotypes negative?
- Do you think stereotyping in humor is harmful?
- Should we stop telling jokes that make fun of certain groups?
- Do stereotypes reflect deeply held beliefs or are they superficial?

3. Madeline Drexler, in a column from The Boston Globe Magazine, examines humor from a different perspective—its importance in battling stress, emotional isolation, and feelings of powerlessness. Read the following article, highlighting any interesting points you want to comment on in your discussion. Don't worry about not understanding every word; read for the main ideas.

IT WORKS! Learning Strategy: Highlighting

The best medicine

by Madeline Drexler

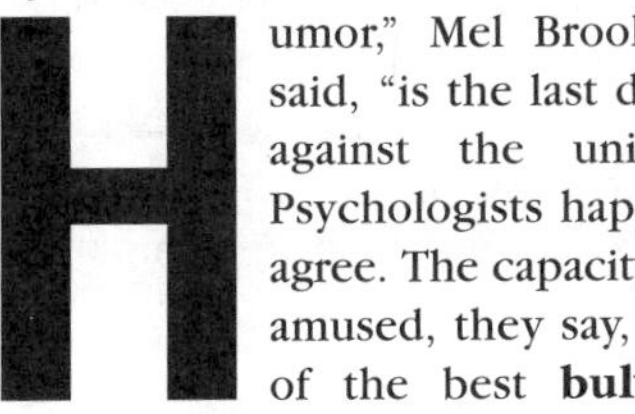umor," Mel Brooks has said, "is the last defense against the universe." Psychologists happen to agree. The capacity to be amused, they say, is one of the best **bulwarks** against stress, isolation, and feelings of powerlessness. Laughter isn't a cure-all, of course, and **relentless** cheer can be downright unhealthy. But a refined sensitivity to double meanings, visual **incongruities,** human **foibles**—an attitude that far **surpasses** joke-telling—can literally make life worth living.

"One of the things humor does is give people **perspective,**" says Robert Pierce, a clinical psychologist in Rochester, New York, who has examined the place of humor in therapy and in life. Intense personal battles, for instance, often involve angry **parties** whose identities are tied up with being right. But shared laughter, which can happen when exaggerating each other's positions or even reversing roles, "is an invitation to look at yourself from a different point of view," a view that is usually revealing, Pierce says.

As humor educator Joel Goodman puts it, "We need to be serious about our goals and work, but to take ourselves lightly." Director of The Humor Project, in Saratoga Springs, New York, Goodman leads seminars about ways to find more comedy in daily life.

Humor gives power. "A lot of adults **shy away from** humor, because they're afraid of losing control," Goodman says. But, in psychological **lingo,** humor actually creates an "internal **locus of control"** when reality is out of control—a way to shape our own reactions to the chaos around us. Gallows humor is the ultimate example. A woman who survived a Nazi concentration camp once told Goodman of a rainswept night when water seeped through a hole in the barracks roof. Summing up the general feeling of desperation, she officiously opened a spoked umbrella whose fabric had been torn away, and stood beneath the leak.

Humor knocks down emotional **boundaries.** When something is so funny that two friends helplessly shake with laughter, they often glance at each other, then look away, again and again. "There's an **intimacy,** so that people can't keep looking," Pierce says. Often this intimacy comes from an unmasking, being confronted with truths about oneself that transform the entire situation.

Usually, the **bonds** forged by humor outlast the joke. In fact, someone else's presence is almost essential—we laugh loudest and longest with other people. Surveys repeatedly show that a sense of humor is one of the top two qualities people look for in a **mate** and that people rarely describe themselves as humorless. "People are more willing to say they have a low sex drive than to say they have no sense of humor," says Midge Wilson, associate professor of psychology and women's studies at DePaul University in Chicago.

Yet, as Wilson's studies show, humor doesn't always translate between the sexes. What's funny to women is frequently incomprehensible to men. What's funny to men is often dopey or **boorish** to women. Women, especially, can be victims of **a double standard** in the way society defines sense of humor. "A man with a sense of humor is one who makes jokes," Wilson wrote in a recent study, "but a woman with a sense of humor is one who laughs at the jokes men make, including those **at her own expense.**" What does that make a woman who tells her own jokes? **A threat,** say many feminist psychologists.

Partly, that's because men's humor often reflects the **sensibilities** of the ruling order, while women's wit takes aim at **the powers that be**. But Wilson's research illuminates more particular **disparities** between male and female humor. Men tend to tell more jokes, laugh at someone else's expense, and compete for the funniest line. Women tell stories out of their own experience, make themselves to be the object of laughter, and use humor to build and celebrate relationships. Wilson keenly understood this last point when she moved to a new house. "It didn't feel like my home until people were there and laughed in it," she says. "That's what made a house a home."

Still, some high spirits seem to require some measure of emotional distance. It isn't easy to laugh when the car has just been stolen, the job lost, or the vacation ruined. "People often say, 'Someday we'll laugh about this,'" Joel Goodman says. The question I pose is: Why wait?"

Source: The Boston Globe Magazine, October 31, 1993

Threads

A difference of taste in jokes is a great strain on the affections.

George Eliot, 1819–1880, in *Daniel Deronda*

bulwarks: strong supports, protection
relentless: continuous
incongruities: events or acts that seem out of place because of their difference from things happening around them
foibles: small, foolish personal habits or weaknesses in character
surpasses: goes beyond, further than
perspective: a view from a distance
parties: persons involved in an activity
shy away from: avoid
lingo: language
locus of control: a position or point of control
boundaries: dividing lines, limits
intimacy: closeness
bonds: shared feelings that unite people
mate: husband, wife, or partner
boorish: rude, insensitive
a double standard: a different level or degree of quality considered acceptable
at her own expense: against her, making her seem silly
A threat: possible danger
sensibilities: feelings about what is correct in behavior
the powers that be: the people in power
disparities: differences

LEARNING STRATEGY

Understanding and Using Your Emotions: Talk with others to discover and express feelings about language learning.

4. In her book, *Lost in Translation,* writer Eva Hoffman talks about what it was like learning to exist in a new language when her family immigrated from Krakow, Poland, to Vancouver, Canada, when she was 13. In the excerpt that follows, she writes about an incident that happened shortly after she moved to Canada, on a day when she was riding in a car with some of her new Canadian classmates. She describes how embarrassed she felt that day because she did not understand the finer points of English well enough to understand the jokes of her teen-age friends, and her efforts at translating the jokes she knows in Polish failed miserably.

"Come on, foreign student, cheer up," one of the boys **sporting** a flowery Hawaiian shirt and crew cut tells me, poking me in the ribs good-naturedly. "What's the matter, don't you like it here?" So as the car caroms off, I try to get in the mood. I try **to giggle** coyly as the girls exchange **insinuating** glances—though usually my **titter** comes a telling second too late. I try to join in the general **hilarity,** as somebody tells the latest elephant joke. Then—it's always a mistake to try too hard—I decide to show my goodwill by telling a joke myself. Finding some interruption in which to insert my uncertain voice, I **launch** into a translation of some slightly **off-color** anecdote I'd heard my father tell in Polish, no doubt hoping to get points for being so **risqué** as well as a good sport. But as I hear my **choked-up** voice **straining** to assert itself, as I hear myself missing every beat and rhythm that would say "funny" and "punch line," I feel a **hot flush** of embarrassment. I come to a **lame** ending. There's a silence. "I suppose that's supposed to be funny," somebody says. I **recede** into the car seat.

Ah, the **humiliation,** the misery of failing to amuse! The incident is as **rankling** as being told I'm **graceless** or ugly. Telling a joke is like doing a linguistic **pirouette.** If you fall flat, it means not only that you don't have **the wherewithal** to do it well but also that you have misjudged your own skill, that you are fool enough to undertake something you can't finish—and that lack of self-control or self-knowledge is a lack of grace.

sporting: wearing
to giggle: to laugh in a silly, childish way
insinuating: suggesting something indirectly
titter: a nervous laugh
hilarity: feeling of cheer, expressed by laughter
launch: to begin forcefully
off-color: sexually improper
risqué: slightly rude and shocking
choked-up: having difficulty speaking because of emotion
straining: making a great effort
hot flush: a sudden feeling of heat in the skin
lame: weak
recede: move back or away
humiliation: feeling ashamed or that you've lost the respect of others
rankling: causing anger and bitterness
graceless: awkward in movement, clumsy
pirouette: a very fast turn made on one toe as by a ballet dancer
the wherewithal: the necessary means

Eva Hoffman had two problems:

- although she understood the words of the jokes in English, she didn't find them funny, and
- when she translated a joke from Polish into English, her friends didn't laugh.

A. Have you ever been in either situation? If yes, describe the situation and try to analyze what happened.

B. Look at these cartoons:

Gary Larson © 1993
Universal Press Syndicate

Gary Larson © 1988
Universal Press Syndicate

Do you understand the words?	YES	NO
Do you get the joke?	YES	NO

If you understand the words but don't get the joke, then probably the difficulty is that the joke is culturally based.

In the first cartoon, the joke relates to a story that many American children read called *The Little Engine That Could.* In the second cartoon, the joke relates to an American toy called Mr. Potato Head.

It's logical, then, that you wouldn't get the joke if it's related to a story or toy that you never heard of, even if you understand the language in the joke. It is common for culturally based jokes to fall flat with people unfamiliar with the culture being targeted.

Don't get discouraged. Ask native speakers why something is funny and take notes. Bit by bit you can add to your store of cultural knowledge.

IT WORKS!
Learning Strategy:
Using Checklists

5. Understanding how you feel about certain language tasks and activities can help you better handle the demands of language learning. The following checklist may help you see how you felt about a particular discussion you participated in.

Check Your Feelings

a. Describe how you feel in relation to one of the discussion tasks you completed in this chapter. On each line, check one of the two descriptors that more closely describes the way you feel. Realize that no single descriptor is necessarily better than its opposite.

_____ happy	_____ unhappy
_____ proud	_____ ashamed
_____ confident	_____ unconfident
_____ peaceful	_____ anxious
_____ unafraid	_____ afraid
_____ risk-taking	_____ cautious
_____ clear-thinking	_____ confused
_____ friendly	_____ unfriendly
_____ interested	_____ bored
_____ calm	_____ angry
_____ strong	_____ weak
_____ energetic	_____ tired
_____ outgoing	_____ shy
_____ accepting	_____ critical
_____ able to tolerate contradictions	_____ unable to accept contradictions
_____ want to learn the language	_____ don't want to learn the language
_____ want to know the culture	_____ don't want to know the culture

Source: *Language Learning Strategies,* by Rebecca Oxford, 1990. Newbury House, pp. 187–189.

b. If you find this checklist useful, you can use it regularly to help you link your feelings with the language tasks and activities in which you are involved. If you decide to use this checklist, you should do so at least once a week. (See Appendix O for a copy of the checklist.)

Movie Review

With a partner or small group, go to the comedy section of your local video store and select a video you would like to watch. Rent a copy of the video and watch it together. Afterwards, discuss the film and make a report to the class. Include the following information in your report:

1. The name of the film
2. The director and cast
3. The main elements of the plot
4. The type of humor used in the film
5. Your opinion of the film

Just for Fun

The following children's poem is by Shel Silverstein, author and illustrator of many delightful books of poetry and prose for children. His humorous poems have a strong rhythm to them, and in addition to being fun to read aloud, they provide useful material for practicing rhythm, stress, and intonation. Why don't you try reading it aloud and see what you think?

Sick

"I cannot go to school today,"
Said little Peggy Ann McKay.
"I have the measles and the mumps,
A gash, a rash, and purple bumps.
My mouth is wet, my throat is dry,
I'm going blind in my right eye.
My tonsils are as big as rocks,
I've counted sixteen chicken pox
And there's one more—that's seventeen,
And don't you think my face looks green?
My leg is cut, my eyes are blue—
It might be instamatic flu.
I cough and sneeze and gasp and choke,
I'm sure that my left leg is broke—
My hip hurts when I move my chin,
My belly button's caving in,
My back is wrenched, my ankle's sprained,
My 'pendix pains each time it rains.
My nose is cold, my toes are numb,
I have a sliver in my thumb.
My neck is stiff, my spine is weak,
I hardly whisper when I speak.
My tongue is filling up my mouth,
I think my hair is falling out.
My elbow's bent, my spine ain't straight,
My temperature is one-o-eight.
My brain is shrunk, I cannot hear,
There is a hole inside my ear.
I have a hangnail, and my heart is—what?
What's that? What's that you say?
You say today is . . . Saturday?
G'bye, I'm going out to play!"

If you enjoyed reading this aloud, go to a library or bookstore and find the book from which this is taken, *Where the Sidewalk Ends,* or other children's poetry books. Find other poems you like and practice reading them aloud, focusing on rhythm, stress, and intonation. Bring one to class and read it aloud to your classmates. If you like, bring extra copies and lead the class in reading it aloud together, emphasizing the key words.

Guest Speaker

Invite an amateur comedian, a newspaper cartoonist, or a folklorist from a local college or university to come to your class to talk about humor. Follow the steps for inviting a guest speaker in Appendix H.

Listening Log Report

Bring your Listening Log to class and report on one entry in a small group. Take turns doing the following:

- Tell your group members what you watched or listened to.
- Give a short oral summary followed by your personal reaction. Do not read what you have written.
- Check your listeners' comprehension by asking questions such as: "Do you understand what I mean?" and "Am I being clear?"
- Rephrase or restate to make your points clear.
- Answer your listeners' questions and ask for their reactions.

FOLLOW-UP

Choose any of the following activities to do outside of class and then report on what happened or what you found out. These activities can be done individually, in pairs, or in small groups. (Refer to Oral Presentation Feedback forms in Appendix L.)

IT WORKS! Learning Strategy: Practice Outside the Classroom

1. Find out if there is a comedy club in your town. Go see a show with some friends.
2. Rent a video from the comedy section of your local video rental store. Watch it with friends. While you are watching it, help each other with vocabulary and cultural references. Make a note of three or four things you don't get and ask a native speaker about them.
3. Start keeping a humor diary of funny things that happen to you.
4. Watch a popular sitcom on TV. Write down some of the lines that were followed by laughter and you wondered why. Be sure to include the context in which the funny remarks were made. Ask a native speaker to explain why they were funny.
5. Go to your public library to the books-on-tape section. Find a tape about humor, check it out, and listen to it. Share your findings with your friends—which tapes you liked, which you didn't.
6. Together with your classmates, compile a list of funny films, books, and tapes that you think are great. Photocopy the list and add to it throughout the year.
7. Go to the humor section of your local library or bookstore. Browse through the books, or ask the librarian or a store clerk to recommend a funny book. Be specific about what you want: a book of jokes or cartoons, a funny novel, a humorous non-fiction book, a collection of funny essays, a humorous autobiography, and so on.
8. Read the comics in the daily newspaper. Ask someone about ones you don't understand. If you find one particularly funny, start a conversation with someone about it. Begin by asking, for example, "Did you read the comics today today? "Calvin and Hobbes" (or whatever your favorite comic strip is) was really funny!"
9. Get in the habit of telling your friends and classmates any new jokes you hear. Start off by saying, "I heard a good joke today. Do you want to hear it?"

LEARNING ASSESSMENT

IT WORKS!
Learning Strategy:
Evaluating Your Progress

1. Look back at Part I (Listening) of this chapter. What activities helped you most in understanding the listening passages?

   ____

   ____

   ____

2. Give an example of when you had trouble understanding what you heard.

   ____

   ____

   ____

   Why did you have difficulty?

   _____ **a.** I didn't know the vocabulary.

   _____ **b.** I wasn't paying attention.

   _____ **c.** The speaker wasn't clear.

   _____ **d.** The speaker spoke too fast.

   _____ **e.** Other: ______________________________

3. Were you more successful than you expected to be in understanding the listening material about humor? Were you less successful than you expected? Why?

   ____

   ____

   ____

4. Look back at Part II (Speaking) of this chapter. Give one or two examples of your most successful efforts at oral communication. Try to explain why you were able to succeed.

   ____

   ____

   ____

5. Give an example of a discussion in which you had trouble communicating with your classmates.

   ____

   ____

   ____

Why did you have difficulty?

_____ **a.** My classmates didn't understand my pronunciation.

_____ **b.** I didn't understand my classmates' pronunciation.

_____ **c.** I had trouble finding the main ideas in the readings.

_____ **d.** There was a lot of new vocabulary.

_____ **e.** Other: ______________________________

6. What could you do next time to:

a. better prepare for a listening passage?

____

____

____

b. improve your effectiveness when speaking in a group?

____

____

____

7. Look back at the goals you set at the beginning of this chapter.

a. Which goals did you achieve?

____

____

____

b. What will be your primary goal in the next chapter?

____

____

____

Little Burnt-Face and Ash Girl—Cinderella in Different Cultures

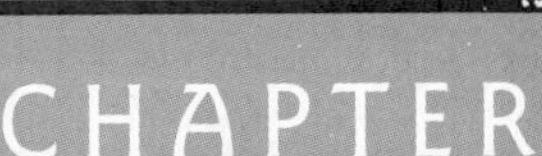

4

CHAPTER

INTRODUCTION

Throughout the centuries, people have communicated cultural values through the oral tradition of storytelling. Common themes across cultures appear in many of these stories, the most famous of which is "Cinderella." In this chapter you will listen to two different versions of the story of Cinderella. These listening passages are much longer than those you listened to in other chapters because they contain whole stories. The first, called "Little Burnt-Face," is a Native American tale, and the second, called "Ash Girl," is one of Grimm's fairy tales from Germany. The name "Cinderella" is used throughout the chapter when generalizing about the girl. In addition to listening to these stories, you will have opportunities to read about and discuss the role of fairy tales in society.

Background Knowledge Check

IT WORKS! Learning Strategy: Using Prior Knowledge

The following items reflect some of the content that you will find in this chapter. Write **a, b, c,** or **d** next to each item in the list according to the following:

(a) I have never heard of this.
(b) I have heard of this, but I don't really know what it means.
(c) I have some idea of what this means, but I'm not sure about it.
(d) I have a clear idea of what this means and can explain it.

_____ **1.** The universality of fairy tales

_____ **2.** The role of fairy tales in teaching morals and values

_____ **3.** The symbolism of nature in fairy tales

_____ **4.** The controversy surrounding the violence and frightening situations portrayed in fairy tales

_____ **5.** Nursery rhymes

_____ **6.** Proverbs

Students who have chosen **d** for any of the items should briefly explain what these items mean. If no one has chosen **d,** don't worry. You will have a chance to learn more about these as you progress through the chapter.

Setting Goals

IT WORKS! Learning Strategy: Setting Goals

Complete the following statement by checking the goals you want to achieve in this chapter.

While working on this chapter, I will make an effort to:

_____ **1.** speak more while I am working in a small group.

_____ **2.** give others more chances to speak while working in a small group.

_____ 3. show others that I am actively listening by looking into their eyes and nodding as they talk.

_____ 4. ask more questions in front of the whole class.

_____ 5. make more comments in front of the whole class.

_____ 6. monitor one aspect of my pronunciation, such as _______________.

_____ 7. monitor one aspect of grammar as I speak, such as _______________.

_____ 8. use some of the new vocabulary when speaking, both in and out of class.

_____ 9. listen to the radio and watch TV outside of class.

_____ 10. learn about the similarity of fairy tales and values across cultures.

_____ 11. try to achieve another goal, such as _______________

_______________________________________.

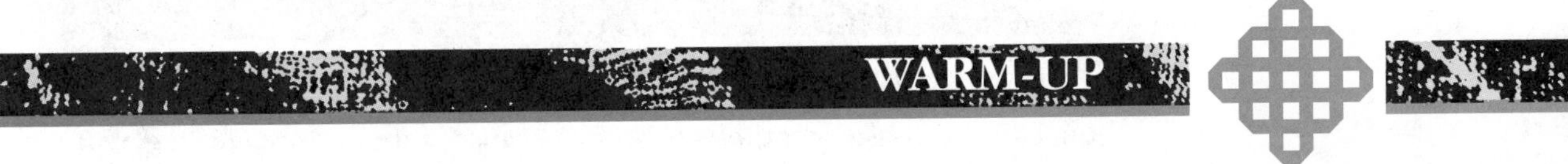

WARM-UP

Read the following passage from the introduction to *The Uses of Enchantment—The Meaning and Importance of Fairy Tales* by child psychologist, Bruno Bettelheim:

"....[N]othing can be as enriching and satisfying to child and adult alike as the folk fairy tale. True, on an **overt** level fairy tales teach little about the specific conditions of life in modern mass society; these tales were created long before it came into being. But more can be learned from them about the inner problems of human beings, and of the right solutions to their **predicaments** in any society, than from any other type of story within a child's comprehension. . . ." (p. 5)

"The fairy-tale hero proceeds for a time in isolation, as the modern child often feels **isolated.** The hero is helped by being in touch with primitive things—a tree, an animal, nature—as the child feels more in touch with those things than most adults do. The fate of these heroes convinces the child that, like them, he may feel **outcast** and abandoned in the world, **groping in the dark,** but, like them, in the course of his life he will be guided step by step, and given help when it is needed. Today, even more than in past times, the child needs the **reassurance** offered by the image of the isolated man who nevertheless is capable of achieving meaningful and rewarding relations with the world around him." (p. 11)

Threads

With the new concern of multicultural diversity, one way of learning about people is through their folklore.

Alan Dundes,
U.C. Berkeley Professor

overt: open, not hidden
predicaments: difficult situations
isolated: separated from others
outcast: rejected
groping in the dark: searching blindly
reassurance: comfort and security

Think about the fairy tales that you heard as a child.

- Who told them to you, and who listened with you?
- What did you learn from them?
- Were the heroes and heroines of the stories at first isolated but then helped, as Bettelheim describes?
- Were the heroes and heroines in touch with nature?
- Why do you think these stories are told all around the world?
- What is the value of analyzing these stories as adults?

PART I: LISTENING

Before You Listen

It is important to note that the two listening passages in this chapter are much longer than those in other chapters because here we are dealing with two complete stories.

LEARNING STRATEGY

Understanding and Using Emotions: Realizing that you already know something about a topic reduces your anxiety.

THINK ABOUT WHAT YOU ALREADY KNOW

If you already know a version of Cinderella, write down the first five words or phrases that come to your mind when you think of the story.

____

____

____

____

____

If you don't know a version of Cinderella, write a list of the characters typically found in fairy tales in your native culture.

____

____

____

____

____

Mill Around: Walk around your classroom and ask at least five of your classmates the following questions. Put their first names in the "YES," "NO," or "DON'T KNOW" boxes.

	YES	NO	DON'T KNOW
1. Was Cinderella helped by a human?	______	______	______
2. Was Cinderella's shoe made of glass?	______	______	______
3. Is there any blood in this story?	______	______	______
4. Are Cinderella's stepsisters forgiven at the end of the story?	______	______	______

Threads

The tale of Cinderella probably originated in 9th century China.

When you are finished, let the class know if any of your classmates' responses were surprising to you and explain why.

LEARNING STRATEGY

Overcoming Limitations: Ask others or use a dictionary to understand words you don't know.

VOCABULARY PREPARATION FOR LISTENING TO "LITTLE BURNT-FACE"

Wigwam

Before you listen to "Little Burnt-Face" from the Native American Micmac tribe, read the sentences on the next page, which are actual lines taken from the story. Then, in the space at the left, write the letter of the definition you think best fits the underlined word or phrase. Since you can't get all the meanings from context here, get help by working with a classmate. Use a dictionary if necessary.

_____ **1.** Once upon a time, in a large Indian village next to a lake, there lived a man who was a <u>widower</u>.

_____ **2.** The second daughter was <u>vain</u>.

_____ **3.** . . . [T]he eldest daughter used to <u>beat</u> the youngest girl, and burn her face with

_____ hot coals; yes, and even <u>scar</u> her pretty body.

_____ **4.** "She is a <u>good-for-nothing</u>! She was forbidden to go near the fire, and she disobeyed and fell in."

_____ **5.** . . . [T]here was a beautiful <u>wigwam</u>. And in that wigwam lived a Great Chief and his sister.

_____ **6.** The Great Chief was <u>invisible</u>; no one had ever seen him but his sister.

_____ **7.** . . . [A]ll they ever saw of the Chief were his <u>moccasins</u>; when he took them off, they became visible. [Little Burnt-Face put her father's *moccasins on* her bare feet . . .]

_____ **8.** "And with what does he pull his <u>sled</u>?"

_____ **9.** Little Burnt-Face's two sisters put on their . . . brightest strings of <u>beads</u>, and

_____ <u>braided</u> their hair beautifully. . . .

_____ **10.** Little Burnt-Face made herself a white dress and cap out of <u>bark</u> from a tree.

_____ **11.** As she passed through the village, the boys and girls <u>hissed</u>, yelled, and

_____ <u>hooted</u>.

_____ **12.** His <u>bow-string</u> is made of the

_____ <u>Milky Way</u>.

_____ **13.** She . . . washed her with <u>dew</u> until the burns and scars all disappeared. . . .

_____ **14.** . . . [T]hey went back to their wigwam in <u>disgrace</u>, weeping with

_____ <u>shame</u>.

Definitions:

a. shoes made of soft leather
b. American Indian dwelling, usually of a rounded shape
c. put three sections of hair together to form a design
d. a man whose wife has passed away (died)
e. made a nasty sound like a snake (ssssssssssss)
f. made a sound like an owl (ooooooooooo)
g. in dishonor
h. hit very hard
i. drops of moisture that appear at night from the atmosphere
j. very concerned about her appearance
k. a vehicle that slides in snow

l. the galaxy containing the earth, sun, and solar system
m. a painful feeling caused by injury to a person's self-respect
n. unable to be seen
o. the string on a bent piece of wood (bow) used to shoot arrows
p. leave a mark on the skin that will stay after the wound heals
q. a person who can do nothing right
r. the outside covering of a tree
s. small, usually round objects put on strings to make bracelets and necklaces

As You Listen: Listening Passage 1

LISTEN FOR DETAILS

Remember that it is not necessary to understand every word. As you listen, write what you can find out about each character in the right column.

CHARACTERS IN "LITTLE BURNT-FACE"	
People	**Some Details**
The old widower	______________________
	______________________
The eldest daughter	______________________
	______________________
The second daughter	______________________
	______________________
The youngest daughter	______________________
	______________________
A Great Chief	______________________
	______________________
The Chief's sister	______________________
	______________________

IT WORKS! Learning Strategy: Getting the Idea

Do the following with a partner:

1. Compare your notes.
2. Using fewer than five words, write a new title for "Little Burnt-Face." The title should reflect the moral of the story (its message).

New title: ______________________

Before You Listen: Listening Passage 2

VOCABULARY PREPARATION FOR LISTENING TO "ASH GIRL," BY JACOB & WILHELM GRIMM

These are actual sentences taken from the listening passage you will hear. Some of the underlined vocabulary items may be new to you, but your classmates may know them. Share your knowledge and work together to define these words. Your teacher will help you with the words you don't know.

1. She closed her eyes and passed away.
2. Every day the girl used to go out to her mother's grave and weep.
3. Then, evil days began for the poor stepchild.
4. Her sisters played all sorts of mean tricks on her, teased her, and used to pour peas and lentils into the ashes so that she'd have to sit and pick them out again.
5. There was no bed for her; she just had to lie down in the ashes beside the hearth.
6. Bring me the first twig that brushes against your hat on the way home.
7. In order that his son might choose a bride, the king proclaimed a festival.
8. Ash Girl wept, for she would have liked to go to the ball.
9. The pigeons bent their heads and began peck, peck . . . and they pecked all the good lentils into the dish.
10. You're not coming along (to the ball). . . . We'd only be ashamed of you.
11. She jumped into a small shack.
12. He painted the stairs with sticky tar, so when she ran downstairs, the girl's left slipper stuck there.
13. She forced her foot into the shoe, and suppressing her pain, went out to the king's son.
14. He looked at her foot and saw the blood oozing out.
15. Her heel was too large (to fit into the shoe).
16. The two sisters were frightened and turned pale.

IT WORKS!
Learning Strategy: Asking Others

As You Listen: Listening Passage 2

This story has been divided into eight parts. Before listening to each part, read the questions. Then, as you listen, listen for the answers. Whenever you hear a beep, stop the tape and write *very brief* answers— just words and phrases.

QUESTIONS	ANSWERS
A.	
1. What happened to the girl's mother?	____________
2. How did the girl feel?	____________
3. What did her father do after one year?	____________
4. How did the stepmother and stepsisters treat the girl?	____________
5. Why was she called "Ash Girl"?	____________
B.	
1. What did the father bring the sisters from the fair?	____________
2. What did he bring Ash Girl?	____________
3. What did she do with it?	____________
4. What did the bird do?	____________
C.	
1. Why did the king call a festival?	____________
2. What did the stepmother throw into the ashes?	____________
3. Who helped Ash Girl pick the lentils out of the ashes?	____________
4. Why did the stepmother say that Ash Girl couldn't go to the ball?	____________
D.	
1. Where did Ash Girl go after everyone had left for the ball?	____________
2. What did the bird do for her?	____________
3. Where did she go after that?	____________
4. Did anyone know who she really was?	____________
E.	
1. Did the king's son let anyone else dance with her?	____________
2. On the first day she jumped into a small shack. Where did she run to on the second night?	____________

F.

1. What did the bird give her on the third day? ______________
2. What was the prince's trick? ______________
3. What did the first sister cut? ______________
4. Who told the prince about this? ______________

G.

1. What did the second sister cut? ______________
2. When he saw the blood, where did the prince go? ______________
3. How did the stepmother and stepsisters feel when the prince found Ash Girl? ______________

H.

1. What happened to the two sisters at the wedding? ______________

From the questions and answers above, retell the story aloud or in writing.

After You Listen

FOCUS ON MAKING COMPARISONS

The two versions of Cinderella you have heard have many similarities and differences. In order to see these clearly, write the headings from the following chart on your blackboard or put newsprint on your classroom walls. Then, with everyone up and out of their seats, walk around the room and insert your responses. (If you prefer, work in pairs to complete the chart.)

LEARNING STRATEGY

Forming Concepts: Systematically comparing and contrasting specific points can clarify new information and help you reuse it.

COMPARISON OF THE TWO STORIES		
	Little Burnt-Face	**Ash Girl**
The girl's father	____________	____________
Examples of treatment by her sisters	____________	____________
Examples of treatment by her stepmother	____________	____________
Magical powers that helped her	____________	____________
Her shoes	____________	____________
The place where she met the man she would marry	____________	____________
The man she married	____________	____________
Punishment of those who hurt her	____________	____________

Threads

In the French version, Cinderella had a *sable* (fur) slipper. In the English version, she had a *glass* slipper. This difference is probably due to a mistranslation from the French.

LISTENING LOG

IT WORKS! Learning Strategy: Practice Outside the Classroom

Reminder: Keep up your Listening Log with as many entries as your teacher requires. At the end of Part II (Speaking), you will report on one of your entries in a small group. (If necessary, see Appendix F for more details on Listening Logs.)

ANY QUESTIONS?

Before you go on to read about and discuss more issues about fairy tales, answer the following questions on a separate sheet of paper. Do not write your name on the paper. Your teacher or a classmate will collect the papers and share everyone's answers with the class.

IT WORKS! Learning Strategy: Clarifying

1. What has been the most valuable aspect of this chapter for you so far?
2. What is still unclear?

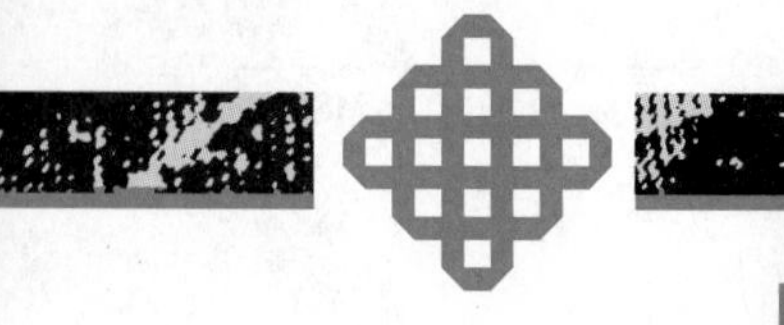

Discussion

The following discussion questions deal with different aspects of fairy tales and folklore. Choose the topic or topics you would like to discuss. Feel free to add related questions of your own to the questions that are asked here. And as always, you should focus on using new vocabulary and appropriate conversation skills.

When appropriate for the activity, work in small groups. Assign one person to act as discussion leader and another person to act as recorder. The discussion leader will make sure that everyone talks and stays on the subject. The recorder will take notes and later report briefly to the class on the main points of your group's discussion.

Before you begin, take a look at the conversation skills questionnaire on page 108 of this section. You will respond to the items on the questionnaire after one of your discussions has been completed. As you work in groups, keep the items on the questionnaire in mind.

1. Look back at the section entitled "Think About What You Already Know" on page 96. When you answered the questions in this activity, were you thinking of another version of Cinderella? If so, you might have been thinking of:

- "Yeh-Shen" (the Chinese version) or
- "Cinderella, or the Little Glass Slipper," (the French version} or
- "____" (You add the name.)

IT WORKS! Learning Strategy: Comparing

a. If you know these or other versions of Cinderella, explain how they are similar to and different from "Little Burnt-Face" and "Ash Girl."

b. After you discuss the similarities and differences, read the following excerpt and see if you can identify the universal phenomenon that it describes:

> [The student of fairy tales] finds himself faced by the astonishing fact that a body of the tales have been found to be not merely ancient but to be traditional in a variety of countries and cultures; and that versions of a story told in widely separated parts of the earth will sometimes not merely bear resemblance, but possess actual points of details in common.
>
> *The Classic Fairy Tales,* by Iona and Peter Opie. Oxford University Press, 1974 (p. 21)

2. Discuss the role of fairy tales and stories in your native culture. You may want to consider some of the following questions in your discussion:

- Are they usually told without books or are they read aloud?
- Are they meant for children only?
- Give examples of how animals are used in fairy tales.
- Are certain animals symbols?
- Is there a wolf in any of the stories? Is it usually good or bad?

3. Read and then comment on one or more of the following excerpts:

a. Little Burnt-Face is the scorched (burned) face of the desert in the burning summer, and the Great Chief, whose symbol is the arching rainbow, is the healing rain. Invisible for a long period of time, he comes at last and restores its original beauty to the face of the waiting earth child. This is typical of the folklore of many tribal cultures in the way that it uses symbolism and also in the concern it shows for natural phenomena.

The Arbuthnot Anthology of Children's Literature, 4th edition, 1976.
Scott, Foresman & Co., p. 392.

b. In all tongues and all times since humanity began, the most familiar words of childhood have probably been "Tell me a story." And the stories have been told, not really for children but for adults. As they always do, children have listened in, beyond the edge of the fire's light, to hear what tales were told. Those they could grasp, they took to themselves, until, over the stretch of centuries, certain stories have become their own. Unfortunately, with the rise of the modern world, grownups have increasingly abandoned the folk tales of simpler times and quieter places as fit for only the young. Now folk tales are mainly the province of children and scholars, but surely anyone who knows the folk tales will agree with Horace: "Change the name and the tale is about you." The *tale* is all tales humans have ever told; the *you* is all of us.

The Arbuthnot Anthology of Children's Literature, 4th edition, 1976.
Scott, Foresman & Co.

IT WORKS!
Learning Strategy:
Learning Through
Reading

c. [The stories] reiterate moral truths that are important for children to know. "Be of good cheer," these stories seem to say. "Use your head, keep a kindly heart, a civil tongue, and a fearless spirit, and you will surely find the water of life and your heart's desire."

The Arbuthnot Anthology of Children's Literature, 4th edition, 1976.
Scott, Foresman & Co.

d. Fairy tales are . . . more realistic than they may appear at first sight; while the magic in them almost heightens the realism. The magic sets us wondering how we ourselves would react in similar circumstances. It encourages speculation. It gives a child license to wonder. And this is the merit of the tales, that by going beyond possibility they enlarge our daily horizon. For a man not given to speculation might as well walk on four legs as on two.

The Classic Fairy Tales, by Iona and Peter Opie.
Oxford University Press, 1974 (p. 20)

4. According to Bruno Bettelheim, "Many parents believe that only conscious reality or pleasant and wish-fulfilling images should be presented to the child—that he should be exposed only to the sunny side of things. But such one-sided fare nourishes the mind only in a one-sided way, and real life is not all sunny. . . . The dominant culture wishes to pretend, particularly where children are concerned, that the dark side of man does not exist. . . ."

The Uses of Enchantment—The Meaning and
Importance of Fairy Tales, p. 7

In other words, Bettelheim believes that it is good for children to learn about evil in fairy tales, because there is evil in life. But there are people today who would like to change fairy tales. . . .

Classic fairy tales don't need PC revisions

by Ray Recchi

Once upon a time, in a land called America, there were parents who told their children exciting stories about children and bears and pigs and bunnies who were constantly being threatened by foxes or witches or big bad wolves.

These stories, called fairy tales, usually taught lessons and ended with the **villains** getting their **just desserts** and the heroes and heroines living happily ever after.

So popular were these fairy tales that it became quite common for children to beg their parents to tell the same stories over and over. When those children grew up and became parents, they enjoyed telling the same stories to their own children.

Thus, traditional fairy tales such as "Little Red Riding Hood," "The Three Little Pigs" and "Goldilocks and the Three Bears" became a part of childhood and parenthood for many generations.

Until recently, that is. Apparently, some of the current crop of parents are not living happily ever after.

In retrospect, many of them seem rather unsatisfied with their childhoods and determined that their children should not suffer the same horrible fate.

Culver Pictures

They **whine** that foods they were served were too high in fat and cholesterol and too low in vitamins. The toys they played with were too dangerous and politically incorrect. And those fairy tales—those violent, horrible fairy tales—were simply too frightening and traumatizing to bear.

So their kids are drinking skim milk, eating unsalted Styrofoam instead of potato chips and low-fat yogurt instead of ice cream. They play with politically correct toys. And they are about to get some nonviolent fairy tales, courtesy of Western Publishing Co, Inc., which puts out those Little Golden Books.

I had an opportunity to preview the first of the new nonviolent fairy tales, "Little Red Riding Hood."

You remember the story. While walking through the woods to bring a basket of **goodies** to her grandmother, Little Red Riding Hood encounters a wolf and tells him where she's going. So he takes a shortcut to Grandma's house, **gobbles up** Grandma and takes her place in bed. When Red arrives and tells him what big teeth he has, the wolf says, "All the better to eat you with, my dear," then swallows her, too. But a passing woodsman hears her screams and comes to the rescue, **slaying** the wolf, then releasing the amazingly alive Red and Grandma from the wolf's **tummy.**

It's a classic.

In the new version, however, the wolf doesn't eat Grandma. He chases her into a closet, where she locks herself in and begins to sew **linens** together. When the wolf starts to chase Red, Grandma bursts out in a ghost costume, says "Boo," and the frightened wolf runs away, never to return. (In fact, Red gets quite a nasty scare, too.)

In the new version of "The Three Little Pigs," the wolf doesn't come down the chimney and fall into a pot of boiling water, he **hyperventilates** from all that huffing and puffing. When he **passes out,** the pigs build a jail around him.

Of course, all this seems harmless enough—unless you take it beyond fairy tales. How will Christian parents, for example, deal with the Crucifixion? That's pretty violent. And what about all those Christians being **devoured** by lions? Will those parents also take all the violence out of classics such as "Treasure Island" and "Huckleberry Finn"?

More to the point, could they take the violence out of real life? By **shielding** children from any and all violence, wouldn't parents be **setting** their kids **up** for some pretty **nasty** surprises when they get older and realize that the world isn't the warm and **fuzzy cocoon** they've been led to believe it is?

Besides, if the parents who heard those "violent" fairy tales in their youth grew up to be such caring, responsible people, why can't their children do so, too?

Source: Reprinted with permission from the Sun-Sentinel, Fort Lauderdale, Florida.

villains: evil characters
just desserts: appropriate punishments
in retrospect: looking back
whine: complain with a nasalized voice
goodies: sweets
gobbles up: eats up
slaying: killing
tummy: stomach
linens: bed sheets
hyperventilates: breathes so rapidly that carbon dioxide in the blood decreases
passes out: faints
devoured: eaten
shielding: protecting
setting . . . up: preparing
nasty: very unpleasant
fuzzy cocoon: soft, cozy place

What do you believe? Should fairy tales remain as violent and scary as they are in order to introduce young children to the darker side of life? Or should the tales be revised so that they become less violent and scary?

If your class has strongly differing opinions on this issue, you might want to have a debate. For details on how to conduct a debate, see Appendix J.

LEARNING STRATEGY

Managing Your Learning: Self-Monitoring helps you focus on your participation in a discussion.

5. Now, think about one group that you worked with while discussing topics in this section. Evaluate your conversational skills by filling out the following questionnaire.

CONVERSATION SKILLS QUESTIONNAIRE FOR DISCUSSION QUESTION # ____			
While talking to classmates	**Often**	**Sometimes**	**Never**
1. I checked to make sure that everyone understood what I said by asking questions such as "Do you know what I mean?" and "Are you following me?"	____	____	____
2. I gave explanations, definitions, and specific examples when I saw that members of my group weren't following me. I used sentences such as "Let me explain that" and "To help you understand, I'll give you an example."	____	____	____
3. I asked specific questions such as "What do you mean by ____________?" and "Could you give an example of ____________?" and "Could you explain the part about ____________?" when I needed clarification.	____	____	____
4. I paraphrased what others said to make sure that I understood. I used sentences such as "In other words, you mean ____________ and "You're saying, then, that ____________."	____	____	____
5. I encouraged others to speak by making such remarks as "I'd like to know what ____________ thinks about that" and "What do you think about ____________?"	____	____	____

Source: Adapted from *The Tapestry of Language Learning,* 1992,
by Robin C. Scarcella and Rebecca L. Oxford.
Boston: Heinle & Heinle, p. 158.

Proverbs

IT WORKS! Learning Strategy: Developing Cultural Awareness

Look at the following list of proverbs and the values they represent. If you can think of a proverb in your native language that represents the same value, translate the proverb into English and write it on the line. Use a dictionary if necessary, and share your work with your classmates. Then, as a class decide which values are transmitted in "Little Burnt-Face" and "Ash Girl."

	PROVERB	VALUE
a.	Cleanliness is next to godliness.	Cleanliness
b.	A penny saved is a penny earned.	Thriftiness
c.	Time is money.	Time Thriftiness
d.	Don't cry over spilt milk.	Practicality
e.	Waste not; want not.	Frugality
f.	Early to bed, early to rise, makes a man healthy, wealthy, and wise.	Diligence; Work Ethic
g.	God helps those who help themselves.	Initiative
h.	It's not whether you win or lose, but how you play the game.	Good Sportsmanship
i.	A man's home is his castle.	Privacy; Value of Personal Property
j.	No rest for the wicked.	Guilt; Work Ethic
k.	You've made your bed, now lie in it.	Responsibility; Retaliation
l.	Don't count your chickens before they're hatched.	Practicality
m.	A bird in the hand is worth two in the bush.	Practicality
n.	The squeaky wheel gets the grease.	Aggressiveness
o.	Might makes right.	Superiority of Physical Power
p.	There's more than one way to skin a cat.	Originality; Determination
q.	A stitch in time saves nine.	Timeliness of Action
r.	All that glitters is not gold.	Wariness
s.	Clothes make the man.	Concern for Physical Appearance
t.	If at first you don't succeed, try, try again.	Persistence; Work Ethic
u.	Take care of today and tomorrow will take care of itself.	Preparation for Future
v.	Laugh and the world laughs with you; weep and you weep alone.	Pleasant Outward Appearance

Source: *Survival Kit for Overseas Living,* 1984, pp. 28–29.
Reprinted with permission of Intercultural Press, Inc.

Just for Fun

IT WORKS! Learning Strategy: Clarifying

The following cartoons require knowledge of fairy tales and nursery rhymes familiar to American children. Do you know the fairy tales and nursery rhymes referred to? If you do, explain them, and try to figure out why the cartoons are funny. For those cartoons whose meanings are unclear, go out and ask Americans to explain them to you.

This woman doesn't know the meaning of the word pain.

CINDERELLA UPDATE

BALL! I thought we were going to the MALL.

NURSERY RHYME UPDATE

THE COW THAT JUMPED OVER THE MOON SIGNS WITH NIKE.

RAPUNZEL
STARTS A BUSINESS
HAIR
$1/LB.
©1992 T.O.SYLVESTER

FAIRY TALE UPDATE
007945
007945
©1990 T.O.SYLVESTER
GOLDILOCKS:
BREAKING AND ENTERING

MODERN FAIRY TALES:
HANSEL AND GRETEL
©1988 T.O.SYLVESTER

I wonder if the FDA has okayed this place.

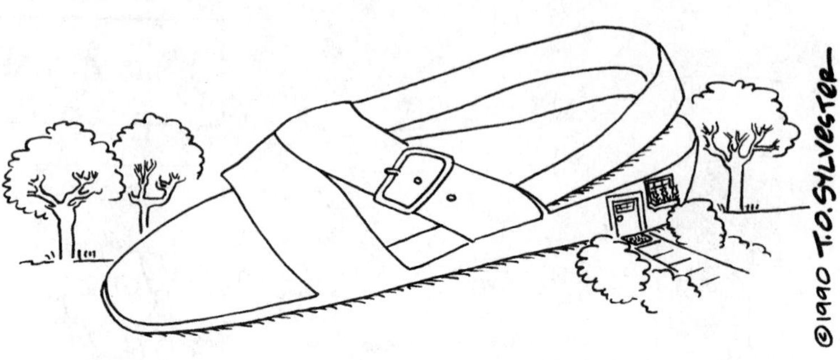

FAIRY TALE UPDATE
©1990 T.O. SYLVESTER
THE SUMMER HOME
OF THE OLD WOMAN WHO LIVED IN A SHOE

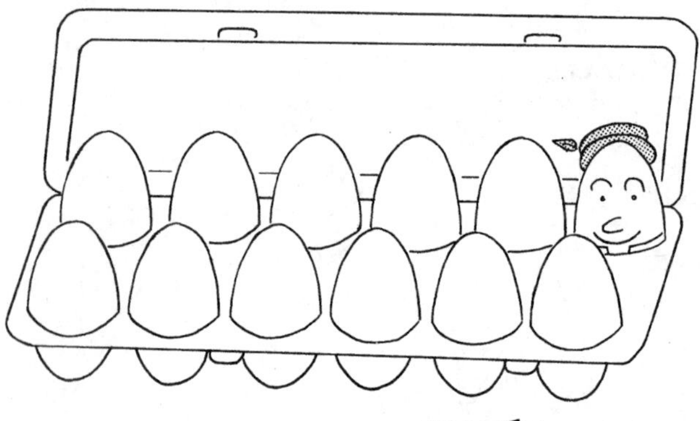

... AND THE DISH RAN AWAY WITH THE SPOON
©1993 T.O. SYLVESTER

This will never work–you're microwave-safe and I'm not.

Source: © T.O. Sylvester

Tell a Story

Choose one of the following assignments to do:

1. At home, think about a fairy tale that made a deep impression on you as a child, and tell it to someone else; or just tell it to yourself to refresh your memory.

   If possible, record yourself telling the story. Listen for any exact translations that wouldn't be clear in English and try to find the English expression to use. Don't write the story—you will tell it to a small group of students in class without notes.

   In class, get into groups of three or four to tell your stories. As you listen to your classmates, remember to be an active listener. That is, smile, nod, make eye contact, and so on. After each story, discuss its moral and the values it teaches.
2. Tell the story of "Ash Girl" from the point of view of one of the stepsisters. Refer to your notes if necessary.

Guest Speaker

Find out if there are any professional or amateur storytellers in your community. Invite one of them to come to your class to talk about the subject of storytelling and why it is important even today. Follow the steps for inviting a guest speaker in Appendix I.

Listening Log Report

Bring your Listening Log to class and report on one entry in a small group. Take turns doing the following:

- Tell your group members what you watched or listened to.
- Give a short oral summary followed by your personal reaction. Do not read what you have written.
- Check your listeners' comprehension by asking questions such as "Do you understand what I mean?" and "Am I being clear?"
- Rephrase or restate to make your points clear.
- Answer your listeners' questions and ask for their reactions.

Choose any of the following activities to do outside of class and then report on what happened or what you found out. These activities can be done individually, in pairs, or in small groups. (Refer to Oral Presentation Feedback Forms in Appendix L.)

IT WORKS! Learning Strategy: Practice Outside the Classroom

1. If you are near a university with courses in cultural anthropology and are interested in folklore,

   - get the class schedule and look for an undergraduate *lecture* class (not a small seminar) on that subject. Visit the class once. If necessary, introduce yourself to the instructor before the class starts.
   - go to the campus bookstore and look at the books that are required for cultural anthropology classes.

2. Divide into groups that will each find information about one item from the following list in the library. After you do your research, give group reports to the class.
   - **a.** "Yeh-Shen" (Chinese version of Cinderella)
   - **b.** "Tattercoats" (English version of Cinderella)
   - **c.** "Cinderella, or the Little Glass Slipper" (by Charles Perrault—French)
   - **d.** "Lon Po Po" (Chinese version of "Little Red Riding Hood")
   - **e.** Information about Charles Perrault
   - **f.** Information about Jacob and Wilhelm Grimm
   - **g.** Information about Hans Christian Andersen
   - **h.** The differences among fairy tales, folk tales, myths, and legends
   - **i.** Examples of nursery rhymes in English
   - **j.** Two or three points made by Bruno Bettelheim in his book, *The Uses of Enchantment—The Meaning and Importance of Fairy Tales*
   - **k.** Roald Dahl's *Revolting Rhymes,* a book that makes jokes out of well-known fairy tales
   - **l.** A book of Native American tales or legends
   - **m.** Fairy tales on tape
   - **n.** Any other material from the folklore section of a library that catches your interest

Threads

Cinderella shouted,
"Get me to the Ball!
There is a Disco at
the Palace!
The rest have gone and
I am jalous!"

Roald Dahl's *Revolting Rhymes*

3. Ask a child whom you know or the child of an adult whom you know to tell you the story of Cinderella or another tale. Interrupt with questions for clarification, and at the end, ask the child what lesson can be learned from the story.
4. Arrange for your class to visit a day care center where
   - **a.** some members of your class tell tales from their native countries, or
   - **b.** you listen to the teacher tell the children stories, or
   - **c.** you listen to the children tell stories.
5. Conduct a survey in which you ask people about the fairy tale they liked the best as children. See Appendix K for guidelines on how to create questions for a survey and how to compile responses.

LEARNING ASSESSMENT

IT WORKS! Learning Strategy: Evaluating Your Progress

1. Look back at Part I (Listening) of this chapter. What activities helped you most in understanding the listening passages?

____

____

____

2. Give an example of when you had trouble understanding what you heard.

____

____

____

Why did you have difficulty?

_____ **a.** I didn't know the vocabulary.

_____ **b.** I wasn't paying attention.

_____ **c.** The speaker wasn't clear.

_____ **d.** The speaker spoke too fast.

_____ **e.** Other: ______________________________

3. Were you more successful than you expected to be in understanding the fairy tales? Were you less successful than you expected? Why?

____

____

____

4. Look back at Part II (Speaking) of this chapter. Give one or two examples of your most successful efforts at oral communication. Try to explain why you were able to succeed.

____

____

____

5. Give an example of a discussion in which you had trouble communicating with your classmates.

____

____

____

Why did you have difficulty?

_____ **a.** My classmates didn't understand my pronunciation.

_____ **b.** I didn't understand my classmates' pronunciation.

_____ **c.** I had trouble finding the main ideas in the readings.

_____ **d.** There was a lot of new vocabulary.

_____ **e.** Other: ______________________________

6. What could you do next time to:

a. better prepare for a listening passage?

____

____

____

b. improve your effectiveness when speaking in a group?

____

____

____

7. Look back at the goals you set at the beginning of this chapter.

a. Which goals did you achieve?

____

____

____

b. What will be your primary goal in the next chapter?

____

____

____

5 CHAPTER

A Medical Question—Should Doctors Always Tell the Truth?

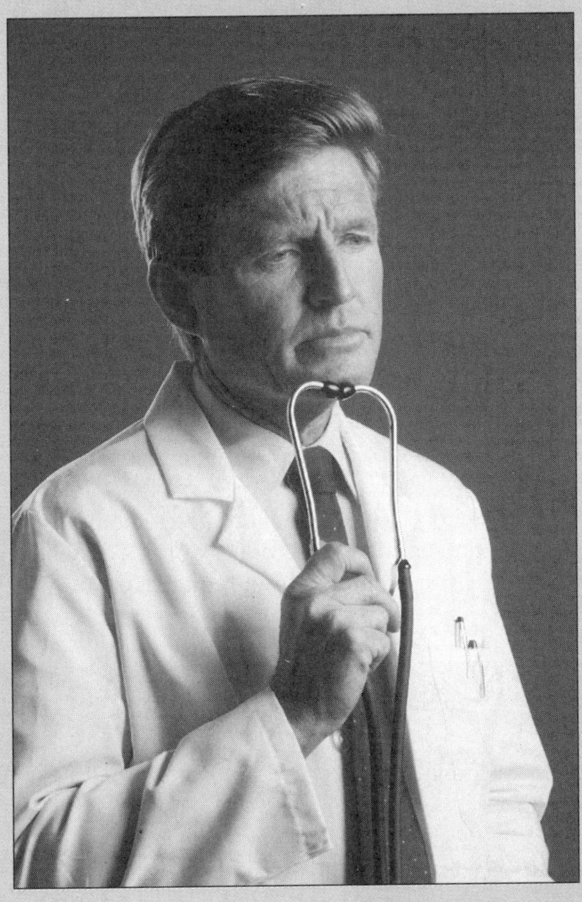

INTRODUCTION

In the previous chapter, you had the opportunity to explore how fairy tales shape the moral attitudes of a culture. In this chapter, you will move into the area of ethics. As the title of the chapter indicates, you will have the chance to explore issues of honesty in medical practice. You will also look at lying as an issue in other areas of society.

Background Knowledge Check

IT WORKS! Learning Strategy: Using Prior Knowledge

The following items reflect some of the content that you will find in this chapter. Write **a, b, c,** or **d** next to each item in the list according to the following:

(a) I have never heard of this.
(b) I have heard of this, but don't really know what it means.
(c) I have some idea of what this means, but I'm not sure about it.
(d) I have a clear idea of what this means and can explain it.

____ **1.** Use of placebos by doctors treating patients

____ **2.** The practice of informed consent in use of placebos

____ **3.** A medical ethicist

____ **4.** A white lie

____ **5.** Reasons a doctor might decide to lie to a patient

____ **6.** Reasons a doctor might decide *not* to lie to a patient

Students who have chosen **d** for any of the items should *briefly* explain what these items mean. If no one has chosen **d,** don't worry. You will have a chance to learn more about these as you progress through the chapter.

Setting Goals

IT WORKS! Learning Strategy: Setting Goals

Complete the following statement by checking the goals you want to try to achieve in this chapter.

While working on this chapter, I will make an effort to:

____ **1.** speak more while I am working in a small group.

____ **2.** give others a chance to speak while working in a small group.

____ **3.** show others that I am actively listening by looking into their eyes and nodding as they talk.

____ **4.** ask more questions in front of the whole class.

____ **5.** make more comments in front of the whole class.

_____ **6.** monitor one aspect of my pronunciation, such as ________________.

_____ **7.** monitor one aspect of grammar as I speak, such as ________________.

_____ **8.** use some of the new vocabulary when speaking, both in and out of class.

_____ **9.** listen to the radio and watch TV outside of class.

_____ **10.** initiate conversations outside of class based on what I am reading and discussing in this chapter.

_____ **11.** try to achieve another goal, such as ______________________________
____.

WARM-UP

Consider the following case, and discuss it with your classmates. What do you think should be done?

A seventy-year-old man, who has just moved to a new city, goes to see a doctor. He has run out of sleeping pills and would like the doctor to write a new prescription. He tells the doctor that he started taking the pills several years earlier, when his wife died, and that he has tried to stop taking them but he cannot. He has become addicted to them and cannot sleep without them. The doctor listens to the old man, and without saying anything to his patient, he considers giving him a **placebo** instead. What do you think the doctor should do? Should he prescribe the medicine even though he knows the man is addicted to the pills, or should he give him a placebo instead?

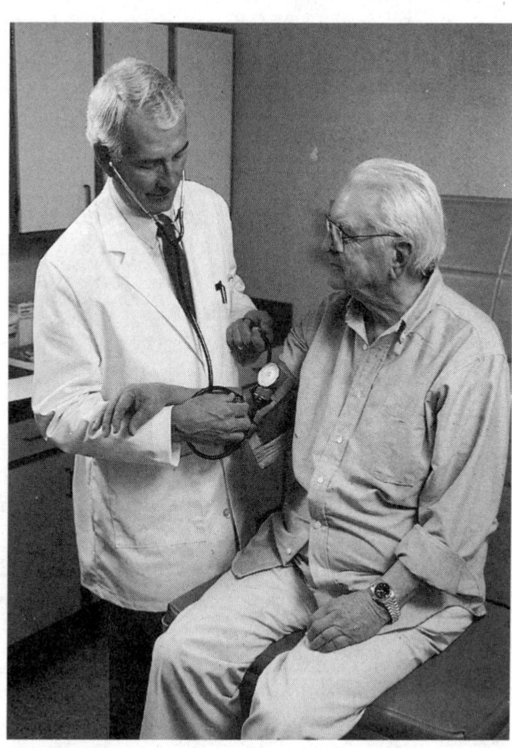

placebo: a substance containing no medication but given to reinforce a patient's expectation of getting medication to make him well

Threads

The word "placebo" comes from the Latin "placere" which means *to please.*

Before You Listen

VOCABULARY PREPARATION FOR LISTENING TO "SHOULD DOCTORS TELL THE TRUTH?"

IT WORKS! Learning Strategy: Guessing Meanings

The following sentences contain vocabulary that you will hear in the listening passage. Read through the sentences and try to get the meaning of any words you don't know from their context. Match the **boldfaced** words with the definitions from the list that follows the sentences. After you have finished, go over your answers with a partner and discuss any words you are not sure of.

1. **On occasion,** a doctor must choose between being truthful or acting in the patient's best interests.
2. There are actually several situations when a doctor might **be tempted to** be less than truthful with a patient.
3. There are times when a doctor might want **to paint a more optimistic (or rosy) picture** of a patient's condition so that the patient won't be unnecessarily frightened.
4. In order to treat the disease, a patient must sometimes undergo a more aggressive treatment, such as **chemotherapy.**
5. Some people believe that **to withhold** information from a person is the same as **outright** lying. In both cases, the doctor is being **paternalistic** by not allowing the patient the right to know and decide.
6. Doctors don't want **to overburden** the patient with too many details that could just be frightening and not useful.
7. A patient came to see the doctor to get a refill of a **prescription** for a sleeping pill. The patient recognized that he **was addicted to** the sleeping medicine, but when he tried to stop taking the medicine, he couldn't sleep and **ended up** taking a sleeping pill. Later, the doctor tried **to wean** the patient from the medicine.
8. An important issue is whether doctors are ever justified in telling these little **white lies** in order to benefit the patient.
9. Chemotherapy has several **side effects,** including physical weakness and loss of hair.
10. When testing the effectiveness of a new drug, researchers conduct clinical trials on two groups, one group receiving the drug, and the second group receiving a **placebo.**
11. A doctor's cultural, religious, educational, and economic background shapes how she interprets the world around her. This background acts like a **filter** that changes and shapes how she perceives things.
12. Most doctors in the United States are reluctant **to deceive** a patient; they believe it is almost always better to tell the truth.

Now, write each vocabulary word from the reading next to the definition that best matches it.

- To result in: ____________________
- Literally, a glass that reduces or changes the quality of the light that enters a camera or telescope: ____________________
- The formula for medicine that a doctor writes for a patient: ____________________
- To overload, to cause strain or stress: ____________________
- A substance that a person thinks contains medication but doesn't: ____________________
- To describe a situation in very positive terms: ____________________
- Treating people in a fatherly way, without allowing them any freedom: ____________________
- Direct, open, clear: ____________________
- To help someone to stop a habit gradually: ____________________
- To cause someone to believe what is not true, to mislead: ____________________
- To hold back something on purpose: ____________________
- The treatment of diseases using chemical substances: ____________________
- Sometimes, at times: ____________________
- To be attracted to doing something: ____________________
- Effects, often undesirable, in addition to the intended one: ____________________
- A lie told so as not to hurt someone else, and therefore not thought of as a bad action: ____________________
- Unable to free oneself from a harmful habit, especially of taking drugs: ____________________

PREDICTING

You are about to hear an interview from National Public Radio's Saturday morning program, Weekend Edition. NPR host Liane Hansen asks two doctors several questions during the discussion. Before you listen to the tape, read over the following questions, which she will ask.

IT WORKS!
Learning Strategy:
Predicting

1. When might a doctor choose not to tell the truth?
2. Have you ever been tempted to be less than perfectly honest with a patient?
3. What does medical ethics tell us is right in the case of the old man addicted to sleeping pills [the same case described at the beginning of the chapter]?
4. Should people be concerned that when they go to their doctor that the doctor might be prescribing a placebo?
5. How often do doctors lie to their patients?
6. What happened to the old man who could not stop taking sleeping pills? [The seventy-year-old man described in "WARM-UP" on page 119]

Can you predict what the doctors will answer?

- With a partner, discuss what you anticipate the doctors will say.
- Write down your predictions.
- After you listen to the tape, come back to your predictions and check them against the information you gather while listening.

As You Listen

LISTEN FOR THE MAIN POINTS

The listening passage is divided into three parts. After each part, when you hear a beep, stop the tape and fill in the chart with short notes on each doctor's general response to interviewer Liane Hansen's questions. As you listen, keep the following points in mind:

- Sometimes only one doctor comments on a question. If one of the doctors does not respond to a question, put **xxx** in the space for an answer under that doctor's name.
- The doctors do not always give direct answers to the questions.
- Focus on the main point they make in response to the questions, even if what they say does not answer the question directly.

The first answer has been done for you.

PART 1.		
Liane Hansen: When might a doctor choose not to tell the truth?	**Dr. Miriam Shuchman:** *several situations—e.g., a patient has cancer and only 6 months to live*	**Dr. Michael Wilkes:** *doesn't say directly—implies doctor should always tell the truth*
PART 2.		
Liane Hansen: Have you ever been tempted to be less than perfectly honest with a patient? What does medical ethics tell us is right in the situation of the old man and the sleeping pills described by Dr. Wilkes?	**Dr. Miriam Shuchman:**	**Dr. Michael Wilkes:**
PART 3.		
Liane Hansen: Should people be concerned that when they go to their doctor, that their doctor might be prescribing a placebo? How often do doctors lie to their patients? What happened to the man who couldn't stop taking the sleeping pill?	**Dr. Miriam Shuchman:**	**Dr. Michael Wilkes:**

Compare your notes with those of a classmate.

- Are they similar?
- What information differs?
- Is any information missing?
- Make a note of anything you are unsure of to check when you listen again.
- How close were your predictions?

LISTEN FOR DETAILS

Listen to the tape again. Stop the tape after each beep and write a short answer for each of the following comprehension questions.

Part 1.

1. What does Miriam think is the difference between what a doctor in the past and a doctor today might tell a patient with a serious illness?

2. What does Michael consider to be the difference between withholding information and lying? Why does he think in both these cases the doctor is being paternalistic?

3. Why does Miriam think that a doctor has to limit the amount of information that he or she gives a patient? Does Michael agree with her?

Part 2.

1. Why did the elderly man come to see Michael?

2. Why couldn't the elderly man give up sleeping pills?

3. What did Michael's colleague suggest he do?

4. What does Miriam feel is the difficulty a doctor faces in this situation?

Part 3.

1. Why is use of placebos in clinical practice rare?

2. What is informed consent?

3. What percentage of medicines commonly prescribed have no biologic activity?

35%.

4. According to Michael, how do cough medicines work?

fact of mind.

5. According to Miriam, why don't patients get the information they need to make decisions?

6. Does Michael plan to continue to prescribe sleeping pills for the old man?

not to use placebo.

Compare your answers with a partner and discuss any differences. Are there any answers you are unsure of or want to change? Listen to the tape once more in case you might have missed something important.

IT WORKS! Learning Strategy: Learning with Others

After You Listen

FOCUS ON LANGUAGE

1. You may have noticed that the interviewer calls both doctors by their first names.
   - **a.** Why do you think she is doing this?
   - **b.** In your native country, would doctors being interviewed on the radio be addressed by their first names?
   - **c.** In your native country, are there fairly clear rules for addressing people? When do you use a first name? a last name? a title? How would you address

     - a doctor?
     - a nurse?
     - a classmate you don't know well?
     - a professor?
     - a high school teacher?
     - the mother of a friend of yours?
     - a close friend's grandfather?
     - a colleague at work?
     - your boss?
     - your hairdresser or barber?
     - a store clerk?
     - your friend's friend, whom you don't know?
     - the ten-year-old child of acquaintances?

   - **d.** Find out how you would be expected to address these same people in the United States.

IT WORKS! Learning Strategy: Developing Cultural Awareness

2. The listening passage contains additional words and phrases that are useful to use. Read over the following excerpts and pay special attention to the **boldfaced** words.

> "Trust was a word that was used early and often during the campaign, and **when it comes to** politicians, people really must think about whether they can trust their representatives to represent them. But **when it comes to** the relationship between a patient and doctor, the word trust should be **a given.** Doctors are, after all, supposed to do what's best for us, and this involves telling the truth."

> "My worry, though, is that doctors might also paint a more rosy picture in order to convince a patient to undergo a more aggressive treatment, **say,** chemotherapy, a treatment that they might not . . . choose to undergo if they had more information."

> "You know, **it's** probably **worth mentioning** here **that** experts feel that about 30 percent of the medicines that we currently prescribe really have no biologic effect."

- Discuss what each of the words or phrases means with your teacher. Find out when it is appropriate to use them.
- Write down three things you can do to make these words part of your active vocabulary.

IT WORKS! Learning Strategy: Managing Your Learning

1. ______________________________
2. ______________________________
3. ______________________________

- For the next week, put your suggestions into practice. After a week passes, write two or three sentences that evaluate the effectiveness of your suggestions and give them to your teacher.

LEARNING STRATEGY

Remembering New Material: Classifying new material into meaningful groups makes it easier to recall later.

3. In this chapter, you will come across a number of words having to do with dishonesty. The chart below contains some of them. Add as many synonyms and related words as you can think of. Continue to add to the list as you learn new words that might fit.

DISHONESTY

VERB	NOUN	ADJECTIVE
to deceive	deception	deceptive
to lie to someone	a lie	lying
to lie about something	a white lie	
to tell a lie		

4. The speakers in the listening passage sometimes use *they* or *them* when referring to one person.

> "It used to be that if a patient was diagnosed with a serious form of cancer, the doctor wouldn't even tell *them*."

> "We're always in the position of deciding what information to give a patient. We don't want to overburden *them* with too many details. But we want *them* to have the information that's really important for making decisions."

> "Before a patient can agree to a given treatment or procedure, the doctor is obliged to inform *them* about the risks and benefits of that treatment."

This is not grammar usage you will find in a grammar textbook; however, you will often hear native speakers of English use *they* or *them* when referring to an unspecified third person, even though they are referring to only one person. People do this, often unconsciously, as a way to avoid using the gender-specific pronouns, *he, she, him,* or *her.*

How can you refer to people without assigning a specific gender? In the past, people always used *he* and *him.* Today you can hear other options. Sometimes people use both pronouns. For example:

- A patient doesn't need to be overburdened with too many details, but *he* or *she* needs to have the information that's really important for making decisions.
- It used to be that if a patient was diagnosed with a serious form of cancer, the doctor wouldn't even tell *him* or *her.*

Another option people use is to choose either he, she, him, or her when referring to a person in general. For example:

- A patient doesn't need to be overburdened with too many details, but *she* needs to have the information that's really important for making decisions.
- It used to be that if a patient was diagnosed with a serious form of cancer, the doctor wouldn't even tell *him.*

A third option is to use plural pronouns to generalize. For example:

- Patients don't need to be overburdened with too many details, but *they* need to have the information that's really important for making decisions.
- It used to be that if patients were diagnosed with a serious form of cancer, the doctor wouldn't even tell *them.*

LISTENING LOG

IT WORKS! Learning Strategy: Planning Ahead

Reminder: Keep up your Listening Log with as many entries as your teacher requires. At the end of Part II (Speaking), you will report on one of your entries in a small group. (If necessary, see Appendix F for more details on Listening Logs.)

ANY QUESTIONS?

IT WORKS!
Learning Strategy:
Clarifying

Before you go on to read about and discuss more issues about lying, answer the following questions on a separate sheet of paper. Do not write your name on the paper. Your teacher or a classmate will collect the papers and share everyone's answers with the class.

1. What has been the most valuable aspect of this chapter for you so far?
2. What is still unclear?

PART II: SPEAKING

Discussion

IT WORKS!
Learning Strategy:
Cooperating

The following discussion questions deal with different aspects of lying . Choose the topic or topics you would like to discuss. Feel free to add related questions of your own to the questions that are asked here. And as always, you should focus on using new vocabulary and appropriate conversation skills.

When appropriate for the activity, work in small groups. Assign one person to act as discussion leader and another person to act as recorder. The discussion leader will make sure that everyone talks and stays on the subject. The recorder will take notes and later report briefly to the class on the main points of your group's discussion.

Before you begin, take a look at the group work questionnaire on page 137 of this section. You will respond to the items on the questionnaire after one of your discussions has been completed. As you work in groups, keep the items on the questionnaire in mind.

Threads

"Ethics" means *the science of morals*. It comes from the Greek.

1. Now that you have listened several times to the passage, what do you think about what the two doctors had to say about whether or not doctors should ever lie or withhold information?

   In small groups, you will discuss the issues raised in the listening passage. Before you begin your discussion:

   a. refer to your notes from the listening passage, and do the following:

   - Write down a couple of interesting points that you reacted to strongly. This will help you focus on the issues you would like to raise in the discussion.

     ____

     ____

   - Write down one or two questions you would like to ask the others in your group.

     ____

     ____

b. Read the following brief excerpt from an essay entitled "Should Doctors Tell the Truth?", which relates closely to the listening passage. Then do the following:

- Highlight any points that tie in with the listening passage or that you may want to comment on in your discussion.
- Make a list of the questions you want to raise in the discussion.

Truth never used to be an issue in medicine. If the news was bad, it was simply not told, a reflex response first identified by Dr. Ronald M. Weintraub, chief of cardiothoracic surgery at Beth Israel Hospital in Boston, as the Uncle Moe Shouldn't Know Syndrome: The family begs the doctor to lie to the patient, which the doctor does and would have done anyway.

The doctor has lied ever since Hippocrates, and in most of the world, truth-telling is still considered bad medicine. Dr. Jimmie Holland, chief of psychiatry at Sloan-Kettering, recently surveyed **oncologists** in 22 countries. She says: "In much of Europe, South America, most of Asia—they consider it unethical to tell. They say, 'America is so **brutal,** you make it so difficult for the patient, and we are kind and gentle.' "

But just yesterday, America was identically kind and gentle. We are, after all, truth **parvenus.** In 1961, in a study published by The Journal of the American Medical Association, 9 out of 10 doctors said they generally concealed a cancer diagnosis from their patients. But by 1977, the ratio had been reversed: More than 9 out of 10 said they usually told the truth.

. . .

For a practice now so broadly **endorsed,** truth-telling is little understood. There is plenty of passionate conviction but no conclusive evidence that disclosure is "better" (or worse), in any medical sense, than the **beneficient** lie.

"I saw a woman whose ovarian cancer had come back after three years," says Dr. Stuart E. Lind of Harvard Medical School, who has written extensively on **disclosure.** "The surgeon had never told her it would probably **recur.** Was it better for her to have those years free of worry? I *think* it's better to know the truth. But I can't be sure. And there may not be a simple answer ever."

Among medical ethicists and philosophers, the issue is not what is "better": "The point is *the right to know,*" says the ethicist George Annas. "You can withhold the truth only if the patient says, directly, 'I do not want to know.' "

oncologists: doctors who specialize in treatment of patients with cancer
brutal: cruel
parvenus: people of low social position who suddenly gain power
endorsed: supported
beneficient: kind or generous
disclosure: the act of making something known
recur: to happen more than once

When you are ready to begin your discussion, share your thoughts on what you have heard and read. Keep your notes in front of you so you can refer to the points you wrote down.

Don't concentrate only on what you want to say. Explore what other members of the group think about the issues. Ask follow-up questions to make sure you understand what others think and to help develop the issues.

2. The following case studies have been used in training doctors. As nonspecialists, what do you think is the best thing to do in each case? As you read each case, write down the questions you want to raise about the issues or any observations you want to make in your discussion.

Case #1

A seventeen-year-old girl visited her pediatrician, who had been taking care of her since infancy. She went to his office without her parents, although her mother had made the appointment for her over the telephone. She told the pediatrician that she was very healthy, but that she thought she

Threads

This deception tortured him—[his doctors'] not wishing to admit what they all knew and what he knew . . . concerning his terrible condition. . . .

Leo Tolstoy,
The Death of Ivan Ilich

had some emotional problems. She stated that she was having trouble sleeping at night, that she was very nervous most of the day. She was a senior in high school and claimed she was doing quite poorly in some of her subjects. She was worried about what she was going to do next year. She was somewhat overweight. This, she felt, was part of her problem. She claimed she was not very attractive to the opposite sex and could not seem to "get boys interested in me." She had a few close friends of the same sex.

Her life at home was quite **chaotic** and stressful. There were frequent battles with her younger brother, who was fourteen, and with her parents. She claimed her parents were always **"on my back."** She described her mother as extremely **rigid** and her father as a disciplinarian, who was quite old-fashioned in his values.

In all, she spent about twenty minutes talking with her pediatrician. She told him that what she thought she really needed was **tranquilizers,** and that was the reason she came. She felt that this was an extremely difficult year for her, and if she could have something to calm her nerves until she got over her current crises, everything would go better.

The pediatrician told her that he did not really believe in giving tranquilizers to a girl of her age. He said he thought it would be a very bad **precedent** for her to establish. She got very insistent, however, and claimed that if he did not give her tranquilizers, she would "get them somehow." Finally, he agreed to call her pharmacy and order medication for her nerves. She accepted graciously. He suggested that she call him in a few days to let him know how things were going. He also called her parents to say that he had a talk with her and he was giving her some medicine that might help her nerves.

Five days later, the girl called the pediatrician back to say that the pills were working really well. She claimed that she had calmed down a great deal, that she was working things out better with her parents, and had a new outlook on life. He suggested that she keep taking them twice a day for the rest of the school year. She agreed.

A month later, the girl ran out of pills and called her pediatrician for a refill. She found that he was away on vacation. She seemed quite **distraught** at not having any medication left, so she called her uncle who was a surgeon in the next town. He called the pharmacy to renew her pills and, in speaking to the druggist, found out they were only vitamins and that she could get them **over the counter** and didn't really need him to refill them. The girl became very distraught, feeling that she had been deceived and betrayed by her pediatrician. Her parents, when they heard, commented that they thought the pediatrician was "very clever."

Source: Reprinted by permission of Dr. Melvin Levine

chaotic: a state of complete disorder and confusion
on my back: idiom meaning "criticizing me"
rigid: strict, unbending, inflexible
tranquilizers: drugs used for reducing anxiety and nervousness
precedent: an action used as an example or rule for present or future action
distraught: extremely upset
over the counter: without a prescription

- As you begin your discussion, you may want to consider some of the following questions in addition to your own questions:

  a. What choices did the pediatrician have in treating the teen-age girl? What would the potential consequences of those choices be?
  b. Do you think he handled the situation well?
  c. Do you think the consequences of the pediatrician's actions were harmful or harmless?
  d. What should he have done once he learned that the girl had discovered that the prescription was merely for vitamins?

Case #2

Martha Lawrence was tense and nervous when she came to the Human Genetics Unit on December 12, 1971. She had been referred by her own physician because, unexpectedly pregnant at the age of 41, she was considered at risk for the birth of a Mongoloid child. She was eighteen weeks pregnant, which would not leave much time for a potential abortion.

Down's syndrome or Mongoloid babies are twenty times as likely to be born to women over 40 as to women under 25. About 50 percent of all such babies are born to mothers over 35, and 25 percent to mothers over 50.

Mrs. Lawrence's first pregnancies had been uncomplicated, and her two sons, ages 16 and 13, were both in good health. The genetic counselor, Dr. Brenda Gould, recommended amniocentesis, the withdrawal of a sample of the amniotic fluid surrounding the **fetus,** drawn from the abdomen with a needle. The fluid contains enough fetal cells for biochemical or **chromosomal** analysis.

The sample showed that the fetus had no extra twenty-first chromosome and thus was free of Mongolism. But the sex chromosomes, rather than being XX for female or XY for male, showed the abnormal XYY composition. Some research suggests that XYY males might be "supermales," **inclined to** violent acts, including sexual offenses, while other recent studies do not **confirm** this finding. Considering the **inconclusive** nature of such research, the possible danger to society and the Lawrence family, and the impact of the information on the way the Lawrences might treat the child, Dr. Gould faced a **dilemma:** what to tell Mrs. Lawrence.

Source: Reprinted by permission of the publishers from *Case Studies in Medical Ethics* by Robert M. Veatch, Cambridge, Mass.: Harvard University Press, Copyright © 1977 by Robert M. Veatch.

fetus: a young baby before birth
chromosomal: having to do with the chromosomes, the threadlike body found in living cells, which passes on and controls a person's characteristics
inclined to: likely to do
confirm: support, agree with
inconclusive: not certain
dilemma: a problem with no easy solution

- As you begin your discussion, you may want to consider the following questions in addition to your own questions:

  a. Dr. Gould has to decide not only which facts to communicate but what the facts actually are. She must determine which facts fulfill her responsibilities as a counselor and which fulfill her moral obligation to the couple who have sought her advice. What are the questions she must ask herself in deciding what to tell Martha Lawrence?

b. What information do you think Dr. Gould should give Martha Lawrence?

c. Now that we have the technology to reveal much more about the condition of a fetus, including defects of varying degree, should a doctor tell the parents everything? What are some arguments in favor of and some arguments against disclosing everything?

3. The following excerpt comes from the diary of Sir Charles Wilson (later Lord Moran), personal physician to Winston Churchill. In it he describes an important time during World War II when he deliberately chose not to be honest with Churchill about his health. The incident he writes about took place on December 26, 1941, when Churchill was in Washington, D.C. meeting with President Roosevelt.

That night, as Churchill lay in bed at the White House, it was so hot that he decided to open the bedroom window. The next morning he told his doctor that the window was so stiff that he had had to use considerable force to open it. As he was opening it, he suddenly felt out of breath and noticed a dull pain over his heart. The pain went down his left arm. "It didn't last very long, but it has never happened before. What is it? Is my heart all right?" Churchill asked.

Sir Charles Wilson examined Churchill and later that day wrote in his diary:

> "There was not much to be found when I examined his heart. Indeed, the time I spent listening to his chest was given to some quick thinking. I knew that when I took the stethoscope out of my ears he would ask me pointed questions, and I had no doubt that whether the **electro-cardiograph** showed evidence of a **coronary thrombosis** or not, his symptoms were those of coronary **insufficiency.**

British Prime Minister Winston Churchill (second from left) during his 1943 voyage by warship to the Middle East for his meeting with the Allied leaders. At far right stands Lord Moran, Churchill's private physician.

The textbook treatment for this is at least six weeks in bed. That would mean publishing to the world—and the American newspapers would see to this—that the Prime Minister was an invalid with a **crippled** heart and a doubtful future. And this at a moment when America has just come into the war, and there is no one but Winston to take her by the hand.

I felt that the effect of announcing that the Prime Minister had had a heart attack could only be disastrous. I knew, too, the consequences of one of his imaginative **temperament** of the feeling that his heart was affected. His work would suffer. On the other hand, if I did nothing and he had another and **severer** attack—perhaps a **fatal seizure**—the world would undoubtedly say that I had killed him through not insisting on rest. These thoughts went racing through my head while I was listening to his heart. I took my stethoscope out of my ears. Then I replaced it and listened again. Right or wrong, it seemed plain that I must **sit tight** on what had happened, whatever the consequences.

'Well,' he asked, looking full at me, 'is my heart all right?'

'There is nothing serious,' I answered. 'You have been overdoing things.'

'Now Charles, you're not going to tell me to rest. I can't. I won't. Nobody else can do this job. I must. What actually happened when I opened the window?' he demanded. 'My idea is that I strained one of my chest muscles. I used great force. I don't believe it was my heart at all.'

He waited for me to answer.

'Your circulation was a bit **sluggish.** It is nothing serious. You needn't rest in the sense of lying up, but you mustn't do more than you can help in the way of exertion for a little while.'

There was a knock at the door. It was Harry Hopkins. I slipped away. I went and sat in a corner of the secretaries' room, picking up a newspaper, so that they would not talk to me. I began to think things out more deliberately. I did not like it, but I determined to tell no one."

Source: Diary entry for 26 December 1941: Lord Moran, *Winston Churchill, The Struggle for Survival, 1940-1965.* London, 1966, page 15.

electro-cardiograph: a machine that records in the form of a drawing the electrical charges that take place in the heart as it beats
coronary thrombosis: heart attack
insufficiency: inadequacy, weakness
crippled: weakened, injured
temperament: a person's nature, esp. as it influences how he thinks, behaves, or acts in general
severer: more serious
fatal seizure: a deadly attack of an illness or medical condition
sit tight: not move, not act on
sluggish: slow moving

Churchill's mild heart attack on that December night in 1941 was to remain a secret for twenty-four years, until, immediately after his death, his doctor published his diary.

This case raises some interesting questions. You may want to consider some of the following in your discussion:

a. Do you think that Sir Charles Wilson did the right thing? If your answer is yes, would it still be yes if Churchill had died shortly after the initial attack?

PART I: LISTENING

Before You Listen

BACKGROUND READING

The following essay about the science of smell appeared in the *Boston Globe Magazine.* It will give you some useful background knowledge for the listening passage you will hear.

IT WORKS! Learning Strategy: Highlighting

As you read, highlight the answers to the following questions. When you have finished, compare your answers with a partner. Feel free also to highlight any points you think you may want to comment on later.

1. What are the two steps that our brain goes through when we smell something?
2. What was the most frequently reported smell to trigger childhood memories?
3. What factors were different among the people whose memories were triggered by various odors?
4. Why is smell research of interest to people in marketing?

Scent of a memory

by Madeline Drexler

As researchers have lately learned, **olfactory** memory is not only individual, but also generational and regional. We are the fragrances we remember, and **gauging** our reactions to smells can be useful to writers, psychiatrists, sociologists, and anyone else interested in the human psyche. Most recently, of course, the science of smell has been taken up by marketers, who seek to **replicate** aromas that send **nostalgic** consumers back in time and ultimately to their wallets.

Smells **evoke** memories better than the **stimuli** to any of the other senses, and there is an anatomical reason why. The nose is connected through the olfactory pathway to the brain to the limbic system, the area of the brain considered to be the seat of memory and emotions. When we first smell something, our brain instantly judges whether we like the smell or whether it signals a **threat** to our well-being. Only afterward does it try to determine exactly what we are smelling. This sequence of **subjective** experience followed by **objective** naming occurs only with smell and taste. The other senses involve the coding of stimuli in the **cerebral cortex,** a process by which we identify sensory impressions before we **assess** them.

At the Smell and Taste Treatment and Research Foundation, in Chicago, **neurologist** and psychiatrist Alan Hirsch surveyed nearly 1,000 people **randomly** selected at a shopping center. He asked if a particular odor had ever evoked a memory of childhood, and if so, which odor. He also asked whether their childhoods had been generally happy or sad.

Eighty-five percent of those surveyed reported that a particular odor had **triggered** a childhood memory. The most common was the aroma of fresh-baked bread. But beyond that **yeasty** association, the memory triggers varied dramatically according to geography, age, and other factors.

People who grew up on the East Coast, for example, were more **likely** to say that the smell of flowers evoked memories of childhood; those from the Midwest mentioned farm animals; Southerners noted fresh air; and people from the West Coast cited cooked or barbecued meat. Personal history also made a difference: People with unhappy childhoods were more likely to report **foul** smells as triggers for childhood memories.

b. Should the doctor have consulted anyone else? Was the doctor taking on too much responsibilty in making his decision?

c. Does the public have a right to know all the details of the health of its government leaders? Does the public even need to know?

d. Do you think a doctor should ever lie about the health of a patient who is a public figure? If yes, under what circumstances? If no, why not?

4. The previous questions all raise the issue of how much information doctors should give to a patient and how much information a patient has the right to know. But what about deception in other areas of life? Is it ever all right to lie? In her book *On Lying: Moral Choices in Public and Private Life,* philosopher Sissela Bok looks at lying and deception in public and private life—in government, medicine, law, academia, journalism, in the family, and between friends. The following excerpt comes from the introduction to her book.

> "Should physicians lie to dying patients so as to delay the fear and anxiety which the truth might bring them? Should professors exaggerate the excellence of their students on recommendations in order to give them a better chance in a tight job market? Should parents **conceal** from children the fact that they were adopted? Should social scientists send investigators masquerading as patients to physicians in order to learn about racial and sexual **biases** in diagnoses and treatment? Should government lawyers lie to members of Congress who might otherwise oppose a much-needed welfare bill? And should journalists lie to those from whom they seek information in order to expose corruption?
>
> We sense differences among such choices; but whether to lie, **equivocate,** or tell the truth in any given situation is often a hard decision. Hard because **duplicity** can take so many forms, be present to such different degrees, and have such different purposes and results. Hard also because we know how questions of truth and lying inevitably **pervade** all that is said or left unspoken within our families, our communities, our working relationships. Lines seem most difficult to draw, and a consistent policy out of reach.
>
> I have **grappled** with these problems in my personal life as everyone must. But I have also seen them at close hand in my professional experience in teaching applied ethics. I have had the chance to explore particular moral **quandaries** encountered at work, with nurses, doctors, lawyers, civil servants, and many others. I first came to look closely at problems of professional truth-telling and deception in preparing to write about the giving of placebos. And I grew more and more puzzled by a **discrepancy** in perspectives: many physicians talk about such deception in a **cavalier,** often **condescending** and joking way, whereas patients often have an **acute** sense of injury and of loss of trust at learning they have been **duped.**
>
> I learned that this discrepancy is reflected in an odd state of affairs in medicine more generally. Honesty from health professionals matters more to patients than almost everything else that they experience when ill. Yet the requirement to be honest with patients has been left out altogether from medical oaths and codes of ethics, and is often ignored, if not actually **disparaged,** in the teaching of medicine.

As I widened my search, I came to realize that the same discrepancy was present in many other professional contexts as well. In law and journalism, in government and in the social sciences, deception is taken for granted when it is felt to be excusable by those who tell the lies and who tend also to make the rules. Government officials and those who run for elections often deceive when they can **get away with it** and when they assume the true state of affairs is beyond the comprehension of citizens. Social scientists **condone** deceptive experimentation on the ground that the knowledge gained will be worth having. Lawyers **manipulate** the truth in court on behalf of their clients. Those in selling, advertising, or any form of advocacy may mislead the public and their competitors in order to achieve their goals. Psychiatrists may **distort** information about their former patients to preserve **confidentiality** or to keep them out of military service. And journalists, police investigators, and so-called intelligence operators often have little **compunction** in using **falsehoods** to gain the knowledge they seek.

. . .

We have a great deal **at stake,** I believe in becoming more clear about matters of truth-telling, both for our personal choices and for the social decisions which **foster** or discourage deceptive practices. And when we think about these matters, it is the reasons given for deceiving which must be examined. Sometimes there may be **sufficient** reason to lie—but when? Most often there is not—and why? Describing how things are is not enough. Choice requires the formulation of criteria. To lie to the dying, for example, or to tell them the truth—which is the best policy? Under what circumstances? And for what reasons? What kinds of arguments support these reasons or defeat them?"

Source: From *Lying* by Sissela Bok. Copyright © 1978 by Sissela Bok. Reprinted by permission of Pantheon Books, a division of Random House, Inc.

conceal: hide
biases: prejudices
equivocate: to not answer yes or no clearly
duplicity: deceit, deception
pervade: spread through every part of
grappled: struggled
quandaries: situations where its difficult to know the right thing to do
discrepancy: difference, lack of agreement
cavalier: thoughtless; informal and easy in manners
condescending: acting in a manner that makes you appear above everybody else
acute: sharp, intense
duped: deceived
disparaged: spoken about without respect for something
to get away with it: to succeed in a deceit
condone: to treat a wrong behavior as harmless
manipulate: control and influence for their own purpose
distort: to twist out of the true meaning
confidentiality: secrecy
compunction: guilt, shame
falsehoods: lies
at stake: at risk
foster: to encourage
sufficient: enough

a. With a partner or in small groups discuss the following questions:

- What is the author's main point? Do you agree with her?
- Do you think that in your native country there is a similar loss of confidence and trust? If so, why? Are there specific examples of lying you can share with your group to support your point of view?
- In your native country is it common to lie in certain circumstances? Is it acceptable? Give specific examples.

b. In the paragraphs you have just read, Bok raises the issue of many different kinds of lies: doctors lying to the sick and dying, professors lying about students in order to help them find jobs in a tight job market, parents not telling their children they are adopted, social scientists using deception to get information for their important research, journalists lying as a means of exposing corruption, government officials and politicians deceiving the public about the state of the government, lawyers manipulating the truth in court to help their clients, advertisers misleading the public in order to sell a product. Often the justification is that the end justifies the means.

- Make a chart of all the areas where Bok sees lying. For each category, list hypothetical examples you can think of where people might lie.
- Can the lies you have put on your list ever be justified?
- What criteria are you using to decide if and when a lie might be justified?

5. What about small white lies casually told to a friend, a classmate, or a teacher? Are they harmful or harmless? Does the end ever justify the means?

a. Look at the following examples and decide what you would do in each case. You might want to try role-playing each incident.

- A close friend has just bought a very expensive oriental carpet. You think it is ugly and not worth the amount your friend paid for it. Your friend asks you if you like it. What do you say?
- You miss an extremely important exam because you overslept. You are afraid the instructor will not let you make up the exam because it is not the first time that this has happened. Do you tell the truth and hope for the best, or do you make up a story about what happened?
- A good friend gets a new haircut that looks terrible and is very unflattering. He or she asks you what you think. What do you say ?
- Someone you know slightly asks you to his house for dinner. You feel you don't have enough time to spend with your good friends, much less spend an evening with a slight acquaintance, so you don't want to go. You are free the night he wants you to come over. When he calls to invite you, what do you say?

b. In a group, make up examples of situations in which white lies might be told. Share them with another group to see what they would do under the circumstances.

c. After you have discussed the different examples, see if the class can come to any agreement regarding when it might be acceptable to tell a white lie.

6. Now, think about one group that you worked with while discussing topics in this section. Evaluate your conversational skills by filling out this questionnaire:

IT WORKS!* *Learning Strategy: Self-evaluation

Group Work Questionnaire for Discussion Question # ____

1. What one word would you use to describe how the group worked together? ____________

2. What one word would describe the way you would have liked the group to work together? ____________

3. Did everybody participate?

   Always ______ Usually ______ Occasionally ______ Rarely ______ Never ______

4. Did you try to help each other feel able to talk and say what each one thought?

   Always ______ Usually ______ Occasionally ______ Rarely ______ Never ______

5. Did you listen to each other?

   Always ______ Usually ______ Occasionally ______ Rarely ______ Never ______

6. Did you show you were listening by nodding at each other?

   Always ______ Usually ______ Occasionally ______ Rarely ______ Never ______

7. Did you use such expressions as "That's good" to each other when you liked something?

   Always ______ Usually ______ Occasionally ______ Rarely ______ Never ______

8. Did you ask each other questions?

   Always ______ Usually ______ Occasionally ______ Rarely ______ Never ______

9. Did you listen and really try to answer those questions?

   Always ______ Usually ______ Occasionally ______ Rarely ______ Never ______

10. Did you pay attention to each other?

    Always ______ Usually ______ Occasionally ______ Rarely ______ Never ______

11. Did your group stay on the assigned task?

    Always ______ Usually ______ Occasionally ______ Rarely ______ Never ______

12. Did any one person do most of the talking?

    Yes ______ No ______

13. Was any one person quiet most of the time?

    Yes ______ No ______

Movie Review

Many films have dealt with lying and deception in a humorous way. In *Tootsie,* Dustin Hoffman plays an out-of-work actor who disguises himself as a woman in order to get a job and ends up being a star on a popular soap opera. In *Working Girl,* Melanie Griffith is a secretary who rises in the brokerage business by masquerading as her boss, who is out of the country. In *Mrs. Doubtfire,* Robin Williams plays a divorced man who disguises himself as an old woman to get a job as a nanny so he can be near his children. In *Dave,* Kevin Kline portrays a man who so closely resembles the President of the United States that he is brought in to pretend to be the President when, unknown to the public, the real President is stricken by a massive stroke. All four films lead to happy endings and treat deception in a lighthearted way.

In "Tootsie," Sydney Pollack plays George Fields, a high-powered New York agent, and Dustin Hoffman stars as Michael Dorsey, a dedicated but struggling actor, who finally manages to land a leading role by auditioning as a woman, Dorothy Michaels.

a. With a partner or in a small group, brainstorm the names of any other films you can think of that contain instances of lying or deception of some kind.

b. With your partner or group, rent from a video store one of the films on your list or from the list above. Watch the film together and then prepare a report for the class. In your report, include:

- the name of the film
- the major characters and the actors who portrayed them
- the general story of the film
- the lies or deception involved in the story
- your opinion of the plot and of the film overall
- your opinion of whether such kinds of deception could ever work in real life

Threads

Tis strange—but true; for truth is always strange; stranger than fiction.

Lord Byron, 1788–1824, in *Don Juan*

Just for Fun

Look at the following cartoon. What do you think? Would you like to have telephone technology that can tell you if someone is lying are not? Can you imagine circumstances where you might prefer to have someone lie to you?

"He's lying"

Source: Drawing by Handelsman; © 1992. *The New Yorker* Magazine, Inc.

Guest Speaker

Invite a health professional, a lawyer, a politician, an ethicist, or anyone else you choose to come to your class to talk about the ethical considerations of lying. Follow the steps for inviting a guest speaker in Appendix I.

Listening Log Report

Bring your Listening Log to class and report on one entry in a small group. Take turns doing the following:

- Tell your group members what you watched or listened to.
- Give a short oral summary followed by your personal reaction. Do not read what you have written.
- Check your listeners' comprehension by asking questions such as: "Do you understand what I mean?" and "Am I being clear?"
- Rephrase or restate to make your points clear.
- Answer your listeners' questions and ask for their reactions.

FOLLOW-UP

Choose any of the following activities to do outside of class and then report on what happened or what you found out. These activities can be done individually, in pairs, or in small groups. (Refer to Oral Presentation Feedback forms in Appendix L.)

IT WORKS! Learning Strategy: Practice Outside the Classroom

1. The newspaper is filled daily with instances of deception of one kind or another. Find and read an article that deals with lying or withholding of information. In your opinion, was the deception justified? Discuss the article with a friend, giving your reaction to what you read, and find out what your friend thinks.
2. Go to a library or bookstore to see what more you can learn about the issue of lying. Are there many books on the subject? You might want to look at these two books:

   - By Sissela Bok: *Lying: Moral Choices in Public and Private Life*
   - By Harry Stein: *Ethics (And Other Liabilities)*

   Choose a book and read it to find out more about the issues of lying. As you read the book, keep either a written or an audio journal of the book's most important points and your reactions to them. Keep a list of any new vocabulary words you want to be able to recognize or use.
3. Conduct a survey on how people feel about lying, both telling lies and being lied to. Refer to Appendix K for guidelines on how to conduct a survey.

LEARNING ASSESSMENT

1. Look back at Part I (Listening) of this chapter. What activities helped you most in understanding the listening passages?

   ____

   ____

   ____

2. Give an example of when you had trouble understanding what you heard.

____

____

____

Why did you have difficulty?

_____ **a.** I didn't know the vocabulary.

_____ **b.** I wasn't paying attention.

_____ **c.** The speaker wasn't clear.

_____ **d.** The speaker spoke too fast.

_____ **e.** Other: ______________________________

3. Were you more successful than you expected to be in understanding the listening material on the subject of whether or not doctors should always tell the truth to patients? Were you less successful than you expected? Why?

____

____

____

4. Look back at Part II (Speaking) of this chapter. Give one or two examples of your most successful efforts at oral communication. Try to explain why you were able to succeed.

____

____

____

5. Give an example of a discussion in which you had trouble communicating with your classmates.

____

____

____

Why did you have difficulty?

_____ **a.** My classmates didn't understand my pronunciation.

_____ **b.** I didn't understand my classmates' pronunciation.

_____ **c.** I had trouble finding the main ideas in the readings.

_____ **d.** There was a lot of new vocabulary.

_____ **e.** Other: ______________________________

6. What could you do next time to:
   a. better prepare for a listening passage?

   ____

   ____

   ____

   b. improve your effectiveness when speaking in a group?

   ____

   ____

   ____

7. Look back at the goals you set at the beginning of this chapter.
   a. Which goals did you achieve?

   ____

   ____

   ____

   b. What will be your primary goal in the next chapter?

   ____

   ____

   ____

Academic Dishonesty—How Common Is Cheating?

6

CHAPTER

INTRODUCTION

In the previous chapter, you examined truthtelling in the field of medicine. In this chapter, you will listen to a passage that relates to academic dishonesty. In the first two parts of the passage, you will hear the radio interviewer give background information. In the third part, the interviewer will talk to two university experts on the subject of cheating. In addition to listening to the tape, you will have opportunities to read about and discuss this interesting and controversial subject.

Background Knowledge Check

The following items reflect some of the content that you will find in this chapter. Write **a, b, c,** or **d** next to each item in the list according to the following:

IT WORKS! Learning Strategy: Using Prior Knowledge

(a) I have never heard of this.
(b) I have heard of this, but I don't really know what it means.
(c) I have some idea of what this means, but I'm not sure about it.
(d) I have a clear idea of what this means and can explain it.

_____ **1.** Cheating

_____ **2.** Plagiarism

_____ **3.** Crib notes

_____ **4.** Honor code

Students who have chosen **d** for any of the items should *briefly* explain what these items mean. If no one has chosen **d,** don't worry. You will have a chance to learn more about these as you progress through the chapter.

Setting Goals

Complete the following statement by checking the goals you want to achieve in this chapter.

IT WORKS! Learning Strategy: Setting Goals

While working on this chapter, I will make an effort to:

_____ **1.** speak more while I am working in a small group.

_____ **2.** give others a chance to speak while working in a small group.

_____ **3.** show others that I am actively listening by looking into their eyes and nodding as they talk.

_____ **4.** ask more questions in front of the whole class.

_____ **5.** make more comments in front of the whole class.

_____ **6.** monitor one aspect of my pronunciation, such as ________________.

_____ **7.** monitor one aspect of grammar as I speak, such as _______________.

_____ **8.** use some of the new vocabulary when speaking, both in and out of class.

_____ **9.** listen to the radio and watch TV outside of class.

_____ **10.** learn about the subject of cheating in schools.

_____ **11.** try to achieve another goal, such as ______________________________

____.

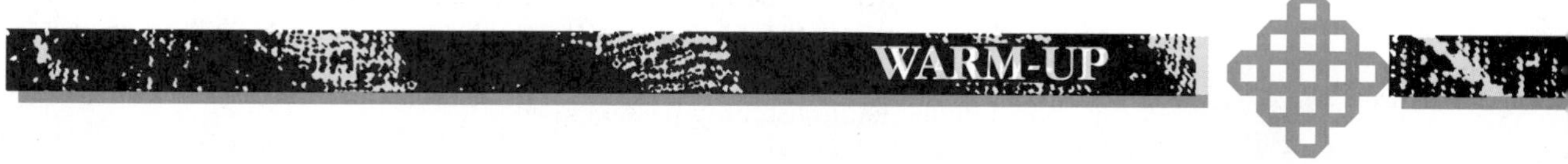

WARM-UP

It is said that a picture is worth a thousand words. Look at the picture below and then answer these questions orally or in writing:

- What is the student doing?
- Why do you think he is doing it?
- Is it common in your native country?
- Do you think it is common in the United States and Canada?
- Should he be punished? Why or why not?
- What adjectives describe this kind of behavior?

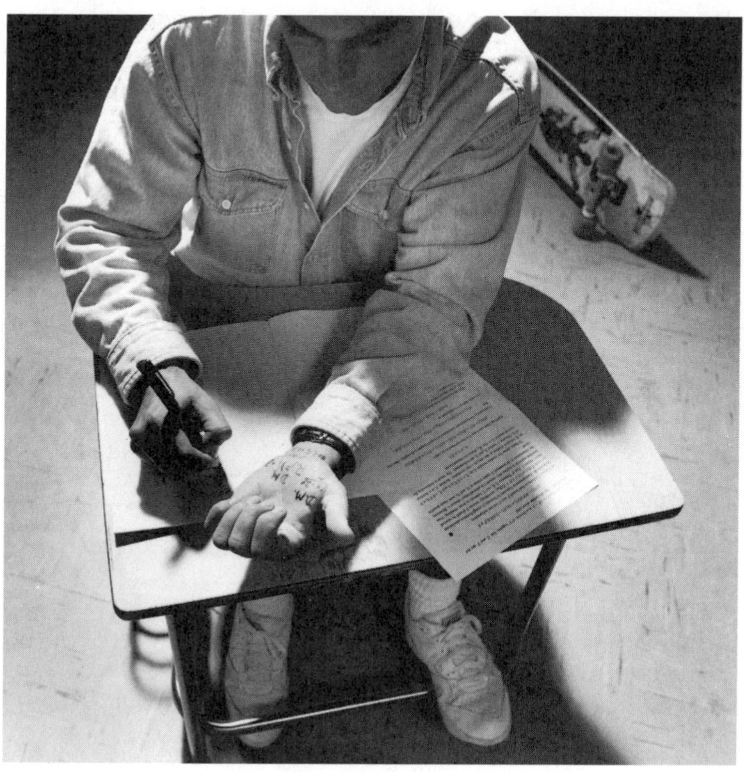

PART I: LISTENING

Before You Listen

BACKGROUND INFORMATION

Read the following excerpt from a *Washington Post* article entitled "College Cribbers . . . Ethics May Be In, but So Is Cheating." The discussion in this article is about the results of the "Academic Honesty" survey conducted by Professor Donald McCabe, one of the speakers that you will soon be listening to in a National Public Radio listening passage:

> "I haven't shocked anyone with my survey," asserts Donald McCabe, an associate professor of business ethics at Rutgers University Graduate School of Management who not long ago conducted a broad-scale study of college cheating. . . . In his four-page questionnaire filled out anonymously by 6,097 students from 31 of America's most scholastically elite schools, 67 percent admitted cheating at least once in college; 41 percent of undergraduates admitted cheating on exams and 19 percent admitted cheating on four or more tests. . . .

Source: *Washington Post,* January 6, 1992, p. C5.

Threads

The word "cheater" comes from "escheator," which was an officer of the King who received dues and taxes.

Below are some of the actual questions from the Academic Honesty Survey that Dr. McCabe is referring to. Try to answer these questions. Your answers should be based on either your high school or college experience.

1. In your opinion, what percentage of your classmates have cheated on a test, exam, or paper?

______ None ______ 1-5 % ______ 6-10% ______ 11-20%

______ 21-30% ______ 31-40% ______ 41-50% ______ Over 50%

2. How frequently do you think any of the following occur?

	Never	**Seldom**	**Very Seldom**	**Often**	**Very Often**
*Stealing from the library	______	______	______	______	______
**Plagiarism	______	______	______	______	______
Cheating during exams/tests	______	______	______	______	______

*Choose two students to ask the school librarian and report to the class at the next class meeting.

**This word is defined in the last item in Question 3 that follows.

Since Question 3 is very personal, you don't have to answer this question in writing. Just *think* about your responses.

3. Have you ever:	**Never**	**Once**	**A Few Times**	**Many Times**
used crib notes (cheat notes) on a test?	____	____	X	____
copied from another student during a test?	____	____	X	____
seen another student cheating on a test?	____	____	____	X
used unfair methods to learn what was on a test before it was given?	X	____	____	____
copied material, almost word for word, from any source and turned it in as your own work (plagiarized)?	____	____	X	____

4. What do you think the typical teacher would do if he/she knew someone had cheated on a test or assignment?

____ Probably nothing

____ Refer the matter to the appropriate authority for handling

____ Give the student a warning

____ Give the student a failing grade on the test/assignment

____ Give the student a failing grade in the course

____ Other (Please specify: ______________________________)

Now, answer these questions:

- Why do you think Professor McCabe conducted this study?
- Do you think that the subject of academic dishonesty should be discussed in classes? Why or why not?
- Dr. McCabe's findings were reported on the radio, on TV, and in newspapers and magazines. Why do you think there was so much interest in his research?

As You Listen

Part A:

1. Listen, and connect what you hear to the concept map below. Then complete the empty circle in the middle.

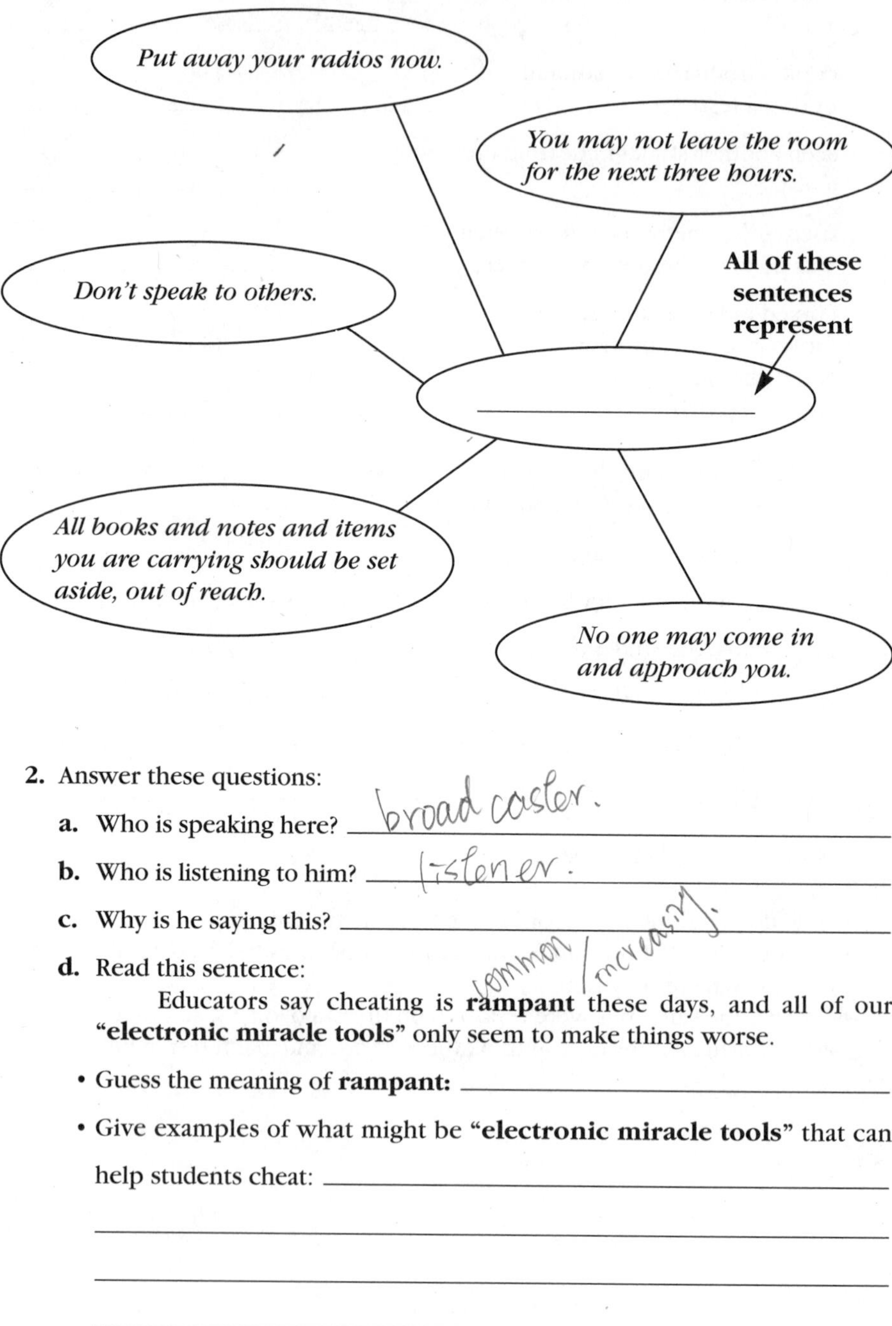

Put away your radios now.
You may not leave the room for the next three hours.
Don't speak to others.
All of these sentences represent
All books and notes and items you are carrying should be set aside, out of reach.
No one may come in and approach you.

2. Answer these questions:

   a. Who is speaking here? ______

   b. Who is listening to him? ______

   c. Why is he saying this? ______

   d. Read this sentence:

   Educators say cheating is **rampant** these days, and all of our **"electronic miracle tools"** only seem to make things worse.

   • Guess the meaning of **rampant:** ______

   • Give examples of what might be **"electronic miracle tools"** that can help students cheat: ______

LISTEN FOR JUST ONE IDEA

Part B: Listen to Part B. First write, and then tell a partner *one* point that you remember most vividly.

One point that I remember: ______________________________

____

LEARNING STRATEGY

Managing Your Learning: By focusing your attention on finding the specific information that you need, you increase your chances for success and have a concrete way to identify parts that you understood.

LISTEN FOR DETAILS

First, read the questions below.
Then listen to Part B again and try to answer the questions.

1. Here's the "pop quiz" that the speaker gives to his listeners. What is the correct answer to his question about how many students admit to cheating?
   - **a.** 1/4 of the student body
   - **b.** 1/2 of the student body
   - **c.** 1/3 of the student body
   - **d.** 2/3 of the student body

   Guess what he means by "the student body." ______________________________

2. List the kinds of cheating that he mentions by completing these phrases:
   - **a.** stealing ______________________________
   - **b.** copying ______________________________
   - **c.** groups of students joining together to ______________________________

3. What happened in India? ______________________________

   ____

   ____

GUESS BY USING BACKGROUND KNOWLEDGE

To answer the questions below, you will need to try to guess the meanings of some words that occur at the end of Part B on the tape.

IT WORKS! Learning Strategy: Guessing Meanings

- First, read the questions below, and then listen again to the end of Part B where *Cheating 101* is discussed.
- Then, try to answer the questions with a partner.
- Listen again to see if the tape now makes more sense to you.

The student author at Rutgers University sold a **"how-to guide for would-be cheaters"** called *Cheating 101.* Figure out what this phrase means by analyzing its separate words:

1. **guide**—Think of a tour guide. What does it tell its readers? ____________
2. **would-be**—Think of conditional sentences such as "I **would be** happy if I got an A on the test." Compare this sentence to "They would be cheaters if they knew how to cheat."

   Would-be cheaters, then, are probably people who ____________
3. At many colleges and universities in the United States, introductory courses are given the number "101." Why do you think, then, that the author of *Cheating 101* gave his book that title? ____________
4. Now, answer this question: What is a "how-to guide for would-be cheaters"?

   ____

   ____

Before You Listen

Part C: In Part C, you will hear a discussion with the interviewer, Professor Donald McCabe of Rutgers University, and Sally Cole, Judicial Affairs Officer at Stanford University.

VOCABULARY PREPARATION FOR LISTENING

Read the following sentences from the discussion, and then, in the matching exercise that follows, try to match up the **boldfaced** words with their definitions.

NOTE: The spaces at the left will be used as you listen to Part C. Leave them blank for now.

_____ **1.** . . . the students who were participating in the survey . . . were asked to indicate whether they had ever **engaged in** any of the following list of activities, each of which, **um,** was dishonest, and therefore a form of cheating, though they certainly **ranged widely in severity** from **padding** a few items on a bibliography . . . to purchasing a term paper from a "paper factory" and submitting it with one's own name on it.

_____ **2.** [Purchasing a term paper from a "paper factory"—] That's when you **hand in** a research paper that someone else has written and you . . . you've . . . paid fifty **bucks** or something for it.

____ 3. I've become convinced after looking at the responses of the over 6,000 students that responded to my survey that students have a somewhat different **perspective** on what **constitutes explicit cheating. . . .**

____ 4. There are many students out there, according to the results I found, that are cheating because everybody else is. It's a very **standard justification,** and as Sally said, that doesn't make it right. But I think I can **appreciate** more now that I've done the survey than I did before, that students today, with all the pressures that graduate schools put on their **G.P.A.s . . .**, feel it very difficult to sit in a class when they see other students cheating in a given course and not cheat themselves.

____ 5. A lot of these issues of what **constitutes** cheating depends . . . especially rules concerning **collaboration,** it will depend on what the instructor's guidelines are. . . .

____ 6. How **widespread** do you think it ["classic cheating"] is?

Matching: Write the letter of the definition on the right next to the word or phrase that you think it defines.

f 1. **engaged in** activities
k 2. **um**
l 3. **ranged widely in severity**
a 4. **padding** a few items on a bibliography
e 5. **hand in** a research paper
b 6. paid fifty **bucks**
c 7. a different **perspective** on
d 8. what **constitutes explicit cheating**
m 9. It's a very **standard justification**
j 10. I can **appreciate** more now
h 11. **G.P.A.s**
g 12. rules concerning **collaboration**
i 13. **widespread**

a. dishonestly adding
b. dollars
c. a different view about
d. what is *real* cheating
e. submit, give
f. participated in
g. rules about working together
h. grade point averages
i. common
j. understand
k. a sound made while thinking
l. varied in seriousness
m. a very common excuse

As You Listen

LISTEN FOR VOCABULARY

Have the Part C Vocabulary Preparation exercise on pages 150–151 in front of you as you listen to Part C. As you listen, quickly put checks (√) in the spaces next to the sentences that you hear.

Dr. Donald McCabe

LISTEN FOR DETAILS

Before you listen again, look at the incomplete notes below. Then, as you listen, try to write down whatever details you can catch. (See Appendix B for information on note-taking.)

IT WORKS! Learning Strategy: Taking Notes

Notes

Definition of cheating:

- Cole:

- McCabe:

Cheating to buy notes?

- Cole:

How widespread at Cole's and McCabe's schools?

- Cole:
- McCabe:

After You Listen

FOCUS ON NOTE TAKING

Join one or two students to compare notes. Fill in what you are missing, and discuss any parts where your notes differ in content. If necessary, listen again to Part C.

FOCUS ON REPEATING WHAT YOU HEARD

LEARNING STRATEGY

Remembering New Material: Learning vocabulary in a structured context enables you to remember it and use it in different situations.

In groups of three, orally *reconstruct,* or rebuild, your notes. One member of each group will present what Cole and McCabe said about the definition of cheating. Another member will present what Cole said about buying notes. The third member will present what Cole and McCabe said about how widespread cheating is at their campuses.

STEPS

a. Get into groups of three. Decide on which section of the outline each student will reconstruct.

b. Listen once more to Part C, giving special attention to *your own* section. Add any new information that you hear to your part of the outline.

c. While glancing at the notes, orally reconstruct the outline:

- Use phrases that indicate whose ideas you are giving, such as "according to," "in x's opinion," "x believes that," and so on.
- Please be careful not to add any information that was not on the tape, and don't add your opinion. Your goal here is to present what was said.
- While each person is speaking, the two listeners should indicate that they are paying attention by making eye contact with the speaker and occasionally nodding and smiling. (See Appendix D for information on how to be an active listener.)

d. Choose three students from different groups to come to the front of the class to present their oral reconstructions.

FOCUS ON SUMMARIZING

LEARNING STRATEGY

Managing Your Learning: Using new vocabulary to express the main idea and give some details demonstrates that you are making specific progress.

On a separate sheet of paper, write a one-paragraph summary of Part C as you refer to your notes. Begin your first sentence as follows: "In the "Academic Dishonesty" discussion, the speakers talk about . . ." Complete that sentence with the main idea of the listening passage. As you write the rest of the summary, be sure to indicate whose ideas you are presenting by using phrases such as "according to."

NOTE: If you use a speaker's exact words, put them between quotation marks. Otherwise, you will be plagiarizing! For instructions on how to summarize, see Appendix A.

Threads

If an author is once detected in borrowing, he will be suspected of plagiarism ever after.

William Hazlitt

FOCUS ON LANGUAGE

LEARNING STRATEGY

Managing Your Learning: By paying attention to the ways native speakers pronounce words and use special expressions in certain situations (such as when asking for clarification), you learn from many models.

Listen once more to Part C. Now that you understand the *content* of Part C, focus on the *way* the speakers communicate with each other. The following questions will be your guide.

1. When he introduces Professor McCabe, the host stumbles on two sounds when he says the words "business ethics." What two English sounds does he mix up? ______________________

   (The message to you: Even native speakers can stumble in pronunciation.)
2. What phrase does the host use to get the discussion started after he finishes introducing the professor?

   I ______________________ (2 words total)

   (The message to you: When you want to start a conversation with someone, you might want to start with, "I understand [that] . . ." or "I've heard [that] . . .")
3. When Sally Cole defines cheating, she gives a long definition. The most important words in her definition are said louder and stronger than the others, and those words are also given higher intonation. Can you catch some of those important words? Try to write five of them here:

   HINT: Most of the words are nouns or adjectives.

   ____

   ____

   (The message to you: The most important words—usually nouns, adjectives, adverbs, and main verbs—usually receive the strongest stress and intonation.)
4. After Sally Cole mentions purchasing a term paper from a "paper factory," the host needs some clarification, so he *rephrases* what she said in a statement. Rephrasing is a method of putting what someone else said into your own words so that you can find out if you understood what you heard. Here is part of what the host said. Try to fill in the missing words:

   That's when you hand in a research paper that ______________

   ____

   and you've paid fifty bucks or something for it.

   (The message to you: When you want to make sure that you understood what someone said, you can try to repeat the idea in your own words.)

5. What does Sally Cole say to the host to let him know that he understood what she meant?

____

(The message to you: After you rephrase what people have said, they will let you know if you accurately caught their point. If your rephrasing is inaccurate, then you will probably hear an explanation.)

6. When the host asks Professor McCabe for his definitions of cheating, the Professor expresses agreement with what Sally Cole said, but he needs to add an explanation. What does he say?

   I think I would generally agree with what Sally said, with possibly

____.

(The message to you: It's important to learn polite ways to express partial agreement and then add more details.)

7. When the host asks Sally Cole about how widespread "classic cheating" is on the Stanford University campus, she doesn't really understand the question.

   First, she pauses, and then what does she ask? ____________________

(The message to you: When you don't understand a particular part of what someone has said, ask, "What do you mean by . . .?")

   How does the host respond to this question?

Well, ____________, isn't it? Uh, I ____________, uh . . .

(The message to you: Phrases such as "That's a good question" and sounds such as "uh" and "um" give the speaker some thinking time before answering an unexpected question.)

LISTENING LOG

IT WORKS!
Learning Strategy:
Practice Outside
the Classroom

Reminder: Keep up your Listening Log with as many entries as your teacher requires. At the end of Part II (Speaking), you will report on one of your entries in a small group. (If necessary, see Appendix F for more details on Listening Logs.)

ANY QUESTIONS?

IT WORKS!
Learning Strategy:
Clarifying

Before you go on to read about and discuss more issues about academic dishonesty, answer the following questions on a separate sheet of paper. Do not write your name on the paper. Your teacher or a classmate will collect the papers and share everyone's answers with the class.

1. What has been the most valuable aspect of this chapter for you so far?
2. What is still unclear?

PART II: SPEAKING

Discussion

The following discussion questions deal with different aspects of academic dishonesty. Choose the topic or topics you would like to discuss. Feel free to add related questions of your own to the questions that are asked here. And as always, you should focus on using new vocabulary and appropriate conversation skills.

When appropriate for the activity, work in small groups. Assign one person to act as discussion leader and another person to act as recorder. The discussion leader will make sure that everyone talks and stays on the subject. The recorder will take notes and later report briefly to the class on the main points of your group's discussion.

Before you begin, take a look at the conversation skills questionnaire on page 164 of this section. You will respond to the items on the questionnaire after your discussions have been completed. As you work in groups, keep the items on the questionnaire in mind.

1. In the cartoon below, Calvin and Hobbes discuss cheating on a test.

CALVIN and HOBBES

TODAY AT SCHOOL, I TRIED TO DECIDE WHETHER TO CHEAT ON MY TEST OR NOT.

I WONDERED, IS IT BETTER TO DO THE RIGHT THING AND FAIL ...OR IS IT BETTER TO DO THE WRONG THING AND SUCCEED?

ON THE ONE HAND, UNDESERVED SUCCESS GIVES NO SATISFACTION. ...BUT ON THE OTHER HAND, WELL-DESERVED FAILURE GIVES NO SATISFACTION EITHER.

OF COURSE, MOST EVERYBODY CHEATS SOME TIME OR OTHER. PEOPLE ALWAYS BEND THE RULES IF THEY THINK THEY CAN GET AWAY WITH IT. ...THEN AGAIN, THAT DOESN'T JUSTIFY **MY** CHEATING.

THEN I THOUGHT, LOOK, CHEATING ON ONE LITTLE TEST ISN'T SUCH A BIG DEAL. IT DOESN'T HURT ANYONE.

...BUT THEN I WONDERED IF I WAS JUST RATIONALIZING MY UNWILLINGNESS TO ACCEPT THE CONSEQUENCE OF NOT STUDYING.

STILL, IN THE REAL WORLD, PEOPLE CARE ABOUT SUCCESS, NOT PRINCIPLES.

...THEN AGAIN, MAYBE THAT'S WHY THE WORLD IS IN SUCH A MESS.

WHAT A DILEMMA!

SO WHAT DID YOU DECIDE?

NOTHING. I RAN OUT OF TIME AND I HAD TO TURN IN A BLANK PAPER.

ANYMORE, SIMPLY ACKNOWLEDGING THE ISSUE IS A MORAL VICTORY.

WELL, IT JUST SEEMED WRONG TO CHEAT ON AN ETHICS TEST.

Source: Cartoon by Watterson; © 1993 Andrews and McNeel, A Universal Press Syndicate Co.

First, choose two students to take the roles of Calvin and Hobbes and have them perform the dialogue that takes place in the cartoon strip.

Then, discuss these issues that are brought up:

a. Is it better to do the right thing and fail, or do the wrong thing and succeed?
b. Undeserved success gives no satisfaction.
c. Most everybody cheats some time or other.
d. People always bend the rules if they think they can get away with it.
e. Cheating doesn't hurt anyone.
f. In the real world, people care about success, not principles.

2. In your native country:
   a. How common is cheating in secondary schools? In colleges and universities?
   b. What are some methods of cheating that students use?
   c. When students enter big exams, do they have to present photo identification?
   d. Is it permissible to copy another writer's words exactly without identifying the writer and without using quotation marks? Explain.
   e. (Make up your own question) ______________________________

3. The following is an explanation of *plagiarism* given in a college policy statement on academic honesty:

> **Plagiarism:** Although difficult to define, plagiarism consists of taking the words or specific substance of another and either copying or paraphrasing the work without giving credit to the source. The following examples are only some of the many forms plagiarism may take:
>
> **a.** Submitting a term paper, examination, or other work written by someone else.
> **b.** Failure to give credit in a citation for ideas, statements of facts, or conclusions expressed by another.
> **c.** Failure to use quotation marks when quoting directly from another, whether it be a paragraph, a sentence, or even a part thereof.
> **d.** Inappropriate paraphrasing (e.g., over-reliance on sentence structure of the original author).

Threads

The Latin origin of "plagiarism" is "plagiarius," which means kidnapper, seducer, literary thief.

In the following chart, indicate whether or not **a, b, c,** and **d** above are considered acceptable in your native country:

	ACCEPTABLE	UNACCEPTABLE
a.	____________	____________
b.	____________	____________
c.	____________	____________
d.	____________	____________

If you indicated that any of the above are acceptable:

- Are you surprised that is not acceptable in the United States? Explain.
- What will you have to do if you take a writing or speech course in the United States?
- Can you remember now any instance in the past in which you were accused of plagiarizing in the United States? If yes, explain.

4. **a.** Read the following authentic letter written to a teacher by a student in a grammar class. Apparently the students sat at long tables rather than at individual desks, and when test time came, guess what happened!

Dear Teacher,

I study very hard every day and well into the night before exams. I do this so I can achieve a good grade I can be proud of. During EVERY test this year some students have been using cheat sheets, then allowing other students at the table to read their tests! They do this while you are in the room. I don't know what to do. I cannot tell on them by name but they are wrong and make my grade look bad. I don't know what you are doing when they pass around their tests, because I am afraid to look up and be accused of cheating. Please stop the cheating during tests. More and more of the other students are using cheat notes under their tests and showing them on to their friends. My grades are important to me and to have all this cheating around me while I work so hard is very depressing.

Sincerely,

A Concerned Student

b. If you were the teacher who received this letter, what would you do?

5. Read the following excerpt from a review of the book *Cheating 101.* You'll recall that this book, mentioned in Part B of the tape that you listened to earlier in this chapter, is a "how-to-cheat" guide written by Rutgers University senior, Michael Moore.

Student markets primer on the art of cheating

by Anthony Flint

One of the hottest books on college campuses isn't the latest collection of Calvin and Hobbes—it's a book about cheating.

Cheating 101 is a how-to guide on shortcuts to a degree—effective places to hide crib sheets, systems of foot signals for sharing multiple-choice answers, places to buy term papers, and dozens of other tips.

Michael Moore, 24, a Rutgers University senior and author of the book, has sold 5,000 copies, mostly at Rutgers, Ohio State, and the University of Maryland. He recently returned from a marketing road trip to Penn State. And he plans to go to Boston, home to 11 colleges and universities, to hawk the $7 book around spring break.

"We're going to hit Boston right after we hit Daytona Beach in March."

Moore, a journalism major, contracts with a printer to produce the 86-page book and sells it mostly out of his home in Hopewell, N.J. But because of the book's popularity, he takes sales operations on the road from time to time. Sometimes aided by a pre-visit article in a student newspaper, he sets up a table in a fraternity house or a room on campus and watches the money roll in.

Source: Reprinted courtesy of The Boston Globe, February 3, 1992.

Now, answer these questions:

- Do you think that it is right or wrong to sell a book that teaches people how to be dishonest?
- Why do you think Moore's book is so popular?
- Reread the book review, and then write your own discussion question about *Cheating 101* to ask your group or class:

____

____?

IT WORKS!
Learning Strategy:
Playing a Role

6. Perform the following role-plays:

   a. You are the student who wrote the letter to the grammar teacher in Discussion Question #4 on page 159. But you decided not to send the letter to the teacher. Instead, you are going to the teacher's office to talk in person about what's going on.

   Suggested first line: "Excuse me. May I come in?"

   b. Three people are on a TV talk show. One is an interviewer who has invited Michael Moore, the author of *Cheating 101,* along with a college teacher who is upset that someone is selling a book that teaches students how to cheat. The interviewer asks questions; Moore and the teacher argue.

   Suggested first lines: "Good afternoon, ladies and gentlemen. Today we have an exciting show for you. My guests are . . ."

7. With a partner, decide on the message of each of the following:

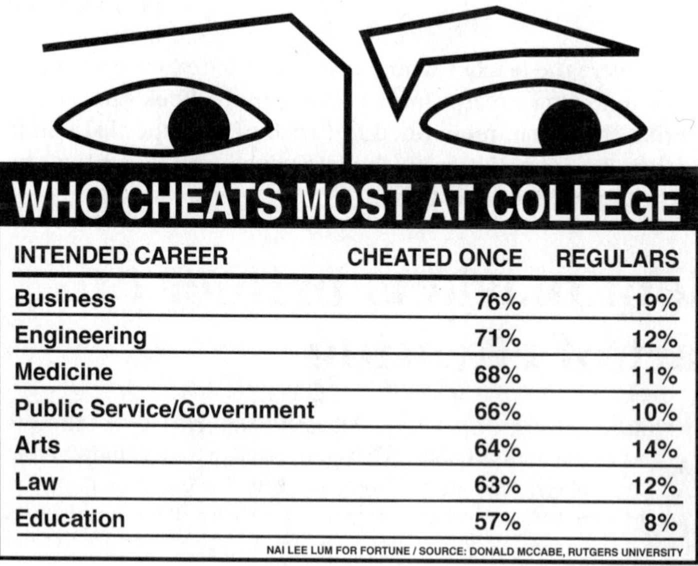

WHO CHEATS MOST AT COLLEGE

INTENDED CAREER	CHEATED ONCE	REGULARS
Business	76%	19%
Engineering	71%	12%
Medicine	68%	11%
Public Service/Government	66%	10%
Arts	64%	14%
Law	63%	12%
Education	57%	8%

NAI LEE LUM FOR FORTUNE / SOURCE: DONALD MCCABE, RUTGERS UNIVERSITY

Source: *Fortune*

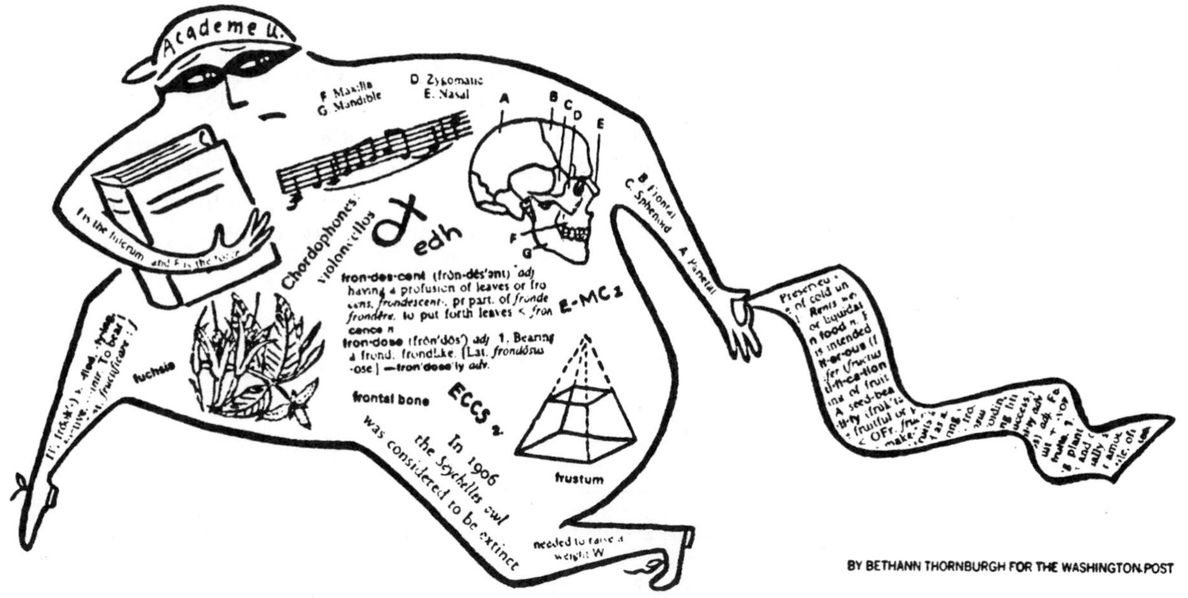

Source: Bethann Thornburgh

LEARNING STRATEGY

Understanding and Using Emotions: Discussing your feelings and reactions with others helps you clarify what you are thinking.

8. The following are excerpts from authentic letters to the editor of a professional journal for teachers. All three letters are by teachers who talk about cheating in their classes. Read the letters, and then for each, write a few words that indicate your reaction. When everyone is finished, discuss reactions in groups or as an entire class.

Letter 1

I have a strategy which prevents cheating rather than requires repair for the later damage.

As I hand out the first quiz or exam of the term, I loudly and clearly state, "Now, if you are going to cheat, make sure you copy from someone much smarter than you are!" The laughter that follows this pseudo-warning usually eases most students into the test. . . .

Karen Russikoff
California State Polytechnic University
Pomona, California, USA

Your Reaction: ____

____

____

Letter 2

I had some problems with students cheating, not because of different definitions but because in the "face-saving" culture in Indonesia, maintaining harmony is more important than maintaining fairness, and avoiding embarrassment is just as important as avoiding embarrassing someone else. Cheating is rampant because the accusing teacher loses more respect than the guilty student.

Bruce T. Sidebotham
Universitas Bung Hatt
Ulak Karang, Padang Indonesia

Your Reaction: ______________________________

____

____

Letter 3

If an entire class is furtively sharing answers under their breath, I warn the group firmly yet gently. If they persist, I say nothing and actually let them continue if they will. At the end of the test, I collect the papers as if nothing happened. That evening, I don't grade the papers or mark them in any way. The next class session, I simply announce that the class decided to do the test as a group effort and not as an individual test, and we will discuss it as class work and no grade will be given. We then go over the answers and say nothing more about it. I usually have fewer problems come next test!

John Wheeler
Štátny pedagogický ústav
Bratislava, Slovakia

Your Reaction: ______________________________

____

____

9. In the listening passage, Dr. Cole referred to the phenomenon of buying lecture notes. Read the following article on this subject. List the pros and cons of buying notes, and then discuss whether or not you agree with this practice.

No, but I bought the notes

by Ben Wildavsky

On page 32 of the Stanford University directory, alongside information on tutoring and study-abroad programs, an equally matter-of-fact listing offers students a scholarly shortcut that makes academic purists cringe.

Undergraduates "stuck in large classes" who want "to ease the boring lecture burden" can—for a modest price—hire an expert to go to class, take notes and type them up neatly for delivery within days.

Many students at Stanford and elsewhere are nonchalant about the practice, calling professional notes a harmless supplement to their own efforts. Even some professors have no objections.

But critics say that students who hire note-takers are, in effect, paying others to do their intellectual heavy lifting. Ultimately, the critics charge, buying class notes erodes the foundation of higher education.

"If you cruise through college just buying the notes and not going to class . . . it doesn't even begin to be a poor substitute for the intellectual engagement" that should be part of campus life, said Ann Franke, counsel to the American Association of University Professors.

Paid note-takers are hardly recent visitors to college lecture halls. One of the first note-taking services was founded in the 1930s to serve students at the University of California at Berkeley. Most other note-taking businesses opened over the past 25 years.

What has changed is the popularity of the services. They are now a fixture at many of the nation's large universities, from several UC campuses to Ohio State and Cornell. In some classes, a majority of students buy the notes.

Note-taking services typically hire juniors, seniors or graduate students and charge from $17 to $25 for a semester's worth of notes. Often printed on hard-to-photocopy red or green paper, the notes include disclaimers warning students not to skip class.

Many undergraduates insist that they really do use commercial notes as a backup, particularly in science and math courses where it can be hard to absorb the torrent of technical information delivered by some fast-talking professors. Other students concede that buying notes allows them to miss lectures, but say that is not necessarily a problem.

One recent morning in the UC Berkeley student union, sophomore Nikesh Desai joined a steady stream of students picking up Black Lightning lecture notes. "This summarizes it pretty well," he said, holding the latest installment of notes for his molecular cell biology class. "If I miss class, I don't feel bad or anything—I'm still studying the material."

Another customer, social-welfare major Nancy Gee, said it is common for students to share their class notes, even without a formal note-taking business. "They might as well make money out of it," she said. "It's a little bit of capitalism. . . . Ethically, well, you become accustomed to certain things."

Most note-taking services are nonprofits run by students, but some are private businesses operated off campus.

Copyright Lawsuit

Officials at the University of Florida sued an off-campus service called "A-Plus Notes" for copyright violation because it does not obtain professors' permission before taking and selling notes. The university lost in December, and an appeal is pending.

Most services do ask instructors' permission. Some even offer to pay professors royalties—50 cents for each subscriber in a class is the going rate at UC Berkeley. Still, a number of scholars refuse to give the go-ahead.

UC Berkeley plant biologist Richard Malkin, irked that students were skipping his 8 A.M. lectures, stopped allowing note-takers into his large introductory biology class several years ago. The quality of the Black Lightning notes also bothered him.

"There were just a lot of gaps," he said.

Stanford political scientist David Abernethy also keeps paid note-takers out of his classroom, saying students learn more actively when they take their own notes. "The more I'm engaged in interpreting things that I'm hearing using my own words and activating my brain to put them in those words, the more I'm likely to retain what goes on in class," he said.

Laissez-Faire

Other professors take a more laissez-faire approach.

"Whatever way they can learn the material is fine with me," said Berkeley chemistry professor Peter Vollhardt, whose organic chemistry class included about 400 Black Lightning subscribers in the past semester. "They're adults."

Vollhardt speaks more highly than Malkin of the quality of the commercial notes. But Black Lightning takes no chances. It includes a line in each subscription contract saying it takes no responsibility for inaccuracies.

An entire body of research on student note-taking has been published in educational journals. Kristin King reviewed it for her University of Oregon master's thesis and found that calling in professionals can be beneficial.

King is hardly a disinterested party—she runs Footnotes, the campus note-taking service. She found that students' own notes often fail to record the most important parts of a lecture.

As for class attendance, King surveyed 637 students and found that three-quarters said they used Footnotes to supplement their own notes.

Even students who defend note-takers admit to some qualms.

Mike Payne, a 20-year-old Stanford sophomore from Los Altos who earns $14 per lecture as a note-taker in a human biology course, said some students have legitimate reasons for buying notes. But, he added, college is so expensive these days that skipping class just seems foolish.

10. Of course, cheating doesn't occur only *in* school; it occurs in all areas of society. Read the following excerpt from a newspaper article about a school district superintendent who falsely wrote on his résumé that he had received a doctorate (Ph.D.) from Stanford University:

School chief resigns—lied about degree San Jose official claimed he had doctorate

by David Sylvester and Dan Turner

The trustees of the San Jose Unified School District accepted the **resignation** yesterday of the district's popular **superintendent** for **faking** his **résumé** and planned to turn the matter over to police for possible prosecution.

James Baughman, superintendent of the district since 1989, confessed to the board Wednesday that he had lied about receiving a doctorate from Stanford University. Baughman, 39, who had **raced up the ladder** in the district, told the board he had a friend **fabricate** the Stanford **transcripts.**

"There were several times he wanted to come forward and say something, but you dig yourself in a hole and you can't get out," said board member Carol Myers.

Richard Couser, board president, said the board decided to file a police report because Baughman had been paid an additional **stipend** for four years based on the false credential. Baughman actually received bachelor's and master's degrees from Santa Clara University.

The board **wrestled** with its decision for eight hours yesterday because Baughman was credited with helping **turn the troubled district around** in the past three years. Couser said he "felt sick" when he learned about the faked resume. "I feel like one of my kids fell off the face of the earth," he said.

Jack Farrell, acting registrar at Stanford, said Baughman was never enrolled there.

"Because this is a matter of public record, I don't understand why a search committee didn't call, said Cecelia Burciaga, a development officer with Stanford's Office of Student Affairs. "This could have been found out at any time by anyone."

Burciaga said she was working as associate dean of graduate studies last summer when a student called asking to see Baughman's doctoral **dissertation** in the psychology department. Burciaga said she checked with the registrar and discovered there was no record that he had received a degree.

resignation: formal statement that one is giving up a job
superintendent: supervisor of a school district
faking: writing lies
résumé: list of educational and professional experience
raced up the ladder: reached success quickly
fabricate: create something false
transcripts: official school documents with grades and degrees
stipend: additional pay
wrestled: struggled
turn the troubled district around: reverse; go from problematic to much better
dissertation: thesis; formal piece of writing required for Ph.D.

Now, answer these questions:

- According to the article, James Baughman was very good at his job. Do you think he should have been fired? Why or why not?
- If you think he should be punished, what kind of punishment would you recommend?
- Do you know anyone who lied about qualifications in order to get a job? If yes, please explain what happened.
- Is lying about your qualifications ever justifiable?

11. Now, think about one group that you worked with while discussing topics in this section. Evaluate your conversational skills by filling out this questionnaire:

CONVERSATION SKILLS QUESTIONNAIRE FOR DISCUSSION QUESTION # ______			
While talking to classmates,	**Often**	**Sometimes**	**Never**
1. I checked to make sure that everyone understood what I said by asking such questions as "Do you know what I mean?" and "Are you following me?"	______	______	______
2. I gave explanations, definitions, and specific examples when I saw that members of my group weren't following me. I used sentences such as "Let me explain that" and "To help you understand, I'll give you an example."	______	______	______
3. I asked specific questions, such as "What do you mean by ______?" and "Could you give an example of ______?" and "Could you explain the part about ______?" when I needed clarification.	______	______	______
4. I paraphrased what others said to make sure that I understood. I used sentences such as "In other words, you mean ______" and "You're saying, then, that ______."	______	______	______
5. I encouraged others to speak by making such remarks as "I'd like to know what ______ thinks about that" and "What do you think, ______?"	______	______	______

Guest Speaker

Invite a teacher or administrator from your school to come to your class to talk about the subject of academic dishonesty (policies, honor codes, punishment, etc.). Follow the steps for inviting a guest speaker in Appendix I.

Listening Log Report

Bring your Listening Log to class and report on one entry in a small group. Take turns doing the following:

- Tell your group members what you watched or listened to.
- Give a short oral summary followed by your personal reaction. Do not read what you have written.
- Check your listeners' comprehension by asking questions such as "Do you understand what I mean?" and "Am I being clear?"
- Rephrase or restate to make your points clear.
- Answer your listeners' questions and ask for their reactions.

FOLLOW-UP

Choose any of the following activities to do outside of class and then report on what happened or what you found out. These activities can be done individually, in pairs, or in small groups. (Refer to Oral Presentation Feedback Forms in Appendix L.)

1. Find out if your school has a policy on academic honesty and/or an honor code. If a policy or code exists, try to get a copy for your class to analyze and discuss.
2. Rent the movie *School Ties,* which is about about a Jewish boy at a private boarding school who witnesses a classmate cheating. After the teacher finds cheat notes on the classroom floor after a test, the teacher announces that all students will be expelled from the school unless the cheater confesses or a witness comes forward. Soon after you see the movie, write down your personal reaction in a paragraph so that you will remember your thoughts when you report to your class.
3. Ask a native speaker of English to explain any of the following idioms that are new to you. If possible, ask for sentences containing these idioms, and share the sentences that you collected with your class.

IT WORKS! Learning Strategy: Asking Questions

- *to stretch the truth*
- *to bend the rules*
- *to take credit for something you haven't done*
- *to get away with something*
- *to keep your eyes on your own paper*
- *to watch someone like a hawk*
- *to be kicked out of school*
- *to turn someone in*
- *to tell on someone*
- *to squeal on someone*

Threads

There was things which he stretched, but mainly he told the truth.

Mark Twain, 1835–1910

4. In your school or local library, explain to a librarian that you are a student and have a few brief questions to ask about library theft for a homework assignment. Here are some questions to ask:

- How common is it for people to steal books and periodicals?
- How common is it for people to rip out pages from books and periodicals? Why do they do this?
- What security measures have been taken to decrease these problems? Report your findings to your class.

5. Conduct a survey about cheating at your own school. See Appendix K for guidelines on how to create questions for a survey and how to compile responses.
6. To gather material for a speech on ethics, go to the library and look up ethics, honesty, lying, and cheating. Look for specific incidents to describe that relate to cheating in school, lying on applications, corporate theft of new technology, and so on.

LEARNING ASSESSMENT

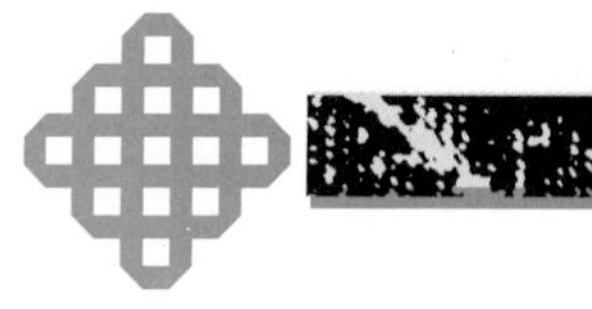

IT WORKS! Learning Strategy: Evaluating Your Progress

1. Look back at Part I (Listening) of this chapter. What activities helped you most in understanding the listening passages?

____

____

____

2. Give an example of when you had trouble understanding what you heard.

____

____

____

Why did you have difficulty?

_____ **a.** I didn't know the vocabulary.

_____ **b.** I wasn't paying attention.

_____ **c.** The speaker wasn't clear.

_____ **d.** The speaker spoke too fast.

_____ **e.** Other: _______________________________

3. Were you more successful than you expected to be in understanding the listening material about academic dishonesty? Were you less successful than you expected? Why?

____

____

____

4. Look back at Part II (Speaking) of this chapter. Give one or two examples of your most successful efforts at oral communication. Try to explain why you were able to succeed.

____

____

____

5. Give an example of a discussion in which you had trouble communicating with your classmates.

____

____

____

Why did you have difficulty?

_____ **a.** My classmates didn't understand my pronunciation.

_____ **b.** I didn't understand my classmates' pronunciation.

_____ **c.** I had trouble finding the main ideas in the readings.

_____ **d.** There was a lot of new vocabulary.

_____ **e.** Other: ______________________________

6. What could you do next time to:

a. better prepare for a listening passage?

____

____

____

b. improve your effectiveness when speaking in a group?

____

____

____

7. Look back at the goals you set at the beginning of this chapter.

a. Which goals did you achieve?

____

____

____

b. What will be your primary goal in the next chapter?

____

____

____

Smells and Behavior—How We Are Influenced

7

CHAPTER

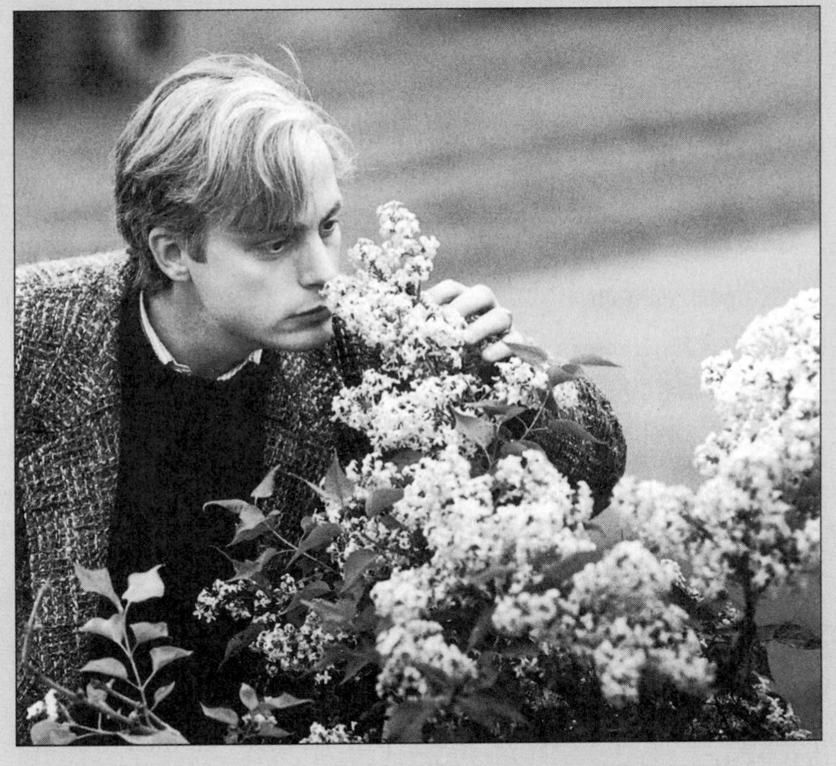

INTRODUCTION

In the previous two chapters, you considered the use of deception in medicine and academia. Now you will have the chance to think about something completely different—smells. Most of us think about smells only in terms of things smelling good or bad. But how often do we consider the effects particular smells might have on our behavior? We may not have thought about this, but scientists certainly have. In this chapter, you will learn more about some of the current research into the effects of smells on behavior and about some of the ways smells are being used in the marketing world.

Background Knowledge Check

The following items reflect some of the content that you will find in this chapter. Write **a, b, c,** or **d** next to each item in the list according to the following:

(a) I have never heard of this.
(b) I have heard of this, but I don't really know what it means.
(c) I have some idea of what this means, but I'm not sure about it.
(d) I have a clear idea of what this means and can explain it.

_____ **1.** The reasons why smells activate our memories more than the other senses

_____ **2.** Smell research

_____ **3.** Why smell research is of interest to people in marketing

_____ **4.** The impact smells could have on our lives in the future

_____ **5.** The Smell and Taste Treatment and Research Foundation

Students who have chosen **d** for any of the above should *briefly* explain what these items mean. If no one has chosen **d,** don't worry. You will have a chance to learn more about these as you progress through the chapter.

Setting Goals

Complete the following statement by checking the goals you want to achieve in this chapter.

mold.

IT WORKS! Learning Strategy: Setting Goals

While working on this chapter, I will make an effort to:

_____ **1.** speak more while I am working in a small group.

_____ **2.** give others a chance to speak while working in a small group.

_____ **3.** show others that I am actively listening by looking into their eyes and nodding as they talk.

_____ **4.** ask more questions in front of the whole class.

_____ **5.** make more comments in front of the whole class.

_____ **6.** monitor one aspect of my pronunciation, such as ________________.

_____ **7.** monitor one aspect of grammar as I speak, such as ________________.

_____ **8.** use some of the new vocabulary when speaking, both in and out of class.

_____ **9.** listen to radio and television interview programs outside of class.

_____ **10.** start a conversation outside of class to discuss the issues raised in this chapter.

_____ **11.** try to achieve another goal, such as ______________________________ ____.

WARM-UP

"Your magazine smells fabulous. May I kiss you?"

Source: Drawing by Weber; © 1992, *The New Yorker* Magazine, Inc.

Threads

The first newspaper with a perfumed advertising page was issued on March 25, 1937 by the *Daily News* in Washington D.C.

1. What point do you think the cartoon is making?
2. What is your reaction to it?
3. What do you think of magazines that come with perfumed pages?
4. Do you think a smell can make people change their behavior?

IT WORKS! Learning Strategy: Using Laughter

Age had a big influence on olfactory recall. People born before 1930 found that fragrances from nature were most evocative. These included pine, hay, horses, sea air, and meadows. People born after 1930 were more apt **to wax** nostalgic over food odors and synthetic smells. The younger the respondent, the more likely that the trigger was **synthetic.** Among people 20 to 30 years old, sentimental scents **emanated** from crayons, men's cologne, chlorine, window cleaner, motor oil, and car exhaust.

These findings are enough to make a marketing manager **salivate. Subliminal** fragrance cues are already common in manufacturing and sales. When supermarkets spray a baked goods scent around cake and cookie displays, sales in those areas go up. Hirsch found that when a pleasant odor **concocted** in his lab was circulated around Las Vegas **slot machines,** customers spent significantly more. By the 21st century, he says, "the use of odors to market products will be as common as Muzak is today."

Source: The Boston Globe Magazine, January 24, 1993

olfactory: of or about the sense of smell
gauging: measuring
replicate: reproduce
nostalgic: feeling fondness for something or some period in the past
evoke: produce a memory or feeling
stimuli: things that cause activity
threat: a possible danger
subjective: influenced by personal feelings
objective: not influenced by personal feelings
cerebral cortex: the gray matter covering the outer surface of the brain
assess: judge, evaluate
neurologist: a doctor who treats or studies diseases of the nervous system
randomly: without any fixed plan
triggered: caused something to happen
yeasty: pertaining to yeast, the material that makes bread rise and become light and soft
likely: probable
foul: evil-smelling
to wax: to grow, to become
synthetic: artificially produced
emanated: came out from
salivate: produce an increased amount of saliva, the liquid in the mouth
subliminal: at a level of the mind that the senses are not conscious of
concocted: made by mixing and combining
slot machines: gambling machines operated by putting coins in a slot

VOCABULARY PREPARATION FOR LISTENING TO "SMELLS AND BEHAVIOR"

IT WORKS! Learning Strategy: Cooperating

The following phrases come from the National Public Radio listening passage you are about to hear. Circle the *italicized* words and phrases that you think you already know. Explain their meanings to a partner.

1. . . . bakers *figured out* a long time ago that *venting* their ovens onto the sidewalk will *lure* in *drooling* customers . . .
2. . . . the study you did involved *odorizing* a Las Vegas *casino* . . .
3. . . . *slot machines* were treated with different smells . . .
4. . . . in the presence of a pleasant *odor* . . .
5. . . . this smells like *baked goods* or whatever . . .
6. . . . we're just at the *tip of the iceberg* . . .
7. . . . this does have other *applications* . . .
8. . . . oh, *by all means* . . .
9. . . . in terms of leisure-time *gambling* . . .
10. . . . it makes you more awake and *alert* . . .
11. . . . depending on how your *spouse* feels . . .
12. . . . our eyes and ears *are* constantly *assaulted by* manipulations . . .
13. . . . can't we just *leave* the nose *alone?* . . .
14. . . . the nose is being assaulted *anyhow* . . .

As You Listen

LISTEN FOR WORDS IN CONTEXT

IT WORKS!* *Learning Strategy: Guessing Meaning

Keep the preceding phrases in front of you, and circle the number of each phrase as you hear it. When the tape stops, discuss with your teacher and classmates the meaning of the vocabulary words and phrases.

LISTEN FOR THE MAIN IDEA

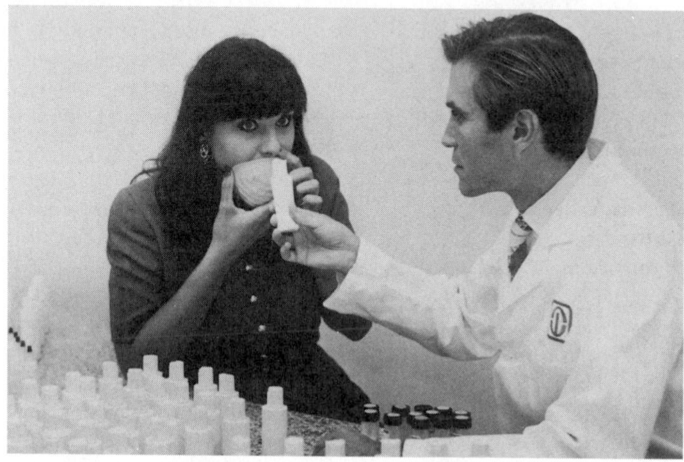

Dr. Alan R. Hirsch, neurological director of the Chicago based Smell and Taste Treatment and Research Foundation, with one of the nearly one thousand participants in his study testing smells associated with childhood memories.

1. Listen to the tape again. After you listen, write down short answers to the following questions.
   a. What kind of research does Dr. Alan Hirsch do?
   ____
   b. How does Dr. Hirsch think understanding smells will have an impact on how we live in the future?
   ____
2. Now combine your answers to **a** and **b** above into one single summary sentence that reveals the main point of the interview that you have just heard. The sentence has been started for you, as follows:

   According to Dr. Alan Hirsch, ______________________________
   ____
   ____

LISTEN FOR DETAILS

First, read the questions below. Then listen to the tape again and circle the letter of the correct answer for each item.

1. Researchers in Chicago released a study which said that
   a. we should take more risks with our money.
   b. smells influence the way we feel.
   c. a good smell will make us spend more money.

2. Dr. Hirsch's research involved
   - **a.** deodorizing a Las Vegas bank.
   - **b.** smell and taste in Chicago.
   - **c.** adding odors to two different areas in a casino.
3. In the presence of a pleasant odor, the amount of increase in money that people put into slot machines was
   - **a.** 4.511 percent
   - **b.** 45.11 percent
   - **c.** 40.51 percent
4. What did this particular odor smell like?
   - **a.** Baked goods or bananas
   - **b.** Baked goods
   - **c.** It's hard to say
5. How does Dr. Hirsch envision smells as part of our life in the year 2010?
   - **a.** They will make us wake up and go to the health club.
   - **b.** They will intensify whatever it is we are doing.
   - **c.** They will have no real impact.
6. How does the interviewer probably feel about having smells added to our environment?

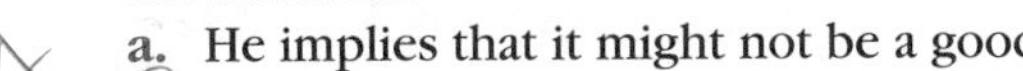

   - **a.** He implies that it might not be a good idea.
   - **b.** He probably likes the idea.
   - **c.** He probably has no opinion.
7. Dr. Hirsch suggests that
   - **a.** the smells of carpet clearner and deodorizer are pleasant.
   - **b.** smells are everywhere and we should use them to help people.
   - **c.** assaulting the nose is not a bad thing.

After You Listen

FOCUS ON SUMMARIZING

IT WORKS! Learning Strategy: Summarizing

Now that you have listened to the tape several times, on a separate sheet of paper, copy the one-sentence summary you wrote when you listened for the main idea on page 174. Add two or three sentences with some details that would help clarify the main idea for someone who hasn't heard this tape.

Then, in a separate paragraph, write your personal reaction.

FOCUS ON IDIOMS

1. When the interviewer asks Dr. Hirsch if there are any applications to this smell research, he answers, "By all means," an idiom meaning "of course" or "without fail." Two more idioms using *means* are "by no means" and "by any means." Do you know what they mean? If not, look them up in a dictionary or ask a native speaker to explain them. Write their meanings here:

   by no means ______________________________

   by any means ______________________________

2. Another idiom that Dr. Hirsch uses is "tip of the iceberg," meaning "only a small visible part of a much larger problem." The idiom comes from the fact that only a small piece of a real iceberg is visible. The much larger and more dangerous part of the iceberg lies hidden beneath the surface of the ocean.

Find other idioms in English with the word *tip*. You can ask a native speaker or consult a dictionary of idioms. Bring what you have learned to class and share it with your classmates. Be sure to explain:

- The idiom and its meaning
- The origin of the idiom (if you can find it out)
- The idiom used in a sentence

FOCUS ON VOCABULARY

1. In the reading and the taped interview, you came across a number of words related to smell. The following list contains those words plus a few more. What is the difference in their meanings?

Nouns	**Verbs**
smell	to smell
odor	to odorize
scent	to deodorize
aroma	to stink
fragrance	to smell up
whiff	to stink up
stench	to reek
stink	

Threads

The most evil of the 17,000 smells so far classified are two substances reminiscent of a combination of rotting cabbage, garlic, onions, burned toast, and sewer gas.

- Individually or with a partner, choose one of the words and look it up in a dictionary, taking notes on all of its meanings. Make sure that all of the words are assigned. Even if you already know some of the word's meanings, it may have additional meanings or connotations that you are not aware of.
- Present the word and its definitions to the class. Give sentences that illustrate its use.
- As your classmates give their presentations, insert the words into the proper column in the Word Connotation Chart below. Some words may have more than one connotation.

IT WORKS! Learning Strategy: Grouping

WORD CONNOTATION CHART

Positive	Neutral	Negative
______	______	______
______	______	______
______	______	______
______	______	______
______	______	______
______	______	______

2. There are many words we can use when describing our other senses—taste, touch, hearing, and sight. To learn some of these words, do the following:

- Divide into four groups.
- Choose one of the four senses above. Your group will research words pertaining to this sense.
- Look in a thesaurus to find words related to the sense you are researching.
- Find at least five words that you will teach to the class. Look up their definitions in a dictionary, and find examples of the words used in sentences.
- Present your words and their definitions to the class.

IT WORKS! Learning Strategy: Using Laughter

3. In the cartoon below, we could say that the pizza delivery man has a sixth sense.

Source: The "Bizarro" cartoon by Dan Piraro is reprinted by permission of Chronicle Features, San Francisco, California

When we speak of the five senses, we mean smell, taste, touch, hearing, and sight. What do we mean, then, when we talk about someone having a "sixth sense"?

LISTENING LOG

Reminder: Keep up your listening log with as many entries as your teacher requires. At the end of Part II (Speaking), you will report on one of your entries in a small group. (If necessary, see Appendix F for more details on Listening Logs).

ANY QUESTIONS?

IT WORKS! Learning Strategy: Clarifying

Before you go on to read about and discuss issues of smell and behavior, answer the following questions on a separate sheet of paper. Do not write your name on the paper. Your teacher or a classmate will collect the papers and share everyone's answers with the class.

1. What has been the most valuable aspect of this chapter for you so far?
2. What is still unclear?

Discussion

The following discussion questions deal with different aspects of smells and behavior. Choose the topic or topics you would like to discuss. Feel free to add related questions of your own to the questions that are asked here. And as always, you should focus on using new vocabulary and appropriate conversation skills.

When appropriate for the activity, work in small groups. Assign one person to act as discussion leader and another person to act as recorder. The discussion leader will make sure that everyone talks and stays on the subject. The recorder will take notes and later report briefly to the class on the main points of your group's discussion.

Before you begin, take a look at the group work questionnaire on page 182. You will respond to the items on the questionnaire after one of your discussions has been completed. As you work in groups, keep the items on the questionnaire in mind.

1. Read the following excerpts in which each speaker recalls a smell that triggered a childhood memory.

> Once a few years ago I was eating a kiwi, an overripe kiwi fruit. Somehow, the taste and smell of the kiwi triggered what must have been a long-buried memory of a day many years before in Poland, when I was a child. . . maybe twenty years ago, when I was in a garden or a forest, and found a bush with berries on it. I remember that I had never seen that kind of berry before, and I picked one and ate it. It had a very particular kind of flavor. I guess I had completely forgotten about eating that berry until the smell and taste of the kiwi brought it all back. My memory of eating the berry was intense. I was surprised by its intensity because I couldn't recall having remembered it before. But the smell of the kiwi fruit, for some reason it connected me very directly to that specific day in the forest when I ate the berry.
>
> –Jerzy K., Exeter, New Hampshire

> A couple of years ago I was in Washington, D.C. on business. I decided to go to Monticello, Thomas Jefferson's home, which is in Charlottesville, Virginia, just a few hours from Washington. I rented a car and drove to Monticello, and I got there in the late afternoon, about 4 o'clock. . . . I got out of the car, and immediately I was overcome by an intense, almost indescribable longing. The feeling was extraordinary because it was a mixture of this powerful longing with an equally intense familiarity, like the feeling of home. I knew immediately what it was. There was something about the air, a fresh, damp, cool smell that was exactly like the smell, the late afternoon smell, of my childhood summers. I spent every summer as a child on my grandfather's farm in Virginia, a couple of hours south of Charlottesville, and this smell took me back thirty years. It didn't make me remember a particular day, but a very exact scene of my grandfather's farmhouse and the surrounding fields and woods flashed through my mind. Maybe it was the smell of the red dirt you find there, maybe some plant. I can't describe the smell but I know I have never smelled it anywhere else.
>
> –Virginia M., Exeter, New Hampshire

In the following questions, you will be asked to describe what triggers memories in you. As your classmates give their descriptions, close your eyes and try to visualize what they are describing.

IT WORKS!
Learning Strategy: Visualizing

a. Is there a taste or smell that triggers a certain feeling or memory in you? If so, what is it? Share your memory with your classmates, giving as many details as possible so you can paint a clear mental picture for them.

b. Do your other senses trigger memories? Does a particular color or visual image or a song make you remember something from the past? If so, what is it? Give as full and rich a description as you can.

2. Read the following summary of and excerpt from a scene from Polish writer Stanislaw Lem's science fiction novel, *The Futurological Congress.* Many of the words will be new to you. Don't worry about them. Just try to get the main idea of the story. Highlight anything you find interesting.

IT WORKS!
Learning Strategy: Focus on Main Idea

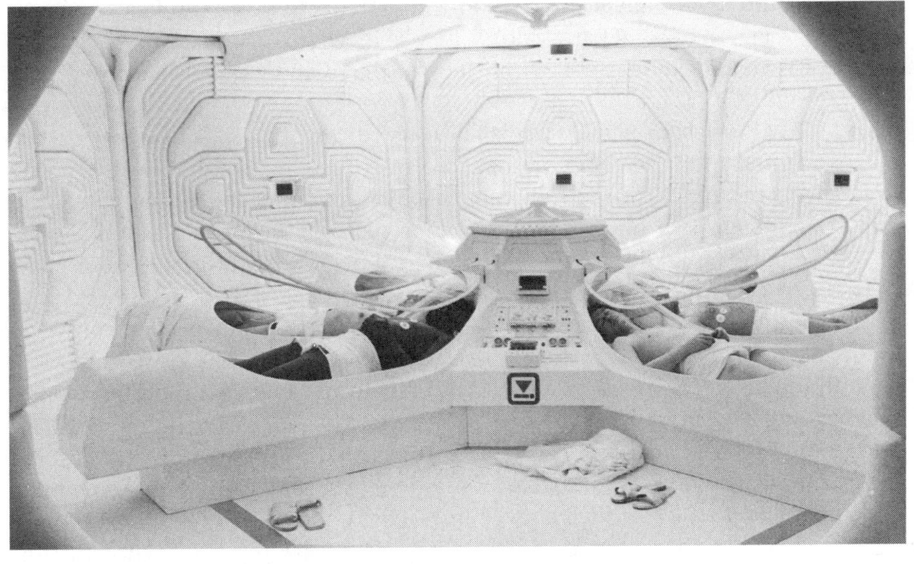

In a scene from "Alien," the crew of the space ship Nostromo is woken up from hypersleep by the ship's computer, "Mother."

In *The Futurological Congress,* the main character, Ijon Tichy, is seriously injured when revolution breaks out in the Third World country where he is attending the Eighth Futurological Congress. He is taken to a hospital where he is flash-frozen to await a future cure for his otherwise **fatal wounds.** When he is finally **thawed out,** he finds himself in the 21st century, in the year 2039. He is shocked and depressed by much of what he finds, especially when he learns a horrifying secret, that in the year 2039, unknown to most people, our sense of reality is controlled by drugs that are pumped into the air we breathe. These drugs, or "mascons" as the author calls them, falsify reality and create the **illusion** of a good life when in fact the reality is exactly the opposite. In the following excerpt from the novel, Professor Trottelreiner, one of the scientists who helped develop the drugs, explains to Tichy what "mascons" are all about.

"Tichy, for you I'll do it. I'll break a professional secret. Everything you've complained of is known to the littlest child. And how could it be otherwise? For progress was destined to travel this path the moment narcotics and early hallucinogens were replaced by the so-called psycholocalizers, drugs whose effects were highly selective. Yet the real revolution in experiential engineering took place only twenty-five years ago, when mascons were synthesized. These are **psychotropes,** whose specificity is so great they can actually influence isolated sites of the brain. **Narcotics** do not cut one off from the world, they only change one's attitude towards it. **Hallucinogens,** on the other hand, **blot out** and totally **obscure** the world. That you have learned from your own experience. But mascons, mascons **falsify** the world."

"Mascons . . .," I said. "I seem to know that word. Yes! Those mechanical dogs they used to have at football games. But how does that tie in with this . . . ?"

"It doesn't. The word has taken on—excuse me, tasted on—an altogether different meaning. From mask, masquerade, mascara. By introducing properly prepared mascons to the brain, one can mask any object in the outside world behind a **fictitious** image—**superimposed**—and with such **dexterity,** that the psychomasconated subject cannot tell which of his perceptions has been altered and which have not. If but for a single instant you could see this world of ours the way it *really* is—undoctored, **unadulterated,** uncensored—you would **drop in your tracks!"**

"Wait a minute. What world? Where is it? Where can I see it?"

"Why, anywhere. Here, even!" he whispered in my ear, glancing nervously around.

The Professor pulls out a small bottle with a worn cork and lets Tichy take a whiff of an illegal chemical that can erase the effects of the mascons. Tichy smells the chemical and suddenly his environment changes completely. The magnificent hall he thought he was in, with its beautiful carpets, crystal chandelier, sparkling tables, and orchestra playing exquisite chamber music disappears. It turns into a concrete **bunker** packed with people, with only a naked light bulb and music playing loudly from a loudspeaker hung on a rusted wire. The silver dish with delicious steaming **pheasant** that Tichy thought he had been eating has turned into a chipped plate containing **unappetizing,** grey-brown **gruel.** What had just moments before appeared to be the overhanging leaves of a nearby potted palm tree turn out to be the drawstrings on the underwear of the person sitting, along with three other people, on a narrow shelf above him. Tichy is horrified, but the effects of the chemical in the bottle begin to wear off and are replaced with the false reality of the magnificent hall again. The Professor informs Tichy that what he has just seen is, in fact, the reality of one of the nicer restaurants, and that there are places even worse. Tichy begs to know if this falsification of reality by pumping substances into the air is some sort of evil scheme. The Professor replies that in a world where more than twenty billion people live in misery, it is out of a deep sense of **compassion** and for the highest **humanitarian** reasons that this chemical **hoax** has been **perpetrated,** that reality has been disguised to mask its true character.

"Come now, is it so **satanical** if, in some extreme case, a doctor chooses to hide the truth from his patient? I say that if this is the way we must live, eat, exist, at least let us have the fancy wrappings. The mascons work perfectly—with one single exception—so what is the harm in them?"

Source: Excerpts from *The Futurological Congress,* by Stanislaw Lem, 1974. New York: The Continuum Publishing Company, pp. 113–114; 119.

fatal wounds: deadly injuries
thawed out: became unfrozen
illusion: false appearance or idea
psychotropes: drugs that change perception
narcotics: addictive drugs that reduce pain, change mood and behavior, and cause sleep
hallucinogens: drugs that cause false or distorted perceptions of objects or events
blot out: cover, hide
obscure: make difficult to see
falsify: make untrue
fictitious: untrue, invented, not real
superimposed: over or on top of something else
dexterity: quick cleverness and skill
unadulterated: pure, complete, not mixed with anything else
drop in your tracks: collapse, drop dead from shock
bunker: a strongly built shelter used by soldiers
pheasant: a large, long-tailed bird shot for food
unappetizing: unappealing food
gruel: a thin liquid food made from grain and water
compassion: sympathy for the suffering of others
humanitarian: concerned with trying to improve people's lives, such as by providing better conditions to live in and by opposing injustice
hoax: a trick that makes someone believe something that is not true
perpetrated: committed, done
satanical: evil

What is your reaction to the situation that science fiction writer Lem describes?

Write your reaction down on a piece of paper and then read it out loud to your classmates.

In small groups, choose one or more of the following questions to discuss.

a. Do you think manipulation of people through substances we smell is a potential danger? Could it ever go as far as science fiction writer Lem imagines? Why or why not?

b. Lem creates a new term, "experiential engineers." What do you think he means by the term? Would you call researching and developing smells to influence behavior experiential engineering?

c. Much has been written about how we are constantly influenced and manipulated by television and other media, by the entertainment industry, and by advertising, even in ways of which we may not be aware. This chapter introduces a new element: manipulating smells to affect people in particular ways. Do you think we need to be worried about how we are either knowingly or unknowingly influenced by any of these factors?

d. Scientists are constantly discovering new technologies that once were unimaginable. Can you think of any recent scientific breakthroughs or discoveries that make possible something that was once impossible? What are the benefits of these discoveries? What are the drawbacks? What, if any, regulation should there be regarding the applications of these discoveries?

e. Do you know of any examples where a science fiction writer or filmmaker imagined something that later actually came true? What? Do you know of any science fiction novels or films that describe things that haven't yet happened but that you think will eventually happen? Explain your answer.

IT WORKS!* *Learning Strategy:* *Using Your Imagination

3. Lem wrote his book in 1971, and envisioned the world 68 years later, in the year 2039. What do you envision the world will be like 68 years from now? With a partner or in groups, create a scenario describing how the world will be different in 68 years. You may want to consider changes in the following categories:

genetic engineering	work	family life
reproduction	leisure time	communication
education	war and piece	shopping
government	food	crime control
transportation	entertainment	international trade

Feel free to add categories of your own.

4. Now, think about one group that you worked with while discussing topics in this section. Evaluate your group experience by filling out this group work questionnaire.

Group Work Questionnaire for Discussion Question # ____

1. What one word would you use to describe how the group worked together? ____________

2. What one word would describe the way you would have liked the group to work together? ____________

3. Did everybody participate?

Always ______ Usually ______ Occasionally ______ Rarely ______ Never ______

4. Did you always try to help each other feel able to talk and say what each one thought?

Always ______ Usually ______ Occasionally ______ Rarely ______ Never ______

5. Did you listen to each other?

Always ______ Usually ______ Occasionally ______ Rarely ______ Never ______

6. Did you show you were listening by nodding at each other?

Always ______ Usually ______ Occasionally ______ Rarely ______ Never ______

7. Did you use such expressions as "That's good" to each other when you liked something?

Always ______ Usually ______ Occasionally ______ Rarely ______ Never ______

8. Did you ask each other questions?

Always ______ Usually ______ Occasionally ______ Rarely ______ Never ______

9. Did you listen and really try to answer those questions?

Always ______ Usually ______ Occasionally ______ Rarely ______ Never ______

10. Did you pay attention to each other?

Always ______ Usually ______ Occasionally ______ Rarely ______ Never ______

11. Did your group stay on the assigned task?

Always ______ Usually ______ Occasionally ______ Rarely ______ Never ______

12. Did any one person do most of the talking? Yes ______ No ______

13. Was any one person quiet most of the time? Yes ______ No ______

Movie Review

Using smells to manipulate human behavior might have seemed like science fiction at one time, but we are now seeing it turn into reality. What about other so-called science-fiction situations? Might they also be predictions of things waiting for us down the road of the future?

The following movie reviews reflect only a tiny percentage of science-fiction films available on video. With a partner or small group, choose one of the films reviewed, or select another science-fiction film that you would like to see. Rent a copy of the video and watch it together. Afterwards, discuss the film and present a report to the class. Be sure to include the following information in your report:

1. The name of the film
2. The director and cast
3. The main elements of the plot
4. Your opinion of the film
5. Your opinion of whether the same situation could someday happen

Cocoon *****
DIR: Ron Howard. CAST: Don Ameche, Wilford Brimley, Hume Cronyn, Brian Dennehy, Jack Gilford, Steve Guttenberg, Barret Oliver, Maureen Stapleton, Jessica Tandy, Gwen Verdon, Tahnee Welch

Cocoon is a splendid entertainment about a group of people in a retirement home who find what they believe is the fountain of youth. The only trouble is that the magic place belongs to a group of extraterrestrials, who may or may not be friendly. Rated PG-13 for suggested sex, brief nudity, and light profanity. 1985; 118 minutes.

Blade Runner **** 1/2
DIR: Ridley Scott. CAST: Harrison Ford, Rutger Hauer, Sean Young, Daryl Hannah, Joanna Cassidy, Edward James Olmos, M. Emmet Walsh.

This Ridley Scott (*Alien*) production is thought-provoking and visually impressive. Harrison Ford stars as a futuristic Philip Marlowe trying to find and kill the world's remaining rebel androids in 2019 Los Angeles. *Blade Runner* may not be for everyone, but those who appreciate something of substance will find it worthwhile. Rated R for brief nudity and violence. 1982; 118 minutes.

In the film "Blade Runner," Daryl Hannah and Rutger Hauer portray rebel androids trying to remain on Earth in defiance of a law forbidding their presence on the planet.

Star Trek IV: The Voyage Home **** 1/2
DIR: Leonard Nimoy. CAST: William Shatner, Leonard Nimoy, DeForest Kelley, James Doohan, George Takei, Walter Koenig, Nichelle Nichols, Catharine Hicks.

Our stalwart heroes journey back to Earth in their "borrowed" enemy spacecraft just in time to witness a new tragedy in the making: an alien deep-space probe is disrupting our planet's atmosphere by broadcasting a message that nobody understands. When Spock identifies the "language" as that of the humpback whale, extinct in the twenty-third century, Kirk leads his crew back to the twentieth century in an attempt to locate two of the great mammals and utilize them for translation duty. Charming and lighthearted, though rated PG for somewhat intense themes. 1986; 119 minutes.

E.T.—The Extra-Terrestrial *****
DIR: Steven Spielberg. CAST: Dee Wallace, Henry Thomas, Peter Coyote, Robert MacNaughton, Drew Barrymore.

The highest-grossing (and we think most entertaining) science-fiction film of all time, this is Steven Spielberg's gentle fairy tale about what happens when a young boy meets up with a very special fellow from outer space. Sheer wonder is joined with warmth and humor in this movie classic. Rated PG. 1982; 115 minutes.

Alien **** 1/2
DIR: Ridley Scott. CAST: Tom Skerrit, Sigourney Weaver, John Hurt, Ian Holm, Harry Dean Stanton, Yaphet Kotto, Veronica Cartwright.

A superb cinematic combination of science fiction and horror, this is a heart-pounding, visually astounding shocker. The players are all excellent as the crew of a futuristic cargo ship that picks up an unwanted passenger—an alien that lives on human flesh and continually changes form. Rated R. 1979; 116 minutes.

Star Wars *****
DIR: George Lucas. CAST: Mark Hamill, Harrison Ford, Carrie Fisher, Alec Guiness, Peter Cushing, Anthony Daniels.

May the Force be with you! Writer-director George Lucas blended the best of vintage pulp science fiction, old-fashioned cliffhangers, comic books, and classic fantasy to come up with the ultimate adventure "a long time ago in a galaxy far, far away." Rated PG. 1977; 121 minutes.

Source: *Video Movie Guide 1993*
by Mick Martin and Marsha Porter © 1992.
New York: Ballantine Books.

Simulation

As farfetched as it may seem, many companies have already begun using certain smells to influence customer behavior. The *New York Times's* article, "The Scent of Money," which you will read before doing the simulation, gives examples of a number of businesses that have utilized scents in one way or another.

IT WORKS! Learning Strategy: Playing Roles

For this simulation, you will be taking on the roles of different people engaged in a debate on whether or not to pump smells into the stores of a small shopping mall to stimulate spending.

The Situation:

Silvergate Mall is a small, exclusive shopping mall consisting of the following: a small traditional men's clothing store, two women's clothing boutiques, an excellent bookstore, a gourmet food and coffee store, a health-food store with a juice bar, a jewelry store, a toy store, a shoe store, a sporting-goods store, a fine quality cookware store, a leather-goods store, and a highly rated seafood restaurant. The mall is special in that none of the stores is a chain or large discount store; they are all individually owned. The mall location is excellent and is a highly desirable place for a store to lease space.

The stores in this mall have traditionally done a brisk business with healthy sales; however, because of the current economic slump, sales have fallen off sharply. Several of the store owners leasing space in the mall have heard about the research done on scents that will stimulate spending and want to have such smells pumped into the mall common areas as well as their individual stores. Several other store owners are against pumping smells into any part of the mall, even if not into their stores.

The real-estate developer who built and owns the mall is the head of the mall board of directors, which decides mall policy. The remaining board members consist of four of the store owners, elected for a three-year term by all the store owners who lease space in the mall. The owner-developer has called a meeting of the board and invited community and employee representatives to join the discussion. The following questions are on the agenda:

1. Should pleasant smells that might stimulate spending be pumped into the common areas of the mall?
2. Should those stores that wish to do so be allowed to pump smells into their shops?

Conducting the Simulation

LEARNING STRATEGY

Managing Your Learning: Organizing your ideas before your discussion keeps you focused later when you are speaking.

Step One: Preparation

- Choose roles. Refer to the role descriptions on pages 189–191.
- Skim the *New York Times's* article "The Smell of Money," which has additional information that will help you play your roles more effectively. As you skim the article, highlight any facts you think are important to the case.

This is a long reading, but it contains a lot of information you have already heard or read. Don't worry about vocabulary in the article. Use the article to (a) help you support what you're going to say and (b) help you anticipate what others will say in the simulation.

- Write down any comments you want to make or questions you want to ask during the discussion. Try to anticipate the points the opposing side will make and think of possible replies. Try to think of workable solutions to the problems faced by the mall.

Threads

Perfume means "from smoke." The original use of perfume was to counteract the offensive smell of burning flesh during sacrifices.

The smell of money

by N.R. Kleinfield

It was bound to happen. Someone thinks he is about to create the Honest Car Salesman in a bottle.

A year ago, one of Detroit's Big Three auto makers hired Dr. Alan R. Hirsch, a **quirky** smell researcher in Chicago, to devise a rather exceptional scent. The hope was that when the odor was sprayed on a car salesman, he would—yes—smell honest.

It sounds absurd. In fact, after she was done laughing, Dr. Susan Schiffman, a smell researcher and professor of medical psychology at the Duke University Medical School, remarked, "I was not aware that honesty had a specific smell associated with it."

But Dr. Hirsch, who refuses to name his Detroit client, is confident that he will have the Honest Car Salesman Odor devised within a year. If he succeeds, he said, the auto maker will entrust the smell to its dealers, who will spray it on their salesmen, and then customers will catch a whiff and cars **will fly off the lots.**

"I see cars selling, yes," Dr. Hirsch said.

The quest is bizarre but its intent is clear: marketers think smells can sell just about anything. Of the senses, smell is the most closely linked to memory and emotions, making it a **potent** weapon in transforming people's moods. Hence, smells are being **embedded in** women's clothing and pumped into the air at stores and might even be **doused on** automatic teller machines—all in the name of moving merchandise.

"Stores have manipulated everything else—the music, the lighting, the color, the layout—and so this is the new thing to play with," says Dr. Susan Knasko, an environmental psychologist at the Monell Chemical Senses Center, a Philadelphia research organization that studies smell and taste. Marketers suggest that in 10 years odors will be as familiar as Muzak in stores.

This **misting** of America, however, is being viewed with decidedly dark suspicions by consumer organizations. "I think it's disgusting and very offensive," said Joan Claybrook, the president of Public Citizen, the research and lobbying group founded by Ralph Nader.

Smell has long been **deployed** in the retail world, but typically to mask foul odors. Supermarkets, for example, use **atomizers** to conceal the smell of rotting produce. And there have been scattered attempts to quicken the buying passion through odorants. Real estate agents long ago discovered the power of an apple pie baking in the oven.

But now marketers are getting **wilier,** flirting with specially engineered smells.

"It's becoming much more sophisticated than the fan in the bathroom," said J'Amy Owens, the head of Retail Planning Associates, a Seattle consulting concern that specializes in positioning retailers in the marketplace. "We're **on the verge** of something very major here."

In the last two years, she said, she has been **prodding** her **phalanx** of clients to use scents to stimulate sales. She feels all stores should pursue a "signature smell" tailored to their **clientele;** for example, a coconut suntan-oil smell for a store targeted at the young and active. Among her projects is a cinnamon, hot-apple-spice smell for a children's clothing store called Storybook Collectibles that is soon to open in San Francisco. Scent people also report that International Flavors and Fragrances, the world's biggest fragrance company, has made a new-car spray that it says will give used vehicles the **palpable** smell of new plastic and carpeting.

Developing a scent can cost $1,000 to more than $50,000, and it can cost tens of thousands more to spread a fragrance throughout a store. One method uses heat-sensitive **pellets** impregnated with fragrance that are dropped in pots of water and slowly heated. A more sophisticated method uses computer-controlled machines that convert a liquid fragrance to **vapor,** then release the scent through a store's ventilation system.

Though researchers are confident that fragrances alter behavior, there is little quantifiable evidence that pleasing the nose **spurs** people to reach for their wallets. Two years ago, Dr. Knasko introduced a floral scent into a Philadelphia jewelry store and found that many people **lingered** a few seconds longer (a second of a customer's attention is a cherished eternity in retail measures), though they did not buy more. Dr. Knasko, noting that consumers don't purchase jewelry **impulsively,** said perhaps those extra seconds might have translated into sales in a cheaper store.

And then there is Dr. Hirsch. He is a neurologist and psychiatrist who calls himself the "Jacques Cousteau of the nose" and once wore a watch that ran backward. Eight years ago, he started the Smell and Taste Treatment and Research Foundation in Chicago, where he and his colleagues treat patients with smell disorders and pursue research. He thinks he became curious about smell after he was hit by a car while he was a medical student and found that for a week afterward everything smelled like cigarettes.

His foundation is **probing** whether the scent of green apples can soothe migraine headaches and whether the smell of Fritos can bring on weight loss. What has gained Dr. Hirsch the most attention, though, is his untiring promotion of the commercial applications of smells. In particular, he did two studies that have had an electric reception among marketers.

The first was the sneaker study. About two years ago, Dr. Hirsch asked 31 shoppers to inspect Nike sneakers in two identical-looking rooms (he could have chosen a Hula-Hoop, but he picked Nike sneakers). One room was filled with purified air, the other with a mixed floral scent. Afterward, Dr. Hirsch said, 84 percent of the subjects said they were more **inclined** to buy the sneakers in the scented room.

Dr. Hirsch said throngs of retailers got in touch with him, and several retail stores and athletic shops bought the scent's formula for about $3,000. Nike did not. "The big thing we try to do is get athletic shoes not to smell," said Liz Dolan, Nike's director of communications. "We never think about adding a smell."

Dr. Hirsch's second venture came a year ago, when he went to Las Vegas, Nev. to scent a casino. He is no gambler himself (on his last visit, he risked all of 35 cents, losing it). Yet, he went to the Las Vegas Hilton and picked out three slot-machine zones to study for a weekend. One zone was left unscented, while each of the other two was misted with a different agreeable odor. Dr. Hirsch is vague about describing the odors. Using numbers furnished by the Hilton, he compared the play at the slots with the previous and subsequent weekends. He found little change in the neutral zone or in one scented zone, he said, but in the other scented area the amount of money gambled **soared** by 45 percent. And the more intense the smell, the more people bet.

Dr. Hirsch announced these results last month and has heard from 20 casinos around the world that feel their dreams have come true. The Las Vegas Hilton, among others, has asked him for a proposal and cost estimate. He has also been approached by 150 other businesses—clothes stores, shopping malls, health clubs, restaurants—praying that the smell may **induce** their clientele to spend more, too. Dr. Hirsch said he would probably start selling the Las Vegas Odor by January, though he had no idea why it worked. "Actually," he said, "I thought the other odor was going to work, too."

Some researchers have greeted the Las Vegas study with considerable **skepticism.** They point out that Dr. Hirsch, who is 36 years old, has published few papers in scientific journals (he counted 11), and they are unaware of his studies being replicated by other scientists. No one else can copy the Las Vegas inquiry, since Dr. Hirsch won't **divulge** the scent.

Dr. Schiffman, the Duke researcher, said she found the 45 percent **surge** in gambling suspicious, since other efforts to stimulate spending—like spreading the smell of popcorn through a movie theater's ventilation system—had not lifted popcorn sales more than 5 to 15 percent.

"We can't evaluate any of this," said Dr. Charles Wysocki, a smell researcher at Monell. "We don't even know what the scent was."

Dr. Hirsch charges up to $50,000 to produce a smell. Chicago Transparent Products bought a "fresh linen" scent for its new Brawny plastic trash bags that supposedly makes consumers feel healthy and clean. A women's clothing maker, which Dr. Hirsch would not identify, hired him to come up with a smell that can be blended into garments and will supposedly make young women more inclined to buy them.

"There's Muzak, there's neon lighting, there are all sorts of bells and jingles being used," Dr. Hirsch said. "Why not smells?"

Consumer groups, however, are **scathing.** They say that nothing has changed about the products that are enveloped in smells and thus marketers are engaging in smell-washing.

"This sounds like Vance Packard needs to write a sequel called, 'The Olfactory Persuaders'," said Mark Silbergeld, the director of the Consumers Union office in Washington, the product-research organization. (Mr. Packard wrote "The Hidden Persuaders," about advertising, in 1957.) "We have taken the position that shoppers should make their purchases based on rational decisions. We advise shoppers, for instance, that they should not shop for food when they're hungry. This sort of technique would not be **conducive to** rational decisions. It's pretty **sleazy."**

He and others say that companies could face liability lawsuits from people allergic to scents pumped into products or stores. "I never heard of anyone allergic to Muzak," Mr. Silbergeld said. 'But a lot of people are allergic to certain smells."

Smells are also **chancy** because people often perceive them in **idiosyncratic** ways. Dr. Wysocki said experience and genetics play a role in response to a smell. "Say someone first smelled roses on a walk through a garden in the springtime with his mother," he explained. "Then as an adult the smell of roses will involve pleasant memories. Another person first smelled roses at the funeral of his mother. So as an adult, he has a negative reaction to the smell."

As for genetic makeup, Dr. Wysocki said what is **luscious** to one person may be **odious** to another. "I'm a walking example of genetics," he said. "I love the smell of skunks."

At Seafirst Bank, which has 285 branches in the state of Washington, the money that **spews** from its teller machines buys as much as the money from any other bank. But Seafirst believes it can make customers think its money is better than the competition's by teasing the nose.

Starting in the next few months, it plans to test fragrances at several dozen of its A.T.M.s. One idea is to apply a mint smell to the money itself, so it will seem newer and fresher, though Jack David, Seafirst's marketing director, confessed that that "might be stupid."

The Seafirst A.T.M.s **discharge** coupons along with money, and an idea that Mr. David finds more promising is to coat coupons promoting auto loans with the smell of the new leather of a car.

The lodging industry is also experimenting with smells. The Miami Dadeland Marriot Hotel installed a $12,000 fragrance system in its lobby that dispenses a floral-citrus smell that it felt would please guests, perhaps leading to longer stays.

The Marriot system was created by Aromasys Inc., a Minnesota company that began marketing fragrance-dispensing machines about six months ago. Mark Peltier, the company's founder, said he had heard from a number of hotels and retail stores, as well as from corporations that want to use smells to raise productivity among workers, another growing area of research. An Aromasys machine for a small store runs about $5,000, he said, while a hotel lobby system could cost $15,000.

Mr. Peltier originally intended to sell his machines to schools because he felt odors could make students more attentive. But he found that schools didn't have much interest.

Shimuzu, a Tokyo construction corporation, is marketing a computerized scent-delivery system in this country through its S. Technology subsidiary. Researchers in Japan have experimented with smells in offices, hotels, and other public spaces since the 1970s.

Mr. Peltier said he thought systems like this would be **commonplace,** though he foresaw some **turbid** times. "Greed drives this planet," he added. "I think this will go through a period of abuse. People will make false claims and put cheap scents in the air. There will be companies that will not market smells with **integrity.**"

Not every odor experiment has worked free of **angst.** Knot Shop, a Chicago-based chain of tie stores, pumped the smell of leather, oak, and pipe tobacco into five stores for about a year. "The idea is that most women buy neckwear," said Ms. Owens, who served as a consultant to the chain. "And so we wanted the stores to smell like the ideal man."

But Gene Silverberg, the president of Bigsby & Kruthers, the parent company, terminated the smell about four months ago. "Frankly, I didn't find it made enough difference," he said. "The upkeep was a lot of trouble, making sure it was not too strong or too weak. Without the smell, I haven't seen any drop in sales."

A new national network of 24 stores called It's Really One Dollar has had early difficulties. If you sell everything for $1, you might think you don't have to use marketing **gimmicks.** Nevertheless, Steven Schultz, the chain's chairman, is a firm believer in smell, and so he had a fragrance-dispenser installed in the store in Louisville, Ky. The machine **emitted** a peach fragrance that consultants found inviting to the young women that the store targets.

Unfortunately, some of the store's departments, like health and beauty aids, already discharged a smell of their own. So much peach had to be released into the air to overcome those odors that the place smelled like a peach warehouse. After three months, the machine was shut off. But Mr. Schultz has not given up. By early next year he hopes to solve the problem and then to put peach odor into all of his stores.

In some cases, the point is to **repulse** customers. Which brings up the case of the Powerful Underarm Odor.

Dr. Wysocki said that several companies in England and Australia are instilling something akin to the smell of fear into the bills they mail.

They are using androstenone, a volatile steroid found in underarm sweat and urine in humans. It is also present in pigs; males emit it to prompt mating behavior in females. About half the human population can't smell it at all; 30 to 35 percent find it an **alluring,** musky smell, and the rest liken it to stale urine or outrageously powerful underarm sweat.

"For people who get a bill in the mail and it stinks like human urine, I can see why they would want to get it the hell out of the house," Dr. Wysocki said. "That's a nasty odor."

quirky: strange
will fly off the lots: will sell quickly
potent: powerful
embedded in: fixed deeply in
doused on: poured on
misting: spraying
deployed: used
atomizers: spray bottles
wilier: trickier
on the verge of: very near
prodding: pushing
phalanx: a group of people packed closely together
clientele: customers
palpable: noticeable
pellets: small balls
vapor: gaslike form of a liquid
spurs: causes
lingered: waited
impulsively: suddenly, without thinking
probing: investigating
inclined: likely
soared: increased
induce: cause
skepticism: doubt
divulge: reveal
surge: quickly increase
scathing: bitterly cruel in judgment
conducive to: likely to produce
sleazy: cheap and poor looking
chancy: risky
idiosyncratic: peculiar to one person
luscious: having a very pleasant taste or smell
odious: very unpleasant
spews: comes out in a rush or flood
discharge: send out
commonplace: common, ordinary
turbid: dark, heavy
integrity: honesty
angst: worry, concern
gimmicks: tricks
emitted: sent out the smell of
repulse: to cause a strong dislike
alluring: attractive, tempting

Step Two: Acting out the Simulation

- Hold the board meeting to discuss the two proposals. The mall owner will run the meeting. In addition to the board members, a representative of the mall employees and two local community members will join the discussion.
- At the end of the meeting the board members will vote. Try to keep an open mind during the discussion, and in the end vote for what you think is the right thing to do based on your role. You will not necessarily give your personal opinion.
- Any of you who do not participate in the simulation should take notes on what is said. Use this format:

ARGUMENTS IN FAVOR	ARGUMENTS AGAINST
______________________	______________________
______________________	______________________
______________________	______________________
______________________	______________________
______________________	______________________
______________________	______________________
______________________	______________________

Step Three: Debriefing

- If you participated in the simulation, discuss how you felt the discussion and vote went.
- If you observed the simulation, voice your reactions to the simulation and the issues presented, referring to your notes.
- If more than one simulation was going on at the same time, compare notes on what took place in each simulation.

THE ROLES

Mall owner: You have a lot of money invested in the physical facilities of the mall, and it is important for both the mall's image and its profits that all of the space for retail stores in the mall be occupied by high-quality stores doing a healthy business. You are very interested in the idea of pumping in smells to stimulate spending, but it involves expensive new technology and you would like the store owners to help contribute to the cost. You realize that there have been mixed reactions to the proposal. You have called today's meeting with the hope of bringing the different groups to consensus on whether or not to try this new technology. You are fair and open-minded. Your job today is to make sure that people stick to the point. After you have heard all the arguments, you should allow ten minutes for general discussion and then take a vote.

Board Member #1: You run a small, family-owned traditional men's clothing store. Business has been slow because of the economy, and you feel you are losing out to larger department stores that can discount clothing prices heavily. Although the mall is a relatively new location for your store, the business has been in your family for four generations, and you want to keep the business going. You feel strongly that small, family-owned businesses can offer a level of personal service that the larger retail stores cannot. You are in favor of pumping in pleasant aromas to encourage buying because you see it as the only way to remain competitive with the larger stores at other malls. You feel it is no different from any other kind of marketing and that it is just a matter of time before everyone is using it as a marketing tool.

Board Member #2: You have invested your life savings in a fancy cookware store. Although the merchandise you carry is of excellent quality and has sold well in the previous years, for the past 18 months sales have been down, and you are worried about losing the store. You are not sure how you feel about having the smells pumped in. You have mixed feelings about the idea, but you would do almost anything to increase sales.

Board Member #3: You own a health-food store with a juice bar, and in addition to your regular customers, you get an overflow of thirsty shoppers from the other stores in the mall. Although you believe in using smells for their therapeutic value (aroma therapy), you have serious doubts about putting chemicals into the air as well as concerns about the ethics of using smells to put people in a mood to spend money. You are very strongly opposed to this happening at the mall.

Board Member #4: You are the owner of the seafood restaurant located at one end of the mall. Many people who come to the mall to shop end up eating at your restaurant afterwards. You are against pumping in smells. You are afraid that if the shoppers spend too freely in the stores, they will be less likely to come over and have a meal in your establishment. You are also afraid that the smells will somehow interfere with the shoppers' appetites and make them less hungry.

Employee Representative: A poll taken of employees' opinions regarding the proposals showed the following result: 42 percent of the employees working in the mall are in favor of adding smells; 37 percent are against the proposals; and 21 percent have no opinion. Those who are against the proposals feel uneasy about the prospect of working daily in a scented environment, when the potential long-term effects are unknown. There is also some suspicion that it could be a first step to introducing smells that have controlling effects on employees. Several employees have also raised concerns that some people might be allergic to the smells.

Local City Council Representative: You realize that a healthy business community in your town means more economic benefits for the town. Because of cutbacks in federal and state spending, your town has not gotten as much aid as in previous years and has had to cut back on many city services, including after-school and summer programs for children and services for the poor and the elderly. You are a practical person and see higher spending at the mall stores as ultimately benefiting the town. You see no harm and many potential benefits in adding smells to the mall. You are in favor of the proposal.

Citizens' Consumer Group Representative: You are the representative of a local citizens' consumer group. The people in the neighboring community around the mall are extremely concerned about this new direction the mall stores may be taking. Pleasant smells are one thing, but smells with a subliminal message (a subtle message that appeals to the unconscious mind) are another. Many members of your group are also concerned because the smells will cause a kind of air pollution in the stores. Your group has discussed the possibility of organizing a boycott of the stores if the smells are pumped in even to only a portion of the shops. Many people in the community are long-time, regular customers of the Silvergate mall stores.

Optional Roles

Additional Store Owners: You attend the meeting and are allowed to ask questions and to voice your opinion. You may try to influence the opinion of the board members. However, since you are not on the board, you may not vote.

Additional Community Representatives: You attend the meeting and are allowed to ask questions and to voice your opinion. You are not allowed to vote.

Newspaper Reporter: Your job is to take notes and to write a short article reporting on the meeting and its outcome. You can ask questions before and after the meeting, but not during.

Threads

What's in a name? That which we call a rose by any other name would smell as sweet.

William Shakespeare

Listening Log Report

Bring your Listening Log to class and report on one entry to a small group. Take turns doing the following:

- Tell your group members what you watched or listened to.
- Give a short oral summary followed by your personal reaction. Do not read what you have written.
- Check your listeners' comprehension by asking questions such as: "Do you understand what I mean?" and "Am I being clear?"
- Rephrase or restate to make your points clear.
- Answer your listeners' questions and ask for their reactions.

FOLLOW-UP

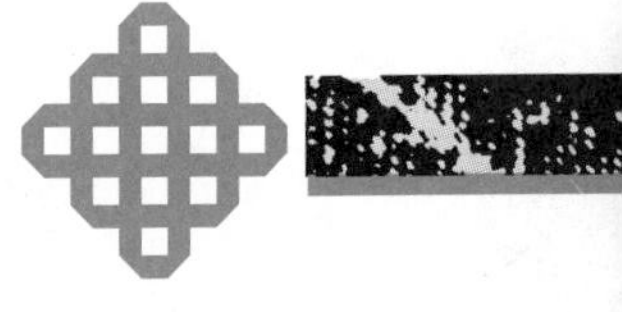

Choose any of the following activities to do outside of class, and then report on what happened or what you found out. These activities can be done individually, in pairs, or in small groups. (Refer to Oral Presentation Feedback forms in Appendix L.)

1. Look up information in a library on subliminal messages that may be contained in print advertising or in music.
2. Many science fiction writers are internationally known and translated. Do you have a favorite that you've read in your native language? Go to a library or bookstore and find a copy (in English, of course) of a book by your

favorite science-fiction author. If you want to practice listening, see if you can find the book on audiotape. Read or listen to it, and when you have finished, summarize the plot for a friend, and explain why you liked the book.

3. Find an article in the newspaper that talks about how the public is being manipulated in some way. Discuss it with a friend, comparing your reactions. If you both agree, try to come up with arguments for the opposing view just for the sake of discussion.
4. Interview five people of differing ages, genders, ethnic backgrounds, and so on about their ideas of how the world will change over the next fifty years. (See Appendix K for information on how to conduct a survey.)
5. Initiate a conversation on one of the topics in this chapter with a friend or colleague. Tape-record the discussion, and afterwards write up a summary of the main points raised in the discussion. Give the summary to your teacher.

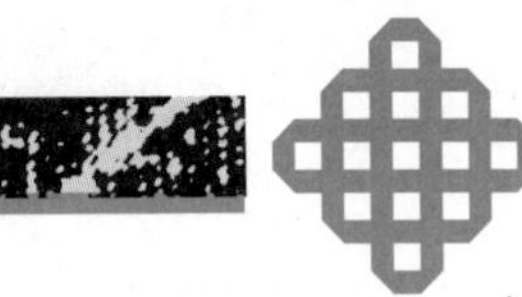

LEARNING ASSESSMENT

IT WORKS!
Learning Strategy: Evaluating Your Progress

1. Look back at Part I (Listening) of this chapter. What activities helped you most in understanding the listening passages?

___

___

___

2. Give an example of when you had trouble understanding what you heard.

___

___

___

Why did you have difficulty?

_____ **a.** I didn't know the vocabulary.

_____ **b.** I wasn't paying attention.

_____ **c.** The speaker wasn't clear.

_____ **d.** The speaker spoke too fast.

_____ **e.** Other: ___

3. Were you more successful than you expected to be in understanding the listening material on the subject of smells and behavior? Were you less successful than you expected? Why?

___

___

___

4. Look back at Part II (Speaking) of this chapter. Give one or two examples of your most successful efforts at oral communication. Try to explain why you were able to succeed.

____

____

____

5. Give an example of a discussion in which you had trouble communicating with your classmates.

____

____

____

Why did you have difficulty?

_____ **a.** My classmates didn't understand my pronunciation.

_____ **b.** I didn't understand my classmates' pronunciation.

_____ **c.** I had trouble finding the main ideas in the readings.

_____ **d.** There was a lot of new vocabulary.

_____ **e.** Other: ______________________________

6. What could you do next time to:
   a. better prepare for a listening passage?

____

____

____

   b. improve your effectiveness when speaking in a group?

____

____

____

7. Look back at your goals you set for yourself at the beginning of this chapter.
   a. Which goals did you achieve?

____

____

____

   b. What will be your primary goal in the next chapter?

____

____

____

Understanding Our World—Science and the Citizen

CHAPTER

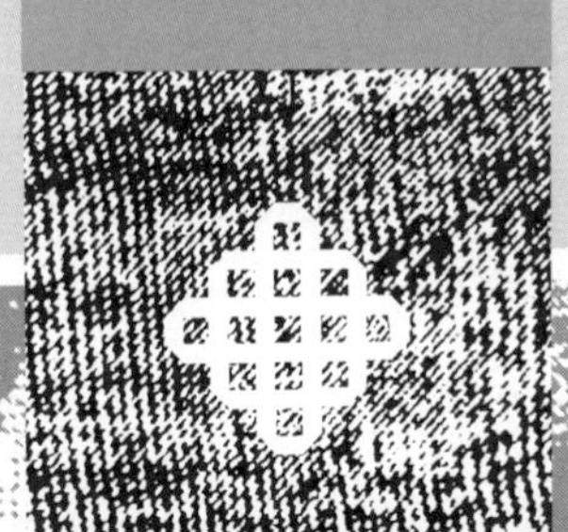

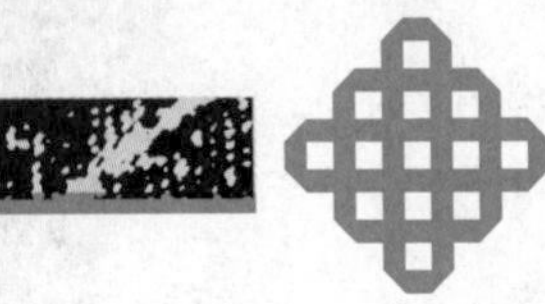

INTRODUCTION

Should our government fund certain space intitiatives or not? Just how concerned should we be about global warming? What should we be doing to stop acid rain? Is it important to put money into research to understand the origin of the universe? Should there be limits on human genetic engineering? These are just a few of the questions that we hear as scientific and technological issues dominate national debate.

How important is it for us as citizens to understand the debates over these issues? How much knowledge of science do we need to be able to cope with the world of the future? How can we get this knowledge? In this chapter, you will explore some of the issues that are being raised today about a citizen's need to know about science.

Background Knowledge Check

The following items reflect some of the content that you will find in this chapter. Write **a, b, c,** or **d** next to each item in the list according to the following:

IT WORKS! Learning Strategy: Using Prior Knowledge

(a) I have never heard of this.
(b) I have heard of this, but don't really know what it means.
(c) I have some idea of what this means, but I'm not sure about it.
(d) I have a clear idea of what this means and can explain it.

_____ **1.** the ozone layer

_____ **2.** ultraviolet radiation

_____ **3.** ozone depletion

_____ **4.** science literacy

_____ **5.** The Planetary Society

_____ **6.** the threat of an asteroid hitting the Earth

_____ **7.** Tunguska, Siberia

Students who have chosen **d** for any of the above should *briefly* explain what these items mean. If no one has chosen **d,** don't worry. You will have a chance to learn more about these as you progress through the chapter.

Setting Goals

Complete the following statement by checking the goals you want to achieve in this chapter.

While working on this chapter, I will make an effort to:

IT WORKS! Learning Strategy: Setting Goals

_____ **1.** speak more while I am working in a small group.

_____ **2.** give others a chance to speak while working in a small group.

_____ **3.** show others that I am actively listening by looking into their eyes and nodding as they talk.

_____ **4.** ask more questions in front of the whole class.

_____ **5.** make more comments in front of the whole class.

_____ **6.** monitor one aspect of my pronunciation, such as ________________.

_____ **7.** monitor one aspect of grammar as I speak, such as ________________.

_____ **8.** use some of the new vocabulary when speaking, both in and out of class.

_____ **9.** listen to the radio and watch TV outside of class.

_____ **10.** discuss the issues raised in this chapter outside of class.

_____ **11.** try to achieve another goal, such as ______________________________

____.

For All Your Needs

SPF 98 ~
Allows wearer to remain in the blazing hot sun 98 times longer than one could without protection.

SPF 457 ~
Allows wearer to stand in front of an open furnace for 25 minutes.

SPF 6,291 ~
Allows wearer to have lunch inside a kiln.

SPF 39,118 ~
Allows wearer to spend afternoon in a bathing suit on Mercury.

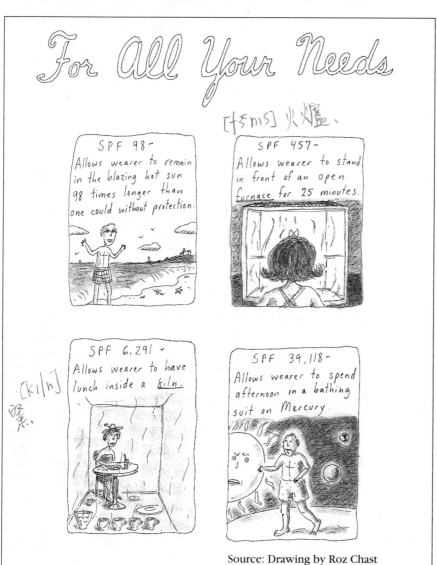

Source: Drawing by Roz Chast

What point do you think the cartoon is making?

PART I: LISTENING

Before You Listen

In this chapter, you are going to hear a listening passage about how the public first began to become aware of the problem of ozone depletion in the atmosphere.

*IT WORKS!
Learning Strategy:
Using Prior
Knowledge*

- Write down the first three things that come into your mind when you hear the word **ozone.**

1. ______________________________

2. ______________________________

3. ______________________________

Compare your associations with a partner. Are they similar?

BACKGROUND READING

Read the following short passages, which talk about ozone. The **boldfaced** words are vocabulary you will also hear when you listen to the tape. Try to get their meanings from the context. Most of the words are used more than once, so you will have more clues to help you guess their meanings. After you finish the readings, clarify the meanings with a partner or your teacher.

*IT WORKS!
Learning Strategy:
Learning from
Reading*

The **ozone** molecule consists of three (as opposed to the usual two) oxygen **atoms.** Only about one molecule per million in the atmosphere is **ozone,** but these molecules play a crucial role in our environment in two ways. **Ozone** near the surface of the earth ("bad **ozone**") is a noxious pollutant, irritating to eyes and lungs. **Ozone** 50,000 feet up, on the other hand ("good **ozone**"), absorbs the sun's harmful **ultraviolet radiation** and thus provides an effective sunscreen for those of us living on the ground. Without **the ozone layer,** humans and other terrestrial life would be constantly bombarded with high-energy radiation and consequently put at risk of medical problems such as skin cancer and eye damage.

The ozone layer is at risk today because of the widespread use of a class of chemicals known as chlorofluorocarbons (CFCs for short). CFCs are used extensively as the working fluids in refrigerators and air conditioners, as cleaners during the manufacture of microchips, and in the manufacture of foam products.

When they were first used extensively in the 1960s, the molecules' stability was considered an asset since they wouldn't break down and add to **pollution.** But that very stability has led to problems, because CFCs last long enough to filter through to the upper atmosphere. There the molecules' chlorine **atoms** act as catalysts in a complex set of reactions that convert two molecules of **ozone** to three molecules of ordinary oxygen, **depleting** the **ozone layer** faster than it can be recharged by natural processes—another example of the Law of Unintended Consequences.

Source: *Science Matters,* by Robert M. Hazen and James Trefil, 1991. New York: Doubleday, pp. 267-268.

With less ozone in the atmosphere, increasing amounts of **ultraviolet radiation** reach the Earth's surface. For humans, increased exposure to **ultraviolet rays** means more cases of skin cancer and cataracts to the eyes. Additionally, increased levels of **ultraviolet radiation** are harmful to crops, and scientists warn that higher amounts threaten the very existence of the delicate microorganisms at the base of the marine food chain. In 1974, 46 years after CFCs were created in a DuPont laboratory, the scientific community began publicly questioning the danger of CFCs to the planet. In an article published in ***Nature*** magazine, University of California-Irvine chemistry professor F. Sherwood Rowland and Dr. Mario J. Molina, his postdoctoral student, warned that CFCs released into the atmosphere would destroy **ozone** in the **stratosphere.** They **estimated** that if CFC emissions continued at the then-present rate (they are now higher), as much as 13 percent of **the ozone layer** would be destroyed within the coming century. Their findings were initially met with skepticism.

In March 1988, the **Ozone** Trends Panel convened by the U.S. government estimated that in the areas of the northern hemisphere where most people live, **the ozone layer** decreased by 2 to 3 percent between 1969 and 1986. Reductions as high as 6 percent, however, were recorded during the winter months in far northern areas such as Alaska and Scandinavia.

Like **global warming, ozone depletion** seems to be happening at a much faster pace than was originally forecast. In fact, we have already experienced more **ozone loss** than scientists previously **predicted** would occur by the year 2020. Some **estimates** translate a 1 percent reduction in **stratospheric ozone** into a 2 percent increase in the amount of **ultraviolet radiation** striking the planet's surface. And certain scientists **estimate** that **ozone loss** could mean a 5 to 20 percent rise in **ultraviolet radiation** reaching our Earth's most populated areas by 2030. Another study **estimated** that a 2.5 percent loss of ozone could translate into a 10 percent increase in skin cancer.

Source: *Our Earth, Ourselves,* by Ruth Caplan and the staff of Environmental Action, 1990. New York: Bantam Books, pp. 51-52.

Before going on, answer the following questions:

1. What is ozone?
2. What is the difference between "good" ozone and "bad" ozone?
3. Why is the ozone layer at risk today?

4. What is the connection between ozone and skin cancer?

VOCABULARY PREPARATION FOR LISTENING TO "UNDERSTANDING OUR WORLD"

The following sentences are based on information from the listening passage you are about to hear. You may already know many of the **boldfaced** vocabulary items. Share your knowledge with a partner, and together read over the sentences and find the definition that best matches each item. You might want to read the sentences aloud to practice saying the vocabulary items you will hear.

1. A number of years ago, the Boeing Aircraft Corporation became interested in building a **supersonic** aircraft to be used in **commercial aviation.**
2. The U.S. government was interested in investing in the Boeing project; however, in order **to justify** any government investment, Boeing needed to produce and sell a certain number of aircraft.
3. About that time, scientists began to suspect that even small changes in the amount of ozone could have a **detectable** effect on the rate of skin cancer around the world. Today this does not seem at all strange, but twenty years ago it was a very **bizarre** idea.
4. Scientists agreed that even a small decrease in the amount of ozone would not be a **trivial** thing.
5. One study showed that two groups of people living in different parts of the country had a difference in the rate of skin cancer they got. This difference was **attributed to** differing amounts of ozone in various regions of the country.
6. This early study was **a first shot** at understanding the relationship between ozone depletion and skin cancer.
7. At that time, scientists estimated that if you had an **x-percent** drop in ozone, you would have **roughly** a 3x-percent increase in the incidence of skin cancer.
8. Because the government was spending **a fair amount** to **subsidize** the early study of the supersonic transport, politicians began **to pick up** information about the possibility of ozone depletion.
9. One politician who was against the project and who wanted **to eliminate** it was a very well-known senator from Wisconsin, Senator William Proxmire.
10. Scientists got to the point where they really **had it down pat.** Anytime anyone called them with a question about ozone, they automatically knew exactly what to answer.
11. When scientists first began to suspect that aerosol sprays could be a cause of ozone depletion, the public found it to be such a **preposterous** idea that

quickly it became a regular joke on *All in the Family,* the most popular **sitcom** on television at that time.

Matching: Write the letter of the definition on the right next to the word or phrase that you think it defines.

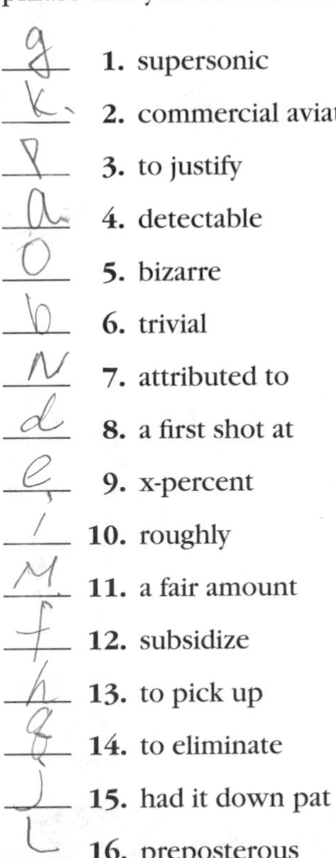

___ **1.** supersonic
___ **2.** commercial aviation
___ **3.** to justify
___ **4.** detectable
___ **5.** bizarre
___ **6.** trivial
___ **7.** attributed to
___ **8.** a first shot at
___ **9.** x-percent
___ **10.** roughly
___ **11.** a fair amount
___ **12.** subsidize
___ **13.** to pick up
___ **14.** to eliminate
___ **15.** had it down pat
___ **16.** preposterous
___ **17.** sitcom

a. noticeable, measurable
b. unimportant
c. a weekly television comedy
d. an attempt
e. an unspecified amount of something
f. pay for part of the cost of something
g. faster than the speed of sound
h. to hear about
i. more or less
j. knew how to do something very well
k. nonmilitary aircraft for paying passengers
l. completely unreasonable or ridiculous
m. quite a large quantity
n. believed to be the result of
o. very strange and odd
p. to give a good reason for
q. to get rid of

As You Listen

You are about to listen to an excerpt from a talk given by Harvard University Professor Michael McElroy, whose specialty is atmospheric sciences. He is speaking to a group of students, telling them how some years ago he and other scientists became involved in the first public discussion of ozone depletion. In this passage, he outlines some of the early factors that led to public awareness of the problem of ozone depletion in the stratosphere.

Michael McElroy, chair of the University Committee on Environment, has done leading work on the stratosphere and global climate change.

LISTEN FOR THE MAIN IDEAS

Although there is a lot of information in the following passage, the main ideas are not as explicit as in earlier chapters. Your job here is to listen and to give each section a title that reflects the main idea of that section. The tape is divided into four sections. Stop the tape at each beep and write a title for that section.

Section 1: ______________________________

Section 2: ______________________________

Section 3: ______________________________

Section 4: ______________________________

NOTE: *Science* and *Nature* are two well-known science journals.

Compare your titles with a partner and discuss your choices. Did you focus on similar information? Make a note of any questions you have.

LISTEN FOR DETAILS

Read over the questions in each section before you listen to the tape again. When you hear the beep, stop the tape and write a short answer for each question in that section.

Boeing concept for a next-generation supersonic airliner would fly at 2.5 times the speed of sound.

Section 1:

a. When did Professor McElroy first start getting involved in public discussions of problems related to global ozone depletion?

____

b. What was a potential problem of the supersonic aircraft that the Boeing Corporation was interested in developing?

____

____

c. What was the U.S. government's involvement in the Boeing Corporation project?

____

____

d. Why was the Boeing Corporation talking about flying large numbers of these supersonic aircraft?

____

____

Section 2:

a. Scientists at that time calculated that there would be ozone depletion from large numbers of supersonic aircraft flying around. How much did they calculate that the amount of ozone would drop?

____

b. Why would changes in ozone have an effect on the rate of skin cancer around the world?

____

____

c. What two population groups did scientists study to determine how the rate of skin cancer might change?

____

____

d. Why were these two population groups selected?

____

____

e. Which population group had the higher rate of skin cancer, and why?

____

____

Section 3:

a. Why did Senator Proxmire first become interested in the early study of the supersonic aircraft?

____

____

b. Did he support the project from the beginning?

____

c. Why was Senator Proxmire's interest in the project important?

____

____

d. What were the two questions that reporters asked scientists about ozone at that time?

____

____

Section 4:

a. What information about the destruction of ozone brought it to the attention of non-science-oriented media?

____

____

b. How long did it take to move from the pages of science journals to the popular media?

____

c. What had now changed about the kinds of questions reporters were asking scientists about global ozone depletion?

____

____

How sure are you about your answers?

Before you check your answers to the questions, fill out the following chart, recording the certainty with which you think each of your answers is correct and complete. Place the number of the question in the appropriate column.

CERTAINTY CHART			
I'M ABSOLUTELY CERTAIN MY ANSWER IS CORRECT	I THINK MY ANSWER IS CORRECT, BUT I'M NOT QUITE SURE	I THINK MY ANSWER IS PROBABLY WRONG, BUT I'M NOT QUITE SURE	I KNOW MY ANSWER IS WRONG

- When you have finished, compare your answers to the comprehension questions with those of a classmate. If your answers differ, discuss them and decide together which answer is right.
- After you have gone over your answers with a classmate, decide whether you want to change any of your responses on the certainty chart.
- Listen to the tape again to verify your answers.

IT WORKS! Learning Strategy: Learning with Others

After You Listen

FOCUS ON SUMMARIZING

Now that you have listened to the tape several times, write two or three sentences that summarize the passage. The first sentence has been started for you.

In his talk, "Understanding Our World," Harvard University Professor Michael McElroy

____

____

____

____

____

After you have written your summary:

- In groups, share what you have written.
- Decide which is the best summary in your group and have the writer put it on the board.
- Discuss the characteristics of a good summary.

FOCUS ON LANGUAGE

LEARNING STRATEGY

Forming Concepts: Analyzing what you hear helps you become aware of language features you can incorporate into your own speaking.

1. As Professor McElroy explains how the public came to be aware of the problem of ozone depletion in the atmosphere, he helps his audience understand the time frame in which this growing public awareness took place.

. . . I remember when I *first* started getting involved. . . .
. . . this goes back to *the early 1970s.* . . .
. . . a supersonic aircraft *at that time* was being discussed. . . .
. . . the Boeing Company *at that time* was talking about large numbers. . . .
. . . our best calculation *at that time*. . .
. . . he made that connection by focusing *for the first time* on . . .
. . . and that was *at the time* a very bizarre idea . . .
. . . and *then* to take the same ethnic grouping in Louisiana . . .
. . . *now* all that has changed. . . .
. . . *in a very short period of time,* it had moved from the pages of *Science* magazine and *Nature* . . .
. . . it became a major subplot on the most popular sitcom on television *at that time*. . . .
. . . it was *a very peculiar time* to be involved in that particular aspect of science. . . .
. . . but what had happened *at this point* is that suddenly ozone was not something you had to explain. . . .

By repeating time expressions, Professor McElroy helps his audience clearly understand the contrasts between different points in time. If a speaker does not make time frames clear in his or her speech, the audience can misunderstand when events actually occurred. Keep this in mind when you are talking about events that took place in past time.

2. Look at the following excerpt from the listening passage. To whom is Professor McElroy referring when he uses the pronoun you?

Now one of the things I find very interesting about this is that at that time, suddenly *you* would find that *you* were on the other end of lots of phone calls from newspaper reporters or radio talk shows from here and there, including Australia and around the world. Suddenly it's a different world *you're* exposed to—and it was interesting how common the questions were. All—essentially 90 percent—of the people who called *you* up asked the same first two or three questions, and *you* got to the point where you really had it down pat. I mean, *you* gave the answer almost before *you* heard the question.

3. Professor McElroy uses the word *now* several times as he speaks. *Now* has a number of definitions, including the following:
   a. At the present time: *They are entering the room now.*
   b. At once; immediately: *Stop talking now!*
   c. In the immediate past; very recently: *He left the room just now.*
   d. At that point in the series of events; then: *The ship was now beginning to sink.*
   e. In these circumstances: *Now we won't be able to stay.*
   f. Used to introduce a command or request: *Now pay attention.*
   g. Used to indicate a change of subject or to preface a remark: *Now let's get down to work.*
   h. Currently fashionable; trendy: *It's the now place to go.*

- In all of the following sentences, Professor McElroy is using only one of the definitions of the word *now* given above. Which of the eight definitions do you think it is?

Now the way the estimate was made was to take a population of a particular ethnic background, a northern European population living in Minnesota, and to look at the incidence rate of skin cancer. . . .

Now one of the things I find very interesting about this is that at that time, suddenly you would find that you were on the other end of lots of phone calls. . . .

Now all that has changed in a pretty drastic way in the case of stratospheric ozone. (This sentence can be interpreted in two ways).

FOCUS ON IDIOMS

In his talk, Professor McElroy talks about the time when ozone depletion stopped being a science issue but became also a political issue—when ". . . the politicians began to *pick it up*. . . ." When he uses the idiom *pick up* here, he means when the politicians first began to hear about the issue. The idiom *to pick up* has well over a dozen different meanings.

- List as many meanings as you can find. Ask a native speaker and/or consult a dictionary.
- For each meaning, write a sentence that illustrates how it is used.
- Compare your list to the lists of your classmates. Add to your list any meanings you may have missed.

FOCUS ON CULTURAL KNOWLEDGE

As an aside remark, Professor McElroy commented that former Senator Proxmire used to issue the "Golden Fleece" award, and when he added that a friend of his had been given the award, you hear laughter from the audience. Do you know what the Golden Fleece award was?

Senator Proxmire was concerned that the government was funding many useless scientific research projects, and periodically he would give the press a list of the projects he considered the biggest waste of government money. This list he called the Golden Fleece awards. The name is a play on words: the Golden Fleece was a golden sheepskin from Greek mythology, and the verb "to fleece" means to defraud someone of money, or to swindle or cheat someone. A "Golden Fleece" award, then, was Senator Proxmire's way of bringing public attention to government-funded projects that he thought were not worth the money. His lists were controversial because often Senator Proxmire and the scientific establishment had very different ideas concerning what kind of research was worthwhile.

When you don't understand a cultural reference, ask someone about it. You will never understand every cultural reference you hear (not even native speakers do), but bit by bit you can build up a large store of cultural knowledge.

Threads

Australia has been called "The Land of the Golden Fleece" from its abundant wool production.

LISTENING LOG

Reminder: Keep up your listening log with as many entries as your teacher requires. At the end of Part II (Speaking), you will report on one of your entries in a small group. (If necessary, see Appendix F for more details on Listening Logs.)

ANY QUESTIONS?

Before you go on to read about and discuss issues of science, answer the following questions on a separate sheet of paper. Do not write your name on the paper. Your teacher or a classmate will collect the papers and share everyone's answers with the class.

1. What has been the most valuable aspect of this chapter for you so far?
2. What is still unclear?

Discussion

IT WORKS! Learning Strategy: Cooperating

The following discussion questions deal with different aspects of science and the citizen. Choose the topic or topics you would like to discuss. Feel free to add related questions of your own to the questions that are asked here. And as always, you should focus on using new vocabulary and appropriate conversation skills.

When appropriate for the activity, work in small groups. Assign one person to act as discussion leader and another person to act as recorder. The discussion leader will make sure that everyone talks and stays on the subject. The recorder will take notes and later report briefly to the class on the main points of your group's discussion.

Before you begin, take a look at the conversation skills questionnaire on page 217. You will respond to the items on the questionnaire after one of your discussions has been completed. As you work in groups, keep the items on the questionnaire in mind.

"I'm beginning to think I need a three-million-year sabbatical from humankind to recover my health."

Source: Drawing by Dedini; © 1992 *The New Yorker Magazine, Inc.*

1. In his talk, Professor McElroy says, "We are concerned with trying to understand the effects of human activity on the global environment." This cartoon also raises the issue of the effects of mankind on the Earth.
   - **a.** What are some of effects of human activity on our planet that the Earth might be referring to in this cartoon? Can we undo the damage?
   - **b.** Do you think technology is part of the problem, or is it the solution? Do you think that advances in technology inevitably bring negative consequences along with the positive? Give specific examples. Who bears the responsibility for the negative consequences?
   - **c.** Are there any modern technological advances that you think we would be better off without?
   - **d.** Scientists continue to develop techniques that allow humans to control their environment in ways that were unimaginable even fifty years ago. Should there be limits to what scientists do? Should scientific research be regulated? If so, by whom?

2. Read the following definition of scientific literacy.

"Scientific literacy **constitutes** the knowledge you need to understand public issues. It is a mix of facts, vocabulary, concepts, history, and philosophy. It is not the specialized stuff of the experts, but the more general, less precise knowledge used in political **discourse.** If you can understand the news of the day as it relates to science, if you can take articles with headlines about genetic engineering and the ozone hole and put them in a meaningful context—in short, if you can treat news about science in the same way that you treat everything else **that comes over your horizon,** then as far as we are concerned you are scientifically literate. . . . But the fact that you don't have to know how to design an airplane doesn't change the fact that you live in a world where airplanes exist, and your world is different because of them. In the same way, advances in fields like microelectronics and molecular biology will affect your life in many ways, and you need to have enough background knowledge to understand how these changes are likely to occur and what their **consequences** are likely to be for you and your children. You must be able to put new advances into a context that will allow you to take part in the national debate about them."

Source: *Science Matters: Achieving Scientific Literacy,* by Robert M. Hazen and James Trefil, 1991. New York: Doubleday, p. xii.

constitutes: consists of
discourse: discussion
that comes over your horizon: that you come in contact with
consequences: results, effects

a. Do you agree with the preceding definition? If not, how would you change it?

- Make a list of three to five things you think a scientifically literate person should know. For example, should a scientifically literate person be able to: explain the difference between an atom and a molecule? explain what the word "superconductor" means? tell when the last ice age was? explain Newton's Laws of Motion? As you make your list, avoid generalities. List some *specific* things you think a scientifically literate person should be able to explain.

____

____

____

____

____

- Compare your list with those of your classmates. Do you agree with what is on their lists? Why or why not?

b. Faculty at Brandeis University in Massachusetts were invited by the university alumni magazine, *The Brandeis Review,* to create a science literacy quiz for the magazine's readers. The purpose of the quiz was to have the readers measure their ability to apply the basic principles of science and math in their everyday lives.

In the following mini-quiz you will find a sample of some of the questions that appeared on the Brandeis quiz. Look over the questions. *You do not need to answer the questions;* just read them. The purpose of this exercise is not to test what you know, but to discuss what kind of scientific knowledge you feel is important to know. After you have read the questions, fill in the chart that follows.

NOTE: If you would like to take the quiz yourself, the answers are given on page 217.

Science Literacy Quiz Excerpt

1. When a newborn baby cries, its face turns very red. This is because:
   - **a.** the brain needs to cool the blood.
   - **b.** crying shuts off blood flow to the rest of the body.
   - **c.** the color acts as an extra sign to the caretaker that the baby needs attention.
   - **d.** the brain's demand for more oxygen is satisfied by the flow of blood and its oxygen to the brain.
2. To hard-boil an egg at high altitudes rather than at sea level requires:
   - **a.** a longer time because the temperature of the air at high **altitudes** is lower.
   - **b.** a shorter time because the temperature of the air at high altitudes is lower.
   - **c.** a longer time because the pressure of the air at high altitudes is lower.
   - **d.** a shorter time because the pressure of the air at high altitudes is lower.
3. The ozone layer needs to be preserved because:
   - **a.** ozone **absorbs** radiation from the sun.
   - **b.** ozone **transmits** radiation from the sun.
   - **c.** ozone absorbs heat given off by the earth.
   - **d.** ozone reflects radiation given off by the earth.
4. Compared with natural vitamin C, **synthetic** vitamin C is:
   - **a.** less effective and slightly **toxic.**
   - **b.** equally effective but more expensive.
   - **c.** equally effective and less expensive.
   - **d.** less effective but less expensive.
5. Both the sun and the moon **exert** force on the waters of the earth. Their relative roles are:
   - **a.** the moon exerts the greater force and is more important than the sun in producing **tides.**
   - **b.** the moon exerts the lesser force but is more important than the sun in producing tides.
   - **c.** the moon exerts the greater force but is less important than the sun in producing tides.
   - **d.** the moon exerts the lesser force and is less important than the sun in producing tides.
6. By consuming one pound of beef:
   - **a.** you barely satisfy your minimum daily protein requirement.
   - **b.** you consume the transferred product of 10 pounds of grain fed to the animal.
   - **c.** you overload the nitrogen elimination capacity of your **kidneys.**
   - **d.** you satisfy an absolute need for red meat.
7. A computer has 8 switches, each of which can be set in 2 positions. The number of possible settings is:
   - **a.** 16.
   - **b.** 64.
   - **c.** 256.
   - **d.** 40,320.

8. While the occurrence of **mutations** is a **random** event in nature, "genetic engineers" can achieve desirable genetic traits by:
   a. moving existing genes into new combinations.
   b. building new genes **from scratch.**
   c. artificially speeding up mutations and waiting for the "right one" to show up.
   d. changing external conditions so organisms will be forced to adapt to them.
9. The hydrogen bomb and the sun both depend upon nuclear reactions for power;
   a. for both, the power is provided by **fusion.**
   b. for both, the power is provided by **fission.**
   c. for the hydrogen atom, the power is provided by fusion, while for the sun the power is provided by fission.
   d. for the hydrogen atom, the power is provided by fission, while for the sun the power is provided by fusion.
10. An **unbiased** coin is **tossed** 1,000 times. The probability of getting 600 or more **heads** is:
   a. less than 1 in 1,000,000.
   b. between 1 in 1,000 and 1 in 100.
   c. between 1 in 100 and 1 in 0.
   d. about 4 in 10.
11. The cause of the **aurora borealis** is:
   a. a reflection off an **ice cap.**
   b. a constellation of stars in our galaxy.
   c. clouds at high altitudes.
   d. particles from the sun interacting with our atmosphere.

Source: *The Brandeis Review,* Winter 1989-1990

altitude: height above sea level
absorbs: takes or sucks in
transmits: sends out
synthetic: artificial, not made naturally
toxic: poisonous
exert: use strength
tides: the regular rise and fall of the seas
kidneys: the two organs in the lower back that separate waste products from the blood
mutations: changes in the cells of a living thing that produce a new quality in the material or the body
random: without any plan
from scratch: starting from the beginning or with nothing
fusion: melting, mixing, uniting, or joining together
fission: the splitting into parts of certain cells or atoms
unbiased: without any tendency to go in one direction or another
tossed: thrown
heads: the side of a coin that bears the image of a person's head
aurora borealis: the bands of light appearing in the night sky in the northern polar regions; also called the northern lights
ice cap: a permanent covering of ice over large areas of land in the polar regions

The questions from this quiz cover a variety of fields of scientific knowledge, but is it really important for citizens today to have an understanding of these fields? Working alone or with a partner, make a list of how important you think it is to know the answers to these particular questions by putting the number of the question in the appropriate column in the chart on the next page.

NOT IMPORTANT TO KNOW	MODERATELY IMPORTANT TO KNOW	VERY IMPORTANT TO KNOW

- How closely does your list match those of the rest of the class? Explain why you put the questions in the categories you did. If you disagree with the way other classmates categorized the questions, explain why.

Calvin and Hobbes

by Bill Watterson

Source: Cartoon by Watterson; © 1991, Andrews and McMeel, A Universal Press Syndicate Co.

3. Why do you think Calvin in the cartoon above is saying math is more like a religion than a science? Have you ever felt that way about math? Do you think many people agree with Calvin? Now that we have electronic calculators, how important is it to study math? Explain your answer fully.
4. How much science and which science courses should be required in high school?
   - Make a list of the science courses that were required in your high school. Next to each course, write the year or years of high school in which you were required to study this subject.
   - Compare your list with the lists of the others in your group.
   - Discuss any differences. Do you think some schools require too much science? Not enough science? Not enough of the right science courses?
   - Design what you think would be the ideal high school science curriculum for today. In your curriculum, make clear which courses should be required and which should be optional.
   - Present your design to the class. Be prepared to defend your choices.
5. Do you think that the street lights in cities and towns affect astronomers' ability to study the night sky through telescopes? Read this article to find the answer. Don't worry about understanding every word.

Astronomers Rage Against the Light

by Malcolm W. Browne

For the past century astronomers have **waged** an unequal battle against the **mounting glare** of electric lighting across night skies—a smog of light pollution that **renders** faint galaxies **all but invisible.**

Two of the latest threats to astronomy **stem from** America's **faltering** economy and a widespread fear of crime.

Mount Palomar Observatory
near Fallbrook, California

One potential victim is the mighty 200-inch telescope on Mount Palomar, Calif., which has led the world in observational astronomy since the late 1940s. In 1984, San Diego, some 40 miles away, **acceded to** astronomers' pleas and replaced its white street lights with low-pressure sodium lamps. Astronomers love the pure yellow light because it is easily filtered from their instruments. But San Diego residents believes it aids thieves (though there is no proof of this).

The San Diego City Council, hoping to **revive** its downtown, is moving to replace its lighting with a lamp that could seriously **degrade** deep-space observations from Palomar.

Meanwhile, a Georgia company, Space Marketing, has announced plans to put a one-mile-wide reflective panel into space sometime in 1996. **Ostensibly** a platform for scientific instruments, this satellite, which would appear nearly as large as the moon, would carry a commercial message or symbol visible from the ground.

"The time may not be distant," said one **anguished** astronomer, "when we'll have to move to the far side of the moon if astronomy is to survive."

waged: fought
mounting : increasing
glare: strong, harsh, unpleasant light
renders: makes
all but invisible: almost impossible to see
stem from: result from
faltering: weakening
acceded to: agreed to
to revive: to make healthy and strong again
degrade: bring down the quality of
ostensibly: supposedly
anguished: feeling pain and suffering

In addition to your own questions and comments, you may want to consider the following questions:

a. Do you agree with the San Diego City Council's plans to replace the low-pressure sodium lights with a form of lighting that could decrease the quality of observations from Mount Palomar, site of a major telescope? Why or why not?
b. What is your opinion of the advertising panel that Space Marketing wants to put into space? What other issues does this plan raise?
c. Are there any additional comments you would like to make or questions you would like to ask?
d. Can you think of another instance in which the interests of scientists and the interests of citizens have collided? What was the problem? What was the outcome?

6. There are a number of private non-profit organizations devoted to furthering scientific knowledge. One of them is The Planetary Society, a group dedicated to the exploration of our solar system. To learn more about this organization, read the following excerpts from a letter that was sent to prospective new members.

"The Planetary Society's innovative Project META is the world's longest running continuous radio search for signals from extraterrestrial civilizations.

We are also playing a major role in preparing for one of the most stirring possibilities of our time—the first mobile robot and human explorers of the planet Mars.

In the future, the Society will try to bring about:

- the development of roving robotic vehicles to traverse the surfaces of nearby worlds.
- new small aircraft which can economically carry out missions to comets, asteroids, the Moon, and Mars.
- development of long-duration flight capability for human crews to prepare for eventual missions to Mars.
- international, multilateral exploration of other planets in our solar system."

In general, what do you think of The Planetary Society's goals?

Now take a look at the U.S. Space Policy Questionnaire that was enclosed with The Planetary Society letter. Answer the questions individually. Compare your answers with a partner or in a group. As you discuss your answers, try to support your opinion as fully as possible.

THE PLANETARY SOCIETY

U.S. Space Policy Questionnaire

Once you've read the enclosed letter... QUESTIONNAIRE # **02465**

please indicate your answers to the following questions and return this survey in the self-addressed envelope *within 14 days.* Your answers will be kept strictly confidential. Tabulated results will be used to help formulate the Society's plans and to influence the future of the U.S. space program.

Your valuable input is greatly appreciated.

A MISSION TO MARS

1. A national goal has been proposed for the American space program: to land a *human* on Mars by 2019, the 50th anniversary of Apollo 11. The cost of human missions to Mars are 10–20 times the cost of robotic Mars missions. But they would define a purpose and goal for all other human space activity.

Do you support a human Mars mission goal?

☐ Yes ☐ No ☐ Not Sure

THE U.S. SPACE PROGRAM

2. President Clinton and Vice President Gore have emphasized their commitment to promoting high technology research and development, arguing that the economic, environmental, and scientific future of the U.S. is at stake.

Do you believe the Clinton Administration should view space research and exploration as a vital and integral part of America's overall technological base?

☐ Yes ☐ No ☐ Not Sure

3. Recent reviews critical of America's space program have recommended that NASA's first priority should be basic space science—such as the exploration of other worlds—and application of space technology to monitoring and researching the Earth's environment.

Do you agree with these recommendations?

A. Space Science and Exploration?
☐ Yes ☐ No ☐ Not Sure

B. Applications to Earth?
☐ Yes ☐ No ☐ Not Sure

NASA

4. Even if NASA's budget is kept at or near current levels, some programs will still have to be eliminated. There is considerable debate about which programs should be maintained and which should be cut.

What is your opinion? Rate the following programs from 1–5 in order of importance (with 1 being most important).

- New robotic planetary missions ____
- Human missions to the Moon or Mars ____
- Shuttle operation ____
- Space station ____
- Earth observation system ____

INTERNATIONAL COOPERATION

5. Increasingly, the other spacefaring nations have expressed a willingness to cooperate with the U.S. on joint ventures to explore the planets. Foremost among them is Russia's Mars '96 mission.

Do you believe that the U.S. should cooperate or compete with space programs of other nations?

☐ Cooperate ☐ Compete ☐ Not Sure

THE SPACE STATION

6. President Clinton has declared his enthusiastic support for joining in partnership with the Russians and other nations on a new plan to build a truly international space station. But there are still powerful forces in Congress who oppose this new approach.

Do you agree that an international space station is the way to go?

☐ Yes ☐ No

Which of these do you see as legitimate rationales for such a project?
(Check all that apply)

☐ Cost reduction
☐ Internaitonal cooperation
☐ Conversion of "swords into plowshares"
☐ Job generation
☐ Expediting of project
☐ Larger, more powerful station
☐ Keeping Russian space capabilities alive
☐ Eliminating redundancy with Russians

SETI

7. The Planetary Society is playing a crucial role in the radio Search for Extraterrestrial Intelligence (SETI), with major programs in the U.S. at Harvard, and in Buenos Aires, Argentina.

Do you believe SETi is a worthwhile endeavor ?

☐ Yes ☐ No

THE PLANETARY SOCIETY

8. Through The Planetary Society, private citizens have been able to directly participate in small, yet vital projects like SETI, the Mars Balloon, the search for near-Earth asteroids, and now, the Mars Rover project with the Russians.

Do you believe that a private citizens' organization should be directly involved in carrying out space science programs?

☐ Yes ☐ No ☐ No opinion

9. Some 100,000 citizens from 131 countries worldwide are now Members of The Planetary Society. They represent the collective voice of those who are interested in — and concerned about — the future of planetary exploration.

Do you believe The Planetary Society should be a strong advocate for a healthy and aggressive U.S. space program, even if it means being critical of present government policy?

☐ Yes ☐ No ☐ No opinion

Thank you very much for your time and participation. Your answers will be most important in helping The Planetary Society influence the future of the U.S. space program.

If you support a vigorous and enthusiastic space program—and want to *personally* make it a reality — then we invite you to join The Planetary Society.

As a Member of the largest and most respected space interest group in the world, you will receive...*The Planetary Report*, our beautiful and informative bimonthly magazine...generous discounts on space-related merchandise...*and* invitations to important conferences, lectures, seminars, and other Society-sponsored events.

☐ **My $20 annual Membership dues are enclosed.**

☐ I prefer to charge my dues to my: ☐ VISA ☐ MasterCard ☐ American Express

Card # ____________________ Exp. Date __________

Signature ____________________

☐ Please bill me. I understand my dues will be payable on receipt.

If you respond within 14 days, we'll send you a special gift with our compliments: *The Solar System in Pictures* — a series of nine full-color 8-1/2" x 11" mini-posters of the planets. Simply complete this form and return it in the enclosed envelope with your Membership dues today.

THE PLANETARY SOCIETY
65 N. Catalina Avenue, Pasadena, CA 91106

DC94

IMPORTANT: Regardless of whether you choose to become a Member of The Planetary Society, it is most important that you send us your completed questionnaire *within 14 days.* Thank you for your participation.

Source: The Planetary Society. Reprinted by permission.

7. What do you think is the most important scientific discovery of the last 100 years? Discuss this question in small groups and then present to the class the main points raised in your discussion.
8. Now, think about one group that you worked with while discussing topics in this section. Evaluate your conversation skills by filling out this conversation skills questionnaire.

IT WORKS! Learning Strategy: Self-Evaluation

Conservation Skills Questionnaire for Discussion Question # ____

While talking to classmates	Often	Sometimes	Never
1. I checked to make sure that everyone understood what I said by asking such questions as "Do you know what I mean?" and "Are you following me?"	____	____	____
2. I gave explanations, definitions, and specific examples when I saw that members of my group weren't following me. I used sentences such as "Let me explain that" and "To help you understand, I'll give you an example."	____	____	____
3. I asked specific questions such as "What do you mean by ____________?" and "Could you give an example of ____________?" and "Could you explain the part about ____________?" when I needed clarification.	____	____	____
4. I paraphrased what others said to make sure that I understood. I used sentences such as "In other words, you mean ____________" and "You're saying, then, that ____________."	____	____	____
5. I encouraged others to speak by making such remarks as "I'd like to know what ____________ thinks about that" and "What do you think, ____________?"	____	____	____

Answers to Science Literacy Quiz (pages 211 and 212)

1. d
2. c
3. a
4. c
5. b
6. b
7. c
8. a
9. a
10. a
11. d

Practicing Explanations

In this section you will have the opportunity to give an explanation. Some of the tasks require short explanations and others require a longer explanation. Choose which task or tasks you would like to do.

1. Did you take the science literacy quiz? If so, choose one of the questions you answered correctly and do the following:

- Explain in detail why your answer is correct and the other choices are incorrect.
- If your answer was correct but was a guess rather than actual knowledge, explain in detail why you chose one answer over the others.
- As you give your answer, from time to time check with your classmates to see how well they are following your explanation.
- As you listen to your classmates' explanations, ask them questions to clarify the subject matter.

2. Why is ice so slippery? Why doesn't water have any calories? How long have butterflies been on the earth? Is it true that lightning never strikes twice in the same place? How does a battery-powered flashlight work? Why is the sky blue? What are some other questions *you* think are interesting? For this exercise, you will ask a question, then research and explain the answer to your classmates.

- Write down a science question that you find interesting.
- If you already know the answer to the question you wrote:

  a. Prepare a short presentation in which you will explain the answer to your classmates.
  b. Make a list of specialized terms or vocabulary you will need to explain.
  c. Use diagrams, charts, and illustrations to help you explain.

- If you don't know the answer to the question you wrote:

  a. Go to the library, or ask a friend who knows about science to explain the answer to you.
  b. Write down any key points and specialized terms, making sure you clearly understand them.
  c. Prepare a short presentation in which you will explain the answer to your classmates.
  d. Use diagrams, charts, and illustrations to help you explain.

3. Find an article in a newspaper or magazine about something that has to do with science.

- Prepare a summary-reaction to the article that you will present orally to your classmates.
- Present your summary-reaction to a small group of your classmates.
- Invite and answer questions from your classmates. Try to find out what *their* reactions are.
- Choose the best summary-reaction from your group for presentation to the entire class.

4. Do you know any interesting stories about scientific discoveries or anecdotes about famous scientists? If so, choose an event or discovery in science or an anecdote about a scientist that you find interesting. Find out as much as you can about what happened. If you need to get more information, interview someone who teaches or studies science, or go to the library for information.

   - Describe the event or anecdote you chose. Make sure you use correct tense forms, appropriate time markers, and rich detail, so that your listeners can visualize what you are describing.

5. You can find numerous science journals in the library or at a newsstand. Many are written for people with a strong science background, but there are also many that present science issues in language that a nonscientist can understand. Go to a library or newsstand and find one of the science journals in the following list or another that you happen to come across. Read an article and make a presentation to the class. In your presentation, include:

   - the name and issue date of the journal.
   - the title and author of the article you read.
   - a summary of the article.
   - your opinion of the article.
   - the topics of the other articles in the journal.
   - whether or not you would recommend this journal to your classmates.

Scientific Journals
*Omni**
*Discover**
*Psychology Today**
*Natural History**
*Smithsonian**
*National Geographic**
*Science Digest**
Scientific American
Nature
*The Sciences**
*World Watch**
*Issues in Science and Technology**
*E: The Environmental Magazine**

* Starred items are journals that can be read and enjoyed by people who do not have a strong background in science and technology.

Debate

IT WORKS! Learning Strategy: Highlighting

Read the following article and then participate in the debate that follows. As you read, highlight what you think are the important points. Do not worry if you do not know every word. Just try to get the main ideas.

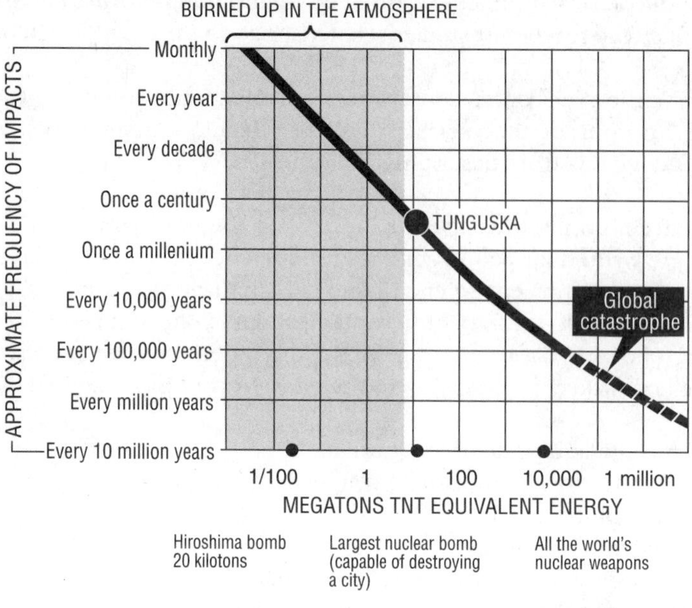

Assessing the threat posed by asteroids

by David Chandler

Someday, scientists believe, an **asteroid** big enough to **decimate** the human race will come **hurtling** toward Earth. It could happen a million years from now, or it could happen tomorrow.

Scientists' awareness of the potential danger of an impact from space has been growing in recent years as photographs from satellites have revealed hundreds of old **craters** on Earth's surface that had never been noticed from the ground, and as astronomers have discovered objects ranging from house-size to mountain-size hurtling by, missing Earth by as little as 100,000 miles.

Last year, two scientific panels came up with recommendations for addressing the threat of cosmic **collisions:** a 20-year, $200-million program to discover any objects that might be headed towards us, and a plan to study ways of heading off the **doomsday** rock if we find one that's on its way.

Last week, the scientists who chaired those panels explained their thinking to a congressional committee that will have to decide what—if anything—to do about it.

The committee must determine how seriously to take the threat, whether to spend **scarce** dollars now to **avert** a danger that may not emerge until long after our great-great-great grandchildren are gone.

David Morrison, an astronomer at NASA's Ames Research Center in California who chaired a workshop organized by the space agency last year on asteroid impacts, told the congressional Committee on Science, Space and Technology that "on a statistical basis, these risks are at least as large as many other natural hazards that are taken very seriously by modern society."

Or as NASA scientist John D. Rather put it: "Impact of large near-Earth objects is a very frequent phenomenon, but potentially more **destructive** than any other threat to life as we know it."

And despite the high-powered telescopes now operating on the ground and **in orbit** and the many spacecraft that have explored the solar system, we could still easily be **blindsided,** the astronomers warn. Space is so **vast** and the asteroids are so **faint,** Morrison said, that only about 100 of the estimated 2,000 asteroids whose orbits cross Earth's have yet been discovered.

That means that, unless and until the 20-year **detection** program is carried out, it is still possible for a **devastating** asteroid to strike the Earth without anyone's seeing it coming. It could, literally, hit tomorrow.

The best-known example of an asteroid's potential for destruction is

A scientist measures one of the craters, 75 feet in diameter, where a giant meteor or asteroid struck near Tunguska, Siberia in 1908

the widely-held theory that a chunk of rock about two miles across smashed into the Earth 65 million years ago and caused a global catastrophe, **wiping out** most of the species then living on the planet, including the dinosaurs.

Impacts big enough to cause devastation on a **global** scale probably only occur every few million years, but smaller asteroids strike the planet more frequently.

Take, for example, what happened over a **remote** stretch of Siberia near the Tunguska river on June 30, 1908. A huge explosion in the air flattened trees for hundreds of square miles and shook the ground hard enough to knock people off their feet 20 miles away from the center of the blast. Scientists now believe it was a **fragment** of an asteroid or comet that exploded, and that a similar impact in the wrong spot would be capable of destroying an average-size city.

Morrison told the panel the latest calculations indicate impacts as large as the Tunguska event could strike in a populated area about once every 3,000 years. And, he said, there's a 1-in-10,000 chance within anyone's lifetime of an impact big enough to cause global damage—climate change that would kill all agricultural crops for a year or longer, causing mass starvation.

Such impacts have probably happened throughout Earth's history, astronomers believe, and will inevitably happen again—unless we see the next one coming and can figure out how to **steer** it away.

The chairman of the workshop last year that studied ways of preventing an asteroid impact told the congressional committee that with enough warning—at least a few years—we could use nuclear weapons **to alter** an asteroid's course and save the planet.

But it would be a **tricky** business at best. The nuclear weapons would have to be exploded nearby the asteroid, pushing it **off course** just enough to miss the Earth. The earlier this is done, the smaller the needed **nudge.** The biggest risk, the panel warned, would be the possibility of creating a **blast** that would shatter the asteroid and shower the Earth with large chunks of the **debris.**

The key is having enough warning time, and that's why the scientists decided the best course would be having a network of six telescopes around the world to seek out all the asteroids in Earth-crossing orbits. The project would cover about 20 years—it takes that long for some of the objects to come close enough to be detected by any existing telescopes.

Groups of astronomers around the world are already conducting searches on a smaller scale. At the present rate, Morrison said, finding all the potentially threatening asteroids might take 200 years.

The National Aeronautics and Space Administration has proposed spending about $500,000 in the next year **to upgrade** the present searches and to work on computer software for a full-scale search. The Australian government recently spent a similar amount to maintain an asteroid search program there. But so far, despite strong support from scientists around the world, no other governments have taken action. In the report from the Morrison workshop, the group wrote that while natural disasters like floods, earthquakes and volcanos may kill thousands of people, and occasionally millions, the impact of a large asteroid "**exceeds** all of these other disasters in that it could kill a billion or more people."

But Morrison stresses that it's important to keep it in perspective. "There are so many other important issues on the table right now it's hard to know what importance should be attached to this."

asteroid: one of many small heavenly bodies between Mars and Jupiter
decimate: destroy
hurtling: rushing with great speed
craters: round rough holes in the ground
collisions: impacts; objects meeting and striking together violently
doomsday: the day when the earth is destroyed
scarce: not many
avert: avoid
destructive: causing great damage
orbit: the path of something moving around a heavenly body, such as the moon or a spacecraft moving around the earth
blindsided: hit unexpectedly
vast: huge
faint: weak
detection: discovery
devastating: completely destructive
chunk: piece
wiping out: destroying
global: worldwide
remote: isolated
fragment: a small piece broken off
steer: guide
to alter: to change
tricky: difficult
off course: off direction
nudge: gentle push
blast: explosion
debris: remains of something broken to pieces
to upgrade: to improve the quality of
exceeds: goes beyond

Threads

The closest measured approach to the earth by an asteroid was 485,000 miles, in the case of Hermes on October 30, 1937.

- After you have read the article, clarify with your teacher or classmates anything you are not sure of.
- Divide the class into two groups (or four groups if you have a large class). One group will argue in favor of public funding of a 20-year asteroid-detection project. The other group will argue against such funding. (See Appendix J for information on debates and panel discussions.)
- Meet with your group, and brainstorm arguments to support your stand. Write down as many arguments as you can in favor of your position. Try to anticipate what the other group will say, and come up with possible counter-arguments. Try to support your opinion with concrete examples to strengthen your argument.
- Bring the two groups together, and intiate a debate. At the end, take a vote on whether or not there should be public funding of an asteroid-detection project.

Guest Speaker

Invite a scientist to come to your class to talk about some of the issues about science that have been raised in this chapter. Follow the steps for inviting a guest speaker in Appendix I.

Listening Log Report

Bring your Listening Log to class and report on one entry in a small group. Take turns doing the following:

- Tell your group members what you watched or listened to.
- Give a short oral summary followed by your personal reaction. Do not read what you have written.
- Check your listeners' comprehension by asking questions such as "Do you understand what I mean?" and "Am I being clear?"
- Rephrase or restate to make your points clear.
- Answer your listeners' questions and ask for their reactions.

FOLLOW-UP

Choose any of the following activities to do outside of class and then report on what happened or what you found out. These activities can be done individually, in pairs, or in small groups. (Refer to Oral Presentation Feedback forms in Appendix L.)

1. Create a questionnaire on attitudes to science literacy. Outside of class, interview several people and then compile the reults. Present the results to the class, and let your classmates know whether or not you were surprised by your findings. (See Appendix K on how to conduct a survey.)
2. Go to a local video store and check out a videotape from one of the following sections: science and nature, documentary, or science fiction. After you watch the video, tape-record your summary of the plot and your reaction to the film. Choose one aspect of pronunciation or grammar to monitor as you are speaking. Re-record your summary-reaction, paying special attention to what you chose to monitor. Give an oral presentation of your summary-reaction to the class.

IT WORKS! Learning Strategy: Self-Monitoring

3. Have you been following any particular science developments in the news (on television, on the radio, in the newspaper)? If so, make a five-minute report about these new developments to the class, and explain why you think these developments are important.
4. Many colleges and universities have an observatory where, on given nights, the public can come to look at the stars and planets through a telescope and also listen to lectures given by the observatory staff. Does your institution have an observatory with a public viewing night? Call the physics and astronomy department to find out. Report your findings to your classmates. If you are interested, visit the observatory, and later let your classmates know what you were able to see.

5. Does your town or city have a science museum? If so, go and spend an afternoon there. Give a short report to your class about what you found most interesting.
6. If you have cable TV, find a science-related program that interests you. Create your own activity to enhance your learning. Report to the class what you watched and what activity you did.
7. Go to a bookstore or library and find *Science Matters: Achieving Scientific Literacy* by Robert M. Hazen and James Trefil. Find a topic in the book that interests you. After you have read about it, tape-record your explanation of what you have just read. Listen to the tape, monitoring one aspect of your speech, then tape-record your explanation again. Did you improve the second time?

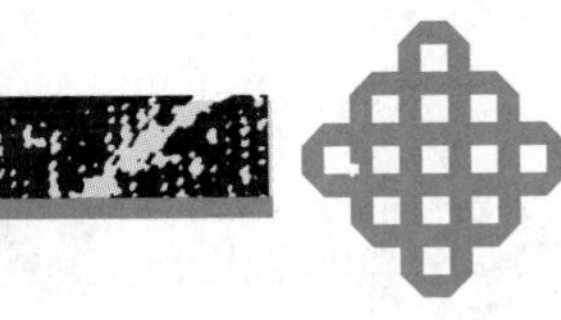

LEARNING ASSESSMENT

1. Look back at Part I (Listening) of this chapter. What activities helped you most in understanding the listening passages?

___

___

___

IT WORKS! Learning Strategy: Evaluating Your Progress

2. Give an example of when you had trouble understanding what you heard.

___

___

___

Why did you have difficulty?

_____ **a.** I didn't know the vocabulary.

_____ **b.** I wasn't paying attention.

_____ **c.** The speaker wasn't clear.

_____ **d.** The speaker spoke too fast.

_____ **e.** Other: ___

3. Were you more successful than you expected to be in understanding the listening material about the first public awareness of ozone depletion? Were you less successful than you expected? Why?

___

___

___

4. Look back at Part II (Speaking) of this chapter. Give one or two examples of your most successful efforts at oral communication. Try to explain why you were able to succeed.

____

____

____

5. Give an example of a discussion in which you had trouble communicating with your classmates.

____

____

____

Why did you have difficulty?

_____ **a.** My classmates didn't understand my pronunciation.

_____ **b.** I didn't understand my classmates' pronunciation.

_____ **c.** I had trouble finding the main ideas in the readings.

_____ **d.** There was a lot of new vocabulary.

_____ **e.** Other: ______________________________

6. What could you do next time to:
a. better prepare for a listening passage?

____

____

____

b. improve your effectiveness when speaking in a group?

____

____

____

7. Look back at the goals you set at the beginning of this chapter.
a. Which goals did you achieve?

____

____

____

b. What will be your primary goal as you continue to learn English?

____

____

____

Appendices

APPENDIX A: SUMMARIZING

1. ***What is a summary?***
   A summary is an oral or written explanation of something you heard, saw, or read. You can summarize a lecture that you heard or a movie you saw. You can also summarize a newspaper article or a reading from a book. A summary is always shorter than the original material.
2. ***Why is it important to learn how to write a summary?***
   You need to learn how to tell other people the main idea of what you heard, saw, or read. If people ask you what a movie was about, you first tell them the main idea of the story. If they are interested, you might give them a few details. Telling *everything* about a movie isn't summarizing.
3. ***What should I put in a summary?***
   Remember that you need to put the **main idea** first. You should add details if you think the people who listen to or read your summary won't understand the main idea without more explanation.

   Also, consider what you are asked to do. If your teacher asks for a **one-sentence** summary, give only the main idea. If your teacher asks for a **brief** (short) summary, write the main idea plus a few details. If your teacher asks for a **detailed** summary, include some, but *not all,* the details.

   Sometimes you will be asked to write a summary and then give your opinion. In this case, be sure to put your opinion in a separate paragraph.
4. ***What should I put in the first sentence?***
   State the main idea in the first sentence. Here are some suggestions for ways to start:

   - According to Lillian Glass, . . .
   - In Lillian Glass's opinion, . . .
   - In the listening passage, Lillian Glass discusses/discussed . . .
   - The listening passage is/was about . . .

   If you know the title of the source, use it in the first sentence between quotation marks. Write, for example:

   - In the article, "Voice Mail: Not the Answer," John Flinn explains/explained that . . .
   - The listening passage, "Voice Mail May Cost Company's Business," is/was about . . .

   NOTE: You can use either simple present or past tense.

5. ***What should I not put in a summary?***
   Don't express your own opinion, and don't add information that was not in what you heard or read.
6. ***Should I use the exact words that I heard? Can I copy from what I read?***
   No. You should try to use your own words. If you must copy, don't copy too much, and be sure to put what you copy between quotation marks.

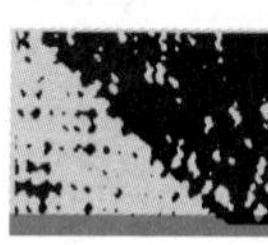

APPENDIX B: TAKING NOTES

It is worthwhile to take notes because:

- it is normal to forget, even after a few hours, what we have heard.
- the act of writing makes the material easier to remember.
- the act of writing forces us to decide what is and what isn't important enough to write down.
- note-taking forces us to focus on and identify main ideas and important details.
- we can identify the areas that we do and don't understand.
- instructors often give assignments and exams based on lectures as well as reading assignments.

Here are a few hints for taking notes:

1. Choose a format that is comfortable for you, but make sure that it is easy to see the difference between main ideas and details in your headings:

Some Ways to Write Headings:

- ***Use capital letters:*** WHY NOTE TAKING IS IMPORTANT
- ***Underline:*** Why note taking is important
- ***Use a box:*** Why note taking is important
- ***Put the heading in a circle in the center of a page with lines for details extending out:***

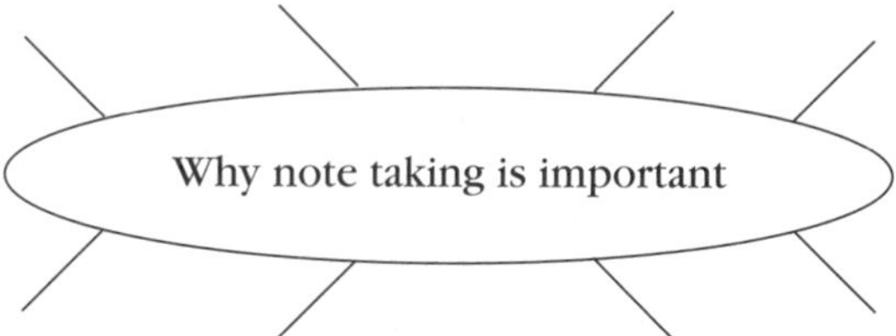
Why note taking is important

Some Ways to Write Details:

- ***Indent below heading and use dashes:***

WHY NOTE TAKING IS IMPORTANT
—we quickly forget what we hear
—material is easier to remember

- ***Indent below heading and use bullets:***

Why note taking is important

- we quickly forget what we hear
- material is easier to remember

- ***Place in circles around main idea:***

we quickly forget what we hear

material is easier to remember

main idea—
Why note taking is important

2. Don't try to write everything you hear, word-for-word, as if you were taking dictation.
3. Use abbreviations to save time. Some examples follow, but use whatever abbreviations you are familiar with. And when you hear long words, try to make up abbreviations for them that you will remember.

w/	with	↑	increases, goes up
w/o	without	↓	decreases, goes down
p	page	#	number
pp	pages	~	approximately
?	question	**re**	regarding
%	per cent	**esp**	especially
$	money	**min**	minimum
eg.	for example	**max**	maximum
i.e.	that is	**&** or **+**	and, plus
etc.	et cetera, and so on	**–**	minus
∴	therefore	**10**	ten
=	the same as	**10th**	tenth
≠	different from	**hr**	hours
>	more than	**min**	minutes
<	less than	**bec**	because
—>	causes, leads to		

OTHER:

Suggestion for Practice

If you are near an American college or university, show this list of abbreviations to some students. Ask them which of these they use, and also ask them for abbreviations that they use that are not on this list. Add theirs to your list, and then share what you have discovered with your classmates.

APPENDIX C: SMALL GROUP DISCUSSION ROLES

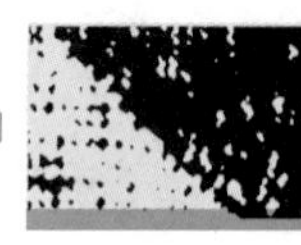

Whenever you have a small group discussion, each member of the group should have a specific role. Each group member already has, of course, an important role—that of participant. However, in the interests of keeping the discussion focused on the task in hand, certain other roles should be assigned. Before you begin your group discussion, always select a discussion leader and a recorder.

ROLE	DUTIES
Discussion Leader	The **discussion leader** makes sure everyone knows everyone else's name; helps the group stay focused on their task; makes sure that no one dominates the discussion; and encourages everyone to participate.
Recorder	The **recorder** writes down all the main points made by the group and reports this information later during the class discussion.
Participant	Every member of the group is a **participant** who actively contributes ideas, facts, and opinions to the discussion.

Here are other roles you may want to assign, depending on the nature of the task:

Timekeeper	The **timekeeper** makes sure the group completes its work within a certain period of time.
Process Observer	After the group-work session, the **process observer** describes the behavior of the group members and how well they worked together as a team.

Source: Adapted from Kate Kinsella & ARC Associates: "Roles of Participants in Groups"

PARTICIPANT RESPONSIBILITY CHART

Participants as well as leaders have interpersonal responsibilities whenever these situations arise:

1. One or two members dominate.
2. Some apparently lack interest.
3. Conflict occurs between members.
4. Some members will not talk.
5. Discussion drifts to irrelevant matters.

A good participant, like a good leader, should, in general:

1. Use tact.
2. Be enthusiastic.
3. Exhibit a sense of humor.
4. Be cooperative.
5. Minimize differences.
6. Be friendly.
7. Identify with the group's goals.
8. Interact.
9. Consider the rewards of membership.
10. Work to help the group.

Source: Raymond Ross, *Essentials of Speech Communication,* 1979, p. 174.

APPENDIX D: HOW TO BE AN ACTIVE LISTENER

It is very important to let speakers know that you are paying attention to what they are saying. You can do this in a number of ways:

Nonverbally

Make eye contact, nod your head, vary your facial expressions.

Verbally

Do some of the following:

1. Show that you understand by saying:

- "Uh-huh" or "Mm-hmmm"
- "That's interesting."
- "I know what you mean."
- "That's right." or "That's true."

2. Ask for repetition with such questions as:

- "Could you please say that again?"
- "Sorry. Could you explain that again?"

3. Ask for clarification with such questions as:

- "I'm not sure I understand. Are you saying that . . . ?"
- "Do you mean that . . . ?"
- "Could you give me/us a specific example of . . . ?"
- "What is a . . . ?" or "What does . . . mean?" or "What do you mean by . . . ?"

4. Summarize, restate, or rephrase what the speaker has said, starting with phrases such as:

- "So you're saying that . . . "
- "In other words, . . . "
- "What you're saying is that . . . "

5. Express agreement or disagreement by saying:

- "Uh-huh" or "Mm-hmmm"
- "I know what you mean."
- "I agree (100 percent)."
- "I disagree with . . . "
- "I'm not sure that I agree . . . "

Suggestion for Practice

You can practice using active listening skills by getting into groups of three. Each of you should take one of the roles below and then switch roles when your teacher asks you to.

The **listener** should listen *actively* to show interest in what the speaker is saying. To do this, the listener should respond both nonverbally and verbally in the ways previously described.

The **speaker** should talk about *one* of the following:

a. An aspect of the chapter you are now working on in *Sound Ideas*
b. A light subject, such as what she or he did or will do over the weekend or on vacation

While speaking, the speaker should make eye contact with the listener and check his or her comprehension occasionally by asking such questions as "Do you know what I mean?" or "Am I being clear?"

The **observer** should be a silent participant and put checks (√) as appropriate in the chart below. After the discussion, the observer should give this feedback to the speaker and listener and ask them how they felt during their discussion.

	SPEAKER	LISTENER
showed comprehension by giving nonverbal feedback	______	______
showed comprehension by giving verbal feedback	______	______
asked for repetition	______	______
asked for clarification	______	______
summarized	______	______
restated in the same words	______	______
rephrased with different words	______	______
expressed agreement/disagreement	______	______
checked comprehension	______	______

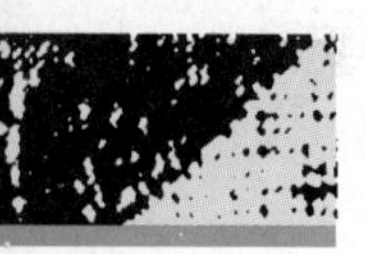

APPENDIX E: TURN-TAKING STRATEGIES

Conversation is a collaborative process. Speakers do not say everything that they want to say all at once; they take turns with other people. In fact, at any moment, the speaker may become the listener. It is not always easy to enter a conversation or to take over the role of speaker. The following tips may help:

Keeping a Conversation Going

- A basic rule of conversation is that only one person speaks at a time.
- Participants work to keep talk continuous by avoiding silence or long pauses, which are considered awkward.

Entering a Conversation

- Indicate that you want to speak by using such interjections as "mm-hmmm," "yeah," "uh-huh," and intonation.
- Use facial expressions and other gestures to show that you want to speak.
- Accept a turn offered by another speaker by responding to a question.
- Complete or add to something the speaker says.

Holding a Turn

- Use language to indicate that you have more to say. You may use intonation or expressions that suggest continuity, such as "First," "Another thing," and "Then."

Bringing Others into the Conversation

- Signal the completion of your turn by slowing down the final syllables of an utterance and dropping the pitch.
- Pause to give someone else an opportunity to take his or her turn to speak.
- Use a gesture or facial expression to signal that your turn is finished.

Using Both Short and Long Turns

Participants in a conversation are continuously evaluating what each other is saying to judge when to take a turn and how much to say. This can sometimes be difficult for a non-native speaker of English.

You need to learn to understand the cues you get in order to use both short and long turns to keep a conversation moving smoothly. If you take only short turns speaking, you may give the impression of being bored and uninterested and unwilling to talk. If you take only long turns, you will be seen as dominating the conversation. To become an effective conversationalist, you need to learn how to balance short and long turns.

Here are some examples of both kinds of turns:

Short Turns

MIKE How was your weekend?

SUSAN It was good. We went to a movie on Saturday and to the Museum of Science on Sunday afternoon. How about you?

MIKE Oh, we didn't do much. We rented a video Saturday night, but that's about it.

Long Turns

You would want to take a longer turn if you want to explain an opinion, describe something, or tell a joke or story.

ALICE So, how was your weekend?

TOM It was good. We finally got to see Jurassic Park.

ALICE Oh really? How was it?

TOM It was fantastic! It's one of the best films I've ever seen. The special effects were incredible. You wouldn't believe how real the dinosaurs looked. It's amazing what these special effects people are able to do.

ALICE Was the film as violent as everybody says?

TOM I didn't think so. I know a lot of people have been saying that it's too violent and too realistic and will scare children, but I disagree. There were a bunch of kids with their parents in the row in front of me, and the parents acted more scared than the kids! Just to give you an example, there was one scene in the film where the two children in the movie were trapped in a room with two particularly vicious dinosaurs who were trying to catch them and presumably eat them—and the kids in the audience seemed to love it. Their faces were glued to the screen. In fact, after the movie was over, I overheard one parent asking his child why he hadn't been scared, and the child told him that he knew it was just a movie and that nothing bad would happen to the kids in the movie. It was like the kid had faith that his father wouldn't take him to a movie where something bad would happen to the kids in the movie.

ALICE Mm-hmmm. . . .

TOM To be honest, I don't know why people are making such a big deal about it. Kids watch a lot more violent stuff on TV. I mean, look at the cartoons they watch on Saturday morning. Those are *really* violent.

ALICE Yeah, it's true. It seems contradictory. It reminds me of an article I saw last week in *Newsweek* about the violence in classic fairy tales and how now everybody's trying to rewrite them so they're less disturbing for kids and they have happy endings and nobody gets eaten. But nobody's doing anything about the violence you see in television cartoons. I don't know about *Jurassic Park,* because I haven't seen it yet, but I think the violence you find in fairy tales is a lot less disturbing than what you see on TV.

TOM Exactly. I agree with you completely.

Many second-language learners find it difficult to take long turns, so they stick to short turns. As a result, they may appear to be uncooperative conversational partners.

Source: Adapted from Jack Richards, *The Language Teaching Matrix.* New York: Cambridge University Press, 1990, pp.68–70.

APPENDIX F: LISTENING LOGS

1. ***What is a listening log?***
   A listening log is like a journal. It is a small book or section of your notebook in which you write information and your thoughts about what you listened to on TV or radio.
   At least twice every week, you will watch or listen to programs and take notes. You will put your notes into your log and then write a short summary of what you saw and heard. After that, you will write your reaction to the program in a short paragraph.
2. ***In more detail, what should go into my log?***
   Twice each week, for each program you watch or listen to, write the following:

   - The name of the program you watched or listened to
   - The date of broadcast
   - Your notes, in list form
   - A short summary in your own words—no more than one paragraph. Don't try to explain everything that you saw or heard. Just give the main idea and a few details.
   - Your personal opinion of the program in a separate paragraph

3. ***Why should we keep listening logs?***
   Logs are useful for a number of reasons:

   - You may be unaware of good programs to watch on TV or listen to on the radio in English. Keeping a listening log encourages you to search them out and listen to them regularly.
   - Listening outside of class helps you to learn English and understand American culture. As you know, it is not enough to speak English only in class.
   - You practice the important skills of notetaking, summarizing, and writing down your reactions. Then, in class you have opportunities to express your ideas orally in a small group.

4. ***How often should I turn in my log?***
   Your teacher will decide. Perhaps it will be turned in every two or three weeks.
5. ***How many entries should be in my log each time I turn it in?***
   Each week you should write two entries. If your teacher collects the log every two weeks, your log will contain four entries each time (and perhaps more if you want extra credit).
6. ***Are logs graded?***
   Your teacher may collect the first logs at the end of the first week to see if everyone understands what to do, and this log may not be graded. Subsequent logs, collected every two or three weeks, often receive letter grades, but your teacher will make the decision.

7. ***How are logs graded?***
Again, that will be your teacher's decision. However, the following are often considered in log grades:

- Whether or not you have made at least two entries per week.
- Whether or not you have three sections per entry—notes, summary, reaction.
- The quality of these three sections.

8. ***Is it okay to watch closed-captioned TV?***
Yes, it's a great idea. For those of you who don't know, closed-captioning prints the spoken words in a TV program along the bottom of the TV screen. This captioning was originally intended for the deaf, but it was also found to be helpful to people learning a language. All new TVs sold in the United States after 1994 can receive closed-captioned programs.
Another advantage would be a VCR. If you have access to a VCR, you might tape a few minutes of a TV program and then play it back over and over. With each replay, your comprehension will increase.
9. ***How can I write about a news program that has a lot of stories?***
You should summarize and react to only one or two of the news stories, not all. If you watch a one-hour news-magazine show that contains three stories, write about only one.
10. ***What should I do if I don't understand what I'm listening to?***
You should write a note to your teacher in your log that you didn't understand a particular program. Then try to find something else to listen to.
11. ***Can I see an example of a log entry?***
Yes. Here's one written by a student who listened to a program on National Public Radio:

NPR
April 27, 1993, 5:30-6:00 P.M.
Denmark's child care system

Notes: careers and motherhood
Denmark's second largest city
nursery—elementary school
rich—pay one third of operating cost
poor—pay nothing

Summary:
Denmark's second largest city has a wonderful child care system. Mothers who want careers as well as motherhood love this system very much. The program is subsidized by the ministry policies. These child care centers are not different from regular kindergartens. They take care of children from three months old to elementary schoolers after school. Only difference is that better off families pay one third of operating cost and poor families pay nothing.

Personal Reaction:
Many women have to struggle with their children to keep their jobs and families at the same time. In U.S., to help and to reduce their hardship, the communities or the government should do something like Denmark.

12. ***What specific TV programs should I watch?***
Programs and schedules can change a great deal, but here are some shows that have been on TV for a long time. Your class could be divided into groups who would find out the day, time, and channel of each show and then report the schedule to the whole class.

TYPE	SHOW	DAY & TIME	CHANNEL
NEWS			
	MacNeil-Lehrer Newshour		
	NBC News		
	CBS News		
	ABC News		
	Nightline		
	Washington Week in Review		
	CNN		
	Other:		
NEWS MAGAZINE SHOWS (short documentaries)			
	60 Minutes		
	20/20		
	Other:		
SUNDAY MORNING NEWS SHOWS			
	Sunday Morning		
	Meet the Press		
	Face the Nation		
	Other:		
TALK SHOWS			
	Donahue		
	Oprah Winfrey		
	Other:		
LATE-NIGHT SHOWS			
	Tonight Show		
	Late Show with David Letterman		
	Saturday Night Live		
	Other:		
COMEDIES			
	The Simpsons		
	Roseanne		
	Other:		
DRAMAS			
	Murder She Wrote		
	Other:		

13. ***What radio programs should I listen to?***
There are a lot of "talk-radio" programs on the radio. If you prefer to listen to noncommercial radio, then you would probably like National Public Radio (NPR). Below is a schedule from a local NPR station in California. Find out the name and address of your local NPR station, write to request a schedule for your area, and compare the two. Of course, you don't need a schedule for the radio. All you have to do is turn it on and you're bound to find something of interest.

Schedule for KQED 88.5FM

	MON	TUE	WED	THU	FRI	SAT	SUN	
mid	All Things Considered							mid
		Sound Ideas						
1am	To the Contrary / Washington Week	BBC World News					Crossroads / Horizons	1am
2am	Sound Money	World Affairs Council	Evening Forum			Commonwealth Club	MonitoRadio Weekend Edition	2am
3am	Morning Edition					Washington Week / Wall Street Week	To the Best of Our Knowledge	3am
4am						Common Ground / Inside Europe		4am
5am						Weekend Edition		5am
6am								6am
7am								7am
8am								8am
9am	Forum							9am
10am						Car Talk		10am
11am	Talk of the Nation					Fog City Radio (live)	A Prairie Home Companion	11am
noon								noon
1pm	Fresh Air							1pm
2pm	All Things Considered							2pm
3pm	The MacNeil/Lehrer NewsHour					BBC World News		3pm
4pm	Marketplace					Living on Earth / Soundprint	MonitoRadio Weekend Edition	4pm
	All Things Considered							
5pm						All Things Considered		5pm
6pm	Marketplace					A Prairie Home Companion	Family Talk	6pm
7pm	Fresh Air							7pm
8pm	World Affairs Council	Evening Forum			Commonwealth Club	Fog City Radio	Sound Money	8pm
9pm	BBC World News						Tech Nation	9pm
10pm	Forum					Tell Me a Story / A Moveable Feast	Crossroads / Horizons	10pm
11pm	All Things Considered					Joe Frank: In the Dark / Latino USA	This Week in N. Cal / Face to Face	11pm

Source: Focus Magazine

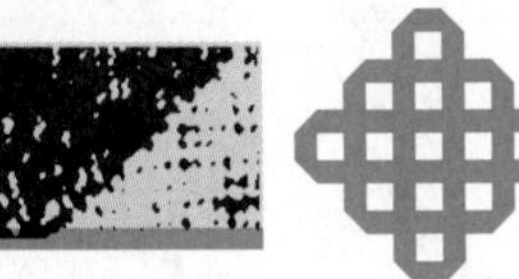

APPENDIX G: ENGLISH USE LOG

Every week keep a daily log of the time you spend listening to and speaking English. Note the activities you do using English and how long you spend on each activity. Also note any special problems you focused on or monitored either in speaking or listening to English. Each week, ask yourself if you are using English *more? less? the same?* Are you monitoring problems *more? less? the same?* Are you consciously using new words *more? less? the same?*

SUNDAY:

MONDAY:

TUESDAY:

WEDNESDAY:

THURSDAY:

FRIDAY:

SATURDAY:

What I will try to do next week:

____

____

____

EXAMPLE OF ENGLISH USE LOG

MONDAY:
- —watched TV news (1 hr.); focused on announcer's intonation
- —had coffee with classmates from Mexico and Japan (35 min.)
- —computer science class; listened to lecture (50 min.)
- —talked with an American classmate about homework after computer science class (15 min.)
- —saw a free film at the Boston Public Library (100 min.)

TUESDAY:
- —asked librarian where to find information for class project (5 min.)
- —ESL class (2 hrs.)
- —worked on ESL class project with classmates (1 hr. 20 min.)
- —watched evening news, took notes for listening log (20 min.)
- —talked on phone to Brazilian, American, and French friends (45 min.)

WEDNESDAY:
- —listened to tapes in the language lab (1 hr.)
- —went to computer science class; took notes on lecture (50 min.)
- —listened to NPR (1 hour) and later talked to friend about an NPR story about an alternative school (35 min.); monitored for past tense
- —called airline company to make reservations (7 min.)

THURSDAY:
- —listened to the radio news (30 min.)
- —went to ESL class (2 hrs.)
- —watched TV program about unsolved mysteries (1 hr.); took notes on words I couldn't understand

FRIDAY:
- —listened to news on radio (30 min.)
- —went to computer science class and listened & took notes (50 min.)
- —asked the professor some questions after class (10 min.)
- —watched the movie "A Room With a View" (2 hrs.)
- —talked with friends about movie (1 hr.)

SATURDAY:
- —spent all day on Cape Cod with friends from ESL class; spoke English together (6 hours); talked to American on beach (45 min.)
- —watched the movie "Star Wars" (2 hrs.)
- —talked with my landlady (45 min.)

SUNDAY:
- —worked on ESL class project w/classmates (2 hrs.)
- —listened to the radio news (30 min.); focused on past tense (10 min.)
- —watched "60 Minutes" on TV and took notes on one of the stories for my listening log (1 hr.); had difficulty w/vocabulary
- —talked to American friend; tried to use new vocabulary (40 min.)

What I will try to do next week: try to increase by 15 min. the amount of time I speak English each day and try to begin conversations with some of the American students in my computer science class. Also monitor myself for correct use of past tense.

APPENDIX H: SELF-FEEDBACK AND MONITORING TASKS

One way to improve performance in language learning is to use feedback. In class, your teacher can give you feedback. Outside of class, you can ask friends who are native speakers of English to give you feedback. However, you can also record yourself speaking alone or with a group and then listen to the recording, focusing on a particular aspect of speech. The following self-feedback tasks are just a few examples of ways in which you can monitor your speech yourself. Your teacher can suggest other ways you can monitor your speech.

Feedback Task #1: Focus on using expressions that encourage the speaker.

1. Record yourself discussing, in a small group, one of the topics from a chapter in this book.
2. Select several minutes from the recording.
3. Listen to your recording and find out whether you used any of the following:
   a. Encouraging expressions, such as:

   - *Really?*
   - *Is that right?*
   - *That's interesting / unusual / nice / amazing / etc.*
   - *It sounds interesting / lovely / odd / fascinating / etc.*

For example:

SAM *"In Japan, a person would never start a speech by telling a joke to break the ice."*

ELLEN *"Oh, really?"*

SAM *"Yes. It would be regarded as frivolous, and the audience would feel that the speaker was not being serious."*

ELLEN *"That's interesting."*

b. Questions that repeat a key word from what the other person has said. For example:

CAROL *"I hate humor that's aggressive"*

JIM *"Aggressive?"*

CAROL *"Yes, jokes or cartoons that are violent or mean."*

These expressions encourage the other person to say more. Listen to the way native speakers use these expressions, and try to introduce these kinds of expressions into your own conversation.

Source: Adapted from *Conversation,* by Nolasco and Arthur, Oxford University Press, 1987, p. 127.

Feedback Task #2: Focus on the strategies to use to keep a conversation going.

1. Record yourself discussing a question from one of the chapters with other members of your small group.
2. Right after your discussion, choose a two- or three-minute section of your recording in which most of the people in the group had something to say. Listen in particular for any examples of questions people asked to encourage the speakers to say more about themselves or their ideas. For example:
   So what did you do then?
   And did that work?
   Do you think you'd do it again?
   When did it all happen?
   Why did you decide to . . . ?
   How did it happen?
   What would happen if . . . ?

   Write down any similar questions you hear in the recording, discuss them in your group, and ask the following questions:
   a. Were the questions grammatically correct?
   b. Were they suitable?
   c. Did they help the conversation go forward?
   d. How could you improve the questions?
3. Now listen for places in the recorded conversation where there was a break or a silence. Discuss these breaks in your group. Were they natural and acceptable? If not, how could you have made the conversation develop more easily? With a question? By showing interest? By asking another person's opinion? Discuss how you would improve the conversation.

Source: Adapted from *Conversation,* by Nolasco and Arthur, Oxford University Press, 1987, p. 129.

Feedback Task #3: Focus on a particular aspect of speech, and monitor yourself for correct usage.

1. Watch a television program, or listen to something on the radio. Take notes, because you will record yourself speaking about what you heard.
2. Check *one* of the following items to monitor as you make your recording:

   _____ Verb tenses

   _____ Word forms (correct forms of nouns and adjectives)

   _____ Adding *-s* to third-person singular verbs in present tense

   _____ Pronunciation of a particular vowel or consonant sound

   _____ Rhythm, stress, and intonation

3. Make a two- or three-minute recording of yourself talking about what you watched on TV or heard on the radio.
4. Listen to your recording, focusing on the aspect of speech that you chose to monitor. Make a note of any mistakes you made or anything you would like to change.
5. Record yourself again, focusing on one area of improvement.
6. Listen to your recording, making a note of where and how much you improved.

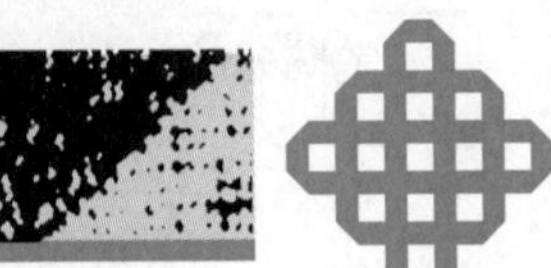

APPENDIX I: GUEST SPEAKERS

Before the Visit

1. Make a list of people in your school or community who can speak on a topic related to the chapter that you are working on. Choose the one that most students agree they would like to invite to speak.
2. Contact the possible speaker and invite him or her to come and speak to the class. (In most situations, your teacher would probably do this.) If the speaker accepts, ask him or her to send a handout or other material before the visit, if possible, so the class can become familiar with the vocabulary related to the topic of the speech.
3. Once the visit has been arranged, decide as a class on a master list of questions you would like to ask. Send this list to the speaker. (Guest speakers can get nervous too, and knowing ahead of time what the audience is interested in will make your guest more comfortable.)
4. Choose a student to contact the speaker and get information for a one-minute speech of introduction. The student should find out where the speaker is from, what job he or she has, and so on, and then should prepare easy-to-read notes on an index card.

   The student "introducer" should include some of the following phrases in the speech of introduction:

- I would like to introduce our guest speaker, ______________________.
- I am very pleased to introduce ______________________.
- ______________ is originally from ______________.
- ______________ is currently ______________.
- ______________ is going to speak to us about ______________.
- Everyone, please welcome ______________________.

During the Visit

5. The designated student should introduce the guest to the class.
6. Everyone should use active listening skills (nodding, eye contact, etc.) and take notes as they listen to the speaker's presentation. It is possible that the speaker will ask the class comprehension questions to make sure that everyone is following what is being said.
7. During the question-and-answer session that should follow the presentation, students should refer to the list of questions that they prepared ahead of time. They should also feel free to come up with new questions and comments. Questions can be related to the content of the presentation, or they can be used to ask for clarification.

After the Visit

8. The class should do the following:
   - Discuss how well they understood the presentation and what aspects of the speaker's style increased or decreased their comprehension.
   - Write a summary of and reaction to the main points that had been covered.
9. One student should send the visitor a thank-you note on behalf of the entire class.

APPENDIX J: INFORMAL DEBATE OR PANEL DISCUSSION

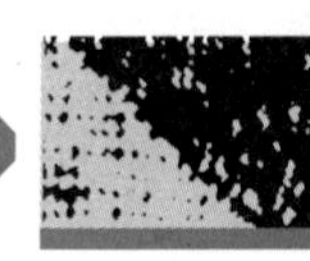

In a regular informal panel discussion, participants provide information to an audience on a particular topic. When a topic is controversial, the discussion resembles a debate, with participants taking sides or positions. Their discussion is guided by an impartial moderator, who makes sure that everyone has a chance to speak and that the discussion stays on target. This is different from a formal debate, in which each participant speaks for a specified amount of time and there is less spontaneous give-and-take of opinion.

In the informal debate or panel discussion, participants discuss a controversial subject. Typically, those who have the same position sit together on one side of the moderator and face an audience, as shown below:

— — — — —	MODERATOR	— — — — —
(Those in favor of something)		(Those against something)

A U D I E N C E

Participants, who express their own opinions or take on special roles, often interrupt each other, which makes it necessary for the moderator to "control traffic." These discussions can become very exciting.

Following a panel discussion, the moderator may invite the audience to ask questions and make comments to the panel members.

The suggested procedure for an informal panel discussion is as follows:

Preparation

1. Each group meets separately to prepare their arguments. They brainstorm their points and make a list, and they also anticipate the points they think the other side will make. The number of panel discussions that go on at the same time will vary according to the size of the class.
2. The moderator plans the introduction. It is helpful for the moderator to think of his or her role as like that of a TV host, who gives background information about the guests and introduces them. The moderator should consult with the teacher about the best way to introduce the subject of the discussion. Once the moderator is ready, if the groups are still preparing, the moderator should visit the groups to get an idea of the points they will raise. This will make it easier for the moderator to prepare some questions in advance. The moderator should always keep in mind that she or he should not express personal opinions in the discussion.
3. If it is possible, arrangements should be made to record the discussion with a video camera.

The Discussion

1. The moderator introduces the topic and then introduces the panel members to the audience. (They could wear name tags or have signs on their desks that indicate their names or roles.)
2. The moderator then poses a question to the last panel member that was introduced.
3. The moderator "controls traffic," giving each panel member a chance to complete his or her thought before the next panel member begins speaking. When there is a silence, the moderator breaks in to ask prepared, specific questions to keep the discussion going.
4. The moderator clarifies, summarizes, restates, or paraphrases arguments when necessary. To do this, he or she will have to try to be alert to signs of possible misunderstanding or lack of comprehension on the part of the audience or panel members.
5. The moderator also tries to keep the discussion coherent. That is, if a speaker brings up a point for discussion, and another speaker makes a remark totally unrelated to the subject, the moderator should interrupt and get the discussion back on track.
6. At the end of the allotted time, the moderator summarizes the main points of the discussion. The moderator then asks for questions and/or comments from the audience and continues to "control traffic."

USEFUL PHRASES IN A DEBATE OR PANEL DISCUSSION

Moderator

To introduce a speaker and "control traffic," say:

I'd like to introduce . . .
Let's start with . . .
First _________ will speak, and then _________
Please don't speak out of turn!
I think _________ has a question.
Now our panel will take questions from the audience.
Sorry to cut you off, but . . .

To restate, say:
If I understand, your idea is that . . .
So, you're saying . . .
In other words, you believe that . . .
Then ask:
Is that right?
Is that what you meant?

Panel Members

To "get the floor," say:

Excuse me for interrupting, but . . .
That's true, but . . .
Yes, but . . .
I'd like to make a point here.
I'd like to ask a question.
I have a question for . . .
I'd like to comment on that.

To express total agreement, say:
Exactly.
That makes sense to me.
That's how I feel about it, too.

To reflect, say:
So, your opinion is that . . .
So, you feel that . . .
You thought it was . . .

To summarize, say:
In summary, then, you think . . .
These, then, are the ideas that you have expressed:

To clarify, ask:
Who? What? Where? When?
Why? How? How much/many?

To get back on the topic, say:
We've gotten off on a tangent. Let's get back on topic.
That's not related to __________. We need to talk about __________.

To respond to an irrelevant remark:
That doesn't relate to what __________ just said.

To express partial agreement, say:
Yes, but . . .
Yes, but on the other hand, . . .
That may be true, but . . .

To express total disagreement, say:
I don't agree.
I disagree with . . .
I don't see it that way.
On the contrary, . . .

To express your opinion, say:
As I see it, . . .
From my point of view, . . .
I (firmly/strongly) believe, think, feel . . .
In my opinion, . . .

If you don't understand what you've heard, say:
I'm sorry. I didn't catch that.
I'm sorry. I didn't get the part about . . .
Could you please repeat . . .
I'm sorry. I'm not following you.
I'm sorry, but I'm lost.
I didn't understand your question. Could you please rephrase it?

To stall (give yourself time), say:
That's a good/interesting question. Let me think about it.

To check for comprehension:
Are you following me?
Do you know what I mean?

APPENDIX K: SURVEYS

Conducting a survey provides an excellent opportunity to practice your English communication skills one-on-one with a variety of people. It also gives you a chance to learn more about how other people view a particular issue you are studying in class or an issue that you yourself are interested in. Use the following suggestions to help make your surveys as successful as possible.

Preparing Questions

1. With a partner or a small group of classmates, decide on a topic for your survey.
2. Decide what kind of format you want to use for your question-and-answer sheet. Do you want to ask only yes/no questions that you can quickly check the answers to as you ask your questions? Do you want to ask "Wh—" questions to get factual information? Do you want to ask more open-ended questions that will allow for a fuller response? Or do you want to ask a combination of question types?
3. Prepare a list of at least ten questions about your topic. Make these questions as specific as possible. If a question is too broad to be answered simply and clearly, compiling your results may be difficult. For example, the question "What do you think about space research?" is more general and thus harder to answer than more specific questions such as "Do you think the space shuttle program is worthwhile? Why or why not?" and "Do you think the benefits of the space shuttle program justify the large amount of money needed to operate the program?"
4. Check over your questions to make sure they are grammatically correct.
5. Decide how many people you want to survey and whether you want to survey people at random or select people with a variety of backgrounds (e.g., age, ethnicity, gender, etc.). For example, if you are conducting a survey on attitudes to space research, you might want to ask men and women of all different ages what they think in order to see if any specific patterns of answers emerge among the subgroups.

Conducting the Survey

1. Decide how you are going to conduct your survey. Do you want to interview people for your survey by yourself or with a partner?
2. Find out where you can find people to interview. You do not have to approach complete strangers on the street. It will be easier if you interview people whom you already know. For example, you might want to interview your neighbors, friends, relatives of people you already know, or people you encounter regularly but don't know well.

3. Explain to each person that you interview what you are doing and why, and give him or her an idea of about how long it will take to answer your questions. You might want to start by saying something like this: "Excuse me, but I am conducting a survey for a class assignment, and I wonder if you would mind answering a few questions." Discuss with your classmates and teacher other opening lines you can use.

   Keep in mind that most people will be happy to answer your questions, especially if they know you are doing it for a class assignment. Many of them may also be interested in why you are doing the survey and what your own opinions are.
4. Even when you have specific questions, you may need to ask for more information on a particular point. Ask follow-up questions when necessary.
5. If you do not hear or do not understand part or all of what the person says, ask for repetition or clarification.
6. If you think you understand what the person has said, but you are not 100 percent certain, try using restatement techniques to help you check your comprehension. (See Appendix D for appropriate phrases to use when you want to clarify or restate something someone has said.)

After the Survey

1. After you have surveyed enough people to obtain the information you want, share your results with the other students in your group. Compile the results so you can summarize the results efficiently and effectively for the class.
2. Make a note about anything that surprises you or that you find interesting in the results.
3. Prepare a short report on the results of your survey.
4. If you want, make a chart or graph to illustrate some of the patterns that emerge from your survey.

Reporting on Your Survey

1. Present to your classmates a short oral report summarizing the results of your survey. Explain first what topic you chose and to whom you chose to direct the questions on your survey. If you made a chart or graph, use it in your presentation. Do not read your report. Instead, speak from notes.

   You can select one person in your group to give the report, or you can give it as a group report, dividing up the information you want to convey to the class.
2. After you have summarized the results, explain what you find interesting, revealing, or surprising about them.
3. Elicit questions from members of the audience to find out their reactions to the results of the survey.

APPENDIX L: ORAL PRESENTATION FEEDBACK FORMS

SPEECH EVALUATION BY TEACHER

Name of Speaker: ______________________

Grade: ______________________

	Disagree Strongly				Agree Strongly
1. The main idea of the speech was clearly stated in a topic sentence.	1	2	3	4	5
2. Enough details were given to clarify the main idea.	1	2	3	4	5
3. The speech was well organized.	1	2	3	4	5
4. The speech was well prepared.	1	2	3	4	5
The Speaker:					
5. showed interest in the topic.	1	2	3	4	5
6. glanced at brief notes and didn't read a written speech.	1	2	3	4	5
7. spoke clearly, at a moderate speed.	1	2	3	4	5
8. spoke in a voice that was neither too loud nor too soft.	1	2	3	4	5
9. recognized when it was necessary to define words and/or give an example.	1	2	3	4	5
10. used the blackboard as necessary.	1	2	3	4	5
11. used eye contact effectively—that is, looked at people in all parts of the room.	1	2	3	4	5
12. used humor and smiled when appropriate.	1	2	3	4	5

Pronunciation Notes

Grammar/Vocabulary Notes

Comments

PEER EVALUATION **Name of Speaker:** ______________________

Name of Peer Evaluator: ______________________

NOTE: Each speech should have at least two peer evaluators.

	Disagree Strongly				Agree Strongly
1. The main idea of the speech was clearly stated in a topic sentence.	1	2	3	4	5
2. Enough details were given to clarify the main idea.	1	2	3	4	5
3. The speech was well organized.	1	2	3	4	5
4. The speech was well prepared.	1	2	3	4	5
The Speaker:					
5. showed interest in the topic.	1	2	3	4	5
6. glanced at brief notes and didn't read a written speech.	1	2	3	4	5
7. spoke clearly, at a moderate speed.	1	2	3	4	5
8. spoke in a voice that was neither too loud nor too soft.	1	2	3	4	5
9. recognized when it was necessary to define words and/or give an example.	1	2	3	4	5
10. used the blackboard as necessary.	1	2	3	4	5
11. used eye contact effectively—that is, looked at people in all parts of the room.	1	2	3	4	5
12. used humor and smiled when appropriate.	1	2	3	4	5

I recommend that next time you

One thing very good about your speech was

SELF-EVALUATION **Name:** ______________________________

NOTE: Do this evaluation after watching the videotape of your speech, if possible.

	Disagree Strongly				**Agree Strongly**
1. The main idea of my speech was clearly stated in a topic sentence.	1	2	3	4	5
2. I gave enough details to clarify the main idea.	1	2	3	4	5
3. My speech was well organized.	1	2	3	4	5
4. My speech was well prepared.	1	2	3	4	5
5. I showed interest in the topic.	1	2	3	4	5
6. I glanced at brief notes and didn't read a written speech.	1	2	3	4	5
7. I spoke clearly, at a moderate speed.	1	2	3	4	5
8. I spoke in a voice that was neither too loud nor too soft.	1	2	3	4	5
9. I recognized when it was necessary to define words and/or give an example.	1	2	3	4	5
10. I used the blackboard as necessary.	1	2	3	4	5
11. I used eye contact effectively. That is, I looked at people in all parts of the room.	1	2	3	4	5
12. I used humor and smiled when appropriate.	1	2	3	4	5

If I could make this speech again, I would

What I especially liked about my speech was

Additional comments:

APPENDIX M: VOCABULARY STUDY TECHNIQUES

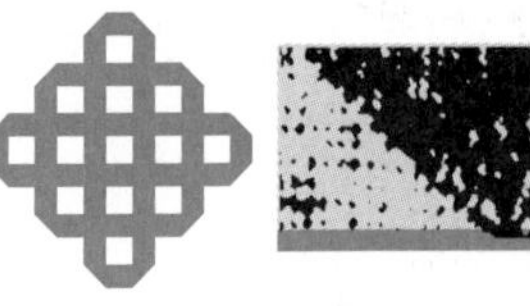

Glossaries and vocabulary lists by themselves are not adequate study aids for students learning English. A more organized, systematic approach to learning can be useful. The following two study systems, *Vocabulary Study Cards* and *Vocabulary Study Sheets,* will help you expand your English vocabulary. Both systems are systematic, manageable, and based on learning and memory strategies: remembering new material, personalizing, categorizing and labeling, associating, visualizing, applying, and reviewing.

Vocabulary Study Cards

new word	Illiterate, adj.	part of speech
related word forms	literate, adj. literacy, n. illiteracy, n.	

1. *"Many illiterate people in the United States are immigrants from cultures where education wasn't available or was denied."*	original context
2. *not literate; unable to read or write*	dictionary definition
3. *"About half the population is still illiterate."*	dictionary example
4. *My grandmother is illiterate in English because she immigrated to the United States at age 70 and is afraid to go to school.*	student's own sentence

Vocabulary Study Sheet

New Word: ______________________________
____

Picture Original Context: ______________________________
____

Definition: ______________________________
____

Dictionary Example: ______________________________
____

My Own Sentence: ______________________________
____

New Word: ______________________________
____

Picture Original Context: ______________________________
____

Definition: ______________________________
____

Dictionary Example: ______________________________
____

My Own Sentence: ______________________________
____

New Word: ______________________________
____

Picture Original Context: ______________________________
____

Definition: ______________________________
____

Dictionary Example: ______________________________
____

My Own Sentence: ______________________________
____

Source: Kate Kinsella and ARC Associates, *Strategies Which Promote Academic Reading Comprehension and Retention for Diverse Learners*

APPENDIX N: EXPRESSING AND ASSESSING WHAT YOU HAVE LEARNED

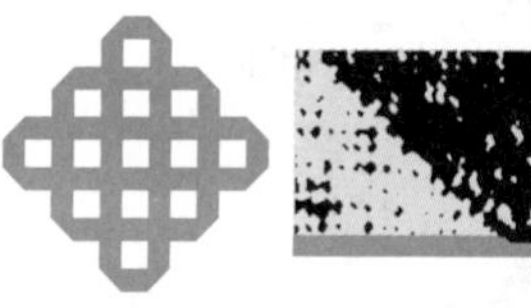

Teachers commonly test, or "assess," students' knowledge and ability by giving an "essay test." This kind of test is not usually given in writing classes, where actual essays are routinely assigned. Rather, these tests are common in "content" classes, where students study particular subjects.

The following series of questions and answers will help you find out exactly what an essay test is and how to prepare for one. Read them over carefully, especially if you know that your teacher plans to use this type of test at the end of a chapter.

1. ***What is an essay test?***
   An essay test is a timed test that requires students to write responses in lists, sentences, or, more commonly, paragraphs. In contrast, "short-answer" tests typically require students to pick an answer or just fill in a blank.
2. ***How do "essay tests" differ from "essays"?***
   a. Essay tests don't require the typical introduction, body, and conclusion of a regular essay. Some essay questions, in fact, may require only a one-paragraph response.
   b. Essay tests are to be answered within a strict time limit, so there isn't time for the typical writing process of prewriting, writing, and rewriting. The most efficient way to prepare and write a response to an essay question that requires a long answer is to:
   - read the essay question through at least twice.
   - immediately write down the thoughts that come to your mind.
   - organize those thoughts into a simple, brief outline.
   - reread the essay question to be sure that you are on target.
   - write the response in paragraph form.
   - reread your response to make sure that it answers the essay question(s) completely and directly.
   - quickly proofread your response.

   Don't spend time on an introduction. With a time limit, you need to get to the point right away.
3. ***What is the biggest problem that non-native speakers of English have with essay tests?***
   You may think that the answer to this question is vocabulary and grammar. But the most common problem is that students often don't answer essay questions directly, don't answer them completely, or don't answer them at all but instead write responses that have nothing to do with the topic.
4. ***What can I do to make sure that I am answering essay questions directly?***
   a. First, it is necessary to **fully understand the question.** You should read the essay question at least twice. It's a good idea to rewrite the question in your own words. If an essay question has two or more parts, then rewrite each question separately. For example:

   Test Directions: In separate paragraphs, first explain the issue discussed in the videotape, and then explain why you agree or disagree with the person who was interviewed.

   You quickly write: *What issue did the videotape discuss?*
   Do I agree or disagree with the person who was interviewed?

b. Answer both parts of the question completely and **in order.** In the answer to the sample above, you would not give your opinion first and then explain what was discussed in the videotape.

c. **Use words from the question directly in the first sentence of your answer** so that you stay focused on the question, and the person reading your answer will see that you were focused and answering directly. For example, in answer to the essay question about the videotape, in the first sentence of the first paragraph you would write:

In the videotape, the issue of ______________________ *was discussed.*

In the first sentence of the second paragraph you would write:

I agree/disagree with . . .

5. ***Any other tips?***

Yes. Look at the specific words in the questions to find out exactly what is being asked for and what **form is expected.** Underline the important **direction words.** Here are a few examples of direction words:

a. **List . . .** (When you *list,* don't use complete sentences.)
   1.
   2.
   3.

b. **Define . . .** (When you *define,* give the meaning of the term with enough detail to show that you really understand it.)

X <u>means</u> that . . .

c. **Explain . . .** (When you *explain,* give enough reasons, facts, and details to make an idea clear.)

X is true <u>because</u> . . .

d. **In a short paragraph, describe . . .**
Follow the rules of paragraph writing: indent the first line; pay attention to margins; write a topic sentence containing the main idea.

Remember, on essay tests, the main idea will come directly from the question.

Suggestion for Practice

After you have finished a chapter in *Sound Ideas,* get together with a few other students and write from three to five essay questions based on topics that your class has covered. Then, choose a student to write those essay questions on the board.

As a class, read the essay questions and point out those with multiple parts and direction words that need special attention. Write the first sentence of your response to each question to make sure you are responding to it directly.

Your teacher may collect the questions the groups come up with and use them to prepare a practice test and then a *real* essay test for the class.

APPENDIX O: CHECKING YOUR FEELINGS

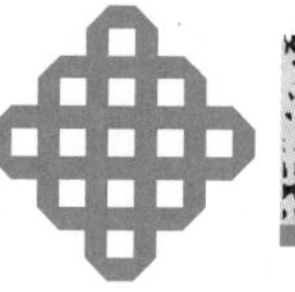

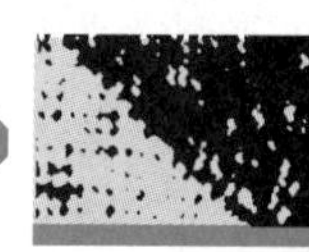

One way to learn more about how you learn best is to keep track of how you feel about the various tasks you perform in English. Once a week, make a list of the various activities in which you used English for that week or, if you wish, for that day. Choose one or more of the activities, and use the checklist below to help you focus on how you felt while doing each activity. Check one of the two descriptors on each line that better describes your feelings during that activity. Realize that nothing is either black or white, and no descriptor is necessarily better than its opposite.

_____ happy	_____ unhappy
_____ proud	_____ ashamed
_____ confident	_____ unconfident
_____ peaceful	_____ anxious
_____ unafraid	_____ afraid
_____ risk-taking	_____ cautious
_____ clear-thinking	_____ confused
_____ friendly	_____ unfriendly
_____ interested	_____ bored
_____ calm	_____ angry
_____ strong	_____ weak
_____ energetic	_____ tired
_____ outgoing	_____ shy
_____ accepting	_____ critical
_____ able to tolerate contradictions	_____ unable to accept contradictions
_____ want to learn the language	_____ don't want to learn the language
_____ want to know the culture	_____ don't want to know the culture

Source: *Language Learning Strategies,* by Rebecca L. Oxford, 1990.
Boston: Heinle & Heinle, pp. 187–189.

After you finish filling out the checklist, try to analyze why doing a particular activity made you feel a certain way. Would you rather have different feelings? If so, list some steps you can take that you think will move you in the direction that's right for *you.*